Educational Social Software for Context–Aware Learning:
Collaborative Methods and Human Interaction

Niki Lambropoulos
London South Bank University, UK

Margarida Romero
University of Toulouse, France

INFORMATION SCIENCE REFERENCE

Hershey · New York

Director of Editorial Content:	Kristin Klinger
Senior Managing Editor:	Jamie Snavely
Assistant Managing Editor:	Michael Brehm
Publishing Assistant:	Sean Woznicki
Typesetter:	Michael Brehm, Michael Killian
Cover Design:	Lisa Tosheff
Printed at:	Yurchak Printing Inc.

Published in the United States of America by
Information Science Reference (an imprint of IGI Global)
701 E. Chocolate Avenue
Hershey PA 17033
Tel: 717-533-8845
Fax: 717-533-8661
E-mail: cust@igi-global.com
Web site: http://www.igi-global.com/reference

Library of Congress Cataloging-in-Publication Data

Educational social software for context-aware learning : collaborative methods
and human interaction / Niki Lambropoulos and Margarida Romero, Editors.
    p. cm.
  Includes bibliographical references and index.
  Summary: "This book examines socio-cultural elements in educational
computing focused on design and theory where learning and setting are
intertwined"--Provided by publisher.
  ISBN 978-1-60566-826-0 (hardcover) -- ISBN 978-1-60566-827-7 (ebook) 1.
Internet in education--Social aspects. 2. Online social networks. 3. Web
2.0. I. Lambropoulos, Niki, 1966- II. Romero, Margarido, 1980-
  LB1044.87.E362 2010
  371.9'0460973--dc22
                          2009031268

British Cataloguing in Publication Data
A Cataloguing in Publication record for this book is available from the British Library.

Dedicated to the memory of Evelyne Corcos (1946-2009): educator, researcher, humanist, behavioralist, and mentor.

Evelyne Corcos was relentless and compassionate in her conviction that with the right tools and incentives, at-risk, alienated teens could improve their learning skills and deepen their relationships with other human beings. She was a specialist in management techniques and interventions for students with behavioral disorders and/or learning disabilities; she worked tirelessly to help them and their teachers make the classroom a place where positive, life-altering learning could occur.

In all her teaching and research activities, Professor Corcos embraced digital and enriched media because she saw these technologies as opportunities to reach out effectively to young people. Her work in French and in English helped teachers to learn and helped students to become their own teachers.

Professor Corcos's life work was exemplary: a portrait of the highest and noblest ideals of a humanist--and humane--education.

Peter Paolucci, PhD
York University, Canada

Table of Contents

Section 1
Introduction to Educational Social Software

Section 2
Educational Social Software Technologies

Section 3
Educational Social Software: The Teacher Perspective

Section 4
Educational Social Software Applicability and Evaluation

Detailed Table of Contents

Section 1
Introduction to Educational Social Software

Chapter 1

Mark J. W. Lee, Charles Sturt University, Australia
Catherine McLoughlin, Australian Catholic University, Australia

The main agents of change in the present era can be posited as globalisation and the diffusion and uptake of technologies that have given rise to a knowledge-based, networked society. The latest evolution of the Internet, Web 2.0, is resulting in significant transformations in terms of how we live, work, and communicate. In the higher education arena, the drive towards self-organising communities and collaboration through social networking applications has triggered widespread debate on the purpose of education, with a growing emphasis on the need not only to facilitate the acquisition of knowledge and information, but also to cultivate in students the skills and digital literacies necessary to engage with social and technological change. In this chapter, the authors discuss the affordances of Web 2.0 and social software tools, and provide examples of current conceptualisations and metaphors of learning that leverage these affordances to support learner choice, autonomy and agency in the creation of ideas and knowledge artefacts. An innovative learning paradigm is proposed that the authors call Pedagogy 2.0, based on the key elements of personalisation, participation and productivity. Finally, the authors argue for a more holistic and evidence-based approach to research and evaluation of Web 2.0-based learning programs and initiatives that supports the development and sharing of best practices across academic disciplines, institutions, and countries.

Chapter 2

Bolanle A. Olaniran, Texas Tech University, USA
Indi M. Williams, Texas Tech University, USA

This chapter explores three facets of Web 2.0: the pedagogical use of social software in a Web 2.0 e-learning environment, social software, and social networking from the perspective of transactional control in fostering student learning, as proposed in the theoretical framework of Dron's (2006) theory. It also examines the implications of Web 2.0 as it relates to learning and e-learning. Using Facebook as a case specific Web 2.0 platform, the researcher pursues understanding of learner control, as well as cultural interactions in Web 2.0 environments in the broader context of cultural implication for Web 2.0 as a learning platform in a global e-learning environment. Accordingly, the Facebook example helps to illustrate how instructors and students can effectively control their learning environment (or relinquish control of their learning environment) within an intracultural setting, in an attempt to create a meaningful learning experience as proposed by the transactional control model. In conclusion, the chapter offers recommendations for Web 2.0 e-learning technology applications in order to create effective and meaningful learning for students and instructors.

Chapter 3

Margarida Romero, Université de Toulouse, France & Universitat Autònoma de Barcelona,
Spain

In recent years, we have witnessed an information revolution. This revolution has been characterised by widespread access to the Internet and by the emergence of information which has been generated by end-users–the so-called user-generated content. The information thus generated has been supported by Web 2.0 applications or social software. These changes in the information society have had an important impact in education, with more and more adults enrolling on life-long learning programs; moreover, the availability of distance learning courses has grown in line with this increase in demand. In this emergent educational paradigm, the new 2.0 technology context implies new competencies for learners. These competencies include literacy in information and communication technology (ICT), learning autonomy, self-regulation and metacognition, while at the same time expanding the opportunities for metacognitive development. We will consider in this chapter these two perspectives of the 2.0 context; on the one hand, the new requirements provided by the environment and, on the other hand, the new learning opportunities which this environment brings.

Section 2
Educational Social Software Technologies

Chapter 4

Filiz Kalelioglu, Baskent University, Turkey
Yasemin Gulbahar, Baskent University, Turkey

In this chapter, numerous educational activities are presented for instructors in order to address each type of multiple intelligences. Most probably, these educational activities are those which are already being experienced by many instructors. The key point here is that although students are exposed to many educational activities, instructors generally don't have any idea or rather don't consider the learning outcomes in terms of multiple intelligences. In general, assessment activities are based only on the chunk of knowledge that the student gains after any particular activity. In fact, instructors should deal with the effects and improvements in students other than just the knowledge, after engagement in educational activities. Thus, instructors should base their instructional plans on a theoretical basis, especially when integrating technology into their courses. Hence, the development and changing activities and other tasks of social software according to the multiple intelligences that underline individual differences were discussed briefly in this chapter.

Chapter 5

Interactive whiteboards (IWB) are the latest technology trend in schools and businesses. The purpose of this chapter is to discuss how social software and IWB technology promotes active engagement and interactive content delivery. Using IWB technology users are able to interact, collaborate, and evaluate. To implement the IWB effectively, there are numerous issues to address: professional development, interactivity, feedback, collaboration, and the future of the IWB.

Chapter 6

We analyze the interactions produced through a Web annotations tool. This communication tool, usually employed as a collaborative tool or as a medium of artistic or social criticism, has been introduced in a mathematics course for online pre-engineering students. The objective of this innovation is to integrate the communication and the subject's contents and to check whether a better level of communication between students and professors improves the acquisition of basic mathematical competencies. As a result of this study, we put forward a model for the analysis of the online interaction, as well as a classification of students in relation to the use of the communication tool.

We present an empirical study investigating how interactions with a popular social tagging system, called del.icio.us, may directly impact knowledge adaptation through the processes of concept assimilation and accommodation. We observed 4 undergraduate students over a period of 8 weeks and found that the quality of social tags and distributions of information content directly impact the formation and enrichment of concept schemas. A formal model based on a distributed cognition framework provides a good fit to the students learning data, showing how learning occurs through the adaptive assimilation of concepts and categories of multiple users through the social tagging system. The results and the model have important implications on how Web 2.0 technologies can promote formal and informal learning through collaborative methods.

Chapter 8

This chapter explores the various facets of screenPLAY, an interactive video intervention for at-risk teens, which presents social skills in a medium that is both familiar and motivating to this age group. The chapter begins with a discussion of the pedagogical ideas that motivated the creation of screen-PLAY, from the necessity to move away from a skill-driven to a content-driven social-skill intervention, to promoting learning from experience, and then to the importance of clarifying learning objectives. In addition to the adoption of a constructivist perspective, a case is made for including cognitive and linguistic concomitants with social skill acquisition. A description is provided of how these additional two variables relate to behavior and the way they are integrated in the structure of the intervention. A cognitive skill is embedded in each of the eleven templates used to present content. Video clips displaying vignettes employing student actors are analyzed in a context that requires users to record their responses, thoughts, and observations in audio or text files that are uploaded to be accessed later by other users. The anonymity of both users and actors is protected, first, by the provision of an avatar to represent the user, and then, by having the video clips transformed into a comic book look. The technical details of the construction of this digital platform are provided, as well as a dialectic analyzing how the obstacles, encountered along the way, ultimately contributed to the overall innovative functionality. Future directions are examined in the context of screenPLAY's modular structure that allows the addition of content and functionality.

Section 3
Educational Social Software: The Teacher Perspective

With this contribution, we briefly explain how both the e-tutor role and competencies have changed since the beginning of the debate about this essential e-learning human resource. Until now, what set of professional functions were requested to be a good e-tutor? What training policies must be identified to give an answer to the needs of e-tutors for them to be able to interact effectively in e-learning scenarios oriented to sharing knowledge and social networking?

As communication and connection are essential instruments for professional educators, this chapter seeks to examine the effectiveness of an online "virtual teacher's lounge" in the framework of offline communities. Essentially, an online discussion forum for educators is evaluated for the purpose of determining whether the forum provides a "space" conducive for the development of a community of professional educators as benchmarked against an understanding of offline community formation and existence. The foundational works of Ferdinand Tonnies, James Coleman, and Ray Oldenburg are used to develop 12 characteristics of community—as understood in the context of social communities. The study finds that online communities closely resemble offline communities in structure and interaction, but only for select participants. The participants observed demonstrating or facilitating the characteristics of community comprise around 10% of the total number of users participating in the analyzed discussions.

Section 4
Educational Social Software Applicability and Evaluation

As the average age of Canada's public servant inches toward 50, it is expected that between 30-40% of the government's key knowledge workers will retire in the next five years. Consequently, the government is challenged with attracting and retaining new employees and ensuring that all public servants have the necessary skills and knowledge to do their jobs well. Since formal learning does not alone prepare employees to perform in complex work environments, the federal Public Service is implementing informal learning strategies to facilitate knowledge creation and exchange and to manage tacit knowledge. This chapter describes how technology-supported communities of practice are being employed across Canada with the support of the Canada School of Public Service. The strategic context, challenges, lessons learned, and vision for the future are also discussed.

The dissemination of university knowledge has been traditionally based on lectures to students organised in homogenous groups. The advantages of this method are that it can give a unified vision of content, guaranteeing equal access to knowledge for all students. The 21st century university must combine its learning and teaching methods and incorporate different strategies and educative resources, as well as seeking to advance individual learning and promote collaborative work. The relevance of Web 2.0 is clear in this university learning context as it enables collaborative work to be carried out using ICT. In this chapter, we will deal with the different possible uses of social software in university teaching. We will show that the proper use of Web 2.0 tools can favour collaborative learning and promote new ways of teaching and learning.

Chapter 13

Paula Roush, London South Bank University, UK
Ruth Brown, London South Bank University, UK

Publishing with friends is the account of an action research cycle in which a print-on-demand Web site, Lulu.com, became a classroom for second and third year digital photography students to publish their photobooks. Building on the earlier use of a blogging platform as a personal learning environment, this narrative explores the pedagogical prospects of the read/write Web, and illustrates the way in which students use social networks for creative produsage (Bruns, 2008). Students were positive about the pedagogical approach, and the opportunities to gain valuable hands-on experience in their chosen field of study.

Chapter 14

Kai Pata, Tallinn University, Estonia

This chapter describes the Web of social software tools with its inhabitants as an evolving and ecological environment, discussing and elaborating the connectivist framework coined by George Siemens in his book Knowing Knowledge. This new perspective to ecological learning in social software environments resides on the ideas of Gibson's and his followers approach to ecological psychology, the rising theory of embodied simulation and Lotman's theory of cultural semiosis. In the empirical part of the chapter, we focus on the methods of investigating how social software systems become accommodated with their users forming learning spaces. Analysis discusses such ecologically defined spaces for individual and collaborative learning.

Foreword

The explosion of the Web in the mid-nineteen nineties promised a revolution in all human activities. In a talk on the use of the Web in education that I gave at that time, I said, "The challenge is to develop effective ways of teaching with the new medium, not to transfer ineffective methods from the old medium."

Like all revolutions, the initial radical fervour was succeeded by a far more conservative regime. The products of that first revolution are with us today; companies, charities, governments, and so forth are all now very adept at pushing information at us via the Web. Likewise within schools and colleges, the first generation of learning management systems still predominate, being used by institutions to push corporate information and tutors to push knowledge at the students. An example of how the ineffective methods from the old medium have found expression in the new.

From the start of the Web revolution, there were places where the visitors were encouraged to talk back to the Webmasters and, even rarer, places where they were encouraged to talk to each other. These capabilities found a more mature application in social networking environments such as blogs, wikis, facebooks, folksonomies, twitters, and online virtual environments.

These so-called Web 2 capabilities provide environments where a second revolution in social and educational practice can take place. But ineffective methods from the old medium can still be transferred into it; one example being a number of colleges who have bought islands in second life, only to construct replicas of their physical campus upon it. Their replicas are complete with lecture halls where the student avatars are expected to assemble in ranks to be lectured at by the avatar of the tutor.

The chapters in this book are at the leading edge of attempts to develop more effective use of Web 2 capabilities in education. What is implicit in all the studies, and explicit in some, is that education is an interactive social process. Knowledge and meaning are actively acquired by engagement and communication within a community of learners. This has always been the case, despite the perception of many that knowledge flows into empty heads as the professor pronounces from the stage. Web 2 capacities augment the channels through which social communication can occur.

But communication, even in the new media, has within itself the possibility of miscommunication. For example, the 21st century student who apologised for not replying to an e-mail by explaining to their not-very-old tutor that they 'only use e-mail to talk to old people!'; communicating with his peers solely by facebook. The YouTube video 'A Vision of Students Today' illustrates the ways in which contemporary students network and communicate, in a format and medium which is alien to many tutors.

It is said that a young person who is not radical has no heart, but an old person who is not conservative has no wisdom. Working in internet time, it will not be long in real time before the revolutionary heart of these studies becomes the accepted pedagogic wisdom of our age.

Fintan Culwin

Fintan Culwin is a Professor of Software Engineering Education and Head of the Department of Software Development & Computer Networking and the Centre for Interactive Systems Engineering at London South Bank University. He holds a BSc in Psychology, PGCE in Secondary Science, from the Open University PG units Software Engineering & Networks and a PhD in Software Engineering. His research interests are: initial software development education, learning objects for SD education, academic misconduct, forensic document analysis and visualisation, and plagiarism deterrence and detection. He has published widely in the fields of his research interests. Outise his office he runs several marathons a year and is an Iron Man in Triathlon.

Preface

The emergence of Web 2.0 triggered a general trend towards online social interactions and brought sociology in the global interactive picture. The emergence of Web 2.0 has brought about the opportunity to create new educational uses of Web 2.0 user centred software. Social software platforms, human networks, and human activities in Web 2.0 refer to a set of technologies for sharing information and communication. Web 2.0 has led to the creation of new technologies at a rapid pace.

The participant as a learning community member is the central point in the learning opportunities provided by 2.0 approaches in e-learning. E-learning 2.0 puts the user as a learner and her community at the centre of the learning process. From a technical viewpoint, the integration of social software has created interesting new possibilities for organizing novel learning and working situations. From an educational viewpoint, this phenomenon created issues related to individual and social learning for internalisation and externalisation of information and knowledge (Vygotsky, 1978). Studies on relationships, practices, and activities with the use of tools in the purpose of learning appear to present contradictive results (EFQUEL, 2006; Cuban, 2001). Current learning management systems support administrative functions; thus, they target teachers' information provision, resulting in most cases in poor learning opportunities for the learner. Studies on social relationships, interactions, and engagement between the e-learning participants, as well as practices and activities with the use of tools for the purpose of learning appear to present contradictive results. Thus, design for socio-cultural learning requires social tools; this means that social and personalised tools should be integrated within a learning platform.

These issues in educational technologies appear to be connected to the computational history. Computing pioneers, such as Engelbart (1963), seemed to adopt a learning summit on using the machine for the 'augmentation of human intellect.' Shackel (1991) suggested that the designers need to enable human's capabilities, while Mumford (1983) proposed that socio-technical systems design assists designers to maximize human gains while achieving business and technical excellence. Therefore, some answers lie in the principles of computing and in particular social computing. Social computing is concerned with the intersection of social behaviour and computational systems. According to Dourish (2004), there is a need to incorporate social understandings into interface design as the systems we use are embedded in systems of social meaning, fluid and negotiated between us and the other people around us. By incorporating understandings of how social practice emerges, we can build systems that fit more easily into the ways in which we work. In other words, tools designed using social understandings of interactions, in turn, enhance social interactions with computation. Is this feasible in educational computing?

EDUCATIONAL SOCIAL SOFTWARE FOR CONTEXT AWARE COMPUTING: COLLABORATIVE METHODS AND HUMAN INTERACTION

Educational social software is Web-based software supporting learning via group interaction. Under this paradigm we can consider a range of applications such as Weblogs, wikis, social bookmarking and syndication systems, multiplayer online games, discussion forums, or even 3D worlds. The knowledge is empowered under social construction relative to the activity and situations in which it has being explored (Brown, Collins, & Duguid, 1989). For Dabbagh & Bannan-Ritland (2005), *"there is a social framework or culture surrounding a learning context and its constituents are the learners, the interactions that those learners engage in, and the tools that enable those interactions."* In interactive educational technology, this is related to context awareness; context is organisational or cultural and the context that surrounds learning activities on the interface. In other words, methods, learning activities, tools, and evaluation are highly interconnected. For example, computer-supported collaborative learning is an interdisciplinary trend to emphasise the use of methods such as ethnography to extract implications for design based on its situated context.

For this reason, the key objective of this book is to look into the socio-cultural elements in educational social computing focused on design and theory driven where learning and the setting are intertwined. The book discusses the basis of a broad framework for learning environments and online in particular, enriched with contributions from domains, sometimes as diverse as computer science (application design and engineering of human interfaces), psychology (the application of theories of cognitive processes and the empirical analysis of user behaviour), sociology and anthropology (interactions between technology, work, and organization), and industrial design (interactive products).

In conclusion, this book is anchored in the concept that by exploiting human skills and experiences, information technology empowers and enhances learners' capabilities. It revisits the socio-cultural learning summit on examining learning quality by using the machine for the augmentation of human intellect, productivity, improvement, and innovation at individual, organizational, societal, and global levels.

The book's objective is to serve all parts involved in computer-supported collaborative learning in both the business and the education sector with regard to educational context-aware social interactions. In addition, the multidisciplinary approaches will attract readers from different fields such as education, communication studies, sociology and anthropology, and computer science.

These are the sections for the organisation of the chapters:

- **Introduction to Educational Social Software**
- **Educational Social Software Technologies**
- **Educational Social Software: The Teacher Perspective**
- **Educational Social Software Applicability and Evaluation**

DESCRIPTION OF CHAPTERS

This edition aims to illuminate aspects of educational social software (ESS) related to human-human and human-computer interactions by employing diverse methodologies and technologies aiming to a better understanding of the online CSCL settings. The Web 2.0 technologies for active engagement and collaboration, as well as networking and social interactions, created a debate in education. The mere provision of knowledge was related to poor learning opportunities, in comparison to the advantages of the co-construction of new knowledge anchored in collaborative creativity in CSCL and e-learning, in particular. Thus, our book is structured in four broad areas: Section 1 introduces ESS. Section 2 refers to the associated technologies. Section 3 presents the teachers' perspective in ESS and Section 4 discusses ESS applied and validated case studies.

The book includes 14 chapters from prominent international collaborating authors from Australia, Canada, Estonia, France, Italy, Spain, Turkey, United Kingdom, and USA.

The following section presents an overview of each chapter.

ORGANIZATION OF THE BOOK

Section 1: Introduction to Educational Social Software

In Chapter 1, the agents of change of Web 2.0 social and knowledge-based society point to the need for self-organising communities and collaboration. In this way, mere provision of knowledge becomes innovation and brings quality in learning and the acquisition of new skills. The authors discuss the ESS affordances and provide examples of contemporary and associated learning analytical frameworks. Pedagogy 2.0 is proposed as the innovative learning paradigm based on the key elements of personalisation, participation, and productivity.

In Chapter 2, the pedagogical use of social software in e-learning 2.0 is related to the technologies and social networking from the perspective of transactional control in fostering student learning. In addition, the chapter examines the implications of Web 2.0 related learner control, as well as pointing to cultural interactions using Facebook. It examines ways and offers recommendations that instructors and students can effectively use to control their learning environment within an intracultural setting.

In Chapter 3, user-generated content within ESS is discussed in regard to its impact in education. As new skills and competencies are needed in one's lifetime, more and more adults attend life-long learning programs. These new learning needs include literacy in information and communication technology (ICT), learning autonomy, self-regulation, and metacognition. Consequently, the author presents the dialogue between the new requirements the era of Web 2.0 for creativity and collaboration brings in education and the new learning opportunities which this environment conveys.

Section 2: Educational Social Software Technologies

In Chapter 4, several educational activities are presented related to each type of the multiple intelligences. The authors present the argument that although students are exposed to many educational activities, instructors generally do not take multiple intelligences into account. For example, assessment activities are still associated with the mere provision of information without considering active engagement in educational activities aiming in collaborative creativity. In the Web 2.0 context, educators may have to revise their instructional plans by seriously considering the integration of multiple intelligences and new technologies into their courses.

In Chapter 5, the interactive whiteboards (IWB) are presented as the latest technology trend in schools and businesses. The author discusses ways to promote active engagement and interactive content with the use of ESS and IWB in particular. IWB technology has several advantages as the users are able to interact, collaborate, and evaluate their own work. IWB integration in the classrooms brings numerous issues to address: professional development, interactivity, feedback, collaboration, user attitude, and the future of the IWB.

In Chapter 6, a Web annotations tool is examined in relation to social interactions. Although it is usually employed as a collaborative tool or as a medium of artistic or social criticism, the tool was introduced in a mathematics course for online pre-engineering students. The aim was to enable communication between the students and their contents and evaluate the acquisition of basic mathematical competencies in relation to the communication improvement. The authors present a model to support online interaction analysis and classification in relation to the use of this communication tool.

In Chapter 7, an empirical study is presented investigating the ways interactions with the popular tagging tool del.icio.us are related to knowledge adaptation via concept assimilation and accommodation. In their case study, the authors observed a relationship between the quality of social tags and the formation and enrichment of concept schemas. Their proposed formal model is based on distributed cognition framework and provides good fits to the associated learning material. The implications are connected to the ways Web 2.0 technologies can promote CSCL in formal and informal settings.

In Chapter 8, ScreenPLAY is presented as an interactive video intervention for at-risk teens to enhance their social skills and motivation. The authors present the pedagogical ideas behind ScreenPLAY and the need for a content-driven social-skill intervention to promote experiential learning. Other than a constructivist perspective, cognitive and linguistic concomitants with social skill acquisition were targeted in relation to learning as change of behaviour. Ethical issues are also presented as of major importance in this age group and are related to interface design challenges.

Section 3: Educational Social Software: The Teacher Perspective

In Chapter 9, the role of the e-tutor and her competencies is discussed in relation to the e-learning 2.0. The author attempts to answer questions on the new set of professional functions that are required and the associated training policies. Such e-tutoring needs are needed so the e-tutor can effectively work in e-learning scenarios from a lifelong, sharing knowledge, and social networking perspective.

In Chapter 10, communication and connection are presented as essential instruments for a community of professional educators. The author was anchored in the community research and developed a 12 characteristics framework to investigate the online and offline community settings. Offline communities and an online discussion forum for educators are observed, analyzed, and evaluated for a "space" conducive for the community development. The author found that, in these communities, the active participation level is directly correlated to the likelihood of benefit.

Section 4: Educational Social Software Applicability and Evaluation

In Chapter 11, the case of the Canadian government is presented related to challenges of attracting and retaining new employees, as well as ensuring that all public servants have the necessary skills and knowledge to do their jobs well. From a life-long perspective, the federal Public Service implemented informal learning strategies to facilitate knowledge creation and exchange and to manage tacit knowledge within communities of practice. The authors also present the strategic context, challenges, lessons learned, and vision for the future.

In Chapter 12, different possible ESS uses are considered for university teaching. The authors argue that if Web 2.0 tools are used properly, they can actually favour collaborative learning and promote new ways of teaching and learning. They present their work on ESS uses in the university campus and propose a hybrid learning model aiming to combine the potential of technology with the possibilities of collaborative learning.

In Chapter 13, the use of the publishing/social network site lulu.com is presented as a virtual learning environment for photopublishing projects with undergraduate digital photography students. The authors employed "e-tivities" and collaborative rubrics that appeared to support learners' daily network practices, namely their use of social network sites to get their work seen and peer-reviewed.

In Chapter 14, ESS and Web 2.0 with its inhabitants is presented as an evolving and ecological environment, discussing and elaborating the connectivist framework. The authors focused on methodologies to examine ESS and the ways they become accommodated with their users forming learning spaces and user-generated context for individual and collaborative learning.

REFERENCES

Dourish, P. (2004). *Where the action is: The foundations of embodied interaction.* Cambridge, MA: MIT Press.

Garrison, D. R., & Vaughan, N. (2008). *Blended learning in higher education.* San Francisco: Jossey-Bass.

Dillenbourg, P. (Ed). (1999). *Collaborative-learning: Cognitive and computational approaches.* Oxford: Elsevier.

Ehlers, U.-D., Goertz, L., Hildebrandt, B., & Pawlowski, J. M. (2006). *PANORAMA report: Use and dissemination of quality approaches in European e-learning.* FEDECOP.

Englebart, D. C. (1962). A conceptual framework for the augmentation of man's intellect. In P. Howerton (Ed.), *Vistas in information handling* (vol. 1). Washington, D.C.: Spartan Books.

Mumford, E. (1983). *Designing human systems-the ETHICS method.*

Shackel, B. (1991). Usability–context, framework, definition, design, and evaluation. In B. Shackel & S. J. Richardson (Eds.), *Human factors for informatics usability* (pp. 21–37). New York: Cambridge University Press.

Vygotsky, L. S. (1978). *Mind in society.* Cambridge, MA: Harvard University Press.

Acknowledgment

The editors would like to acknowledge the help of everyone involved in the collation and review process of the book, without whose support the project could not have been satisfactorily completed. This book would not be in our hands without IGI Global. Special thanks to our editors, Rebecca Beistline and Tyler Heath, as well as Jan Travers. We are grateful to them for their expert guidance, support, and incredible spirit.

In closing, we wish to thank our reviewers who improved the chapters with their expert help and advice: William L. Anderson, Stamatina Anastopoulou, Susan M. Beebe, Daniel Burgos, Ben Daniel, Carmen Elena, Alex Sandro Gomes, Agostino Marengo, Julianna Mrázik Nóra, Manuel Perez, Niels Pinkwart, and last but not least, Karen Stepanyan.

Niki Lambropoulos
London South Bank University, UK

Margarida Romero
University of Toulouse, France

March 2009

Section 1
Introduction to Educational Social Software

Chapter 1

Social Software as Tools for Pedagogical Transformation:
Enabling Personalization, Creative Production, and Participatory Learning

Mark J. W. Lee
Charles Sturt University, Australia

Catherine McLoughlin
Australian Catholic University, Australia

ABSTRACT

The main agents of change in the present era can be posited as globalization and the diffusion and uptake of technologies that have given rise to a knowledge-based, networked society. The latest evolution of the Internet, Web 2.0, is resulting in significant transformations in terms of how we live, work, and communicate. In the higher education arena, the drive towards self-organizing communities and collaboration through social networking applications has triggered widespread debate on the purpose of education, with a growing emphasis on the need not only to facilitate the acquisition of knowledge and information, but also to cultivate in students the skills and digital literacies necessary to engage with social and technological change. In this chapter, the authors discuss the affordances of Web 2.0 and social software tools, and provide examples of current conceptualizations and metaphors of learning that leverage these affordances to support learner choice, autonomy, and agency in the creation of ideas and knowledge artifacts. An innovative learning paradigm is proposed that the authors call Pedagogy 2.0, based on the key elements of personalization, participation, and productivity. Finally, the authors argue for a more holistic and evidence-based approach to research and evaluation of Web 2.0-based learning programs and initiatives that supports the development and sharing of best practices across academic disciplines, institutions, and countries.

DOI: 10.4018/978-1-60566-826-0.ch001

INTRODUCTION

In the present landscape of technological and social transformation, significant and ongoing changes are underway that are impacting how we live and work. Concurrent social trends, such as the diversification of life trajectories, multiple career paths, re-skilling, and flexible working hours, are leading to new paradigms of education and learning. There is a change in the view of what education is for, with a growing emphasis on the need to support not only the acquisition of conceptual knowledge in a specific subject area or domain, but also the development of life skills and resources necessary to engage with social and technical change, and to continue learning throughout life (Owen, Grant, Sayers, & Facer, 2006; Fischer & Konomi, 2005).

The rapid diffusion of information and communications technologies (ICTs), in particular the Internet and World Wide Web, has fuelled the growth of the "information age" and "knowledge-based society," and in recent years we have been witnessing the rise of "Web 2.0" (O'Reilly, 2005). Epitomized by the proliferation of social technologies that are less about "narrowcasting" to individuals, Web 2.0 tools are more focused on the creation of communities that allow people with common interests to meet, collaborate, learn from each other, and build new digital resources. Web 2.0 is therefore not merely a technological shift or new suite of tools; it is also a social movement that opens up new opportunities to communicate, interact, and share data. The new ease of connectivity enables greater participation and thereby offers users a range of pathways, modes, and styles of working and learning. The increased emphasis on user-generated content, data and resource sharing, and collaborative effort, together with the availability of a raft of innovative social software applications, signals that the Web is a powerful platform for generating, repurposing, and remixing content.

Robinson (2005) talks of the "people-centric Web," which is all about "conversations, interpersonal networking, personalization, and individualism" (Abram, 2005, p. 44). When we consider the constantly expanding lexicon of Web 2.0 applications (Web logs [blogs], wikis, podcasts, Really Simple Syndication [RSS] feeds, social tagging, mash-ups, Twittering, modding, and the list goes on) it becomes clear that they signal changes in the learning landscape. Applied to education, we are invited to envision learners as active participants, creators of knowledge, and seekers of personal, engaging experiences. In what has been called a culture of participation, the line separating consumers and producers of content is becoming blurred, as the term "prosumers" indicates. As Web 2.0 users, our students are often actively creating and sharing content and ideas in this new knowledge space. The independence and digital skills displayed by Generation Y stand in stark contrast to the control culture of education, in which teacher-controlled syllabi and assessment tasks dominate, and in which learning is commonly perceived as the absorption of information from textbooks and other "authoritative" sources. Beyond the walls of formal places of learning (schools, colleges, universities), there is a plethora of online networks populated by self-directed, vital, self-managed learners who are capable of generating new ideas. These are thriving knowledge-creating communities that are open to all who wish to participate.

In discussing the implications of Web 2.0 for education, we must expand our vision of pedagogy so that we view students as active participants or co-producers of knowledge rather than passive consumers of content, and strive to create learning opportunities that are participatory, social processes supportive of personal life goals and aspirations. There is a compelling need not only to engage with and capitalize on the digital literacies and tools that learners are already conversant with, but also to equip them with the competencies and attributes needed to be successful in the knowledge economy (Jenkins, 2007). Of paramount importance is to encourage learners to exercise agency in shaping their own learning trajectories. In this chapter, the authors identify the specific educational affordances of social software tools and provide examples of current innovative pedagogies that attempt to address these demands, within a framework that they call Pedagogy 2.0.

WEB 2.0 AND SOCIAL SOFTWARE: CONNECTIVITY, COLLABORATION, AND CUSTOMIZATION

Web 2.0 applications, including but not limited to wikis, blogs, RSS, podcasting, social networking sites, tag-based folksonomies, and peer-to-peer (P2P) media sharing utilities, are attracting intense and growing interest across all sectors of education and training (Allen, 2004; Alexander, 2006). Also referred to as the "Read-Write Web" (Richardson, 2006), as it goes beyond the provision of viewable/ downloadable content to enable members of the general public to actively contribute and shape online content, Web 2.0 is seen to hold considerable potential for addressing the needs of today's diverse students, enhancing their learning through the facilitation of customized, personalized experiences (Bryant, 2006; Green, Facer, Rudd, Dillon, & Humphreys, 2005). While course management systems (CMS's) that integrate geographically-dispersed learners in asynchronous educational interactions have been widely available for a number of years, many educators and institutions are discovering that new approaches to teaching and learning are required to meet the needs of a generation of learners who seek greater autonomy, connectivity, and socio-experiential learning. In contrast to earlier e-learning efforts that simply replicated traditional, didactic models of teaching in online environments, Web 2.0 offers rich opportunities to move away from the highly-centralized

industrial model of learning of the past decade, towards achieving individual empowerment of students through learning designs that focus on collaborative, networked communication, and interaction (Rogers, Liddle, Chan, Doxey, & Isom, 2007). Later in the chapter, we explore the themes of what pedagogical options and dynamic modes of social interaction and learning are now relevant to millennial learners.

Although it is arguable that the Internet has always comprised a network of individuals, connected through social technologies such as email, chat rooms, and newsgroups/discussion boards, a key difference is that while "portal" was the Web 1.0 buzzword, "platform" is the current keyword (O'Reilly, 2005), indicating that users can both create and use the tools to create content. Institutions of higher learning have yet to come to terms with this high-powered environment, and what it implies for teaching and learning (Ryberg, 2008). The most relevant aspects of Web 2.0 for education are digital tools that bridge personal and social worlds, and are endowed with both flexibility and modularity that enables collaborative remixability, a term coined to describe "a transformative process in which the information and media... organized and shared [by individuals] can be recombined and built on to create new forms, concepts, ideas, mashups and services" (Dybwad, 2005, "From personalization to glocalization and back again," para. 1). The term "social software" came into use in 2002, and is broadly defined as "software that supports group interaction" (Shirky, 2003, para. 2). Many social software applications straddle the virtual and real social worlds, as they entail online and offline interactions and various forms of visual and verbal connectivity in both synchronous and asynchronous modes. For example, *Flickr* (Yahoo! Inc., 2008) and *YouTube* (YouTube, LLC, 2008) facilitate the sharing of photos and videos with both "real world" and "virtual" friends; social networking sites like *MySpace* (2008), *Friendster* (2008), and *Facebook* (2008) allow users to build an online identity by customizing their personal profiles with a range of text and multimedia elements, as well as interacting with existing contacts and establishing new relationships. Another social networking site, *Stickam* (Advanced Video Communications, Inc., 2008) is "polysynchronous" (Robbins-Sponaas & Nolan, 2005) in that it additionally allows users who are online simultaneously to interact through real-time video and audio using their Web cameras (Webcams) and microphones. Mejias (2005) commented that "… social software can positively impact pedagogy by inculcating a desire to reconnect to the world as whole, not just the social part that exists online," referring to the isolating and decontextualized experience of much text-based traditional education. Mejias also has a much broader definition of social software that includes the categories

depicted in Table 1, which encompass both Web 1.0 and 2.0 technologies. For the purposes of the current discussion, the definition adopted here, to link in with the key notion of learner control and choice, is that proposed by Dron (2007): "social software… is [where] control and structure can arise through the process of communication, not as a result of design, but as an emergent feature of group interaction" (p. 233).

With this rich and varied functionality in mind, it is necessary to consider the affordances, limits, and potential value adding of social computing tools for millennial learners. Evidence for this can be found in emerging debates that argue a case for a conceptualization of learning as a networked, collaborative, and social activity, supported by a range of ICT affordances, including those provided

Table 1. Social software categories and examples (based on the work of Mejias, 2005)

Type of social software	Examples
1. Multi-player online gaming environments / virtual worlds	Multi-User Dungeons (MUDs); Massively-Multiplayer Online Games (MMOGs) such as World of Warcraft; 3D Interactive Virtual Worlds (IVWs) such as Second Life, Active Worlds
2. Discourse facilitation systems (Synchronous)	Chat rooms; instant messaging (e.g. MSN Messenger / Windows Live Messenger, AOL Instant Messenger, Yahoo Instant Messenger, ICQ); Voice-over Internet Protocol (VoIP) applications (e.g. Skype, Gizmo5)
3. Discourse facilitation systems (Asynchronous)	Email; bulletin boards; discussion boards; moderated commenting systems (e.g. K5, Slashdot, Plastic)
4. Content management systems	Blogs; wikis; document management systems (e.g. Plone); Web annotation systems
5. Product development systems	Sourceforge; Savane; LibreSource
6. Peer-to-peer file sharing systems	BitTorrent; Gnutella; Napster; Limewire; KaZaA; Morpheus; eMule; iMesh
7. Selling/purchasing management systems	eBay, Amazon Marketplace
8. Course management systems (CMS's)	Blackboard/WebCT; ANGEL; Moodle; .LRN; Sakai; ATutor; Claroline; Dokeos
9. Relationship management systems	MySpace; Friendster; Facebook; Faceparty; Orkut; eHarmony; Bebo; LinkedIn
10. Syndication systems	List-servs; RSS; Atom
11. Distributed classification systems	Social bookmarking (e.g. Delicious; Digg; Furl); Social cataloguing (e.g. LibraryThing, neighborrow and Shelfari for books, RateYourMusic.com and Discogs for music, Flixster, DVD-Spot and DVD Aficionado for DVDs/movies, BibSonomy, Bibster, refbase, CiteULike and Connotea for scholarly citations). Image and video sharing sites like Flickr and YouTube also make use of tag-based folksonomies, a type of distributed classification system, to facilitate the organization and retrieval of media content.

by social software tools (Mejias, 2005; Brown & Duguid, 2000). In summarizing the value and impact of learning networks for learning and knowledge creation, researchers suggest that pedagogical innovation is needed: "… [the new emphasis of education] requires the development of learning episodes for pupils that have dialogue and communication as core features. From this perspective, there is a far greater emphasis on networked rather than linear models of learning and on providing culturally relevant experiential and purposeful learning episodes than the consumption of abstract knowledge alien to that in which the knowledge was both created and will be applied in the future" (Rudd, Sutch, & Facer, 2006, p. 5).

The importance of integrating digital resources and social software tools stems from the fact that such resources are part of the knowledge society and economy, and are becoming more and more tightly woven into how we communicate, think, and generate knowledge and ideas in everyday life. Knowledge is no longer controlled and stable, but open to interpretation, modification, and recreation by anyone, anywhere (Breu & Hemingway, 2002). The traditional macro-structures of the disciplines are being replaced by dynamic micro-structures created by networked individuals working collaboratively. These communication networks are able to link people and summon the "wisdom of crowds" (Surowiecki, 2004), so that the collective intelligence of groups can be harnessed to generate ideas that are fresher, richer, and more sophisticated than the contributions of individual users. Lindner (2006) quotes Parkin (2005, p. 31), who observes: "it's not content or even context, but process that gets us going," indicating that participating, doing, and experiencing rather than knowing what or where, and creating knowledge rather than consuming it, is the new mindset and *modus operandi* of learners, online communities, and the knowledge economy at large. All in all, we have an environment in which digital

technology and innovation are paramount, and in which "learning to learn" (know-how) is now far more important than the memorization of explicit knowledge and facts (know-what).

IMPLICATIONS AND AFFORDANCES OF WEB 2.0 FOR EDUCATION

In many ways, the terms "co-creation" and "users add value" encapsulate the practices and ethos of those who participate in and use social software, showing that that is not just an assembly of applications or tools, but a set of concepts, practices, and attitudes that define its scope. This can be exemplified by contrasting two popular Web sites, *Encyclopædia Britannica Online* (2007), and *Wikipedia* (2007), the former maintained by a commercial institution and the latter by members of the public at large. In Wikipedia, an example of community publishing, users can participate and create content, thereby becoming active "prosumers." This openness is a hallmark of Web 2.0, as it allows users to mix, amend, and recombine micro-content, collaboratively and open to the world, inviting revision and commentary. Through an "architecture of participation," which entails the generation and sharing of digital documents by groups, teams, and individuals, the responsiveness of Web 2.0 to users is ensured. This process thrives on the aforementioned concept of "wisdom of the crowds" (Surowiecki, 2004), recognizing that when working cooperatively and sharing ideas, groups can be significantly more productive than individuals working in isolation. In Wikipedia, for instance, users create and evaluate content for other users, resulting a dynamic and ever-expanding repository of shareable, communal information.

So what are the specific implications of Web 2.0 for education, and what unique opportunities are afforded by the new wave of social software tools? One of the most well-known commentators on the Web 2.0 phenomenon, Danah Boyd (2007), claims that it is the sociability aspects that have the most potential for enhancing education, and for supporting three activities that characterize learner-centered instruction: support for conversational interaction, support for social feedback, and support for social networks and relationships between people. In this way, social software tools can also be viewed as pedagogical tools that stem from their affordances of sharing, communication, and information discovery. An affordance is an action that an individual can potentially perform in his or her environment by using a particular tool (Affordance, 2008); for example, blogging entails typing and editing, which are not affordances, but which in tandem with other functions lend themselves to the affordances of idea sharing and interaction. Educational affordances, then, can be defined as the relationships between the properties of an educational intervention and the characteristics of the learner that enable certain kinds of learning to occur (Kirschner, 2002). Some examples of the affordances of social software tools are listed below. These affordances stimulate the development of a participatory culture, where there is genuine engagement and communication in a learning community, and where learners feel socially connected with one another:

i)   *Collaborative information discovery and sharing.* Information sharing is enabled through a range of software applications, and experts and novices alike can make their work available to the rest of the digital world, for example through personal publishing (Downes, 2004) tools like blogs and podcast channels. Social bookmarking tools (e.g. *Delicious* [2008], *Furl* [LookSmart, Ltd., 2008]) allow people to build up collections of Web resources or bookmarks, classify and organize them through the use of tags, and share both the bookmarks and tags with others. In this way, users can find people with similar interests and learn from one another

as they jointly contribute to the continuous evolution of a "folksonomy" of Web-based content.

ii)   *Content creation.* Web 2.0 stresses the preeminence of content creation over content consumption. Anyone can create, assemble, organize, and share content to meet their own needs and help address the needs of others, as manifested in the most visible wiki project, Wikipedia, which allows users to add and modify encyclopedia entries in an open editing and review structure. Open source and open content initiatives (cf. Massachusetts Institute of Technology, 2008; *MERLOT*, 2008), as well as copyright licensing models like *Creative Commons* (2008; Beshears, 2005), are acting as a major catalyst for the growth of user-generated content in education.

iii)   *Connectivity and social rapport.* Social networking and rapport-building sites like *MySpace*, *Facebook*, and *Friendster* attract and support networks of people and facilitate connections between them. They are representative of what Gee (2004) calls affinity spaces, in which people acquire both social and communicative skills, and at the same time become immersed in the participatory culture of Web 2.0. In these spaces, users engage in informal learning and creative, expressive forms of behavior and identity seeking, while developing a range of digital literacies and competencies.

iv)   *Knowledge and information aggregation and content modification.* The advent and growth of syndication technologies like RSS and Atom, as well as related technologies such as podcasting and vodcasting, are indicative of a move to collecting material from many sources and using it for personal needs. The aggregated content can be remixed and reformulated (the concept of a mash-up) before being fed forward, either to be consumed by other individuals or to become the raw material for further remixing and reformulation.

RETHINKING METAPHORS OF LEARNING IN A WEB 2.0 WORLD AND KNOWLEDGE ERA

Taking a broad view of the affordances—sharing, customization, collaboration, etc.—has given rise to a number of alternative paradigms for learning, examples of which follow. First, the concept of a Personal Learning Environment, or PLE, is an excellent example of how learners are using digital tools to access information that is relevant to them, and to learn informally. PLEs are learning environments in which learners manage their own learning using various software and services; the environment provides contextually-appropriate toolsets by enabling the learner to adjust and select options based on his/her needs and circumstances, resulting in, ideally, a model where learner needs rather than technology drives the learning process. Downes (2005) describes the PLE as an approach, not an application, one that protects and celebrates identity as well as supporting multiple levels of socializing and the building of communities of inquiry. While the current generation of CMS's allows each student to have their own personal view of the course(s) they are enrolled in, most do not accommodate the social connectivity tools and personal profile spaces that students might choose. They are firmly set in frameworks and decisions made by teachers and institutions, and often conform to a classroom or lecture hall metaphor, which can have constraining effects on both learners' and teachers' willingness and ability to adapt to new learning modes and paradigms. Perhaps this explains, at least in part, why we can't stop lecturing online (Sheely, 2006).

Another pedagogical approach that draws on a range of Web 2.0 affordances is the knowledge building paradigm, proposed by Scardamalia and Bereiter (2003), based on the dynamics of how communities work. It privileges a less hierarchical form of learning based on small teams, sharing, content creation, and use of ICTs to access, share, create, and continually improve ideas. In general, learning processes can be said to evoke a number of possible scenarios or metaphors. Sfard, for example in (1998) distinguished between two metaphors of learning, the acquisition metaphor and the participation metaphor. The former views learning mainly as a process of acquiring chunks of information, typically delivered by a teacher or instructor, while the latter perceives learning as a process of participating in various cultural practices and shared learning activities. In Web 2.0, individuals, groups, and environments contribute to the processes of cognition, and learning is embedded in multiple networks of distributed individuals engaging in activities. The participation metaphor is characteristic of how learners engage with social software tools in joint processes that involve conversation, cooperation, and sharing, in ways that are closely tied to socio-cultural theory (Lave & Wenger, 1991; Vygotsky, 1978; Bijker, Hughes, & Pinch, 1987). However, learners are also capable of creating and generating new ideas, concepts, and knowledge, and one of the ultimate goals of 21st-century education is arguably to engender this form of creativity. Current views of knowledge regard the notion of a teacher-dominated classroom and curriculum as obsolete, and embrace learning environments where students assume control of their own learning, make connections with peers, and produce fresh insights and ideas through inquiry. Thus, to keep pace with the content creation processes enabled by social software tools, it appears to be necessary to venture beyond the acquisition and participation dichotomy. Paavola and Hakkarainen (2005) propose the knowledge creation metaphor of learning, which builds on common elements of Bereiter's (2002) theory of knowledge building, Engeström's (1987, 1999) theory of expansive learning, and Nonaka and Takeuchi's (1995) model of knowledge creation.

Figure 1. The three Ps of Pedagogy 2.0

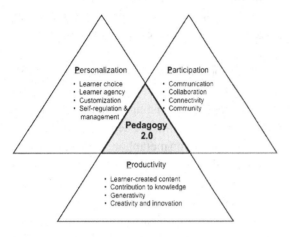

WHAT ARE THE PRINCIPLES UNDERPINNING PEDAGOGY 2.0?

As social software tools become widespread and ubiquitous, several questions are being posed by educational practitioners and researchers, many of whom observe the changing trends and the power of Web 2.0 for connecting teachers, learners, and resources. Alexander (2006) asks: "How do we respond to the possibilities of what some call "E-learning 2.0," based on environments, microcontent, and networking?" (p. 42). One reply would be to reiterate the conventional principles of constructivist learning, which tell us that effective learning is conversational in nature, and that it necessitates a social dimension, including both teacher–learner and learner–learner communication and dialogue (Laurillard, 2001). If used in conjunction with sound instructional strategies, the benefits of making connections to others and conversing through instant messaging, blogs and *Twitter* (2008) can provide an impetus for inquiry-based approaches, and support collaborative, discovery-based learning and exploration.

In an effort to overcome the limitations of existing models of learning, and exploit more fully the affordances and potential of social software tools, it is possible to depict how an individual might operate and learn in a networked society, having access to diverse ideas, resources, and communities, and actively engaging in knowledge creation rather than solely in passive consumption. Figure 1 shows the various overlapping elements that the authors believe enable the realization of a learner-centered, participatory, and personalized approach to pedagogy.

The diagram shows how individuals link with communities and networks in the process of information sharing, knowledge construction, and the development of shared understanding. The interdependence existing amongst ideas, individuals, communities, and information networks, appropriately supported by technology, underpins the demands of what the authors call Pedagogy 2.0, and offers a range of choices to individuals to suit their personal needs and goals. This echoes the core principles of the Web 2.0 era, that social software is about bringing minds, communities, and ideas into contact with one another, while ensuring personalization, collaboration, and creativity, leading to the generation of new and innovative ideas and artifacts.

Other aspects of social software can also be embedded in learner-centered pedagogical frameworks. Apart from the conversational affordances of social software tools, there are further social constructivist principles that apply to Pedagogy 2.0. Learning occurs as a socio-cultural system, within which many learners use tools and multiple forms of interaction to create a collective activity framed by cultural constraints and practices. Typically, learners are scaffolded through the learning experience through the help of others (peers, teachers, virtual community sources, technology) (Vygotsky, 1978, 1987; Wood, Bruner, & Ross, 1976; Bandura, 1997; see also Brush & Saye, 2001; Dabbagh, 2003). Coaching, modeling, mentoring, and the broader notion of cognitive apprenticeship (Collins, Brown, & Newman, 1987; Brown, Collins, & Duguid, 1989) also lend themselves well to the application of Web 2.0 and social software tools in ways that can be said to exemplify Pedagogy 2.0.

Another critical component of effective learning involves active participation with others, including peers, experts, and community. Collaboration and cooperation have long been recognized as ingredients of effective pedagogy; wikis and collaborative writing and editing tools such as *Writeboard* (37signals, n. d.) and *Google Docs* (Google, Inc., 2008) are useful extensions to conventional writing approaches. Linked with this principle of collaborative production, there is the additional facility of sharing and publishing the artifact of the learning activity, and inviting feedback from peers—another form of scaffolding. By publishing and presenting their work to a wide audience, learners benefit from the opportunity to appropriate new ideas, and transform their own understanding through reflection (Williams & Jacobs, 2004). Researchers recognize that communication is often shaped by the use of different tools and technologies. For example, Farmer (2004) proposes that blogs offer "new opportunities in the development of social, cognitive and teacher presence online" (p. 274). In examining the potential for social software tools to support social constructivism and communities of inquiry, Farmer is guided by Garrison and Anderson's (2003) framework for the creation of a successful online learning community, comprising "teachers and students transacting with the specific purpose of facilitating, constructing and validating understanding, and of developing capabilities that will lead to further learning" (p. 23).

Last but not least, a further link between current social software applications and established theory that is relevant to Pedagogy 2.0 is evident in the principles of learner agency, self-direction, and personal meaning construction. A primary goal of learning is that learners should learn to learn, and become capable of making their own decisions and developing their personal learning styles and approaches. For example, the "blogosphere," as well as social networking sites, though they are often viewed negatively by educators, are nonetheless social interactive spaces where learners can choose to explore facets of their own identity, as well as engage in personal self-expression, dialogue, and knowledge sharing with others.

With its three Ps of participation, personalization, and productivity (Figure 1), Pedagogy 2.0 highlights that in a networked society, powered by a range of high-speed technologies, learners have access to ideas, resources, and communities to support their learning, driven by personal needs and choice (personalization), and they are able to develop self-regulatory skills in the process. Pedagogies need to engage learners in the social processes of knowledge creation rather than the mere consumption of instructor-supplied information (productivity), in addition to scaffolding linkages, dialogue, and connections in and across communities and global distributed networks (participation) for the purposes of idea sharing, inquiry, and problem solving. Although not dependent on the technology, Pedagogy 2.0 capitalizes on the core energies and affordances of Web 2.0—a raft of tools that support user autonomy, increased levels of socialization and interactivity, access to open communities, and peer-to-peer networking—in order to move beyond instructor-centered classroom environments, prescribed curricula and content, and the "walled garden" approach of course management systems. While the three Ps represent principles that are congruent with the philosophy of the relatively new concept of Web 2.0, they nevertheless are well supported by established and accepted learning concepts and theories including motivation and self-regulation (Pintrich, 1995; Pintrich & Schunk, 1996), information processing theory (Miller, 1956), multimedia learning theory (Mayer, 2001), socio-cultural learning theory (Vygotsky, 1978; Brown et al., 1989; Lave & Wenger, 1991), and experiential learning theory (Kolb, 1984; Kolb & Fry, 1975).

The three Ps of Pedagogy 2.0 and how they apply to the design of learning activities and environments are discussed in greater detail in the sub-sections that follow. It is important to note that the elements depicted in Figure 1 seek not only to identify desired learning outcomes, but also to provide a foundation upon which guidelines and principles can be derived, to help inform the processes of instructional and learning design. For example, while student-generated content is a valued outcome of learning as it provides evidence of knowledge construction, the principle of active learner contribution must underpin the learning task design (Burgos, Hummel, Tattersall, Brouns, & Koper, 2008), to ensure that there are ample opportunities for learners to become producers of resources as opposed to merely being consumers of content.

Participation

More engaging, socially-based models for teaching and learning are needed to replace the traditional, "closed classroom" models, which place the spotlight on the institution and instructor. A defining feature of Pedagogy 2.0 is that, alongside the increased socialization of learning and teaching, there is a focus on a less prescriptive curriculum and a shift towards teacher–student partnerships in learning, with teachers as co-learners or "associates" in learning (Eustace, 2003). This stance is echoed by Lee (2005), according to whom "we have already managed to overcome the confines of the physical classroom, but... still remain unknowing prisoners of the instructor-centred online classroom. To move further ahead, we will need to demolish these virtual walls so as to create social learning spaces, in which learners and... [teachers]... become associates in a community of practice, participating in networks of interaction that transcend the old-fashioned constructs of institutions and organisations" (p. 17).

Now, social software tools make it easy for learners to engage deeply with their peers, instructors, other subject-matter experts, and the community at large. Through these tools, individuals can create and maintain their own collections of ideas, photos, and bookmarks online. These creations, while enabling personal expression and publication, also allow for social constructivist forms of participation by allowing comments and annotations by others, and by facilitating contributions to extant communities of interest through the sharing of resources. Therefore, not only is this element of Pedagogy 2.0 reflective of the "participation" model of learning (Sfard, 1998), as opposed to the "acquisition" model, but it also adds a further dimension to participative learning by increasing the level of socialization and collaboration with experts, community, and peer groups, and by fostering connections that are often global in reach. Jenkins (2007) fittingly sums up the process as follows: "Learning in a networked society involves understanding how networks work and how to deploy them for one's own ends. It involves understanding the social and cultural contexts within which different information emerges... and how to use networks to get one's own work out into the world and in front of a relevant and, with hope, appreciative public" (p. 51).

Personalization

Research attests to a growing appreciation of the importance of the learner's self-direction and control over the whole learning process (Fazey & Fazey, 2001; Narciss, Proske, & Koerndle, 2007). Evidence suggests that we can improve learning effectiveness by having learners take active responsibility for their own learning in a variety of technology-enhanced and technology-mediated educational settings (Dron, 2007; Nesbit & Winne, 2003). Learner self-direction and self-regulation are cornerstones of such approaches as problem-based and inquiry-based learning (Desharnais & Limson, 2007; Edelson, Gordin, & Pea, 1999), and are central to the grand vision of Pedagogy 2.0, where learners have the freedom to decide how to engage in personally-meaningful learning.

In fact, the notion of personalization is not entirely new to educators, and it is often linked to the term "learner-centered" education, a desirable state where learners know how to choose and make decisions relating to their personal learning needs. Despite the efforts of many constructivist teachers, however, the control culture of education prevails, and pre-packaged content and pre-designed syllabi continue to dominate, denying students choice and autonomy in shaping their own learning trajectories. According to Dron (2006), such approaches lead to de-motivation, boredom, and confusion. Web 2.0 and social software tools enable choice and allow learners to make decisions about how to best meet their goals and needs for connection and social interaction. Apart from choosing which resources and sites to subscribe and contribute to, which tools to use, and how and where to use them, we are witnessing a shift in the modalities of expression that are now available (Jenkins, 2007). Text alone is not always preferred mode of communication, as Web-based multimedia production and distribution tools incorporating rich audio (podcasting, *Skype*), photo (*Flickr*), and video (vodcasting, *YouTube*) capabilities are constantly growing.

The use of social software also presents exciting prospects in the way of authentic learning and assessment opportunities that are personally meaningful and relevant to learners. With "Mobile Web 2.0" (Cochrane, 2008), the wireless connectivity and data gathering capabilities (e.g. photo-blogging, video recording, voice recording, text input) of modern wireless mobile devices can be used to deliver peer-generated content in multiple media forms to members of a distributed workforce for just-in-time learning, such as in preparation for a real task in the workplace. Students can capture text, sound, images, and video *in situ* within "real-world" contexts and locations, to be shared with their peers and instructors, and receive assistance with and feedback on job tasks through opportunities for observation, correction, and remediation. This potential to bridge pedagogically-designed learning contexts and to facilitate learner-generated contexts (Luckin et al., 2005; Luckin, 2006) paves the way for a new level of personalization that capitalizes on the affordances of Web 2.0.

By harnessing digital technologies and social software tools, three key areas pivotal to the development of personalization in education are aptly summarized by Green et al. (2005). According to these researchers, pedagogy must: (i) ensure that learners are capable of making informed educational decisions; (ii) diversify and recognize different forms of skills and knowledge; and (iii) include learner-focused forms of feedback and assessment.

Productivity

As argued earlier in this chapter, students are capable of creating and generating ideas, concepts, and knowledge, and the ultimate goal of learning in the knowledge age may be to enable such forms of creativity and productivity. In recent times, the value of textbooks is being questioned (Moore, 2003; Fink, 2005) and the open source and open content movements are gaining increased attention and traction. Clark (2003) points towards the "Napsterisation" of e-learning through P2P file and media content sharing services. Today's students perceive little value in the rote learning of factual information, particularly given the accessibility and ease of use of search engines and Web-based reference sites such as *Google* and *Wikipedia*. Educators are thus beginning to realize that instructor-supplied content has limitations, particularly if it pre-empts learner discovery and research, and active student involvement in the knowledge creation process. They are starting to comprehend how social software tools make it easy to contribute ideas and content, placing the power of media creation and distribution into the hands of "the people formerly known as the audience" (Rosen, 2006, para. 1), which includes their students.

Mirroring the massive outpouring of information and dynamic, user-generated content between peers on the Web, dubbed personal publishing (Downes, 2005), is the rise of student-generated content and student performance content (Boettcher, 2006), the latter of which is defined as student-generated content in the form of artifacts that are products of real or authentic task performances. For example, in recent years the e-portfolio (Love, McKean, & Gathercoal, 2002; Abrami & Barrett, 2005) has emerged as popular strategy for capturing and organizing student-generated content, which, in addition to completed project/assignment work or deliverables, may also incorporate evidence of the process of learning that is representative of the complexity and "messiness" of an authentic, problem-based learning experience, such as successive drafts of solutions, descriptions of mistakes made, or reports of difficulties encountered. Lyons and Freidus (2004) demonstrate how e-portfolios can be used to scaffold inquiry-based learning and reflection on practice.

Student-generated content may also include computer-mediated communication (CMC) discourse such as chat logs and discussion board postings, reflective writing in the form of blog-based diaries, summaries, and reviews, created by students working individually or in teams. Last but not least, it may also include "found" content, including the results of students' own wide reading, gathered from Web sites, journals, magazines, and news articles that are brought to and shared with others in the learning environment.

EVALUATING THE EFFECTIVENESS OF WEB 2.0-BASED LEARNING TOOLS AND APPROACHES

Alongside the evolution of Web 2.0 tools and their application to teaching and learning, there have also been changes in evaluation theory and practices, with a greater emphasis on taking the per-spective that student learning and engagement are at the heart of whether technology can be deemed to be effective (Salaberry, 2001). Combined with appropriate strategies, Web 2.0 technologies have the potential to impact student learning, and may call for new and expanded definitions of student learning outcomes, that include, for instance, the development of digital literacies and the fostering of creative, diverse modes of expression using social media (Katz & Macklin, 2007; Lorenzo & Dziuban, 2006; Jenkins, 2007). Evaluative studies on the adoption and effectiveness of Web 2.0 tools in education are limited; one of the most significant reports in this area was recently commissioned by the British Educational Communications and Technology Agency (Becta). Although the project was primarily aimed at examining practices in K-12 schooling, the following quote can also be applied to questions on how Web 2.0 and social software are being used in higher education: "Confident adoption of Web 2.0 practices must be grounded on convincing research that shows its appeal and its impact. Yet empirical studies in this area are rather rare. This may reflect the neglect of researchers or it may be an indication that Web 2.0 practices themselves are still poorly represented in the curriculum and, therefore, hard to investigate *in situ*" (Crook et al., 2008, p. 49). The authors of the report claim that while there is a dearth of research and evaluation at the primary and secondary levels, there is considerably more activity surrounding practices in higher education.

As Web 2.0 is relatively recent, and adoption by educational institutions has been piecemeal rather than systemic, much of the published work reflects initial attempts by individuals who are experimenting with new tools and applications. Crook et al. (2008) are critical of existing evaluation efforts, pointing out that "there is relatively little reporting of the learning process and rarely a comparison point that helps evaluate the impact of an intervention relative to alternative learning structures" (p. 54). Clearly, there is a need for contextualized studies and evaluations that report on changes to pedagogy and student learning that accrue from integration of Web 2.0 tools and approaches in learning environments, but existing attempts are often isolated, experimental, and focused on the technological design rather than providing holistic, in-depth analyses of the learning environment and the changes that have been effected. In addition to large-scale, longitudinal studies, case studies are needed that contribute to the development of best practice. In order to be of use, such case studies must be theoretically grounded and go beyond the provision of descriptive accounts to include in-depth analysis of the context, participants, instructional design, and pedagogical approaches adopted. They should seek to establish their relevance and application outside their local settings, providing others with practical advice and guidelines, supported by concrete evidence, on how to design, implement, and evaluate pedagogical improvements within their own ecologies of practice.

In describing the impact of the recent technological changes affecting higher education, Hilton (2006) uses two competing metaphors to depict the challenges of the Web 2.0 era: "a perfect storm, born from the convergence of numerous disruptive forces… [and] the dawn of a new day, a sunrise rife with opportunities arising from these same disruptive forces" (p. 59). These contrasting images underpin the uncertainty surrounding the benefits and advantages of emerging technologies and how, when and where Web 2.0-based learning interventions should be planned. Crook et al. (2008) warn against the dangers of a utopian vision of transformative learning and a bright future that is rich in Web 2.0 tools, and instead advocate a more conservative and pragmatic approach of pedagogical enrichment, at least until there is compelling evidence to the contrary.

SUMMARY AND CONCLUSION

In this chapter, the emphasis has been on Web 2.0 as more than a technological shift or raft of new tools; instead, it is social movement that opens up new opportunities for communication, interaction, and sharing. Greater and easier connectivity enables greater participation, thereby offering users a range of pathways, modes, and styles of working and learning. In education, pedagogies are increasingly beginning to encourage student-generated content, resource pooling, and collaborative effort among learners through the adoption of social software applications. To encapsulate these changes, the framework of Pedagogy 2.0 was proposed by the authors to serve as a conceptual model that distills the range of choices being made available to teachers and learners to suit their personal needs and goals, while promoting participation in and contribution to diverse communities and networks that transcend the walls of the classroom. Pedagogy 2.0 therefore resonates with the core principles of the Web 2.0 era, in which individuals generate, share, and refine knowledge, ideas, and artifacts in concert with and for the benefit of a worldwide audience on the Internet.

This chapter has delineated some of the affordances and constraints of social software, and defined it as an open architecture that facilitates user-controlled, collaboratively-generated knowledge and community-focused enquiry. It is the combination of the technological affordances of social software with new educational agendas and priorities that offers the potential for radical and transformational shifts in teaching and learning practices. How should educators bring these principles into the design of learning and assessment tasks in higher education? The key is to strike a balance between enabling learner self-direction and control by providing options and choice while still supplying the necessary structure and scaffolding. Moving on from the hierarchical, structured approach of institutional CMS's, the concepts of personalization and collaborative, creative production represent current steps towards an alternative approach to technology-mediated learning. The idea is to have learners exercise greater control over their own learning experiences and knowledge creation efforts, rather than be constrained by centralized, instructor-controlled learning interventions.

Such approaches are admittedly not without their challenges, as they call for educators and educational administrators to relinquish some degree of control and to look beyond the traditional view of classroom authority, a departure from the manner in which their jobs have traditionally been done and are expected to be done. Developments in Web 2.0 present fertile opportunities for innovative forms of knowledge building and networking, with an increased constituency of participants. Contemporary learning theories resonate with Web 2.0 affordances by enabling greater learner autonomy and self-direction, while encouraging a broader array of expressive modalities (for example, through podcasts, blogs, wikis, and user-generated video) and therefore give learners more choice, control, and agency in the learning process. The trend towards greater personalization of learning and assessment is apparent, as learner achievements can be showcased through e-portfolios and authentic tasks that are linked to global audiences.

With the prevalence of learner-centered discourse, there are also increased demands on teachers, not only to re-skill in the technical aspects of the new tools, but also to find time to develop the competencies needed to integrate them effectively in their face-to-face and online teaching practices. For example, Web 2.0 endorses strongly collaborative forms of learning that may cast teachers as co-learners rather than experts, thereby requiring professional adjustment to new roles. Pedagogical

change does not happen overnight, and teachers need time and professional development to acquaint themselves and become proficient with alternative approaches. Often the pedagogies that could lead to innovation are not known, not valued, or are perceived by teachers as too onerous or time consuming to implement in practice (Collis & Moonen, 2008). Other issues are related to the management of group and individual achievement through well-designed assessment tasks that are congruent with the spirit of Web 2.0. Many practitioners worry about the ease with which students can use digital media to "cut-and-paste" resources when navigating the Web and engaging in research. There is universal concern over the rise of plagiarism and of the need to educate students in the dispositions of academic integrity, and the skills of establishing the authenticity and authority of Web-based publications. On the positive side, Web 2.0 provides scope and freedom for users to develop confidence and fluency in new modes of inquiry and literacy. Teachers need to keep pace with developments and assist their students to acquire the skills needed to critique and assess the value of new and evolving information sources and interactive knowledge spaces.

In learning institutions internationally, we are witnessing small-scale experiments and the integration of a variety of social software resources in instructional designs and pedagogies. Given the new and dynamic educational landscape, there are richer and more engaging pathways to learn than ever before, creating massive potential for the building of rich and inclusive learning environments that cater to the needs of millennial students. For these environments to expand and flourish, we will need to support innovation at all levels, and to ensure dialogue between educational leaders, researchers, teachers, learners, and the wider community about new approaches to learning that involve collaboration across sectors, industries, and disciplines. While there is a groundswell of enthusiasm for social computing applications and innovative pedagogies, there needs to be research-based investigation into how practices are changing, along with evidence-based practice in analyzing how learning processes and outcomes can be improved. The emerging body of research cited in this chapter reflects a strong level of confidence that learner-centered pedagogies and personalized approaches are being adopted by institutions worldwide. The potential for strategic application of Web 2.0 tools in higher education clearly exists; however, the tools alone do not provide the basis, rationale, or impetus for change, and there is a danger that novel Internet configurations may overshadow the need to ensure that pedagogical considerations are foregrounded so that practitioners recognize the centrality of learner needs and desired learning outcomes, and seek to apply technology constructively. While there is nothing new in this call for pedagogy-before-technology, the plethora of innovative technological applications should serve as a call to refresh teaching practices and acknowledge that the best learning outcomes can be achieved by adopting a multi-perspectival approach that leads to the creation of participatory learning environments, capitalizes on both formal and informal opportunities for learning, and connects academic learning to real-world contexts. An overall change in mindset is needed, that sees and appreciates the possibilities enabled by the different kinds of representational, communicative, and collaborative tools and affordances of the Web 2.0 era.

REFERENCES

Abram, S. (2005). Web 2.0—huh? Library 2.0, librarian 2.0. *Information Outlook, 9*(12), 44–46.

Abrami, P. C., & Barrett, H. (Eds.). (2005). Electronic portfolios [special issue]. *Canadian Journal of Learning Technology, 31*(3).

Advanced Video Communications, Inc. (2008). *Stickam—the live community, live streaming video*. Retrieved on December 3, 2008, from http://www.stickam.com/

Affordance. (2008). In *Wikipedia, the free encyclopedia*. Retrieved on December 4, 2008, from http://en.wikipedia.org/wiki/Affordance

Alexander, B. (2006). Web 2.0: A new wave of innovation for teaching and learning? *EDUCAUSE Review, 41*(2), 32–44.

Allen, C. (2004). *Tracing the evolution of social software*. Retrieved on June 4, 2007, from http://www.lifewithalacrity.com/2004/10/tracing_the_evo.html

Bandura, A. (1997). *Social learning theory*. Englewood Cliffs, NJ: Prentice Hall.

Bereiter, C. (2002). *Education and mind in the knowledge age*. Hillsdale, NJ: Erlbaum.

Beshears, F. M. (2005, October 4). Viewpoint: The economic case for creative commons textbooks. *Campus Technology*. Retrieved on May 10, 2007, from http://campustechnology.com/articles/40535/

Bijker, W., Hughes, T., & Pinch, T. (Eds.). (1987). *Social construction of technological systems: New directions in the sociology and history of technology*. Cambridge, MA: MIT Press.

Boettcher, J. V. (2006, February 28). The rise of student performance content. *Campus Technology*. Retrieved on February 11, 2007, from http://www.campustechnology/article.aspx?aid=40747

Boyd, D. (2007). The significance of social software. In T. N. Burg & J. Schmidt (Eds.), *BlogTalks reloaded: Social software research & cases* (pp. 15–30). Norderstedt, Germany: Books on Demand.

Breu, K., & Hemingway, C. (2002). Collaborative processes and knowledge creation in communities of practice. *Creativity and Innovation Management, 11*(3), 147–153. doi:10.1111/1467-8691.00247

Brown, J. S., Collins, A., & Duguid, P. (1989). Situated cognition and the culture of learning. *Educational Researcher, 18*(1), 32–42.

Brown, J. S., & Duguid, P. (2000). *The social life of information*. Boston: Harvard Business School Press.

Brush, T., & Saye, J. (2001). The use of embedded scaffolds with hypermedia-supported student-centered learning. *Journal of Educational Multimedia and Hypermedia, 10*(4), 333–356.

Bryant, T. (2006). Social software in academia. *EDUCAUSE Quarterly, 29*(2), 61–64.

Burgos, D., Hummel, H. G. K., Tattersall, C., Brouns, F., & Koper, R. (2008). Design guidelines for collaboration and participation with examples from the LN4LD. In L. Lockyer, S. Bennett, S. Agostinho & B. Harper (Eds.), *Handbook of research on learning design and learning objects: Issues, applications, and technologies* (Vol. 1, pp. 373–389). Hershey, PA: IGI Global.

Clark, D. (2003). *The napsterisation of learning (P2P)*. Brighton, England: Epic Group.

Cochrane, T. (2008). Mobile Web 2.0: The new frontier. In *Hello! Where are you in the landscape of educational technology?* [Melbourne, Australia: Deakin University.]. *Proceedings Ascilite Melbourne, 2008*, 177–186.

Collins, A., Brown, J. S., & Newman, S. E. (1987). *Cognitive apprenticeship: Teaching the art of reading, writing, and mathematics*. (Tech. Rep. 403). Washington, D.C.: National Institute of Education. (ERIC Document Reproduction Service No. ED 284 181).

Collis, B., & Moonen, J. (2008). Web 2.0 tools and processes in higher education: Quality perspectives. *Educational Media International, 45*(2), 93–106. doi:10.1080/09523980802107179

Creative Commons. (2008). Retrieved on December 30, 2008, from http://creativecommons.org/

Crook, C., Cummings, J., Fisher, T., Graber, R., Harrison, C., Lewin, C., et al. (2008). *Web 2.0 technologies for learning: The current landscape—opportunities, challenges, and tensions*. Coventry, England: Becta. Retrieved on December 29, 2008, from http://partners.becta.org.uk/upload-dir/downloads/page_documents/research/web2_technologies_learning.pdf

Dabbagh, N. (2003). Scaffolding: An important teacher competency in online learning. *TechTrends, 47*(2), 39–44. doi:10.1007/BF02763424

Delicious. (2008). Retrieved on December 30, 2008, from http://www.delicious.com/

Desharnais, R. A., & Limson, M. (2007). Designing and implementing virtual courseware to promote inquiry-based learning. *Journal of Online Learning and Teaching, 3*(1), 30–39.

Downes, S. (2004). Educational blogging. *EDUCAUSE Review, 39*(5), 14–26.

Downes, S. (2005, October). *E-learning 2.0. ELearn*. Retrieved on June 3, 2007, from http://www.elearnmag.org/subpage.cfm?section=articles&article=29-1

Dron, J. (2006). Social software and the emergence of control. In *Proceedings of the Sixth International Conference on Advanced Learning Technologies* (pp. 904–908). New York: ACM.

Dron, J. (2007). *Control and constraint in e-learning: Choosing when to choose*. Hershey, PA: Information Science Publishing.

Dybwad, B. (2005, September 29). Approaching a definition of Web 2.0. *The social software weblog* [weblog]. Retrieved on January 10, 2007, from http://socialsoftware.weblogsinc. com/2005/09/29/approaching-a-definition-of-web-2-0/

Edelson, D. C., Gordin, D. N., & Pea, R. D. (1999). Addressing the challenges of inquiry-based learning through technology and curriculum design. *Journal of the Learning Sciences, 8*(3/4), 391–450. doi:10.1207/s15327809jls0803&4_3

Encyclopædia Britannica Online. (2007). Retrieved on August 10, 2007, from http://www. britannica.com/

Engeström, Y. (1987). *Learning by expanding.* Helsinki, Finland: Orienta-Konsultit Oy.

Engeström, Y. (1999). Innovative learning in work teams: Analyzing cycles of knowledge creation in practice. In Y. Engeström, R. Miettinen & R.-L. Punamäki (Eds.), *Perspectives on activity theory* (pp. 377–404). Cambridge, England: Cambridge University Press.

Eustace, K. (2003). Educational value of e-learning in conventional and complementary computing education. In S. Mann & A. Williamson (Eds.), *Proceedings of the 16th Annual Conference of the National Advisory Committee on Computing Qualifications* (pp. 53–62). Hamilton, New Zealand: NACCQ.

Facebook. (2008). Retrieved on December 4, 2008, from http://www.facebook.com/

Farmer, J. (2004). Communication dynamics: Discussion boards, weblogs, and the development of communities of inquiry in online learning environments. In R. Atkinson, C. McBeath, D. Jonas-Dwyer & R. Phillips (Eds.), *Beyond the comfort zone: Proceedings of the 21st ASCILITE Conference* (pp. 274–283). Perth, Australia: University of Western Australia.

Fazey, D. M., & Fazey, J. A. (2001). The potential for autonomy in learning: Perceptions of competence, motivation, and locus of control in first-year undergraduate students. *Studies in Higher Education, 26*(3), 345–361. doi:10.1080/03075070120076309

Fink, L. (2005, September 16). Making textbooks worthwhile. *Chronicle of Higher Education.* Retrieved on March 10, 2007, from http://chronicle. com/weekly/v52/i04/04b01201.htm

Fischer, G., & Konomi, S. (2005). Innovative media in support of distributed intelligence and lifelong learning. In *Proceedings of the Third IEEE International Workshop on Wireless and Mobile Technologies in Education* (pp. 3–10). Los Alamitos, CA: IEEE Computer Society.

Friendster. (2008). Retrieved on December 4, 2008, from http://www.friendster.com/

Garrison, D. R., & Anderson, T. (2003). *E-learning in the 21st century: A framework for research and practice.* London: Routledge Falmer.

Gee, J. P. (2004). *Situated language and learning: A critique of traditional schooling.* New York: Palmgrave-McMillan.

Google, Inc. (2008). *Google docs.* Retrieved on December 4, 2008, from http://docs.google. com/

Green, H., Facer, K., Rudd, T., Dillon, P., & Humphreys, P. (2005). *Personalisation and digital technologies.* Bristol, England: Futurelab. Retrieved on October 23, 2007, from http://www.futurelab. org.uk/resources/documents/opening_education/ Personalisation_report.pdf

Hilton, J. (2006). The future for higher education: Sunrise or perfect storm? *EDUCAUSE Review, 41*(2), 58–71.

Jenkins, H. (2007). *Confronting the challenges of participatory vulture: Media education for the 21st century*. Chicago, IL: MacArthur Foundation. Retrieved on January 4, 2008, from http://www.digitallearning.macfound.org/atf/cf/%7B7E45C7E0-A3E0-4B89-AC9C-E807E1B0AE4E%7D/JENKINS_WHITE_PAPER.PDF

Katz, I. R., & Macklin, A. S. (2007). Information and communication technology (ICT) literacy: Integration and assessment in higher education. *Systemics, Cybernetics, and Informatics*, *5*(4), 50–55.

Kirschner, P. A. (2002). Can we support CSCL? Educational, social, and technological affordances for learning. In P.A. Kirschner (Ed.), *Three worlds of CSCL: Can we support CSCL?* (pp. 7–47). Heerlen, The Netherlands: Open University of the Netherlands.

Kolb, D. A. (1984). *Experiential learning*. Englewood Cliffs, NJ: Prentice Hall.

Kolb, D. A., & Fry, R. (1975). Toward an applied theory of experiential learning. In C. L. Cooper (Ed.), *Theories of group process* (pp. 33–58). London: John Wiley.

Laurillard, D. (2001). *Rethinking university teaching: A framework for the effective use of educational technology* (2nd ed.). London: Routledge.

Lave, J., & Wenger, E. (1991). *Situated learning: Legitimate peripheral participation*. Cambridge, England: Cambridge University Press.

Lee, M. J. W. (2005). New tools for online collaboration: Blogs, wikis, RSS, and podcasting. *Training and Development in Australia*, *32*(5), 17–20.

Lindner, M. (2006). Use these tools, your mind will follow. Learning in immersive micromedia and microknowledge environments. In D. Whitelock & S. Wheeler (Eds.), *The next generation: Research proceedings of the 13ᵗʰ ALT-C conference* (pp. 41–49). Oxford: ALT.

LookSmart, Ltd. (2008). *Furl*. Retrieved on December 30, 2008, from http://www.furl.net/

Lorenzo, G., & Dziuban, C. (2006). *Ensuring the net generation is net savvy*. Washington, D.C.: EDUCUASE.

Love, D., McKean, G., & Gathercoal, P. (2002). Portfolios to webfolios and beyond: Levels of maturation. *EDUCAUSE Quarterly*, *25*(2), 29–37.

Luckin, R. (2006). Understanding learning contexts as ecologies of resources: From the zone of proximal development to learner generated contexts. In T. Reeves & S. Yamashita (Eds.), *Proceedings of World Conference on E-Learning in Corporate, Government, Healthcare, and Higher Education 2006* (pp. 2195–2202). Chesapeake, VA: AACE.

Luckin, R., du Boulay, B., Smith, H., Underwood, J., Fitzpatrick, G., Holmberg, J., et al. (2005). Using mobile technology to create flexible learning contexts. *Journal of Interactive Media in Education, 22*. Retrieved on December 4, 2008, from http://jime.open.ac.uk/2005/22/luckin-2005-22.pdf

Lyons, N., & Freidus, H. (2004). The reflective portfolio in self-study: Inquiring into and representing a knowledge of practice. In J. J. Loughran, M. L. Hamilton, V. K. LaBoskey & T. L. Russell (Ed.), *International handbook of self-study of teaching and teacher education practices* (pp. 1073–1107). Dordrecht, The Netherlands: Springer.

Massachusetts Institute of Technology. (2008). *MIT OpenCourseWare*. Retrieved on December 30, 2008, from http://ocw.mit.edu/

Mayer, R. E. (2001). *Multimedia learning*. Cambridge, England: Cambridge University Press.

Mejias, U. (2005). A nomad's guide to learning and social software. *The Knowledge Tree: An E-Journal of Learning Innovation, 7*. Retrieved on December 10, 2006, from http://knowledgetree.flexiblelearning.net.au/edition07/download/la_mejias.pdf

MERLOT. (2008). Retrieved on February 19, 2008, from http://www.merlot.org/

Miller, G. A. (1956). The magical number seven, plus or minus two: Some limits on our capacity for processing information. *Psychological Review, 63*(2), 81–97. doi:10.1037/h0043158

Moore, J. W. (2003). Are textbooks dispensable? *Journal of Chemical Education, 80*(4), 359.

MySpace. (2008). Retrieved on December 4, 2008, from http://www.myspace.com/

Narciss, S., Proske, A., & Koerndle, H. (2007). Promoting self-regulated learning in Web-based environments. *Computers in Human Behavior, 23*(3), 1126–1144. doi:10.1016/j.chb.2006.10.006

Nesbit, J. C., & Winne, P. H. (2003). Self-regulated inquiry with networked resources. *Canadian Journal of Learning and Technology, 29*(3). Retrieved on November 4, 2007, from http://www.cjlt.ca/content/vol29.3/cjlt29-3_art5.html

Nonaka, I., & Takeuchi, H. (1995). *The knowledge-creating company: How Japanese companies create the dynamics of innovation*. New York: Oxford University Press.

O'Reilly, T. (2005). *What is Web 2.0: Design patterns and business models for the next generation of software*. Retrieved on December 15, 2006, from http://www.oreillynet.com/pub/a/oreilly/tim/news/2005/09/30/what-is-web-20.html

Owen, M., Grant, L., Sayers, S., & Facer, K. (2006). *Social software and learning*. Bristol, England: Futurelab. Retrieved on April 11, 2007, from http://www.futurelab.org.uk/resources/documents/opening_education/Social_Software_report.pdf

Paavola, S., & Hakkarainen, K. (2005). The knowledge creation metaphor–an emergent epistemological approach to learning. *Science and Education, 14*(6), 535–557. doi:10.1007/s11191-004-5157-0

Pintrich, P. R. (Ed.). (1995). *Understanding self-regulated learning: Vol. 63. New directions for teaching and learning*. San Francisco: Josey-Bass.

Pintrich, P. R., & Schunk, D. H. (1996). *Motivation in education: Theory, research, and application*. Upper Saddle River, NJ: Merrill.

Richardson, W. (2006). Blogs, wikis, podcasts, and other powerful tools for classrooms. Thousand Oaks, CA: Sage.

Robbins-Sponaas, R. J., & Nolan, J. (2005). MOOs: Polysynchronous collaborative virtual environments. In K. St. Amant & P. Zemliansky (Eds.), *Internet-based workplace communications: Industry and academic applications* (pp. 130–155). Hershey, PA: Information Science Publishing.

Robinson, K. (2005). *Web 2.0? Why should we care?* Retrieved on January 11, 2006, from http://www.publish.com/article2/0,1759,1860653,00.asp

Rogers, P. C., Liddle, S. W., Chan, P., Doxey, A., & Isom, B. (2007). Web 2.0 learning platform: Harnessing collective intelligence. *Turkish Online Journal of Distance Education, 8*(3), 16–33.

Rosen, J. (2006, June 27). The people formerly known as the audience. *PressThink* [weblog]. Retrieved on October 2, 2007, from http://journalism.nyu.edu/pubzone/weblogs/press-think/2006/06/27/ppl_frmr.html

Rudd, T., Sutch, D., & Facer, K. (2006). *Towards new learning networks.* Bristol, England: Futurelab. Retrieved on July 5, 2007, from http://www.futurelab.org.uk/resources/documents/opening_education/Learning_Networks_report.pdf

Ryberg, T. (2008). Challenges and potentials for institutional and technological infrastructures in adopting social media. In V. Hodgson, C. Jones, T. Kargidis, D. McConnell, S. Retalis, D. Stamatis & M. Zenios (Eds.), *Proceedings of the Sixth International Conference on Networked Learning 2008* (pp. 658–665). Lancaster, England: Lancaster University.

Salaberry, M. R. (2001). The use of technology for second language learning and teaching: A retrospective. *Modern Language Journal, 85*(1), 39–56. doi:10.1111/0026-7902.00096

Scardamalia, M., & Bereiter, C. (2003). Knowledge building. In J. W. Guthrie (Ed.), *Encyclopedia of education* (2nd ed., pp. 1370–1373). New York: Macmillan.

Sfard, A. (1998). On two metaphors for learning and the dangers of choosing just one. *Educational Researcher, 27*(2), 4–13.

Sheely, S. (2006). Persistent technologies: Why can't we stop lecturing online? In L. Markauskaite, P. Goodyear & P. Reimann (Eds.), *Who's learning? Whose technology? Proceedings of the 23rd ASCILITE Conference* (pp. 769–774). Sydney: CoCo, University of Sydney.

Shirky, C. (2003, April 24). *A group is its own worst enemy: Social structure in social software.* Paper presented at the O'Reilly Emerging Technology conference, Santa Clara, CA. Retrieved on April 19, 2005, from http://www.shirky.com/writings/group_enemy.html

37signals. (n. d.). *Collaborative writing software online with writeboard, write, share, revise, compare.* Retrieved on December 4, 2008, from http://www.writeboard.com/

Surowiecki, K. (2004). *The wisdom of crowds.* New York: Doubleday.

Twitter. (2008). Retrieved on December 5, 2008, from http://twitter.com/

Vygotsky, L. S. (1978). *Mind in society: The development of higher psychological processes.* Cambridge, MA: Harvard University Press.

Vygotsky, L. S. (1987). Thinking and speech (N. Minick, Trans.). In R. W. Rieber & A. S. Carton (Eds.), *Problems of general psychology, including the volume thinking and speech: Vol. 1. The collected works of L. S. Vygotsky* (pp. 39–285). New York: Plenum. (Original works published in 1934 & 1960).

Wikipedia. (2007). Retrieved on August 10, 2007, from http://www.wikipedia.org/

Williams, J. B., & Jacobs, J. (2004). Exploring the use of blogs as learning spaces in the higher education sector. *Australasian Journal of Educational Technology, 20*(2), 232–247.

Wood, D. J., Bruner, J. S., & Ross, G. (1976). The role of tutoring in problem solving. *Journal of Child Psychiatry and Psychology, 17*(2), 89–100. doi:10.1111/j.1469-7610.1976.tb00381.x

Yahoo! Inc. (2008). *Welcome to Flickr–photo sharing.* Retrieved on December 4, 2008, from http://www.flickr.com/

YouTube. LLC. (2008). *YouTube–broadcast yourself*. Retrieved on December 4, 2008, from http://www.youtube.com/

KEY TERMS AND DEFINITIONS

Architecture of Participation: A term that describes the nature of innovation in the open source movement, whereby individuals can share, create, and amend software, thereby participating in the creation of improved forms of software. This can help turn a good idea or piece of software into a best-quality product as many users and developers can adapt, change, and improve it.

Blogosphere: A term used to describe the cultural and social milieu surrounding blogging and its users, conceived by observers who liken blogging communities to a large, intricate ecological network or biosphere. The blogosphere is an example of a Web-based social network. *See also* social networking.

CMS: Course Management System. An integrated suite of software tools designed to manage academic or training courses. Commercial examples are *Blackboard* and *WebCT*, although many open source alternatives, such as *Moodle* and *Sakai*, exist. In addition to the provision of online learning content and activities and the facilitation of online assessment, CMS's typically support a range of administrative functions including learner enrolment, workflow, records management (e.g. reporting of assessment results/outcomes) and resource management (e.g. instructors, facilities, equipment).

Collective Intelligence: A form of intelligence that results from the cooperation, collaboration, and/or competition of a large number of individuals.

Course Management System: *See* CMS.

Digital literacy: Encompasses the knowledge and skills required to locate, understand, evaluate, organize, and create information in various forms using digital tools. While it implies a working knowledge of current technology, it transcends the technical aspects to incorporate the ability to select and use digital information and information sources to achieve particular goals/outcomes. In the information age and knowledge economy, digitally literate people are better placed to communicate and work efficiently, and to participate in society at large.

E-Portfolio: An electronic collection comprising self-assembled evidence demonstrating a learner's knowledge, skills, and abilities, including learner-generated artifacts in multiple media forms that showcase both the products and processes of learning. e-Portfolios are excellent tools for facilitating students' reflection on their own learning, and are increasingly used for both learning and assessment purposes (including recognition/assessment of prior learning) within an academic course or program. Lifelong e-Portfolios are increasingly being used for professional purposes such as certification/accreditation and career advancement (e.g. job promotion).

Knowledge Creation Metaphor of Learning: Unlike theories that emphasize learning as knowledge acquisition (the acquisition metaphor) and as participation in a social community (the participation metaphor), a third metaphor views learning as a process of knowledge creation (the knowledge creation metaphor). This view focuses on mediated processes of knowledge creation that have become especially important in a knowledge society.

Mash-Up: Content or material that is collected from several Web-based sources, then modified, re-mixed, and/or re-combined to create a new formulation of the material. A mash-up typically includes one or more the following digital formats: text, graphics, audio, video, and animation. Mash-ups are commonly seen in "Web 2.0" services and social software tools such as blogs, wikis, RSS and podcast feeds, media sharing applications (e.g. *YouTube*), and social networking sites (e.g. *MySpace*, *Facebook*). *See also* micro-content.

Micro-Content: Very small, basic units of digital content or media that can be consumed in unbundled micro-chunks and aggregated and re-constructed in various ways. *See also* mash-up.

Pedagogy 2.0: Digital tools and affordances call for a new conceptualization of teaching that is focused on participation in communities and networks for learning, personalization of learning tasks, and production of ideas and knowledge. Pedagogy 2.0 is a response to this call. It represents a set of approaches and strategies that differs from teaching as a didactic practice of passing on information; instead, it advocates a model of learning in which students are empowered to participate, communicate, and create knowledge, exercising a high level of agency and control over the learning process.

Personal Learning Environment: *See* PLE.

Personal Publishing: A process in which an individual actively produces his/her own content and information and publishes it on the World Wide Web. For example, the maintenance of a personal blog as an online diary is an instance of personal publishing. *See also* user-generated content.

PLE: Personal Learning Environment. A system, application, or suite of applications that assists learners in taking control of and managing their own learning. It represents an alternative approach to the CMS, which by contrast adopts an institution-centric or course-centric view of learning. Key PLE concepts include the blending of formal and informal learning, participation in social networks that transcend institutional boundaries, as well as the use of a range of networking protocols (RSS, peer-to-peer [P2P], Web services) to connect systems, resources, and users within a personally-managed space. *See also* CMS.

Prosumer: A portmanteau formed by contracting word "producer" with the word "consumer," signifying the blurring of the distinction between the two roles with respect to content and ideas in today's knowledge economy.

Social Networking: A social network is a social structure comprising various nodes, which generally represent individuals or organizations, that are tied together by one or more specific types of interdependency, e.g. common values, shared visions, exchange of ideas, mutual financial benefit, trade, friendship/kinship, or even dislike and conflict. In the context of the Web 2.0 movement, the term is commonly used to refer to Web sites like *MySpace*, *Facebook*, *Ning*, *Friendster*, and *LinkedIn*, which attract and support networks of people and facilitate connections between them for social and professional purposes. The "blogo-sphere" may also be viewed as an example of an online social network. *See also* blogosphere.

Student-Generated Content: Content that is produced by students, often for sharing with peers or a wider audience on the Internet, as distinct from instructor-supplied content such as course notes and textbooks. It is arguable that the main benefits to be gained from student-generated content lie in engagement in the processes of content creation and knowledge construction, as opposed to the tangible end products themselves. *See also* user-generated content.

User-Generated Content: A term that refers to Web-based content created by ordinary people or users, e.g. pictures posted on *Flickr* or ency-cloaedia entries written in *Wikipedia*. Such "Read-and-Write" applications are key characteristic of the Web 2.0 movement, which encourages the publishing of one's own content and commenting on or augmenting other people's. It differs from the "Read-Only" model of Web 1.0, in which Web sites were created and maintained by an elite few. *See also* personal publishing.

Wisdom of Crowds: A concept that relates to the aggregation of information in groups and communities of individuals. It recognizes that the innovation, problem-solving, and decision-making capabilities of the group are often superior to that of any single member of the group. The term was used as the title of a book written by James Surowiecki, published in 2004. *See also* collective intelligence.

Chapter 2
Web 2.0 and Learning:
A Closer Look at Transactional Control Model in E-Learning

Bolanle A. Olaniran
Texas Tech University, USA

Indi M. Williams
Texas Tech University, USA

ABSTRACT

This chapter explores three facets of Web 2.0: the pedagogical use of social software in a Web 2.0 e-learning environment, social software, and social networking from the perspective of transactional control in fostering student learning, as proposed in the theoretical framework of Dron's (2006) theory. It also examines the implications of Web 2.0 as it relates to learning and e-learning. Using Facebook as a case specific Web 2.0 platform, the researcher pursues understanding of learner control, as well as cultural interactions in Web 2.0 environments in the broader context of cultural implication for Web 2.0 as a learning platform in a global e-learning environment. Accordingly, the Facebook example helps to illustrate how instructors and students can effectively control their learning environment (or relinquish control of their learning environment) within an intracultural setting, in an attempt to create a meaningful learning experience as proposed by the transactional control model. In conclusion, the chapter offers recommendations for Web 2.0 e-learning technology applications in order to create effective and meaningful learning for students and instructors.

THE WEB 2.0

Web 2.0 is not a term that refers to any specific or new form of World Wide Web, or Internet 2.0; instead it refers to conglomerate of social software that uses the internet as a platform for which such devices can be connected (Kenney, 2007; O'Reilly,

DOI: 10.4018/978-1-60566-826-0.ch002

2005). In essence, the social software enables an architecture platform that brings about the network effects where people are able to participate. Some specific examples of social software that enable Web 2.0 for collaboration includes blogs and its multimedia companion such as pods and videocasts (Cameron & Anderson, 2006; Kenney, 2007), wikis, distributed classification systems, and RSS feeds (Mejias, 2005). Dron (2007) however has a narrower view of what counts as social software by limiting the technology platforms to Flickr, Ning, Collaborative filtering / Recommender systems, Shared tagging and Social navigation.

Despite views on the variations of what counts as social software, one idea that seems consistent and without debate is the fact that each of these tools fosters a self-emergent collaboration. In order words, social software in relation to Web 2.0 allows and provides ways for transitioning static websites into fully interlink and often interactive computing platforms where users can create, as well as use, contents from other participants. The primary driver of Web 2.0 is the recent development in people's ability to create and publish content online, or in what has been termed as "read/write web" (Richardson, 2007). However, the social component of the Web 2.0 platforms should not be underestimated as users engage in high level of interactivity with the technologies and other users. More important to this discussion, however, is the role of Web 2.0 in educational pedagogy. Unlike distance education that focuses on independent study and student learning, Web 2.0 adds an additional dimension to learning in two ways. First, Web 2.0 helps fosters the idea and tool for e-learning; Second, Web 2.0 allows students to move away from tighter control of teacher or instructor organized activities and curriculum to a context, or platform, where varieties of loosely constructed learners are able to establish and control how they learn. In the words of Terry Anderson (2007), students have the freedom to create their own learning. As a result, this chapter will explore the implication of Web 2.0 as it relates to learning and e-learning. Specifically, the issue of learner control in Web 2.0 environments will be analyzed along with the cultural implication for Web 2.0 as learning platform in global e-learning environment. At the same time, this chapter will explore *Facebook* as a case specific Web 2.0 platform.

CONTROL IN WEB 2.0

First, however, is the issue of control. One of the general arguments in favor of incorporating newer communication technologies into education and learning curriculum is the fact that it enhances learners' capacity to determine how they learn (Olaniran, Savage, & Sorenson, 1996). It is not surprising that a similar argument has been made for e-learning and in particular as one of the major reasons for using Web 2.0 in learning (Dron, 2006; 2007). Dron

(2006) extended the concept of control to what he terms as *Transactional Control* – which he described as choices people make in learning environment regardless of whether the environment is offline or online. Dron (2007) argues that choices are made by both teachers and learners in e-learning environment; however, the degree to which a person dictates the choice determines the amount of transactional control in a given setting. Dron (2007) went on to categorize types of control on a continuum taking into consideration both structure – which is the control that a teacher has on the learning content and the students, and autonomy – that is the level of control the students has. Notwithstanding, the two levels of control are mediated or regulated by the dialogue, or negotiated control, which involves the negotiation between teachers and students regarding how much control one is willing to give up or allow the other to have.

TRANSACTIONAL CONTROL AND LEARNING

The idea of transactional control is useful when one subscribes to the transactional nature of communication, which argues that communicators influence one another and the notion of absolute power is perchance nonexistent in the sense that a teacher may choose to wield tighter control on the learners, but the learners also have choices as to whether, or not to comply. Nevertheless, the choice made is accompanied by potential consequences that can be either negative or positive. Furthermore, the transactional control in any learning environment subscribes to the notion that students must delegate, or give up, a certain level of their control to succeed. The reason for the delegation of control is important given that students are students for a reason--the reason being that learners lack certain knowledge which makes them students to begin with and hence must yield some of their control to the teacher who is believed to have the knowledge to share.

Notwithstanding, the idea of transactional control in Web 2.0 learning environment becomes important because it subscribes to the constructivists' ideology of allowing students to have increased control in how they choose to learn. According to constructivists, how learners choose to learn is believed to be a direct consequence of the level of choice they are given in learning. For example, Jarvis (2000) talks about futuristic learning where a society in an attempt to meet the requirement of global learning needs, stresses the idea that knowledge is fostered through the use of technologies and computers, and when developed, is a way to provide equal opportunities for every individual to receive as much education as they are believed to be capable. The learning society under the futuristic approach is aimed at the central goal of allowing individuals to develop their capabilities. However, it appears that the educational community accepts this notion as a fact without challenge regardless of whether it is in traditional offline or online learning environments. For instance, there are several questions worthy of exploring as one discusses the idea of control and specifically transactional control in e-learning. They include: Is it really possible for learners to learn on their own without being taught or without guidance? Can technologies in and of themselves substitute for teachers and

their guidance role in learning environments? How does one best attain the goal of providing learners adequate control in a way that helps foster their learning without overwhelming them or destroying their motivation to learn? These are important questions that are worthy of attention as one continues to explore Web 2.0 for learning and educational curriculum.

According to Dron (2007), most learning transactions occur by control either by the learners or the teachers. From the learners' perspective, to have control without the ability to exercise the control is useless, and learners are often not knowledgeable enough to make effective decisions about certain aspects of their learning or course materials. Teachers, on the other hand, can also abuse their control or have too much of it, so that it can negatively influence learning experiences. This can occur to the extent that the learning experience may result in boredom, lack of motivation, and confusion. To this end, Dron (2007) suggests that the best way to resolve the two extremes is to allow learners to determine whether, and when, to delegate control at any point in a learning transaction, or environment. It would seem that this approach is no better than allowing students to have all the control in a learning environment while the teachers simply go along with whatever learners decide to do. In particular, this is a perspective with which discussion in this chapter will take issue. However, in an attempt to determine how much control is given to both learners and teachers in the Web 2.0 learning environment, it is useful to examine the different type of learner interaction in e-learning as a whole. These interactions are teacher-student, student-student, and student-group / others (Olaniran, 2004a, 2006, 2007a). However, Dron (2006) identifies four interaction types that he proclaims as important, which include the three well established interaction modes, although they are described differently. These include student-group, teacher-group, content-group, and group-group which are explained below.

The student-group describes a social software environment where learners are considered to be part of a group. Also, learners become part of the process, and product of influence. In other words, they are influencing others, and yet are being influenced by the social collectives.

A teacher-group describes the role of teachers as less significant in the interaction than in traditional e-learning environments even though it is the teacher who usually initiates or suggests the use of social software. The teachers' role may include determining learning goals and eventual outcomes of the learning process. For the most part, a teacher is relegated to front end organizational structure, usually to identify the assignment and provide general guidance regarding what the expected outcomes should be.

Content-group interaction focuses on the social software creating its own structure that is not intended by users. The structure emerges from members' behaviors in the group which consequently affects individuals' actions as members of the group. According to Dron (2007) "The content is a reification of the group's behavior, and the group's behavior is at least partially a consequence of the content" (p. 63).

Group-group interaction focuses on the open sources, or standards, that group members use to make the exchange of information simple and unequivocal. For example multiple social software platforms (e.g., Google maps, Flickr images, blogs, and others) can be used simultaneously to interconnect information and create greater levels of interconnectivity (i.e., community) among users, rather than one individual, or a socially static space.

With Dron's (2007) argument or resolve that social software be used in a manner where learners are given as much control as needed, teachers are suppose to take a passive role, or a back seat, and relegate most of their control to learners. This idea is similar to the one proposed by Jarvis (2000) where he argued that the learning society is a phenomenon of the market, and as such learning should be commoditized, or packaged, in a way that helps foster the goal of customer satisfaction. This claim goes beyond mere customer satisfaction, by stressing that people do not want to learn because learning is not fun. Thus, there is the need to make people learn by making learning a fun process, or by making learning whatever students want (see Jarvis 2000). It is difficult, and almost impossible, even with the best of planning and intention to make learning whatever students want. Thus, it is not feasible for learners to learn when there is no instructor guidance about what needs to be learnt. Furthermore, students have different motivational levels when it comes to learning that must be addressed before they are given the freedom to go it alone (Olaniran, 2007a). The challenge and benefits of the system is that providers of the learning materials are not all educational institutions, and this fact is forcing educational institutions to change their approach with a great deal of alacrity in order to keep up with market demands, while remaining competitive as well. One of the benefits that Web 2.0 offers learning and learners as a whole is the assistance it could offer lifelong learners. Also the fact that it creates a forum and structure that emerges through group participation although the structure is always in the process of constant and continuous change. The technologies are able to adapt to the changing needs of learners and the group they serve (Dron, 2007). Specifically, social software that make up Web 2.0 offer structure that is not confined to the boundaries of teachers and is believed to help circumvent, or reduce, the cost of traditional institutional learning while saving time. One way that social software helps with efficiency in learning is the ability to allow learners, or researchers, to stay ahead of the latest and cutting edge research in a field. For example, Dron (2007) contends that the traditional forum takes more time or in general lags behind the current state of the art, whereas social software is believed to have the capability to provide yesterday's information on a whim, along with users' capacity to participate in the development of such information.

Surely, RSS, blogs among others, allow users to be notified of information without one necessarily searching for them individually, and save time in doing so. But even at that, one must be careful because information readily available at one's fingertip, or at the speed of light, does not necessarily constitute valid information, or authenticate that the information comes from a reliable source, or even assure that the information has not been tampered with. Similarly, Dron (2007) alludes to the fact that social software can be manipulated to offer a one sided view of information, when he offers an example of a Google search for the phrase "miserable failure" which lead to links about President Bush's legacy. Conclusions drawn on such information may be dependent upon how one feels about the president, its administration, and its policies. What is unfortunate about social software, however, is that it is now a commonplace welded into the social fabric of our lives, and it is not surprising that a majority turns to the likes of Google and wikis as authoritative sources and at times the first and only source of information. Thus, if care is not taken, one might assume that the social software is an end in itself. It is not surprising that as much as Dron argues for giving learners as much structure as they need, he admitted to the fact that social software, because of its structure, *may not be useful* pedagogically. Similar concerns has been noted with social software use in educational content (Anderson, 2007, Mejias, 2005, 2007; Vassileva, 2004). While knowledge is still important, its implications on social and cultural values remain unknown and challenges remain in determining its appropriate usage. The discussion will now turn to address a few of the cultural implications of social software in e-learning.

CULTURE, VALUE PREFERENCES, AND SOCIAL SOFTWARE TECHNOLOGIES

Despite decentralization of power and opportunity for increased participation, facilitated by social software, certain cultures remain high context and power distant (e.g., African countries, Japan, South East Asian countries) when considering Hofstede's dimensions of cultural variability (Hofstede, 1980; see also Olaniran, 2007a for full discussion of the dimensions and implications for e-learning). In a high-context culture, information is internalized in the person, or situations, while power distant cultures recognize, or accept, the fact that power is not evenly distributed (see Hall, 1976; Hofstede, 1980). These cultural categories have implications for implicit and explicit communication, and learning tendencies along with the willingness to use technologies. Specifically, Devereaux and Johansen (1994) argue that it might be difficult to get people to use certain technology, such as the CMC systems in power distant cultures, where status dictates every aspect of interpersonal communication. More germane to learning environments is the fact that power distant cultures, such as most African and Asian cultures, subscribe to learning approaches that differ from the social constructivist ideology of giving control to learners. On the contrary, learners expect teachers to set the tone and determine directions for how students learn. Consequently, teachers are viewed as the authoritative figure on subjects and it is the teacher's job to impart their knowledge on the students. Anything short of that would be perceived to be incompetent behavior, and negatively affect the decision to adopt or reject communication technologies in the learning environment (see Kawachi, 1999; Lee 2002; Olaniran, 2001, 2004b, 2007a, 2007b). Japanese designers acknowledge the effect of culture that not all types of communication can be supported by communication technology such as the computer-mediated communication (CMC) systems (Heaton, 1998). Therefore, not accounting for cultural nuances in Dron's proposition of transactional control is a major oversight with significant implication for Web 2.0 and e-learning communities.

The challenge of determining what social software can offer e-learning, and the hindrance by traditional local culture are not to be taken lightly. In high power distance cultures, people tend to view a technology system as threatening to their existence and traditional learning methods. The threat creates anxiety about technologies, and negative feelings toward using these technologies. Henning (2003) found the anxiety in learners with communication technologies to be real and vivid in a study looking at accounts of teachers, and learners, in South Africa. She found high levels of anxiety among e-learners along with the issue, of accessibility to technologies needed for instruction.

Henning concludes that individuals, or learners, face confusion with who is in charge of the learning environment (i.e., the teacher or the student), and rightfully so, as predicted by the power distance dimension. In essence, the idea of putting learners in control may be a biased view of how Western culture constructs, and interprets reality of how learners learn, or need to learn, and a view not necessarily shared by other cultures (Olaniran, 2007a).

Attention to how learners learn along cultural differences suggests the need to examine the differences in oral versus written traditions. The read/write web that characterizes social software and e-learning is more tailored to the written tradition in individualistic cultures whereas collectivistic cultures foster the oral tradition. Therefore, implication for e-learning, and learning in general, is consequential. For instance, e-learning in oral tradition cultures might be better in allowing for more interpersonal interactions where instructors get to explain and establish rules for students to follow (Wang, 2007). On the other hand, the concept of self-paced independent focus for e-

learning works, and can be nurtured, in written or non-oral tradition cultures (Olaniran, 2007a; Wang, 2007).

In essence, cultural differences can influence the use and selection of technologies in e-learning. For example, it was reported that some instructors from the United Kingdom (i.e., non-oral culture) succeeded in e-learning contexts when using certain software, while counterparts from the United Arab Emirates (UAE) saw the same software as unnecessary and additional work that did not fit into its oral culture where learners explain ideas to one another about what they read and what instructors teach (Selinger, 2004). Formulated in a different way, the concept of transactional control can be viewed as two different pedagogical approaches to learning - objectivist, that is, instructor focused learning, versus constructivist, student created learning.

Waterhouse (2005) explains that "constructivist practices encourage students to undertake activities that engage their interests and to build on their experiences" (p. 42). In this manner, students actively participate in their learning environment, choosing between alternatives and seeking answers needed to reinforce knowledge acquisition and foster lifelong learning. This especially is true when a learning environment consists of adult learners who bring a wealth of life experience into the classroom. These learners are characterized as having more autonomy and by being more self-directed/persistent in classroom activities (Picciano, 2001). However, the reality is that not all learners fall into the adult learner category. For example, it has been found that students from certain cultures (i.e., Chinese and Koreans) felt lost when they interact online, or electronically, because they seek rules and rituals similar to those that govern their face-to-face encounters and traditional classrooms (He & Yu, 2005; Wang, 2007).

STUDENT-INSTRUCTOR CONTROL OF THE LEARNING ENVIRONMENT

Within Web 2.0 environments, the teacher may by nature have a very small role in regards to direct student instruction; however Dron (2007) believes that the interactions that occur within the social software present an instructor with a wealth of detail as to how the class as a whole interacts. These details may also include, but are not limited to, the class's learning preferences, interests, needs, strengths and even their weaknesses. So ultimately, when presented with this wealth of information, the question that arises is, how do students know how much control they need within the learning environment, or is the control they are asking for is what they really need?

The answer is that as instructors, we do not know. It may be true that the learning environment reveals information about the class/group, or learners as a whole; however, it does not always adequately predict learning outcomes of each and every student. It may be true that within a social software learning environment that the content is more easily adaptable to more relevant student inquiries, however, it cannot affect the learning negotiation that a student may or may not make. In a constructivist environment, the instructor must accept that he/she is solely a facilitator of knowledge and that the student is in control of individual learning (Waterhouse, 2005). For this reason, a "dependent learner can choose to be controlled, while a more autonomous learner can take more control" however both may be influenced or may influence the environment in a way that suits individual learning styles (Dron, 2007, p. 63).

Furthermore, does an instructor's yielding of control to students always equate effective learning? The answer to this question, again, is no. In an attempt to investigate failure within constructivist learning environments, Clark (1989) examined 70 aptitude-treatment interaction studies to determine how various instructional methodologies influence student aptitudes. His study discovered that in a number of cases, when lower aptitude students chose, or were assigned, to weaker or unguided instruction, they scored significantly lower on post-test measures when compared to pre-test measures. From these findings, Clark (1989) concluded that it was the failure to provide stronger scaffolding, or support mechanisms for less experienced students within the instruction that produced learning loss as measured by the aptitude examinations. In a separate study Clark (1982) determined that when less able learners choose less guided instruction, their scores indicate that they learn less than they would from a structured learning environment. From these results, Clark (1982) postulated that less experienced learners gain more from task-specific structured learning activities as provided by instructors through instructional presentations. Therefore, it appears that the act of an instructor yielding control within a learning environment does not necessarily cause or encourage learning to occur.

Also, Dalsgaard (2006) found that different social software tools create integration problem in supporting e-learning (i.e. integration vs. separation). He concludes that only few social software tools are integrated in existing learning management systems (LMS). At the same time, attempts to integrate social software tools is doomed to failure if not placed in the context of pedagogy (Dalsgaard, 2006), and different course content will pose different problems for integration and separation concerns, and consequently learning with social software.

When re-examining the constructivist perspective with respect to Dron's (2007) theory of transactional control, an organic social software allows for a "negotiation of control" between the learner and the instruction, leading to a "reified structure to which control may be delegated" (p. 63). For this reason an autonomous learner is in a greater position to wield greater control over the environment because it is the independence of the learner, or their autonomy, that dictates whether or not learning occurs. This is due to the fact that within a constructivist learning environment, the guidance by the instructor "is provided to facilitate the individual's efforts and understandings" (Hannafin & Hill, 2002, p. 74). For it is an individual learner's choice to "control their learning or to delegate that control" to others that determines how the learner interacts or makes demand on the environment around him/her (Dron, 2007, p. 63). These demands ultimately determine cognitive development, or effective learning. Kirschner, Sweller, and Clark (2006) state that "the goal of instruction is rarely to search for or discover information" but to "give learners specific guidance about how to cognitively manipulate information in ways that are consistent with a learning goal, and store the result in long-term memory" (p. 77). When these goals are not reached, failure within the learning environment occurs. This is especially true in a social software website such as Facebook. Dron (2007) observes that although these sites have millions of users, "all of whom are contributing to the overall shape of the system" the simple formation of smaller clusters or groups does not allow "significant parcellation" to occur (p. 64). This fact alone can be devastating to a virtual learning community, simply due to the tremendous amount of distractions that are available in the surrounding network. These networks can be equated to "vacuum cleaners of the social world" incorporating both the good and the bad (Dron, 2007, p. 65). So without situating the learning environment within a firm framework, structured solely for learning to occur, there is no guarantee that it will. At the same time, it is the responsibility of the instructor to create and set such structure for learning in motion. For example, the learning process does not exist in the tools themselves because the social networks provide inputs to learning. Dalsgaard (2006) indicates that a networks of weblogs for instance only provides access to other sources (i.e., students, teachers, etc.) and their information. Thus, it is not enough to merely have access, rather, it is important to be

able to transform the information by presenting, reflecting, and constructing knowledge. Then how can a social software and Web 2.0 overcome challenges with learning and meeting both students and instructors' goals? We argue that Web 2.0 may be best applied in sameculture learning environments rather than cross-cultural encounters. Therefore, we examine Facebook as a social networking site to explore possible ways to overcome some of the learning challenges indicated above.

FACEBOOK AS SOCIAL SOFTWARE

Facebook, founded in 2004, was regarded as the seventh most trafficked website in the United States in 2005. Its popularity among students has been well noted to the extent that membership was restricted to individuals with academic based e-mail addresses (Read, 2006). Facebook has a membership of approximately 8 million students from over 200 colleges and 22,000 high schools across the nation. These members have constructed personal WebPages which have been used to post personal information, pictures, messages, and even used Facebook to hold "conversations" and to communicate with friends, family, and instructors (Lahinsky, 2005). According to Facebook spokesperson Chris Huges (personal communication as cited in Mazer et al., 2007) "approximately 297,000 Facebook members identify themselves as faculty or staff" (p. 3), however this is completely understandable, because up until 2006, Facebook restricted registration solely to individuals with a valid college e-mail address (Read, 2006). Due to the popularity of the site within the college environment, many educators and administrations find themselves under pressure to use or formulate an adequate response to the Facebook phenomenon. Facebook may overcome challenges to learning and can meet both instructors and learners' goals through the power to create a social presence within a virtual environment. The site allows students, teachers and class members to create a virtual persona for the strengthening of the face-to-face or online learning environment. Social networking sites like Facebook also have the power to connect.

Anderson (1995), notwithstanding, questions the social structure of cyberspace and characterizes the Internet as occupying "a social space between 'hard' institutions and 'soft' culture" (p. 13). He postulates in accordance with Rheingold's (1993) definition of virtual community that this type of virtual association is characterized by an intimacy and a distance that juxtapose one another by displaying a narrow "slice of life" that is engaging yet limiting. According to Anderson (1995), virtual communities contain a prevalent pattern in which pre-existing communities migrate to the Internet while new communities form and reform online, intersecting with face-to-face and creating new forums altogether. This especially becomes evident with capability for mixed media. For example, pictures, video, and text based chats can be used on sites such as Facebook. For this reason, Shayo, Olfman, Iriberri, and Magid (2007) believe that "virtual communities have emerged from a surprising intersection of human needs and technology" (p. 206). This type of community emerges through electronic interactions where people may or may not meet one another face-to-face, and the lack of face-to-face interactions "make new kinds of communities possible" (p. 206). Notwithstanding, the lack of face-to-face interactions do not in any way nullify, or render the role of instructors void for guiding students toward learning or occurrence of learning.

Mark Zukerberg, the 23 year old founder of Facebook, refrains from calling Facebook a true social networking site, but regards it as a utility or "a tool to facilitate the information flow among users and their compatriots, family members and professional connections" (Levy, 2007). Zukerberg believes that the true vision of Facebook lies in what he calls the "social graph." This graph is "a mathematical construct that maps the real-life connections between every human on the planet"

in which each of us is a "node" linking to the people we know. Therefore, as our ties become stronger with one another online, we begin to utilize different types or combination of media to strengthen ties. Thus, simple online text communication is no longer sufficient. We desire to see photographs, have voice conversations and see films, digital video and moving pictures in order to solidify our sense of identification with the other. So, as our needs begin to change, so do our online communities, and for this reason exclusively, social networking sites such as Facebook emerge and flourish.

The irony of this truth, and what many educators may not understand, is that many students today have a need to create online identities. However these online identities are often drastically different from face-to-face identities, despite the fact that they adversely affect one another. Individuals who have a face-to-face knowledge of one another, such as a teacher's relationship with his/her students, have a need to nurture the relationships already built when online. Whereas, individuals who have not met face-to-face are faced with the challenge of developing and nurturing relationships online depending on their perception of the importance and need for such relationships. Consequently social networks, or Facebook in particular, users have the choice of whether to continue with the relationship, or to terminate it based on personal assessments. This idea creates the intersection of the virtual and the real facilitating the development of social networking, for even when individuals are apart, the need for a virtual social presence and connection remains (Garrison & Anderson, 2003; Short, Williams, & Christie, 1976) and it is not easily achieved because people find it challenging to express themselves as "real persons" especially in text based and institutionally dominated environment (Cameron & Anderson, 2006; Rourke & Anderson, 2002). On one hand, social networking sites like Facebook foster a way to supplement face-to-face interactions rather than replacing them altogether. For example, Facebook allows users, and especially learners, the freedom to create a sense of personal identity and the freedom to do it, which is found to be critical to social presence enhancement (Cameron & Anderson, 2006). Therefore, when the face-to-face class ends and the out of class assignments are given, application of social software and Web 2.0 can be geared towards students' learning processes in ways that maintain their connection to the classroom and to the instructor. From this standpoint, social software and Web 2.0 can offer solutions. On the other hand, social software may help adult learners who already possess certain experiential knowledge to continue their life-long learning and consequently, instructors may be better adept and justified in yielding more control in the learning process while fostering an effective learning and learner environment.

INTEGRATION

Regardless of social software, or Web 2.0 environment, the challenge that different cultures and learning styles pose for e-learning cannot be taken for granted. It goes without saying that how learners view the role of teachers and other learners will affect the selection and use of the technology media (Heaton, 1998, Olaniran, 2004a, 2007a). Specifically, Heaton (1998) contends that if communication technologies are to be useful in Japan, it is important that a familiar sense of atmosphere, or feeling, that must be conveyed through the system. Her research on computer supported collaborative work (CSCW) systems in Japan suggests that it is problematic for groups to use computers for collaborative activities without first meeting face-to-face to establish an environment of trust (see also Barron, 2000; Mason, 1998). Tools wise, Web 2.0 technologies may enable students and users to be in a greater control of how they access information. However, more still needs to be done to address the fact that

Web 2.0 solutions must be context and community specific rather than universal (see also Boulos & Wheelert, 2007). For instance, we presented in this chapter the different value preferences that interfere with Web 2.0 applications in cross-cultural learning environments. At the same time, we provide, the Facebook example to illustrate the use in same culture learning environments to present our points.

Therefore, Web 2.0 environments may still be able to provide rich environments for learning in spite of the challenges facing it. Software designers would need to be cognizant of these challenges, and consequently design systems in a way that helps to overcome some of the potential pitfalls (Olaniran, 2007a, Varela de Freitas & Valente, 2001). For example, there is the need to allow instructors to determine how much control they and their learners' need. One way of doing this is to apply software that allows both teachers and learners to negotiate such control, perhaps through an open source system. For instance, Poftak (2006) talks about her school's use of Elgg system – which allows teachers to share lesson plans and photos through the system's file repository. The system also allows parents of the students to subscribe and have access to certain areas of the community without betraying privacy concerns. The Elgg is community oriented like Facebook and other social software, but it is user driven, low maintenance, and wide open. Users, in essence, can chose to add other social software tools as they deem necessary and appropriate, and are not restricted to the Elgg tools. As Poftak (2006) indicated, it is impossible for one particular software to satisfy everybody's needs. Perhaps one of the most important aspects of Elgg is the recognition that not all forms of openness are good when it comes to learners' information, and as a result the systems designers are adding a plug-in module that offers extra privacy, and administrative control for schools and users (see Poftak, 2007).

IMPLICATIONS

Social software like Facebook can increase effective learning from the stand point of both instructors and learners. For example, Berg, Berquam, and Christoph (2007) suggested that a careful consideration of "how students use social technologies can help [educators] build a strong network of information," and aid us in how to "think differently about how [educators] communicate with students and with each other" (p. 44). Therefore when incorporating Facebook into the Web 2.0 "classroom" it is essential to focus on the modes of interactions and find ways to expand upon systems already put in place. Berg, Berquam and Christoph (2007) explain that when utilizing social networking, core activities such as communication, teaching, tutoring and study groups, have their own unique needs, however they can also be incorporated into various interactive activities such as those found on Facebook.

For teacher-student communications, instructors can utilize Web 2.0 such as the Facebook network to help orient students to the learning environment, facilitate online icebreakers to help students get to know one another, and assist instructors in getting to know their students. Instructors can also create various student groups for group projects and use their own individual Facebook page to provide the student with a greater knowledge of who their instructor is, and a little more insight as to his/her interests or life (see Olaniran 2004a). The Facebook "wall" can be used to facilitate discussion about upcoming assignments, and to clarify any student concerns or questions. This functionality can also be used to provide students with a type of "status check" in regard to classroom schedules and alleviate confusion that may have occurred during face-to-face or e-learning classroom based lectures, or learning materials. By placing the class into a unified Facebook group, instructors can also email the entire class at once, sending updates or other important class related information. To enhance these interactions, instructors can facilitate tutoring sessions, or hold office hours online in order to allow their students to contact them through a more student accessible mode of communication. Teachers can also send reminders to students about impending deadlines.

For student-student interactions, students on Facebook can connect with other students, view photos and other self disclosure information and get to know one another based upon their online virtual identities. Using Facebook privacy settings, students also have the flexibility to decide which photographs they choose to share with their classmates and instructors. For increased learning, students can form teams for studying, or completing projects and assignments with one another. Students can also create online groups that allow for real time interactions. Most importantly, students can remind one another when deadlines are approaching and/or when assignments/grades are in jeopardy (Berg, Berquam, & Christoph, 2007).

For student-content and instructor-content interactions, instructors can design or utilize the wealth of online resources to allow students to explore, in-depth, various aspects of the subject matter being taught. For example, the provision of additional resources through tag links, or other online resources can be used as supplemental course material. Instructors can create problems, or case studies, that require the students to participate in online "webquests" or online "field trips" and "scavenger hunts" in order to suggest a viable solution. For science related courses, instructors can direct students to online experiments, simulations or research sites in order to help facilitate understanding of textbook, or e-learning instructional materials (Waterhouse, 2005). Students can conduct personal research on subject matter, and provide or broadcast their findings to their group or the entire class in addition to the instructor provided, or required information. Utilizing the Facebook network can be a starting point for online inquiry, and may be as simple as a point and click, especially since the interface is intricately integrated into the internet which can be easily brought into the learning environment. Mejias (2007) argues that social software helps students to participate in distributed research communities, which extend beyond class term or session, and technologically beyond tools and resources that schools can provide to students (See also, Achterman, 2006; Jakes, 2006).

CONCLUSION

In spite of the learning benefits of Web 2.0 identified above, it must be stressed that they do not overcome some cross-cultural challenges in e-learning environment. Thus, Web 2.0 environments must be restricted to same or intra cultural settings to account for different needs that apply, or are attributable to different cultures. For example, social networking spaces provide a podcasting and videocasting platform ideal for supporting digital storytelling, where students and teachers can create audio and video along with other multimedia contents. Even at that, students from non constructivist learning pattern and cultures have different perceptions of the role of teachers and how to approach teachers and other students. Therefore, Wang (2007) cautioned in an environment like Web 2.0 for supporting e-learning, instructors need to build team work into curriculum, post guidelines about what constitutes appropriate teamwork etiquette and should not assume that teamwork is a given especially when dealing with Chinese and Korean cultures. Squires (1999) also suggests the need to design and develop social software that allows "freedom and flexibility" such that users (i.e., teachers and learners) can then adapt the software to their idiosyncratic needs and styles.

This chapter raises important questions such as: is it possible for learners to learn on their own without guidance? The answer from our arguments is no and only "maybe" at best. Similarly, can tech-nologies in of themselves substitute for teachers, and their guidance role in learning environments? The answer is possibly, but other variables such as the types of technologies and the pedagogy have to be taken into account. The third major question we raised involves how to best alter the goal of providing learners adequate control in a way that helps foster their learning without overwhelming them, or destroying their motivation to learn. We do not have a concrete answer; however, we suggest that future research and investigation of Web 2.0 and the accompanying technologies will continue to explore these areas. In the interim, we suggest a closer look at other available work on web 2.0 such as Dalsgaard (2006) and Boulos and Wheelert (2007) among others.

REFERENCES

Achterman, D. (2006). Beyond wikipedia. *Teacher Librarian, 34*(2), 19–22.

Anderson, J. (1995). Cybarites, knowledge workers and the new Creoles on the superhighway. *Anthropology Today, 11*(4), 13–15.

Anderson, T. (2007, June). Book review–control and constraint in e-learning: Choosing when to choose. *International Review of Research in Open and Distance Learning, 8*(2), 1–3.

Berg, J., Berquam, L., & Christoph, K. (2007, March/April). Social networking technologies: A "poke" for campus services. *EDUCAUSE Review, 42*(2), 32–44.

Cameron, D., & Anderson, T. (2006). Comparing weblogs to threaded discussion tools in online educational contexts. *International Journal of Instructional Technology and Distance Learning, 3*(11), 3–15.

Clark, R. E. (1982). Antagonism between achievement and enjoyment in ATI studies. *Educational Psychologist, 17*, 92–101.

Clark, R. E. (1989). When teaching kills learning: Research on mathematics. In H. N. Mandl, N. Bennett, E. de Corte, & H. F. Freidrich (Eds.), *Learning and instruction: European research in an international context* (Vol. 2, pp. 1–22). London: Pergamon.

Dalsgaard, C. (2006). Social software: E-learning beyond learning management systems. *European Journal of Open, Distance, and E-learning.* Retrieved on January 3, 2009 from [REMOVED HYPERLINK FIELD]http://www.eurodl.org/materials/contrib/2006/Christian_Dalsgaard.htm

Dron, J. (2006). The teacher, the learner, and the collective mind. *AI & Society, 21*(1), 200–216. doi:10.1007/s00146-005-0031-4

Dron, J. (2007). Designing the undesignable: Social software and control. *Educational Technology & Society, 10*(3), 60–71.

Garrison, D. R., & Anderson, T. (2003). *E-learning in the 21ˢᵗ century. A framework for research and practice.* New York: Routledgefalmer.

He, K. K., & Yu, S. Q. (2005). The education innovating in information age. *Basic Education Reference, 5,* 1–6.

Heaton, L. (1998). Preserving communication context: Virtual workspace and interpersonal space in Japanese CSCW. In C. Ess & F. Sudweeks (Eds.), *Cultural attitudes towards communication and technology* (pp. 163-186). Australia: University of Sydney.

Henning, E. (2003). I click therefore I am (not): Is cognition 'distributed' or is it 'contained' in boderless e-learning programmes? *International Journal of Training and Development, 7*(4), 303–317. doi:10.1046/j.1360-3736.2003.00188.x

Hofstede, G. (1980). *Culture's consequences.* Beverly Hills, CA: Sage.

Jakes, D. (2006). Wild about wikis: Tools for taking students and teacher collaboration to the next level. *Technology and Learning, 27*(1), 6.

Jarvis, P. (2000). Globalisation, the learning society, and comparative education. *Comparative Education, 36*(3), 343–355. doi:10.1080/713656613

Kamel Boulos, M., & Wheeler, S. (2007, March). The emerging Web 2.0 social software: An enabling suite of sociable technologies in health and healthcare education. *Health Information and Libraries Journal, 24*(1), 2–23. doi:10.1111/j.1471-1842.2007.00701.x

Kenney, B. (2007, January). You 2.0. *School Library Journal, 53*(1), 11.

Kirschner, P. A., Sweller, J., & Clark, R. E. (2006). Why minimal guidance during instruction does not work: An analysis of the failure of constructivist, discovery, problem-based, experiential, and inquiry-based teaching. *Educational Psychologist, 41*(2), 75–86. doi:10.1207/s15326985ep4102_1

Lashinsky, A. (2005). Facebook stares down success. *Fortune, 152,* 40.

Levy, S. (2007, August 20). Facebook grows up. *Newsweek, 8,* 40-46.

Mazer, J. P., Murphy, R. E., & Simonds, C. J. (2007). I'll see you on Facebook: The effects of computer-mediated teacher self-disclosure on student motivation, affective learning, and classroom climate. *Communication Education, 56*(1), 1–17. doi:10.1080/03634520601009710

Mejias, U. (2005). A nomad's guide to learning and social software. *The Knowledge Tree.* Retrieved on October 20, 2007, from http://knowledgetree.flexiblelearning.net.au/edition07/html/la_mejias.html

Mejias, U. (2007). Teaching social software with social software. *Innovate: Journal of Online Education, 2*(5). Retrieved on December 2, 2007, from http://www.innovateonline.ifo/index.php?view=article&id=260

O'Reilly, T. (2005). Compact definition. O'Reilly radar. Retrieved on November 15, 2007, from [REMOVED HYPERLINK FIELD]http://radar. oreilly.com/archives/2005/10/web_20_compact_definition.html

Olaniran, B. A. (2001). The effects of computer-mediated communication on transculturalism. In V. Milhouse, M. Asante & P. Nwosu (Eds.), *Transcultural realities* (pp. 83-105). Thousand Oaks, CA: Sage.

Olaniran, B. A. (2004a). Computer-mediated communication as an instructional learning tool: Course evaluation with communication students. In P. Comeaux (Ed.), *Assessing online teaching & learning* (pp. 144-158).

Olaniran, B. A. (2004b). Computer-mediated communication in cross-cultural virtual groups. In G. M. Chen & W. J. Starosta (Eds.), *Dialogue among diversities* (pp. 142-166). Washington, D.C.: National Communication Association.

Olaniran, B. A. (2006). Applying synchronous computer-mediated communication into course design: Some consideration and practical guides. *Campus-Wide Information Systems, 23*(3), 210–220. doi:10.1108/10650740610674210

Olaniran, B.A. (2007a). Challenges to implementing e-learning and lesser developed countries. In A. Edmundson (Ed.), *Globalized e-learning cultural challenges*. Hershey, PA: Idea Group.

Olaniran, B. A. (2007b). Culture and communication challenges in virtual workspaces. In K. St-Amant (Ed.), *Linguistic and cultural online communication issues in the global age* (pp. 79-92). Hershey, PA: IGI Global.

Olaniran, B. A., Savage, G. T., & Sorenson, R. L. (1996). Experiential and experimental approaches to face-to-face and computer mediated communication in group discussion. *Communication Education, 45,* 244–259. doi:10.1080/03634529609379053

Picciano, A. G. (2001). *Distance learning: Making connections across virtual space and time.* Upper Saddle River, NJ: Merrill/Prentice Hall.

Poftak, A. (2006). Community 2.0. *Technology & Learning, 27*(144). Retrieved on October 31, 2007, from http://newfirstsearch.oclc.org/images/WSPL/wsppdf1/HTML/00427/2VVDD/1SW.HTM

Read, B. (2006). A week of change at Facebook, as it expands its membership. *The Chronicle of Higher Education, 53*(5), A35–A35.

Rheingold, H. (1993). *The virtual community: Homesteading on the electronic frontier.* Reading, MA: Addison-Wesley.

Richardson, W. (2007). Teaching in a Web 2.0 world. *Kappa Delta Pi Record, 43*(4), 150–151.

Rourke, L., & Anderson, T. (2002). Exploring social presence in computer conferencing. *Journal of Interactive Learning Research, 13*(3), 259–275.

Selinger, M. (2004). Cultural and pedagogical implications of a global e-learning programme. *Cambridge Journal of Education, 34*(2), 223–239. doi:10.1080/0305764041000170058 9

Shayo, C., Olfman, L., Iriberri, A., & Magid, I. (2007). The virtual society: Its driving forces, arrangements, practices, implications. In J. Gackenbach (Ed.), *Psychology and the Internet: Inrapersonal, interpersonal, and transpersonal implications* (2nd ed., pp. 187-219). Boston: Academic Press.

Shirky, C. (1998). And nothing to watch: Bad protocols, good users: In praise of evolvable systems. [-ff.]. *AMC Net Worker, 2*(3), 48.

Short, J., Williams, E., & Christie, B. (1976). *The social psychology of telecommunication.* London: Wiley.

Squires, D. (1999). Educational software and learning: Subversive use and volatile design. Retrieved on December 10, 2007, from http://csdl2.computer.org/comp/proceedings/hicss/199/0001/01/00011079.pdf

Varela De Freitas, C., & Valente, L. (2001). Uses of Internet in Portugal. *Educational Technology Research and Development, 49*(4), 117–120. doi:10.1007/BF02504953

Vasileva, J. (2004, August 30-September 3). *Harnessing P2P power in the classroom.* Paper presented at the ITS 2004, Maceio, Brazil.F

Wang, M. (2007). Designing online courses that effectively engage learners from diverse cultural backgrounds. *British Journal of Educational Technology, 38*(2), 294–311. doi:10.1111/j.1467-8535.2006.00626.x

Waterhouse, S. (2005). The power of e-learning: The essential guide for teaching in the digital age. Boston: Pearson.

Wilson, B. (1995). Metaphors for instruction: Why we talk about learning environments. *Educational Technology, 35*(5), 25–30.

WEBSITES

Digg: http://www.digg.com

Del.icio.us: http://del.icio.us

Google: http://www.google.com

JIME: http://www-jime.open.ac.uk/

Myspace: http://www.myspace.com

Piczo: http://piczo.com

WikiProfessional: http://www.wikiprofessional.info

You Tube://www.youtube.com

Chapter 3
Metacognition on the Educational Social Software:
New Challenges and Opportunities

Margarida Romero
Université de Toulouse, France & Universitat Autònoma de Barcelona, Spain

ABSTRACT

In recent years, we have witnessed an information revolution. This revolution has been characterised by widespread access to the Internet and by the emergence of information which has been generated by end-users–the so-called user-generated content. The information thus generated has been supported by Web 2.0 applications or social software. These changes in the information society have had an important impact in education, with more and more adults enrolling on life-long learning programs; moreover, the availability of distance learning courses has grown in line with this increase in demand. In this emergent educational paradigm, the new 2.0 technology context implies new competencies for learners. These competencies include literacy in information and communication technology (ICT), learning autonomy, self-regulation and metacognition, while at the same time expanding the opportunities for metacognitive development. We will consider in this chapter these two perspectives of the 2.0 context; on the one hand, the new requirements provided by the environment and, on the other hand, the new learning opportunities which this environment brings.

1. INTRODUCTION

The development of information and communications technology (ICT), and the Internet in particular, are producing a paradigm shift for the diffusion of information and the creation of knowledge. This revolution is even more pronounced in the context of the user-generated approach of Web 2.0. It is interesting to note that the "2006 Time Person of the Year" was none other than *You*. The reason for this surprising choice was the growth and influence of user-generated content on the Internet during the early years of the 21st century.

DOI: 10.4018/978-1-60566-826-0.ch003

In education, this technological revolution is occurring in a context of globalisation, which challenges higher education organisations to structure and harmonise the length of their programs in order to improve quality standards and facilitate student mobility. In the context of the European Community, these changes are outlined in the Bologna Agenda, which sets targets for convergence within the European Higher Education Area (EHEA). This agenda imposes a greater responsibility on the learner – the learner's autonomy is to be developed by a shift from a system of teacher-driven provisions towards a student-centred approach.

From a teaching and learning perspective, we are experiencing two important changes. Firstly, the focus on knowledge construction by the learner, mostly through collaborative contexts; secondly, the willingness to globalise and standardise the information exchanges, the learning processes and the tools. In this new context, it is essential to become the manager of one's own learning. The challenge for the learner is about learning to learn; about developing individual skills for self-regulated learning and for enhancing metacognitive abilities. For this purpose, it is useful to take advantage of the new opportunities offered by Educational Social Software (ESS).

Metacognition, the knowledge about knowledge and how we learn, can be promoted by the social construction of knowledge and by its diffusion. This social construction and diffusion is facilitated by ESS, which provides new opportunities to develop inter-subjective awareness. However, the new facilities offered by Web 2.0 require learners to develop new competencies (ICT literacy, autonomy, metacognition, ...). At the same time, social software is expanding the opportunities for the development of the competencies of learners in the 21st century. Thus, we will consider in this chapter these two perspectives of the new 2.0 context – on the one hand, the new requirements provided by social software and, on the other hand, the new learning opportunities

which this new context brings. Thus, in the first part we explore the changes in both learning and in social software. In the second part, we focus on the implications of Educational Social Software in regard to the needs created by ESS for the new competencies the learner must develop in order to succeed. Lastly, we will focus on the opportunities that ESS provides for the development of metacognitive learners.

2. TOWARDS A NEW LEARNER IDEAL: SELF REGULATION, METACOGNITION AND ENGAGEMENT IN LIFE-LONG LEARNING

The profound changes in the information society have also transformed the learner ideal. In a context of growing obsolescence of knowledge (Brandsma, 1998), subjects and organisations must learn throughout life (life-long learning), developing a willingness to learn continuously, encouraged by educational bodies at the highest national and international level (UNESCO, OECD, European Commission). In this context, autonomous learning is now regarded as a social issue (Moisan and Carré, 2002) fostered by ICT possibilities.

The rapid growth of the Internet in recent decades and the emergence of Web 2.0 have together developed a set of new learning opportunities. This has been achieved through a revolution in the social relations of learning, which can now take place at different times and in different places. These profound changes reshape the competencies of the 21st century learner; these competencies must now include a greater degree of autonomy. Learning skills need to be self-regulated; there is a requirement for a better metacognitive development and an increasing need for those following life-long learning courses to be able to use ICT. The latter implies a certain computer literacy. Learners in the 21st century should develop a complex set of skills before starting to take advantage of the learning potential offered by ICT solutions, and more specifically by social software. Next, we will continue the discussion by analysing four main ESS prerequisites, with special attention to the prerequisite for metacognitive competence.

2.1. Prerequisite I: The Use of ICT

Technology enhanced learning involves the use of technologies to aid learning, and a growing number of courses use Information and Communication Technologies (ICT). In the case of blended learning courses, ICTs are a technological complement to traditional face-to-face learning. With virtual distance courses, ICTs become the main learning environment. However, to take part in distance learning, learners must develop ICT skills in order to navigate through the information, choose the best sources, communicate with peers and professors and contribute to co-creation or information tagging. Computer literacy has become a basic skill for life-long learning and professional integration. In an ICT society, and even more in a 2.0 perspective, ICT skills are a prerequisite.

2.2. Prerequisite II: Learner's Autonomy and Self-Regulation

Students engaged in distance learning courses are free to participate at the time and place of their choice. This freedom is both an opportunity and a heavy responsibility in terms of autonomy and self-regulation. Learner autonomy involves the ability to work alone without external regulation (teacher's instructions, timetables, etc.). Being a self-regulated student implies being able to manage one's own learning times and rhythms, planning one's own activities and their execution (revision, work, ...) and even managing emotions and motivations during the learning process.

2.3. Prerequisite III: Learner's Metacognitive Development

In order to manage his learning, the student must be aware of his current knowledge and should know his strong and weak points. This awareness of one's own cognition and the control of the cognitive processes is known as metacognition. For Marzano (1998) "metacognition is the engine of learning". A student with a good metacognitive development will be able to assess his own achievements, self-evaluate what he knows and what he still needs to learn or review, thus allowing him to plan and regulate the process. Having acquired the metacognitive skills to manage his own learning, he becomes manager of the task and gains a strategic approach to knowledge acquisition.

Learners with good metacognitive development will more than likely be *"people who possess self determination or autonomy in learning and problem solving. They will be able to refer to the what, how, when, where and why of learning when carrying out complex cognitive activities"* (Gordon, 1996). Metacognition has been defined as the *"conscious control of learning, planning and selecting strategies, monitoring the progress of learning, correcting errors, analysing the effectiveness of learning strategies, and changing learning behaviours and strategies when necessary."* (Ridley et al, 1992), but also as *"cognitive strategies"*, (Paris and Winograd, 1990), *"monitoring of cognitive processes"* (Flavell, 1976), *"resources and self regulating learning"* (Osman and Hannafin, 1992) and *"evaluating cognitive states such as self appraisal and self management"* (Brown, 1987).

In other words, being a metacognitive student also means becoming a strategic learner who will choose a strategy to plan and regulate his learning. In this way, if I plan to master the English irregular verbs and know that I find it useful to read aloud,

I will avoid the library, where silence is required, and find a place without such a restriction.

In a context of autonomous learning, metacognition is an important factor for learning performance (Osborne, 2000; Zimmerman and Martinez-Pons, 1990; Pintrich, 2002). In the context of distance learning, metacognition is also a key factor of success (Houssman, 1991). Learning with social software requires learners' metacognition to deal with the non-linear mass of information without wasting time and losing the learning objectives.

2.4. Prerequisite IV: Learner's Willingness to Engage in Life Long learning

However, there is a risk that the proliferation of learning opportunities will be meaningless unless participants and those offering such programs are willing to develop a new approach to learning. In a knowledge society, learning is an on-going requirement for citizens and businesses – both risk losing their competitiveness if they do not update their knowledge on a regular basis. This involves creating a new approach to learning – one not solely confined to secondary education. ICTs have contributed both to the consolidation of the knowledge society as well as to the development of e-learning and blended learning solutions. More informally, the emergence of social software helped to build learning communities (Lave and Wenger, 1991).

To sum up, a pre-requisite for the emergence of continuous learning and the use of ICT is a set of higher order skills – these skills must be acquired before the new e-learning opportunities can be exploited. Next, this chapter will focus on metacognition as a pre-requisite for effective learning in social software. In addition, Educational Social Software (ESS) will be stressed as a great opportunity to enhance metacognitive development activities.

3. METACOGNITION ON EDUCATIONAL SOCIAL SOFTWARE

3.1. The Emergence of New Learning Theorie Towards the ESS Approach

The 2.0 revolution opens up new educational opportunities based on collaborative learning and collective intelligence co-construction, going further than the mere transmission of information. For some authors, traditional pedagogical models no longer serve to explain learning in the context of social technologies. Instead they propose the introduction of a new learning model – connectionism.

From the earliest days of information technology, computers were considered as potential tools to facilitate learning and thus enhance human capabilities. The first approaches tried to implement the behaviourist approaches, creating DILL (digital and library learning) and practice programs (Bottino, 2004). These were followed in turn by MicroWorlds (Papert, 1980) and some educational interactive tools. With the development of the Internet, professors viewed the possibilities of the global network for publishing their learning resources, even if these resources were mostly designed for a traditional face-to-face use in the classroom, without the reengineering needed to fulfil web-based learning specificities (e.g. file formats and weight, human computer interaction and ergonomic rules, etc.). Broadly speaking, this consisted of PowerPoint presentations exported as pdf, and then uploaded into web sites or specific learning platforms. Fortunately, this approach has been modified and gradually enriched. Educational institutions and professors are beginning to reconsider the model in order to exploit the interactive possibilities of the Internet. The Internet is now seen as a tool for social construction of knowledge recommended by the socio-constructivist approach. Groupware has emerged and a new generation of Learning

Management Systems (e.g. Moodle - *Modular Object-Oriented Dynamic Learning Environment*) has started to allow the development of constructivist learning through collaborative activities such as forums, co-constructed glossaries, wikis, or even, WebQuests. This decisive step has brought about the ESS revolution, breaking the learning and learners' atomization which had been imposed by traditional educational software and platform-based approaches. The activities and the learner community have been extended into a wider sphere. The World Wide Web as a global network promotes interaction among users and the collective intelligence generated by large communities of practices and learning. In this context, the emergence of social technologies is a great opportunity to develop the connectionist learning approach.

The connectionism (Siemens, 2004, inspired by Rumelhart and McClelland, 1986) considers learning as the result of connecting different sources of information, adopting a non-linear learning structure. In this approach, learning is a dynamic process – a process that requires our knowledge to be up-dated in order to take into account the evolution of information in the network. Consequently, the *"capacity to know more is more critical than what is currently known"* (Siemens, 2004). That places self-regulation and metacognitive abilities as a key factor for learning performance in a pervasive knowledge network which exhibits information in a continuous state of flux.

3.2. Metacognitive Requirements when Learning with ESS

The pre-requisites for 21st century learners to respond to the new opportunities for learning with ICTs were addressed at the beginning of this chapter, where ICT competence, autonomy and self-regulation and metacognitive development are identified as important. In this section we will explain the metacognitive needs related to

ESS specificities: the complexity, the non-linear structure of knowledge and the continually changing network of people involved in the production and development of knowledge.

Metacognition is highly important for learning in complex situations. Students must manage their own learning in a context of continuous change where they need to regulate themselves as learners and take a large number of decisions concerning both their learning objectives and structure (what to learn and in which order) and the learning modalities (individual or collaborative learning, study time and rhythm, etc.). In urgent situations, metacognition could be supported by just-in-time context-aware mobile devices (Romero and Wareham, 2009), allowing flexible learning solutions adapted to the context.

The learning complexity with educational social software is due to the specificities of 2.0: a network-based structure of non-linear information and interactions. Already, in traditional educational software and web 1.0, interaction and information were limited by the software top-down approach of information workflow. In the bottom-up approach of social software, the number of participants and their contributions makes the system very complex.

The traditional web is already a complex metacognitive challenge for students (Veenman, Wilhelm and Beishuizen, 2004) because of the vast amount of information available and all the possible choices. This complexity is even more important in the case of Web 2.0, where we have an almost infinite number of knowledge contributors and their contributions. In this networked architecture, the information is not always displayed by its original author. Thus, we often reach information aggregations displayed in third sites. Websites like NetVibes or Google News can show a personalized information aggregation for each user. It is no longer a direct source of content, but a remix of external information sources. *"The content disappears behind the architecture. Speech is no longer anchored in a device (technology) but the device anchors speech."* (Ertzscheid, 2005). The information architecture as recovered by a search engine (e.g. Google, Kartoo ...) is also an information aggregation. In these levels of information remix, the original author of the content is often lost. In this sense, we can observe that the aggregation structure becomes even more important that the content structure (Saffer, 2005).

It is already difficult for learners to identify the structure of a linear content in an unknown area of knowledge. For this reason, identifying the information structure and the author in non-linear 2.0 aggregates of information presents a major challenge. Learners' metacognitive capabilities are required in social software more than in the traditional learning context, where the progressive linearity of teacher-led contents transmission, require fewer metacognitive capabilities.

Because of its complexity, ESS involves some learning risks that Thalheimer (2008) has summarized as follows:

1. Learners can learn bad information.
2. Learners can spend time learning low-priority information.
3. Learners can learn the right information, but learn it inadequately.
4. Learners can learn the right information, but learn it inefficiently.
5. Learners can learn at the wrong time, hurting their on-the-job performance.
6. Learners can learn good information that interferes with other good information.
7. Learners utilize productive time in learning. Learners can waste time learning.
8. Learners can learn something, but forget it before it is useful.
9. Previous inappropriate learning can harm learners' on-the-job learning.

To avoid these difficulties, learners need to be placed in the role of managers of their own learning. This implies taking into account the learning objectives, choosing what they will learn, then,

planning and regulating their learning process. Learners who are not able to work in this level of complexity will have difficulties taking advantage of 2.0 learning opportunities.

Thus far, we have analysed the ESS learning requirements, and more especially, the metacognitive pre-requisite. From this point, we will address ESS proactively, as an opportunity to develop the metacognitive abilities of learners in order to better exploit the learning opportunities of this specialised software.

3.3 Metacognitive Development Opportunities in ESS

As metacognition has been a key issue in successful learning, and autonomous learning contexts in particular, many authors have studied how to develop learners' metacognitive capabilities. The nature of the learning interventions for the development of metacognitive learners is mainly based on the awareness of the learning process during the resolution of a specific task. Awareness implies the learner's ability to be conscious of the learning process. The learner must be conscious of his own knowledge – his metaknowledge (the knowledge about knowledge and the way we learn) – and of his own learning strategies. This awareness can be developed through metacognitive guidance, modelling activities or even collaborative dialogues.

In the field of ICT, the work of Jonassen (1990) introduced computers as cognitive tools and extended research has been done in the field. Recently, Azevedo (2005) introduced the potential of computer environments in the development of metacognitive learners. Until now, consideration of the use of computers for metacognitive development has held computers in a traditional perspective, without exploring the new possibilities of social software. This is probably due to the novelty of the 2.0 approaches.

Next in this chapter we will explore the various possibilities of ESS for metacognitive development. First, ESS could be considered as a metacognitive development opportunity because of its social aspects. Secondly, we will focus on activities that can be designed to develop the metacognitive abilities of the learner.

3.3.1 ESS: Social-Based Opportunities for Metacognitive Development

Collaborative activities play an important role in the development of metacognition. Social interaction is considered a pre-requisite in the learning of metacognition (Von Wright, 1992). According to Marzano (1988) metacognition is, initially, the result of a process of social interaction which, gradually, becomes internalized. According to Marzano, language and social relations play an important role in the interactions which will lead to metacognition. Manion and Alexander (1997) also demonstrated that collaborative work helps the development of metacognitive strategies.

We could consider three main social perspectives of metacognition. The first is the consideration of metacognition as an essential part of collaborative work (Salonen, Vauras, and Efklides, 2005). The second considers metacognition as a social interaction product (Goos et al, 2000). In the third perspective, metacognition is considered as socially distributed (socially shared metacognition) (Iiskala, Vauras and Lehtinen, 2004). The first two approaches are mainly accepted by the scientific community. However, a metacognition approach which is socially distributed faces the same criticism as that faced by distributed cognition; for example, the consideration of an external consciousness. For a large number of authors, cognition and metacognition are individual processes that could occur in a social context, but nevertheless remain individual functions because they are produced in one's brain.

Taking the same approach, Pata (2008) suggests that awareness or inter-subjective consciousness (inter-subjective awareness) could reflect the awareness of the individual cognitive and meta-

cognitive process of others. Ligorio, Pontecorto and Talamo (2005) tried to develop metacognition during a distance learning collaborative activity. In this activity, Greek and Italian students were required to write a fairy tale. According to Ligorio and his colleagues the development of metacognition during this activity helped to foster interdependence among participants during the task.

3.3.2 Metacognitive Development through ESS-Based Learning Activities

The previous sections discussed the potential of ESS in metacognitive development because of its associated social aspect. However, despite the opportunities of their context, learners do not necessarily develop all their potential metacognition naturally (Hofer, Yu and Pintrich, 1998). We will now consider activities that could foment and support metacognition learning through the use of Educational Social Software.

Metacognitive Development through Tutored use of ESS: Metacognitive Dialogue and Modelling

During the learning activity, teachers and tutors could go beyond the traditional role of information transmitters and become metacognitive coaches, helping learners to develop their potential through metacognitive dialogue or modelling activities. Metacognitive development through dialogue helps to develop the awareness of learning strategies already used by the learner (Paris and Winograd, 1990).

Metacognitive modelling aims at a gradual internalization of metacognitive strategies through an initial explicit example given by the teacher or tutor. In this way, the teacher could show how to search for and to select information in Wikipedia or other 2.0 websites, making explicit the cognitive strategies he followed during the process of the planning, execution and regulation of this learning task. Thereafter, learners could try to reproduce the same cognitive and metacognitive strategies, describing their strategic behaviour in a written form or expressing it as a thinking aloud process. The explanation allows the teacher to check if the modelling activity served correctly to transfer the cognitive and metacognitive strategies to the learners.

Metacognitive Development through the use of ESS during Peer Tutoring Activities

In a certain way, peer tutoring could become a metacognitive development activity, assigning a *"metacognitive tutor"* role to some learners. That could be achieved by putting learners into pairs where one plays the *"metacognitive tutor"* while the other performs the task. This activity could have collaborative variations and be done by groups of learners or by assigning more specific roles (planning tutor, regulation tutor, ...) that could later be reassigned to another group member.

Metacognitive peer tutoring facilitates metacognitive development because of the closest zone of proximal development (ZPD) between peers. This ZPD allows a more effective metacognitive dialogue because of the close language and references employed between students of the same level. In such situations, learners may explain some examples of the ways they could use the social software that they already use (e.g. MySpace, Facebook) for achieving their learning tasks; they could also make explicit their strategic use of ESS solutions (e.g. Slideshare).

Metacognition Development through the Multiple and Complexity Perspectives of Social Software

Computers as cognitive tools allow outsourcing and expliciting knowledge in multiple perspectives (e.g. texts, static and interactive graphics, videos,...). For Clements and Nastasi (1999), using a microworld such as LOGO engenders a high-level type of conflict resolution involving coordination of divergent perspectives. In this situation, the teacher can explain the metacognitive experience. On the other hand, Witherspoon, Azevedo

and Baker (2007) consider learning as the result of the confrontation of multiple representations, particularly effective in the context of external regulated learning (ERL). In the case of Web 2.0 applications, knowledge develops a myriad of different perspectives during a continuum of information which is continuously evolving. In this continually changing information, knowledge continues to evolve. For example, a definition in Wikipedia may change frequently during a single day. Thus someone who read the article at 9 am will get different information from that obtained by a person who reads it at 5 pm.

To foster learning through these multiple perspectives, and taking into account previous research, we suggest that the use of ESS as a source of multiple representations should be led by the teacher or tutor at primary and high school levels in order to make sure that the activity is correctly modelled. If not, there is a risk that the complexity of representations will render learning through multiple perspectives counter-productive.

Development of Metacognition through the Active Contribution to Web 2.0 Content Production

Participation in social software can contribute to the development of metacognition in different manners. The first way we could consider is the learner 2.0 participation that could be oriented to the sharing of metaknowledge about learning strategies of individual learners. During these activities, learners - individuals or teams - may communicate to the community (e.g. class, school, Internet) their learning process as they perform specific tasks. For example, how to find information by asking experts found in social networks. This metaknowledge sharing activity may also be achieved with distant learners. An example of this might be two students learning a foreign language and sharing their *"metacognitive tips"* or strategies for language learning. It may have even greater significance, and a real external impact, if students contribute to a Wikipedia article after previous work done in class or autonomously. In this set of metacognitive activities based on 2.0 participation and contribution, it is essential to ensure the explanation of metacognition strategies and the metaknowledge gained and developed during the activities. This will ensure a correct transfer to other learning situations.

CONCLUSION

The information society and the emergence of new social web approaches has changed our approach to teaching and learning and, more especially, changed the metacognitive strategies and metaknowledge that we engage when using social software for educational purposes. It has now become necessary to engage in a life-long learning approach, both at the individual level and at the organizational level. This implies a new relationship to knowledge – a relationship where we need to move to higher-level, becoming not just learners, but also managers of our own learning. This involves developing metacognitive skills in order to act more strategically when planning and regulating our learning. However, it also implies integrating social software as a potential life-long learning opportunity.

Throughout this chapter we addressed ESS from a metacognition point of view, first, analysing the metacognitive challenges of ESS, and secondly, considering ESS possibilities for learning and metacognition development. In a context where learning is no longer enough and we must learn to learn, the use of social software for educational purposes adds, firstly, new cognitive and metacognitive prerequisites to the learning process. At the same, ESS opens up new opportunities for metacognition development and life long-learning. Henceforth, learning passively will not be enough to maintain our competitiveness as knowledge workers or learners. We will need to develop our metacognition for learning strategically in an inter-connected world – a world

where knowledge evolves permanently, but where we have a new universe of learning opportunities through social software.

REFERENCES

Azevedo, R. (2005). Computers environments as metacognitive tools for enhancing learning. [Special Issue on Computers as Metacognitive Tools for Enhancing Student Learning]. *Educational Psychologist*, *40*(4), 193–197. doi:10.1207/s15326985ep4004_1

Brandsma, J. (1998). Financement de l'éducation et de la formation tout au long de la vie: Problèmes clés. In *Peut-on mesurer les bénéfices de l'investissement dans les ressources humaines. Formation professionnelle . Revue Européenne*, *14*, 1–6.

Brown, A. L. (1987). Metacognition, executive control, self-regulation, and other more mysterious mechanisms. In F. E. Weinert & R. H. Kluwe (Eds.), *Metacognition, motivation, and understanding* (pp. 65-116). Hillsdale, NJ: Lawrence Erlbaum Associates.

Clarke, E., & Emerson, A. (1981). Design and synthesis of synchronization skeletons using branching-time temporal logic. *Logic of Programs*, *1981*, 52–71.

Clements, D. H., & Nastasi, B. K. (1999). Metacognition, learning, and educational computer environments. *Information Technology in Childhood Education Annual*, *1*, 5–38.

Ertscheid, O. (2005). Google a les moyens de devenir un guichet d'accès unique à l'information. *Le Monde*.

Flavell, J. H. (1976). Metacognition aspects of problem solving. In L. B. Resnick (Ed.), *The nature of intelligence*. Hilldale, NJ: Lawrence Erlbaum.

Goos, M., Galbraith, P., Renshaw, P., & Geiger, V. (2000, July 31-August 6). *Classroom voices: Technology enriched interactions in a community of mathematical practice*. Paper presented at the Working Group for Action 11 (The Use of Technology in Mathematics Education) at the 9th International Congress on Mathematical Education, Tokyo/Makuhari.

Gordon. (1996). Tracks for learning: Metacognition and learning technologies. *Australian Journal of Educational Technology, 12*(1), 46-55.

Hofer, B., Yu, S., & Pintrich, P. (1998). Teaching college students to be self-regulated learners. In D. Schunk & B. Zimmerman (Eds.), *Self-regulated learners: From teaching to self-reflective practice* (pp. 57-85). New York: Guilford.

Houssman, J. (1991). Self monitoring and learning proficiency. In *Computer classroom*. Hofstra University, EDD.

Hurme, T.-R., & Merenluoto, K. (2008, June 9-13). *Socially shared metacognition and feelings of difficulty in a group's computer supported mathematical problem solving*. Kesäseminaari pidetään Physicumissa, Helsingin yliopistossa. Retrieved on October 1, 2008, from http://per.physics.helsinki.fi/Tutkijakoulun_kesaseminaari_2008/Hurme.pdf

Iiskala, T., Vauras, M., & Lehtinen, E. (2004). Socially-shared metacognition in peer learning? *Hellenic Journal of Psychology, 1*, 147–178.

Jonassen, D. H., & Harris, N. D. (1990). Analyzing and selecting instructional strategies and tactics. *Performance Improvement Quarterly, 3*(2), 29–47.

Lave, J., & Wenger, E. (1991). *Situated learning: Legitimate peripheral participation*. Cambridge: Cambridge University Press.

Ligorio, M. B., Talamo, A., & Pontecorvo, C. (2008). Building intersubjectivity at a distance during the collaborative writing of fairytales. *Computers & Education, 5*, 357–374.

Manion, V., & Alexander, J. (1997). The benefits of peer collaboration on strategy use, metacognitive causal attribution, and recall. *Journal of Experimental Child Psychology, 67*, 268–289. doi:10.1006/jecp.1997.2409

Marzano, R. J. (1988). *Metacognition: The first step in teaching thinking. Professional handbook for the language arts*. Morristown, NJ: Silver Burdett and Ginn.

Marzano, R. J. (1998). *A theory-based meta-analysis of research on instruction*. Mid-continent Aurora, CO: Regional Educational Laboratory.

Moisan, A., & Carré, P. (2002). *L'autoformation, fait social? Aspects historiques et sociologiques*. Paris: L'Harmattan.

Osborne, J. W. (2000). *Assessing metacognition in the classroom: The assessment of cognition monitoring effectiveness*. Unpublished doctoral dissertation, University of Oklahoma.

Osman, M. E., & Hannafin, M. J. (1992). Metacognition research and theory: Analysis and implications for instructional design. *Educational Technology Research and Development, 40*(2), 83–99. doi:10.1007/BF02297053

Papert, S. (1980). Mindstorms: *Children, computers, and powerful ideas*. New York: Basic Books.

Paris, S. G., & Winograd, P. (1990). How metacognition can promote academic learning and instruction. In B. F. Jones & L. Idol (Eds.), *Dimensions of thinking and cognitive instruction* (pp. 15-51). Hillsdale, NJ: Lawrence Erlbaum Associates.

Pata, K. (2008). *Sociocultural and ecological explanations to self-reflection*. Retrieved on October 2, 2008, from http://tihane.wordpress.com/category/intersubjectivity/

Pintrich, R. (2002). The role of metacognitive knowledge in learning, teaching, and assessing. *Theory into Practice, 41*(4), 219–225. doi:10.1207/s15430421tip4104_3

Ridley, D. S., Schutz, P. A., Glanz, R. S., & Weinstein, C. E. (1992). Self-regulated learning: The interactive influence of metacognitive awareness and goal-setting. *Journal of Experimental Education, 60*(4), 293–306.

Romero, M., & Wareham, J. (2009). Just-in-time mobile learning model based on context awareness information. *IEEE Learning Technology Newsletter, 11*(1-2), 4–6.

Rumelhart, D., & McClelland, J. (1986). *Parallel distributed processing*. MIT Press

Saffer, D. (2005). *The role of metaphor in interaction design*. Master's thesis, Carnegie Mellon University, Pittsburgh, PA.

Salonen, P., Vauras, M., & Efklides, A. (2005). Social interaction—what can it tell us about metacognition and coregulation in learning? *European Psychologist, 10*(3), 199–208. doi:10.1027/1016-9040.10.3.199

Siemens, G. (2004). *Learning management systems: The wrong place to start learning. E-learnspace*. Retrieved on October 1, 2008, from http://www.elearnspace.org/Articles/lms.htm

Thalheimer, W. (2008, August 18). Evaluation e-learning 2.0: Getting our heads around the complexity. *Learning Solutions*.

Veenman, M. V. J., Wilhelm, P., & Beishuizen, J. J. (2004). The relation between intellectual and metacognitive skills from a developmental perspective. *Learning and Instruction, 14*(1), 89–109. doi:10.1016/j.learninstruc.2003.10.004

Von Wright, J. (1992). Reflection on reflections. *Learning and Instruction, 2*(1), 59–68. doi:10.1016/0959-4752(92)90005-7

Witherspoon, A., Azevedo, R., & Baker, S. (2007, July). *Learners' use of various types of representations during self-regulated learning and externally-regulated learning episodes*. Paper presented at a Workshop on Metacognition and Self-Regulated Learning at the 13th International Conference on Artificial Intelligence in Education, Los Angeles, CA.

Zimmerman, B. J., & Martinez-Pons, M. (1990). Student differences in self-regulated learning: Relating grade, sex, and giftedness to self-efficacy and strategy use. *Journal of Educational Psychology, 82*, 52–59. doi:10.1037/0022-0663.82.1.51

Section 2
Educational Social Software Technologies

Chapter 4
Use of Social Software in Education:
A Multiple Intelligences Perspective

Filiz Kalelioglu
Baskent University, Turkey

Yasemin Gulbahar
Baskent University, Turkey

ABSTRACT

In this chapter, numerous educational activities are presented for instructors in order to address each type of multiple intelligences. Most probably, these educational activities are those which are already being experienced by many instructors. The key point here is that although students are exposed to many educational activities, instructors generally don't have any idea or rather don't consider the learning outcomes in terms of multiple intelligences. In general, assessment activities are based only on the chunk of knowledge that the student gains after any particular activity. In fact, instructors should deal with the effects and improvements in students other than just the knowledge, after engagement in educational activities. Thus, instructors should base their instructional plans on a theoretical basis, especially when integrating technology into their courses. Hence, the development and changing activities and other tasks of social software according to the multiple intelligences that underline individual differences were discussed briefly in this chapter.

INTRODUCTION

Innovations in technology have lead to the transformation of face to face interaction to online environments in past two decades. Many virtual communities have been constituted, for realizing different purposes by means of various technologies. Starting with the oldest and inevitably used technol-

ogy, which we call e-mail, communication patterns and thus technologies have changed into discussion lists, forums, chat rooms and more recently blogs and wikis. These technologies are primarily used in business, nevertheless they have swiftly entered into and extended education. Hence, the latest technologies are used widely in most educational institutions today. The three common approaches for using of technology are to support to traditional instruction, blended learning, and e-learning. Among

DOI: 10.4018/978-1-60566-826-0.ch004

these alternatives, blended learning is the most prevailing as it has much more advantages than traditional instruction and e-learning (Horton, 2000). Blended learning takes the advantages of the strengths of classroom techniques together with web based training. Thus, the teaching-learning process occurs both in the classroom setting and the virtual environment, and all stakeholders can communicate both face-to-face and online.

Together with integration of the popular approaches, the usage of educational social software has moved forward greatly in distance education and e-learning at first. Afterwards, traditional learning and e-learning have begun to be used together - under the title of blended learning - by possessing the different benefits of both traditional learning and e-learning. In that process research studies have begun to be conducted in order to find out how effective all existing technologies are? Since the emergence of communication tools, many research studies have been conducted to maintain the effectiveness of these tools. Moreover, the results of these research studies have brought about the existence of the field known as computer-mediated communication (CMC).

In order to determine the success of these platforms, studies about students' and instructors' preferences and opinions about social software, content analysis of written posts or logs from the systems, interaction patterns and levels, which point out the usage of these social tools were conducted. Although the effectiveness of communication tools has been investigated from multiple perspectives by using different research methods in various settings, these studies currently do not contain the necessary theoretical framework. Nevertheless a number of conceptual frameworks, such as individual differences, social learning, collaborative learning and constructivism, frequently seemed to be used by many studies for establishing the theoretical foundation. However, the effectiveness of learning is a major concern in these environments since online environments are social platforms. It is necessary to make different

theories for clarifying available communication patterns or educational activities in order to reach a more generalized and reliable result.

Under the lights of discussions, educational activities and tasks in these platforms must be constructed according to the theoretical framework. Thus, this chapter aims to discuss the development and changing activities and other tasks of social software according to the multiple intelligences that underline individual differences.

MULTIPLE INTELLIGENCES THEORY

"Multiple Intelligences Theory", proposed by Gardner (1993), approaches learning and instruction from a different perspective. Some researchers have claimed that our intelligence or ability to understand the world around us is a changing process, where people show diversity in terms of understanding and learning. Abilities in performing different skills may differ from individual to individual. One person may be good at playing a musical instrument; one individual may be good at playing football and another maybe good at writing poems. These differences among people are addressed in the multiple intelligences theory. To give an example, if an individual has strong spatial or musical intelligences, instructors should encourage those students to develop these abilities. Gardner points out that the different intelligences represent not only different content domains but also learning modalities.

Howard Gardner viewed intelligence as the capacity to solve problems or to fashion products that are valued in one or more cultural setting (Gardner & Hatch, 1989). Although Gardner initially proposed a list of seven intelligences, he later made additions to this list. For this chapter, eight intelligences are taken into consideration: Verbal-Linguistic (Word Smart), Logical-Mathematical (Number Smart), Visual-Spatial (Picture Smart), Bodily-Kinesthetic (Body Smart), Musical-Rhythmic (Music Smart), Interpersonal

(People Smart), Intrapersonal (Myself Smart) and Naturalistic (Nature Smart) (Smith, 2002, 2008; Brualdi, 1996; Gardner, 1993, 2006; Gardner & Hatch, 1989; White, 1998).

In the light of these facts, educational social software can be investigated in terms of different intelligence types. Furthermore, the tasks given to students may be organized in a way that addresses multiple intelligences. In this way, not only will technology be integrated into teaching-learning processes in an effective manner, but students will also have the opportunity for improvement in the different multiple intelligences. As also suggested by McCoog (2007), one of the best ways to make students acquire 21st century skills such as global awareness and social responsibility, is to differentiate instruction through the use of Gardner's multiple intelligence and technology.

For this chapter, blogs, wikis, instant messaging, forums and e-mail technologies have been selected for investigation from a multiple intelligences perspective. Before going any further, it will be useful to understand these technologies in more detail.

BLOGS

Blogs are called as a method of effective communication in online environments, and innovative ways to use them in education are frequently appearing nowadays. Originally, a blog was an online diary posted on the web that included the publication of personal thoughts, feelings, hobbies, and experiences in a chronological order.

Blogs can also be defined as online writing tools that help their users to keep track of their own online records (Hsu & Lin, 2008). Anyone who doesn't have advanced computer and Internet usage skills can still create such web pages, and express their feelings to others with the help of blogs. Furthermore, blog users and non-blog users

Table 1. Multiple intelligences

Type of Intelligence	Description
Verbal-Linguistic intelligence (Word Smart)	Interested in spoken and written language, the ability to learn languages, and the ability to use language to accomplish certain goals like effectively use language to express ideas.
Logical-mathematical intelligence (Number Smart)	Addresses the capacity to analyze problems logically, solve mathematical operations, and investigate issues scientifically. Examples maybe detecting patterns, reasoning deductively and thinking logically.
Visual-Spatial intelligence (Picture Smart)	Involves the potential to visualize graphics such as three-dimensional objects, imagine the details of an object mentally and draw visually appealing graphics and arts.
Bodily-kinesthetic intelligence (Body Smart)	Includes the potential to use one's whole body or parts of the body mentally and physically in harmony. The coordination of bodily movements in a rhythm, balanced and flexible way is the core of this type of intelligence.
Musical-Rhythmic intelligence (Music Smart)	Involves skills in the performance, composition, and appreciation of musical patterns. The ability of recognition and composition of musical pitches, tones, and rhythms are also among the important tasks of this type of intelligence.
Interpersonal intelligence (People Smart)	Deals with the abilities to understand and interpret the intentions, motivations and desires of other people emphatically. Effective communication and collaboration is also covered in this type of intelligence.
Intrapersonal intelligence (Myself Smart)	Involves an individuals' ability to recognize herself / himself in terms of trust, problems, feelings, fears and motivations. Knowing one's own capacity and deciding on what to achieve is also among the properties of this type of intelligence.
Naturalist intelligence (Nature Smart)	Deals with sensing patterns in and making connections to features and elements in environment and nature. It also enables individuals to recognize, categorize and draw upon certain features of the earth.

can post their comments on the written issues easily. Depending on the authors' preferences, these online writing tools can include features such as links to other blogs, the author's detailed profile, and most importantly feedback from readers (Ellison & Wu, 2008). Blogs can be used for many purposes, but when they are used for educational goals, they can enrich the classroom environment and facilitate social interaction among students. Instructors can integrate blogs in blended and online learning to facilitate specific strategies: posting student work, exchanging hyperlinks, fostering reflective approaches to educational genres, forming and maintaining knowledge communities (Oravec, 2003).

Moreover, usage of blogs can address some of the theoretical underpinnings that are summarized below (Glogoff, 2005):

- In instructional blogging, as a knowledge-centered instructional tool, the instructor designs research activities that engage students in discussions with practitioners, and lead them through developmental concepts of the discipline's knowledge domain.
- In learner-centered blogging (that acknowledges the important attributes of learners as individuals and as a group), the instructor gives positive feedback to students regarding their comments and by posting comments for discussion. In this way, learner-centered blogging offers particularly useful opportunities for learner-centered feedback and dialogue.
- For providing community-centered instruction, blogging supports the importance of social and peer interaction.
- As a receptive learning tool, blogging can encourage students to acquire information from resources and reflect on what they have gathered.
- In a directive learning environment, blogs provide students with equal access to information, to expand students' understanding

of specific issues, and to direct students to explore additional material.

- As a guided discovery and knowledge construction, blogs can also be used to present information architecture and explore more from web sites for other content.

To briefly summarize their many purposes, blogs can easily be used in educational environments. Publication of any materials, course notes, reflections may lead others to review, comment or study. At the same time, blogging not only supports individual sharing, but also allows other visitors to interact with the archived content, blog readers and the owner.

WIKIS

A wiki is a collection of web pages linked to each other which reflect the collaborative effort of many students working together. "Although it is not known as content management systems, wiki systems are another approach to publishing on-line information and a different way to collaborate" (Pereira & Soares, 2007, p. 88). Unlike blogs, which are chronologically reverse-organized, wiki pages are loosely structured but are linked in different ways (Beldarrain, 2006). Namely, "a wiki is a web site in which users can create and collaboratively view, edit, track changes, and save information by means of web browser" (Butcher & Taylor, 2008, p. 34). In these wiki pages, the instructor can also assess, edit or delete the information posted by the students, while students in a team can revise-edit, comment, contribute, reference or study.

One of the most well known examples of a wiki is Wikipedia, an online encyclopedia with entries authored and edited by different people from around the world. Wikis are very useful tools for educational purposes, since they encourage student participation and also a sense of group community. "Indeed, an important element of this

Table 2. General information on blogs (adapted from Hsu, 2007)

BLOGS	
Description	A technology that allows a sequence of entries to be posted and published online
Advantages	Reflection and critical thinking Authenticity through publication Social presence Development of a learning community Active learning Ability to receive and respond to feedback
Disadvantages	Controlled primarily by blog author Editing/modifications not open as in a wiki
Educational applications	Online learning journal Problem solving/manipulation space Online gallery space (writings, portfolio, other work) Peer review exercises
Course/ subject suitability	Writing courses Foreign language courses Research seminars
Theoretical foundations	Activity theory Guided discovery Cognitive scaffolding Receptive learning Social cognition Community practice Communities of inquiry

is the relaxed sense of control over the content, allowing students to have a greater role in managing its focus and direction" (Hsu, 2007, p. 80).

The attractive characteristics of wikis can be summarized as follows by Shih, Tseng and Yang (2008).

- **Rapidity:** The wiki pages can be rapidly constructed, accessed and modified, in hypertext form.
- **Easy:** A simple markup scheme (usually a simplified version of HTML) is used to format the wiki pages, instead of the complicated HTML.
- **Convenience:** Links to other pages, external sites, and images can be conveniently established by keywords. Moreover, the targets of the keywords, links, need not exist when the links are built. They can be appended later.

- **Open source:** Each member can create, modify and delete the wiki pages. Wiki content is not reviewed by anyone before publication, and is updated upon being saved.
- **Maintainability:** Wiki maintains a version database, which records its historical revision and content, thus enabling version management.

In summary, a tool for collaboration and a form of groupware, wikis can be used for courses and activities where there is a document, text, or other project to be worked on jointly by a class or group. The compilation of a class or group report or project, the creation of a knowledge base, or brainstorming sessions appear to be viable applications (Hsu, 2007).

Table 3. General information on wikis (adapted from Hsu, 2007)

WIKIS	
Description	A technology that allows for material to be easily published online, and also allows open editing and inputs by a group
Advantages	Contributions and editing by a group Open access to all users Collaborative
Disadvantages	Lack of organization and structure may result in an unmanageable wiki Tracking of contributions and modifications can be difficult Quality control
Educational Applications	Collaborative writing/authoring Group project management Brainstorming activities Knowledge management
Course/ subject suitability	Knowledge management Writing Group work in courses
Theoretical foundations	Conversational technology Constructivist learning tool

INSTANT MESSAGING (CHAT)

Synchronous discussion, or chat or instant messaging, refers to online dialogue occurring in real time. In chat sessions, there is no time delay between the sender's transmission and the receiver's receipt of the message unlike asynchronous communication (Borowicz, 2004).

Instant messaging engages geographically-distanced students in synchronous dialogues and offers a flexible platform for knowledge construction. Moreover, chat can be used to enhance out-of class learning activities by supporting collaborative learning and improving communication (McCreary & Ehrich, 2001).

Chat can be used in educational settings for many purposes. For example, in distance education it can be used for meeting with students once a week or twice a week, thus facilitating regular meetings, since online discussion lies at the core of distance courses. Moreover, in a blended environment, other activities can be arranged in which all students from a variety of locations are given a problem to solve collaboratively, meaning virtual problem solving

groups. Students can invite people such as expert in various fields, community leaders, and others to their chat sessions. Furthermore, it is possible to communicate other people to practice language skills with the help of chat programs (Ingram, Hathorn & Evans, 2000).

For effective usage of instant messaging in courses, and to affect the quality of educational discussions, Ingram, Hathorn, and Evans (2000) identify a number of critical issues for instructors:

- **Environment:** As the graphical environment of the chat rooms is important, it is advised to use a chat program supporting graphical-based programs instead of text-based ones.
- **Task:** A clear discussion topic or detailed description of the expected product at the end of the discussion should be offered to the students. A second important issue for offering task is type of task, i.e. tasks that require research and review of other materials would not be appropriate for this type of synchronous online discussion tool.

- **Rules:** A clear set of rules is useful for controlling and directing discussions in the chat sessions. It is also important for students to know when to write and when to read.
- **Group-size:** Synchronous online discussion tools usually work best with small groups of three to five students. When group size is larger than this range, it is advisable to divide discussion groups into separate groups in different chat rooms.
- **Identity:** To prevent a student from hiding their own identity, it is advised for students use their own name and not to mislead the rest of the group and the teacher with nick names.
- **Moderation:** According to factors such as large group size, task type or level of students, the instructor may prefer to find a moderator to lead the discussion and keep it on track.

Instant messaging, which is a synchronous tool mostly used to communicate, can also be used to support distance and blended learning to enhance learning activities by supporting collaborative learning. Possible activities may be performed by using chat programs in educational settings in a way of short discussions individually or as a group. Some activities may consist of role playing, conversation in different languages, word games in different languages, grammar games in different languages, brainstorming, summary of a subject taught previously, problem solving activities, case studies and peer review/editing.

FORUMS

A forum is an asynchronous platform where students can communicate by posting messages and responding to them for collaboration or discussion. If it is used for academic discussions or out-of class activities, online forums can enhance learning processes (Chen & Chiu, 2008). The most useful educational advantage of online discussion forums is to provide the time available for reading a message and think about a response, which can help to improve reflection upon and development of a topic (Guiller & Durndell, 2007).

Table 4. General information on instant messaging (adapted from Hsu, 2007)

INSTANT MESSAGING	
Description	Synchronous communications that allow for informal communications to be conducted easily and quickly
Advantages	Availability and acceptance by students Social presence Synchronous communications Encouraging collaboration Reduces formality in communications
Disadvantages	Distracted attention Expectations of 24-7 instructor access Can be time consuming for instructors Benefits are uncertain in classroom settings
Educational applications	Virtual office hours Collaboration on group projects Synchronous class discussions Mentoring
Course/ subject suitability	Courses with group projects and assignments Distance learning support
Theoretical foundations	Active learning Dual (verbal and visual) processing

Discussion forums can be used for many different purposes in different educational environments. The forums may be used as a support to distance or blended learning for social interaction, for discussion of topics towards answering the frequently asked questions, and for individual homework or group projects as a collaborative tool. Differentiated according to the purpose of the forum, instructors may:

- "limit discussions to one or more instructor-initiated themes,
- lead more general discussions,
- assume the role of answering most of the questions from students,
- moderate the discussions but maintain a low profile in them, or even be entirely absent from the discussions" (Mazzolini & Maddison, 2003, p. 238),
- assign a student as a moderator, and
- support discussion and motive to join non-participants into debate.

The discussion in the forum can often be carried out easily within small groups, which made up of four to eight students for learning sets or medium sized group with 20 to 30 students for discussions. If the forum is supposed to set up for very large groups, there may be disappointment with the levels of participation and there may be disorder of posted messages, so that it becomes unmanageable. Conversely, in small groups it is easy to control and follow the messages and information and also the participation level of the students. The participation in the discussion is not only important in face to face environments, but also it is an important concern within any small group in an online environment (Hammond, 2000).

E-MAIL

E-mail (electronic mail), which is a service for sending messages electronically, allows communication among people regardless of the status of people, i.e. whether they are online or not. Moreover, the exchange of electronic text messages and computer file attachments between computers requires people to have a mail account, which is a place where someone can contact another person.

Table 5. General information on forums

FORUM	
Description	Asynchronous communications that allow for communication and discussion to be conducted easily
Advantages	Availability and acceptance by students Social presence Asynchronous communication Encouraging collaboration Reducing formality in communication
Disadvantages	Distracted attention
Educational applications	Collaboration on group projects Asynchronous class discussions Mentoring Peer review exercises
Course/ subject suitability	Courses with group projects and assignments Distance learning support
Theoretical foundations	Active learning Dual (verbal and visual) processing

Furthermore, an e-mail address is a unique name that identifies an e-mail recipient for the transfer of information from one computer to another. It is possible to store, send, compose, forward and receive messages over electronic communication systems by means of the using e-mail.

E-mail can also be used for many purposes. These purposes may be mainly for communication and the transformation of information. Palmer (2000) illustrated internet usage in education, noting that the WWW (for the delivery of multimedia content) and e-mail (for basic electronic communication) are the two important Internet services for teaching and learning. If the students and instructors cannot easily arrange face-to-face meetings, it is important to use e-mail communication (Lightfoot, 2006; Le & Le, 2002).

Martin (1996) chose the e-mail method in his courses in a research study because "student assessment was through requiring students to summarize, comment or discuss the content of each lecture", and "most of the students were part time, visiting the campus only for the scheduled classes" (p. 823).

Being an easy method to send messages, information or other kind of materials by just a few mouse clicks, the instructor want to take into consideration some issues. Instructors can:

- choose a topic for which individualized communication can take place and create links outside of regular space, time,
- support detailed analysis and reflection,
- give participants insight into others' perspectives, and
- keep records of the dialogues and messages (Cook-Sather, 2007).

CREATIVE IDEAS TO USE SOCIAL SOFTWARE IN EDUCATIONAL SETTINGS FROM MI PERSPECTIVE

Considering the advantages, opportunities and educational applications, social software can be integrated into many courses in various ways. Differentiating among intelligence types, social software can be used to create, modify, share, publish, and store course content while also offering communication flexibility. A list of educational activities addressing multiple intelligence types are presented in table 7. The concept and subject can be varied according to the type of intelligence

Table 6. General information on e-mail

E-MAIL	
Description	Asynchronous communications that allow for communications and discussion to be conducted and send messages electronically
Advantages	Asynchronous communications Encouraging writing and communication skills Reducing formality in communications Sending messaging to more than one person
Disadvantages	Distracted attention Time consuming for answering complicated questions
Educational applications	Asynchronous class discussions Peer review exercises
Course/ subject suitability	Courses with group or individual projects and assignments Distance learning support
Theoretical foundations	Active learning Dual (verbal and visual) processing

Table 7. Activity chart for multiple intelligences

	Verbal-Linguistic	Logical-Mathematical	Bodily-Kinesthetic	Visual-Spatial	Musical-Rhythmic	Inter-personal	Intra-personal	Naturalist
Brochure about a place	•		•	•			•	•
Course document	•		•	•			•	
Concept map	•	•	•	•			•	
Story telling presentation	•		•	•	•		•	
A short play	•		•	•	•		•	
A scenario	•		•	•			•	
A poem	•		•				•	
An essay	•		•				•	
A newspaper	•		•	•			•	
An interview	•		•			•	•	
Scoring excel sheet		•	•	•			•	
Self-improvement Graph in excel		•	•	•			•	
A talk show	•		•			•	•	
A puzzle	•	•	•	•			•	
A drawing in graphical editor program			•	•			•	•
Curriculum vitae	•		•	•			•	
Documentary film about global warming	•		•	•	•		•	•
Strategy game		•	•	•	•	•	•	•
Drill and practice		•	•	•	•		•	
Word game	•		•	•	•		•	
Simulations		•	•	•	•		•	•
Sound edit			•		•		•	
Video edit			•	•	•		•	
Sound record			•		•		•	
Video Record			•				•	
Write a song	•		•		•		•	
Create animations			•	•	•		•	
Discussion in chat-forum-email	•	•	•			•	•	
Database creation	•	•	•				•	
Program coding		•	•				•	
E-portfolio	•		•	•			•	

and activities can be enhanced in this way.

For example, if students are required to complete a brochure with a word processor, the tasks and requirements should include steps such as: download a brochure template from the web site, modify the style and formatting of the template, choose a place to introduce or create a place never seen, search for images and information for that place, place images and information into the brochure template, and save and share this product via appropriate educational software. Adding details not only makes educational activities more extensive, but also addresses more than one type of intelligence. In this example, it is thought that Verbal-Linguistic, Bodily-Kinesthetic, Visual-Spatial, Intrapersonal and Naturalist intelligence types are emphasized through the completion of this kind of brochure.

For the effective integration of educational social software into existing curricula and courses, instructors should take into consideration the following suggestions. These suggestions will lead instructors to being able to achieve two major goals. The first goal is the improvement of the ICT skills of students through proper use of recent technologies. Use of the latest technologies to communicate and share resources will provide students the chance of having or improving their ICT skills and become lifelong learners which is expected of them as 21st century students. The second goal addresses the improvement of multiple intelligences. Performing tasks addressing different multiple intelligences will not only yield the manifestation of the dominant intelligent types but also provide opportunities for improving the less dominant intelligence types. In order to enhance students' ICT skills by addressing various types of multiple intelligences, instructors should be aware of the capabilities and opportunities that the software provides.

As previously mentioned, blogs provide users with a platform where people can post messages and others may view and respond to these posts. Moreover, the blog users can upload files, images,

sounds, video, etc. to create more amusing content for their viewers. All the content elements are kept in a certain section or category named by owner. Distinct from blogs, a wiki is a type of web site which enables the students to add, remove, and edit the available content and includes the collaboration of work from many different author that is wikis can be seen as a community for collaborative documentation. Discussion forums, applications allow users to post messages and replies, also the linking of images, videos, sounds or other types of files with the help of other web sites offering opportunities to upload files. Chat programs and e-mail provide the opportunity for sharing all types of file with attachments. Transmission of information is sent in real-time in chat programs, whereas there is a little time delay in the e-mail method according to the status of servers.

Moreover, after realizing the potential benefits of the software, an instructor should take into consideration which multiple intelligence domains is mostly covered by the selected software. Hence, as also suggested by Nelson (1998), instructors can design their lessons including new learning activities fitting the individual strengths of all their students by using internet and web tools. Thus, the list in table 8 is provided to serve as a guide for instructors while addressing multiple intelligence types.

In the light of these facts, some suggestions for instructors in order to support courses with the use of social software for improving multiple intelligences of students are listed as follows. For each type of intelligence, possible computer software, educational tasks and activities have been explained separately.

Suggestions for Verbal-Linguistic Intelligence (Word Smart)

Students may prepare a composition, a story, a poem, a report (on a film, a theatre play...), a summary report, a newspaper, a brochure or a scenario through word processors. Using audio editing

Table 8. Software chart for multiple intelligences

	Verbal-Linguistic	Logical-Mathematical	Bodily-Kinesthetic	Visual-Spatial	Musical-Rhythmic	Inter-personal	Intra-personal	Naturalist
Word Processor	✓	✓	✓	✓			✓	✓
Desktop Publishing	✓	✓	✓	✓			✓	✓
Animation Software	✓		✓	✓	✓		✓	✓
Audio Editing Software			✓		✓		✓	
Video Editing Software			✓	✓	✓		✓	✓
Graphics/Image Editor			✓	✓			✓	✓
Simulation Software		✓	✓	✓	✓	✓	✓	✓
Educational Games		✓	✓	✓	✓	✓	✓	✓
Tutorials			✓	✓	✓		✓	
Drill and Practice		✓	✓	✓	✓		✓	
Multimedia Editing Software	✓		✓	✓	✓		✓	
Web Development Tools	✓		✓				✓	
Audio Conferencing			✓		✓	✓	✓	
Video Conferencing			✓	✓	✓	✓	✓	
Mathematical Software		✓	✓				✓	
Concept Mapping Software		✓	✓	✓			✓	✓
Musical Software			✓		✓		✓	
Web-based Educational Software	✓		✓				✓	
Modeling (3d) Programs			✓	✓			✓	
Database Management Software		✓	✓				✓	
Search engines	✓	✓	✓	✓	✓	✓	✓	✓
Virtual Courseware	✓		✓			✓	✓	
Research Tools	✓	✓	✓				✓	
Collaborative Software	✓		✓			✓	✓	
Programming languages		✓	✓				✓	
Architecture software		✓	✓	✓			✓	✓

tools, students create recordings of a sketch, a composition, a poem, storytelling, news program, interview, scripting, choral reading and retelling. Through audio-video conferencing, students make discussions on a previously given topic. Using presentation software, students may design a narrated presentation on a given topic.

Suggestions for Logical-Mathematical Intelligence (Number Smart)

Students may create scoring pages by using spreadsheets. With the help of puzzle maker programs, students may prepare puzzles. Through mathematical and scientific software, it is possible to solve equations and draw graphs and moreover, students may report causes and effects of solutions. With the help of programming languages and database management programs, students may write codes to create databases. Playing strategic, logic and mind games and simulations is another type of activity to be completed according to lesson objectives.

Suggestions for Visual-Spatial Intelligence (Picture Smart)

By using a graphics/image editor, students can design graphics, cartoons, posters, and can create concept maps with concept map software, worksheets and flowcharts with word processing. Moreover, through 3D modeling programs, students may 'architecturize' real-life objects. It is also possible to integrate actual taken photos into animation programs to present a slide show or create a video in video editing programs. Through architecture software, students can create samples of buildings according to the given scale.

Suggestions for Bodily-Kinesthetic Intelligence (Body Smart)

Students may have the chance to drag and drop cards, elements, objects etc. in the computer-aided environment by using drill and practice software. Playing any games, simulations, strategy and card games, or any programs reinforce this type of intelligence.

Suggestions for Musical-Rhythmic Intelligence (Music Smart)

Audio editing software makes it possible for students to create audio clips by mixing sounds and adding effects. It is also easy to add sounds and audio clips to animations designed in multimedia software or authoring languages. Moreover, PowerPoint slides including sounds or sound effects can be produced. Besides these kinds of activities, it is easy to play virtual instruments with the help of musical software.

Suggestions for Interpersonal Intelligence (People Smart)

By playing video games that involve hundreds of players simultaneously, for example massive multiplayer online games, students can interact and communicate with others. Communication, consensus, and collaboration are the other main concepts underlined by group projects completed in any software in project-based learning. Likewise, the completion of a WebQuest requiring role playing enables students to empathize with one another in different situations. Moreover, joining a video conference, a type of connection of groups via satellite or codec technology, also can be recorded and shared via educational social software. By moderating a chat session or a discussion in a forum, students are able to follow the flow of discussion, communicate and interact with others in a more responsible manner.

Suggestions for Intrapersonal Intelligence (Myself Smart)

Through the usage of word processing, students can design curriculum vitae including the individuals' life history, job history, achievements and skills. With the help of virtual courseware, tutorials and drill and practice, students may study and repeat their lessons at their own pace. Through search engines, students can make research on a topic individually and prepare a reflection paper via word processor. To publish personal feelings, photographs, interests and hobbies, a personal web page can be created using web page development tools.

Suggestions for Naturalist Intelligence (Nature Smart)

Video editing programs provide students to create a documentary film covering possible environmental problems and solutions: i.e. environmental pollution, weather pollution, sea pollution and global warming. Through graphic/image editing software, students can design a poster that announces the issue of waterlessness and smart usage suggestions for it. Again in the same software, it is possible to create a banner that gives a message to stop forest fires for use at the top of web page. In animation programs, students can create season timelines to depict the differences between seasons.

DISCUSSION AND CONCLUSION

Today, all these tasks require technological literacy to some extent. Since the traditional curriculum does not promote the acquisition of contemporary technology skills, many attempts at integrating technology into the curriculum have been made and are still continuing. Being aware of the potential contributions of technology during and after graduation, instructors should use technology for its anticipated effects on students. Instructors should be aware of how children learn through technology, and should facilitate students' pursuit of inquiries, and their development of critical thinking and problem solving skills through the use of collaboration, communication and technology.

These issues notwithstanding, the method of integration of educational social software should be based on one or more of these learning theories. The answers to questions, "how do students learn with technology" and "how can the content be delivered through technology", which are related to educational practices and activities, should follow a learning theory. Moreover, the integration of social software should also meet basic learning needs and goals for students. Some technologies like internet and web tools supporting individual and collaborative learning, classroom presentation, discovery/exploration, synchronous and asynchronous communication and distance learning, provide environments for teaching that focuses on students' individual strengths (Nelson, 1998). Hence, instructors should effectively integrate social software into their courses, and should prepare their students for their future careers as lifelong learners, by providing a variety of activities promoting the development of the multiple intelligences.

A review of educational social software and multiple intelligences theory has shown that no single educational software and no single educational activity based on computer software may not address the expectations of all students. Thus, educational social software and activities which are to be performed by students should be carefully selected in order to meet the diverse needs of all students, and make them achieve expected learning outcomes. Moreover, the selected social software should also support the type of content to be shared with students.

In this chapter, many educational activities are presented for instructor use in order to address each type of multiple intelligences. Probably, these educational activities are those which are already being utilized and experienced by many instructors. The key point here is that although students are exposed to many educational activities, instructors generally don't have any great idea about, or don't consider the learning outcomes in terms of multiple intelligences. Generally, assessment activities are based only on the chunk of knowledge that the student has gained after the particular activity. In fact, instructors should be dealing with the effects and improvements in students other than their knowledge after engagement in educational activities. A curriculum that combines technology and some learning theories such as multiple intelligence supplements students' strengths and expands their possibilities (McCoog, 2007). Thus, instructors should base their instructional plans around a theoretical basis, especially when integrating technology into their courses.

Technology, especially computers, are multimedia tools which provide students with many attractive features such as sounds, pictures, animations, films, visual appeals, virtual field trips and three dimensional visions. When instructors encourage students to use their different intelligences creatively, students may have the opportunity of extending and enhancing their own capabilities and multiple intelligences. Noting that "technologies set out to be mobilized for better instruction" (Gardner, 2000, p. 33), we need to realize how various technologies can help students to develop different capabilities and skills. It is not the presumption that all technologies can help all students equally, but that certain technologies can help certain students (Veenema & Gardner, 1996).

Each type of multiple intelligences supports certain instructional strategies. The ultimate goal of instructional strategies is to meet the overall needs of each learner in the class and therefore might require designing multiple lessons (McCoog, 2007). In order to support a student who possesses strong verbal-linguistic intelligence; activities should be mainly in the scope of the world of words. These educational activities may for example include researching the origins and meanings of the words from online dictionaries, online encyclopedias or e-books, learning how to speak in other languages, learning the grammatical structures of other languages, playing word games such as hangman, puzzles etc, preparing an online book or e-book on a given subject, writing a composition, a story, a poem, a report, a newspaper, a brochure or a scenario via word processor, etc. These activities mainly address the improvement of the quality of the students' writing and expressing his/her feelings.

From the logical-mathematical perspective of the students, by means of educational software students can conduct an experiment and see its results, prepare a crossword or any type of puzzle, write scripts using programming languages, draw graphs, play strategic, logic and mind games and simulations, etc. These activities mainly help to improve the analytic, critical thinking and also problem solving skills.

For empowering students who have visual-spatial intelligence; activities should cover the 'visuals'. It is easy to hold this kind of students' attention on a topic by allowing them to prepare movie clips, timelines, posters, graphics, and cartoons, integrate photos into animation programs to present a slide show or create a video in video editing programs, etc. Moreover, through 3d modeling programs, students may 'architecturize' real-life objects. Also, publishing or sharing his/her products to the visitors via web pages, blogs and other types of educational software will encourage the student to produce more.

All the educational activities completed with the use of a computer-based environment support the usage of the skills of students with bodily-kinesthetic intelligence. The fact that computer applications are required to be used with a keyboard, joystick, mouse or other kind of hardware, students have to use these with physical skills, which is the scope of this intelligence. Therefore, using drill and practice software, playing any games, simulations, strategy and card games, and students may have to drag and drop cards, elements, objects, etc. in the computer-aided environment.

To support students with musical-rhythmic intelligence, educational activities should include activities based on music or musical forms. For example, activities may include adding sounds to presentations, animations, creating audio clips by mixing sounds and adding effects. Moreover, allowing students to play virtual instruments may keep interests in lessons alive.

For the students who have strong interpersonal skills, educational social software serves as a communication tool. It is easy to interact with other students by completing a project, playing video games with other players, joining a video conference, etc. Moderating a chat session or a discussion in a forum allows students to follow the flow of discussion, communicate and interact with others in a more responsible manner.

Individualized learning for the students possessing strong intrapersonal intelligence type is also applicable with all type of computer-based software. For example, tutorials, drill and practice software, simulations, web-based courses, educational games allow students to progress at their own pace. Through the usage of word processing, students can design curriculum vitae including the individuals' life history, job history, achievements and skills. Through search engines, students can conduct research studies on a given topic individually and prepare a reflection paper via word processor. To publish personal feelings, photographs, interests and hobbies, personal web pages can be created using web page development tools. Also, a self-improvement report with graphs prepared via word processing make this kind of student aware of their capacity, meaning things which are in the range of his/her ability and things which are not.

In order to support students with naturalistic intelligence, computers and the internet help them to explore the world as a virtual world. For ex-

ample, virtual museums about dinosaurs, nature, or history offer a journey to the ancient times. Image galleries about underwater life, e-books about the environment, and videos including different scenes of the world may hold the attention of this type of student in educational applications. Moreover, some self-prepared activities will cover this kind of intelligence, such as creating a documentary film including global warming, a poster describing waterlessness and a banner giving a message to stop forest fires, etc.

The creation of educational applications underlining multiple intelligences and usage of a medium for delivering these via educational social software may motivate students to hold their attention on various topics. Moreover, it is possible to make them like the topics they may have previously disliked. Through a variety of intelligences, educational activities can be enhanced and attract the students' attention. Therefore, instructors try to use these technologies or explore new technologies in order to get an answer to the question as to how students learn best through technology. Furthermore, instructors should facilitate their students' sense of inquiry for their development of critical thinking and problem solving skills. Finally, instructors can keep in mind that technology-based activities enhance their intelligence, interest, and improve their communication and collaboration with each others.

CALL FOR RESEARCH

Some possible research studies can be conducted in order to discover answers to the following questions:

- What are the preferences and perceptions of the students about artifacts they produce in terms of sharing them in educational social software?
- What is the contribution of completed educational activities to the development of

different type of intelligences?

- Which educational activity may lead students who have dominant or innate intelligence types to learn more easily?
- What are the suggestions of the instructors about the integration of these activities into the curriculum as an integration model according to their experience?
- How can educational activities addressing multiple intelligence be best assessed? What are alternative assessment types?
- How can an e-portfolio be used from multiple intelligence perspective?
- How to design courses where the communication and collaboration is based on educational social software from a multiple intelligences perspective?
- How can technology-based educational activities be differentiated according to levels of primary, secondary and high school students?

REFERENCES

Anderson, T., & Elloumi, F. (Eds.). (2004). *Theory and practice of online learning*. Canada: Athabasca University.

Beldarrain, Y. (2006). Distance education trends: Integrating new technologies to foster student interaction and collaboration. *Distance Education*, *27*(2), 139–153. doi:10.1080/01587910600789498

Borowicz, S. (2004). The effect of synchronous chat on student performance in an undergraduate introductory accounting course. In G. Richards (Ed.), *Proceedings of World Conference on E-Learning in Corporate, Government, Healthcare, and Higher Education 2004* (pp. 1790-1793). Chesapeake, VA: AACE.

Brualdi, A. C. (1996). Multiple intelligences: Gardner's theory. *ERIC Digest*. Retrieved on June 15, 2008, from http://www.ericdigests.org/1998-1/multiple.htm

Butcher, H. K., & Taylor, J. Y. (2008). Using a wiki to enhance knowing participation in change in the teaching-learning process. *Visions*, *15*(1), 30–44.

Chen, G., & Chiu, M. M. (2008). Online discussion processes: Effects of earlier messages' evaluations, knowledge content, social cues, and personal information on later messages. *Computers & Education*, *50*, 678–692. doi:10.1016/j.compedu.2006.07.007

Cook-Sather, A. (2007). Direct links: Using e-mail to connect preservice teachers, experienced teachers, and high school students within an undergraduate teacher preparation program. *Journal of Technology and Teacher Education*, *15*(1), 11–37.

Ellison, N. B., & Wu, Y. (2008). Blogging in the classroom: A preliminary exploration of student attitudes and impact on comprehension. *Journal of Educational Multimedia and Hypermedia*, *17*(1), 99–122.

Gardner, H. (1993). *Frames of mind: The theory of multiple intelligences*. USA: Basic Books.

Gardner, H. (2000). Can technology exploit our many ways of knowing? In D. T. Gordon (Ed.), *The digital classroom: How technology is changing the way we teach and learn* (pp. 32–35). Cambridge, MA: Harvard Education Letter.

Gardner, H., & Hatch, T. (1989). Multiple intelligences go to school: Educational implications of the theory of multiple intelligences. *Educational Researcher*, *18*(8), 4–9.

Gardner, H. (2006). *Changing minds. The art and science of changing our own and other people's minds*. Boston, MA.: Harvard Business School Press.

Glogoff, S. (2005). Instructional blogging: Promoting interactivity, student-centered learning, and peer input. *Journal of Online Education, 1*(5). Retrieved on August 9, 2008, from http://www.innovateonline.info/index.php?view=article&id=126

Guiller, J., & Durndell, A. (2007). Students' linguistic behaviour in online discussion groups: Does gender matter? *Computers in Human Behavior, 23*, 2240–2255. doi:10.1016/j.chb.2006.03.004

Hammond, M. (2000). Communication within online forums: The opportunities, the constraints, and the value of a communicative approach. *Computers & Education, 35*, 251–262. doi:10.1016/S0360-1315(00)00037-3

Horton, W. (2000). *Designing Web-based training.* USA: John Wiley & Sons, Inc.

Hsu, C.-J., & Lin, J.-C. (2008). Acceptance of blog usage: The roles of technology acceptance, social influence, and knowledge sharing motivation. *Information & Management, 45*, 65–74. doi:10.1016/j.im.2007.11.001

Hsu, J. (2007). Innovative technologies for education and learning: Education and knowledge-oriented applications of blogs, wikis, podcasts, and more. *International Journal of Information and Communication Technology Education, 3*(3), 70–89.

Ingram, A. L., Hathorn, L. G., & Evans, A. (2000). Beyond chat on the Internet. *Computers & Education, 35*, 21–35. doi:10.1016/S0360-1315(00)00015-4

Le, T., & Le, Q. (2002). The nature of learners' email communication. []. Auckland, New Zealand.]. *Proceedings of the International Conference on Computers in Education, 1*, 468–471. doi:10.1109/CIE.2002.1185979

Lightfoot, J. M. (2006). A comparative analysis of e-mail and face-to-face communication in an educational environment. *The Internet and Higher Education, 9*, 217–227. doi:10.1016/j.iheduc.2006.06.002

Martin, P. T. (1996). Email and the Internet as a teaching tool: A critical perspective. *Proceedings of the 26th Annual Frontiers in Education Conference* (pp. 823–825). Salt Lake City, UT.

Mazzolini, M., & Maddison, S. (2003). Sage, guide, or ghost? The effect of instructor intervention on student participation in online discussion forums. *Computers & Education, 40*, 237–253. doi:10.1016/S0360-1315(02)00129-X

McCreary, F. A., & Ehrich, R. W. (2001). Chat rooms as "virtual hangouts" for rural elementary students. *Information Technology in Childhood Education Annual.*

McCoog, I. J. (2007). Integrated instruction: Multiple intelligences and technology. *Clearing House (Menasha, Wis.), 81*(1), 25–28. doi:10.3200/TCHS.81.1.25-28

Nelson, G. (1998). Internet/Web-based instruction and multiple. *Educational Media International, 35*(2), 90–94. doi:10.1080/0952398980350206

Oravec, J. (2003). Blending by blogging: Weblogs in blended learning initiatives. *Journal of Educational Media, 28*(2-3), 225–233. doi:10.1080/1358165032000165671

Palmer, S. (2000). On- and off-campus computer usage in engineering education. *Computers & Education, 34*, 141–154. doi:10.1016/S0360-1315(00)00014-2

Pereira, C. S., & Soares, A. L. (2007). Improving the quality of collaboration requirements for information management through social networks analysis. *International Journal of Information Management, 27*, 86–103. doi:10.1016/j.ijinfomgt.2006.10.003

Rosenberg, M. J. (2001). *E-learning strategies for delivering knowledge in the digital age.* USA: McGraw-Hill.

Sherry, L. (2000). The nature and purpose of online discourse. *International Journal of Educational Telecommunications, 6*(1), 19–52.

Shih, W.-C., Tseng, S.-S., & Yang, C.-T. (2008). Wiki-based rapid prototyping for teaching-material design in e-learning grids. *Computers & Education, 51*, 1037–1057. doi:10.1016/j.compedu.2007.10.007

Smith, M. K. (2002, 2008). Howard Gardner and multiple intelligences. *The encyclopedia of informal education.* Retrieved on August 9, 2008, from http://www.infed.org/thinkers/gardner.htm

Veenema, S., & Gardner, H. (1996). Multimedia and multiple intelligences. *The American Prospect, 7*(29), 70–75.

White, J. (1998). *Do Howard Gardner's multiple intelligences add up?* London: Institute of Education, University of London.

Chapter 5
Learning Together with the Interactive White Board

Linda Larson
McNeese State University, USA

Sharon VanMetre
McNeese State University, USA

ABSTRACT

Interactive whiteboards (IWB) are the latest technology trend in schools and businesses. The purpose of this chapter is to discuss how social software and IWB technology promotes active engagement and interactive content delivery. Using IWB technology users are able to interact, collaborate, and evaluate. To implement the IWB effectively, there are numerous issues to address: professional development, interactivity, feedback, collaboration, and the future of the IWB.

INTRODUCTION

With current trends toward global social interactions, classrooms incorporating interactive educational technologies, such as the interactive whiteboard (IWB), provide their users with the tools for effective expression and delivery of information. By using IWB technology, schools and businesses find it easy for their users to interact, collaborate, and evaluate. This chapter discusses how social software and IWB technology promote active engagement and interactive content delivery. Users need to be actively engaged to promote critical thinking and develop strategies for effective teaching and learning. The IWB software addresses all types of learners, including those with special needs and integrates formative assessment, resources, and dynamic instructional tools. IWB systems are truly innovative learning environments. Not only can the user interact with the software on an individual work station, it also allows for group interactivity, active participation, and collaboration while providing immediate feedback with the use of supplemental equipment and/or software.

BACKGROUND

IWBs or Internet–age chalkboards are giant touch sensitive boards that control a computer connected

DOI: 10.4018/978-1-60566-826-0.ch005

to a digital projector. They are all the rage among teachers. At first glance, it looks very much like a dry erase whiteboard. IWBs were first developed for business (Greiffenhagen, 2002) and the technology is relatively new to education. Teachers struggling to engage students raised on the web find this innovative technology an essential classroom tool. The U. K. has placed a high priority on implementing IWBs and 70% of all primary and secondary classrooms have IWBs compared to just 16% in the United States (Philips, 2008). The price tag for the IWB is about $3,000.00, and teachers find many creative ways to raise the funds to purchase this highly coveted piece of technology. Several companies sell interactive whiteboards, including Hitachi, Panasonic, Mimio, Promethean, and Smart Technologies.

IWB systems provide the user with a variety of software and hardware tools to aid in interaction with the board. The software allows the user to create interactive lessons, activities, and multimedia presentations. The software not only allows the users to write text or display users graphics on the board as they would on a traditional chalkboard but also extends the media possibilities with audio, video, and hyperlink capabilities. By hyperlinking to other pages within the presentation, other documents on- and off-line, as well as other software applications, the user can manipulate the content as needed.

In some IWB systems, the physical touch of a finger or hand activates the sensitive areas of the board. For other systems, a pen or wand is used to activate available options. The pen, which is similar to a stylus, usually has a pressure sensitive tip to act as the left mouse key and a button on the body of the pen to generate right-key action. The wand or 'extended reach' device has similar abilities but with a longer range for accessing hard to reach areas.

Slates and/or tablets are also used by IWB systems to allow for interaction with the board without close physical proximity to the board. The users can access anything on the board even

usersfrom the back of the room as long as they have the IWB in view. This allows for quick interaction between students while they remain at their individual desks. The slate also allows the teacher, from perhaps the back of the room, to interject and assist students who are at the board with an IWB activity.

Use of IWB is often supplemented with response tools such as handheld voting, and texting devices are individual response systems used exclusively with the IWB to encourage student participation while allowing quick assessment of content knowledge. Students communicate with each other and the teacher in named and un-named modes. The anonymous capability of the response tools allows the student to respond without the fear of an incorrect answer. The students are able to type in their responses from anywhere in the room without fear of embarrassment. The teacher is able to determine the percentage of the class that has selected correctly and the percentage that has not and continue the discussion based on that analysis.

LITERATURE REVIEW (RESEARCH)

In a review of the current research Somekh et al, (2006) found "a consistent finding across all data that the length of time pupils have been taught with an interactive whiteboard is the major factor that leads to attainment gains. This appears to be the result of the IWB and IWB software becoming embedded in teachers' pedagogy: that is, when teachers have had sustained experience (around two years) of using an IWB they are able to change their teaching practices to make best use of its facilities."

Currently, the data on the effectiveness of IWBs in U.S. classrooms is inconclusive, but the research is limited because of the "newness" of the technology. Multiple recent studies suggest that the IWB positively impacts attendance and student participation. A district in Summerville,

S.C., installed 1,200 interactive boards in its classrooms, and reported the disciplinary incidents are way down. "Students were bored" before the IBWs arrived, says Superintendent Joe Pye. "Trips to the principal's office are almost nonexistent now" (Philips, 2008). This could possibly be due to the Hawthorn effect or increased classroom management in order to protect the new equipment in the classroom.

As teachers implement IWBs, there can be some real challenges. Some teachers experience a huge learning curve with the IWB. Many times, teachers are not used to integrating technology and they are still accustomed to writing lesson plans with a pen and paper. Many older educators are "petrified" of the boards, says Peter Kornicker, a media specialist at P.S. 161 in Harlem. To implement IWBs effectively, teachers must be provided relevant and long term professional development. Andy Rotherham of Education Sector, a Washington, D.C.-based think tank says, "We have to train them to use it. Otherwise, it's just another underused, expensive gizmo" (Philips, 2008).

IWB IMPLEMENTATION ISSUES

Professional Development

Interactive whiteboard technology is a remarkable tool that has been placed in many schools and school districts. As with any new technology, IWBs are met with both excitement and resistance. With the introduction of any new technology, implementation largely depends on initial and ongoing training. Professional development and technical support must be provided for teachers to feel comfortable utilizing the equipment in their classrooms. Software capabilities and idiosyncrasies should be explored and discussed. Resources such as prepared flipcharts and templates for content modification should be provided. Calibration of the IWB is a requirement and should be reinforced during each PD session.

Quite often, students are more confident interacting with the IWB than are their teachers (Hall, 2005). Hall and Higgins refer to this as "teething troubles" and do not see them as long-term difficulties. Through daily contact the teachers become more familiar with the equipment and the software. Teachers and students develop and maintain skill with the IWB over time through regular use. Additional PD sessions could showcase pedagogical aspects and classroom possibilities. Training must be continuous and detailed in future PD plans and budgets.

IWBs are most effective when both student as well as teacher have direct access manipulating components such as pen, wand, tablet, slate, and response devices. Professional development sessions which exemplify activities for each helps the teachers conceptualize use in their own classrooms. With student access to the IWB generally viewed as important, examples, strategies, and interactive possibilities should be provided during professional development sessions. As more student involvement becomes apparent, the more the teacher's role as facilitator rather than controller becomes necessary.

With the increased interactivity of students on the IWBs comes the need for reconsideration of pedagogical style and content presentation. School systems need to commit to the development of technological competencies of their teachers as well as support teaching strategy skill development so as to incorporate a hands-on learning approach.

In some instances the professional development itself has been accomplished through IWB technology (O'Hanlon, 2007). The time taken from class time or personal life has always been an issue for the implementation of professional development of any kind. Teachers realize that having a substitute teacher carry their class for the duration of PD offered during the school day is not as effective as having taught the class themselves. PD offered after school hours, even with stipend provided, is often poorly attended and is unusually taxing to the teacher after a full teaching day. By offering the professional development online, flipcharts and other forms of IWB presentations can be posted for participants to download and use directly in their classrooms for content or IWB interactive skill build. Online chats and discussion areas provide the participants with a means to ask questions and pose situations for comments from the PD provider as well as from peer participants. Tutorials designed by the PD staff or those available on the web can provide additional resources for user to get acclimated to the IWB and software. Hybrids, instruction provided through face-to-face contact and web mentoring, are sometimes the best approach. By archiving online content training, teachers can access the information many times and from many places. The teachers learn at their own pace and are not taken from their classrooms and the archived materials provide an ever-present resource for review. In this format, school districts are able to disseminate a plethora of information at minimal expense. Teachers are able to access the information without the cost of travel and class time. Due to time constraints and diverse needs of the teachers to be trained, still other school districts opt to provide on-demand, individualized instruction. They may have on-site specialists who work with the teachers on a one-to-one basis providing technical support as well as course content development. The PD specialists are able to research and organize resources specific to their teachers' needs. After the initial training and skill build sessions, teachers often want to maintain contact through electronic bulletin boards. In this way, they continue to share resources with their peers and request help from the specialists.

Glover and Miller suggested that there is an IWB 'culture' that resides within schools incorporating the boards (Glover, Miller, Averis, & Door, 2007). They noted (among the teachers in their study that) there were varying degrees of interactive approaches and sometimes the need for the 'conventional exposition' requiring less hands-on approach. All the teachers studied seemed "enthusiastic about the technology and argued that the nature of their teaching had changed since the introduction of IWB technology" (Glover, Miller, Averis, & Door, 2007). In most school districts, there is a broad range of technology skill levels exhibited among teachers. Those that are already comfortable with using some form of technology for teaching are usually more likely to approach the use of the IWB with a positive attitude. Those that are leery of using technology of other types normally have a less than positive attitude toward IWB use as well. Being less confident, they are also less self-reliant when questions arise in the classroom. These users need a more sustained approach to professional development and seem to work better with assistance on a need-to-know basis.

Regardless of the amount of funding invested in the hardware and software for IWB, it is of little value without the commitment of teachers to adopt and use the technology (Hall, 2005). If initial teacher training programs introduce the latest technologies and in-service teachers receive ongoing professional development, resource materials, and technical support the chances of implementation improve significantly. "Training in the technical and pedagogical aspects of IWB should be viewed as a continuous process rather that a discrete one, requiring regular training session so that teachers can maintain and develop their skills."

Interactivity

Interactivity by teachers and students is the key capability of the IWB. Students can interact with the IWB hardware/software as well as with other students and the teacher. For many in-service teachers, to enhance interactivity in lessons and activities requires pedagogical change. This change is often met with resistance or uncertainty. The benefits seem wide-spread, however. Research indicates an improvement in motivation, concentration, and attention span when students are allowed to interact with course content and equipment is used beyond merely a presentational aid. With considerable financial investment in the interactive whiteboards themselves, the same does not hold true in the training of teachers to truly incorporate its interactive capabilities. Teachers need training to develop and further their approaches to interactive teaching/learning. Being made aware of the potential for interactivity, teachers are enamored by the possibilities but need to move beyond the 'wow' factor into effective implementation in their own classrooms. Without significant change in the approach to teaching and learning, the financial investment may outweigh the benefits. Students need to move beyond passive learning into the interactive possibilities of the IWB.

Following the analysis of 50 videos of lessons taught by 'successful' secondary mathematics and foreign language teachers, Glover and Miller found three types of interactivity (Glover D. e., 2007).

They reported IWB use in the following ways:

Supported didactic. In this approach, the teacher used the IWB as a presentational aid and incorporated many of its tools for demonstration purposes but did not allow the students to interact with the IWB for any length of time.

Interactive. This approach showed an improvement in implementation as students were challenged to participate in course discussions by use of tools integrated into the IWB such as individual response systems. The IWB had moved beyond the novelty stage to students and was truly seen as their means of providing input.

Enhanced interactivity. At this level, students responded to content provided via the IWB individually, in pairs and in groups both large and small. "The IWB was used to prompt discussion, explain processes, develop hypotheses and then test these by varied application."

The IWB was a tool to coordinate the kinesthetic learning taking place in the classroom.

The closer the teachers were to the 'enhanced interactivity' stage, the more pre-planning was involved in the organization of the lesson for use with the IWB. To take full advantage of what the board had to offer, the teachers were planning activities that offered student input through a variety of tools. By interacting and responding via response tools, the students were shaping and driving the activities to better explore the content. Confusion in content areas were more visible and could be reviewed and revisited using IWB content management capabilities. Assessment could be incorporated via the response systems as well as through multimedia/multimodal developed lessons. Lessons could be saved and reused each semester or year and adjustments made to the content quickly and easily to fit the needs of each particular class. According to Wall, Higgins, and Smith, IWB use depends on teacher confidence, level of training. and availability (Wall, Higgins, & Smith, 2005).

Because students enjoy touching the board and manipulating the hardware, there is a higher level of motivation and focus. Students can manipulate text and images already present on the board as well as import text and graphics to the board themselves (Smith, Higgins, & Miller, 2005). Smith and Higgins reveal that even though research indicates the desire of students to physically manipulate the content, teachers do not all involve students to this extent. The board offers teacher-student interaction in the question-response realm but Smith and Higgins refer to this as a 'surface feature' reminiscent of the recitation model of classrooms without IWB technology. For a deeper interactive experience, the quality and depth of the interaction must go beyond question response. Strong visual and conceptual appeal of the information encourages the students to become involved in the exploration and analysis of content. Slates and tablets allow teachers to be positioned among the students rather than necessarily in front of the classroom or near the IWB. Students can use the tablets at their own desks to interact with the IWB as though they were physically at the board, making accessibility simpler. Allowing students to share with their classmates and review work done by their peers, students are able to contextualize the information at a higher level.

Smith, Hardman and Higgins (2006) noted that literacy and numeracy standards improve in 'interactive whole class teaching' when higher quality dialogue and higher pupil ratios are invoked. Research indicates that through interactive lessons student engagement, motivation, and attention improve (Smith, Hardman, & Higgins, 2006). Although when asked, students respond favorably to the physical interaction with the board, too often the activities are prescriptive as noted by Hall and Higgins (2005), designed by the teacher to show a capability of the board for a specific purpose. The students are interacting with the IWB but suggest that it is teacher directed access. Students and teachers alike must be confident enough with the hardware in order to engage in self-directed activities. Knight *et al* (2005) found the interactive whiteboard had a positive impact on motivation and engagement and the ability to revisit prior learning. It also appeared to contribute to raising student self esteem (Knight, Pennant, & Piggott, 2005).

Feedback

All technologies contain characteristics that facilitate or even encourage specific teaching approaches. On one level, the IWB supplemented with an individual response (voting) system only supports multiple choice questions and this could result in a behaviorist teaching model. For example, the teacher might script a lesson and plan the students' responses throughout the lesson. During the lesson, the students receive immediate feedback on their answers. By receiving immediate feedback, the student and the teacher know immediately if the students understand the content. In the paper and pencil mode of learning, the students may not know they are doing a math procedure incorrectly until the teacher grades the work. This immediate feedback may allow the

student to self correct or at least not make the same mistake over again. With these devices, teachers have a choice if they want the students to remain anonymous. If the teacher allows other students to see the identity of each students' response, this could embarrass the student and be a potential problem. When teachers use these devices, they must be aware of this potential problem.

On the other hand, if the teacher shifts the focus from just the 'right' answers and forces students to explain the 'whys' and rationale behind their answers, this can shift the focus to a more constructivist use of the system. The constructivist implementation would require students to engage in a peer discussion about the content of the question. In this model, the teacher reveals a question and the students discuss it in small groups or with partners. They select an answer and compose the rationale for their answer. All can be text messaged by the student using the response system. Students are actively engaged beyond the button pushing of a voting device. In this model, the students have an opportunity to discuss content before selecting an answer.

Many IWBs also include devices that allow the students to input text, numbers, and mathematical symbols. Response systems allow the students to input a text message that can be displayed on the IWB. This input could be used to determine correct responses or to brainstorm ideas. If the teacher chooses, the responses can be displayed or the user can remain anonymous. With these devices, students do not need to wait their turn to contribute their response. For example, students can work collaboratively on digital storytelling, writing and editing exercises, math lesson, and science experiments. The interactive features of the IWB encourage students to collaborate and discuss as they are working on assignments and experiments. In project based learning, students can create Power Point and multimedia presentations in real time and share it with their peers. The IWB will also display streamed or downloaded videos, artwork, or on-line museum presentations. Finally, any software or internet site that can be displayed on the computer screen can also be projected on the IWB. Once projected on the screen, the image becomes fully interactive. With so many internet resources available, there are limitless opportunities available to explore educational relevant material.

Collaboration

Some IWBs offer multi-user input. These interactive devices facilitate real time collaboration, project-based learning, and small group learning. Students can work together on creative projects simultaneously because students have their own input devices. This increases the opportunity for increased interactivity for more students. For example, the students in 6th grade can create interactive storybooks out of an existing story or theme and produce a talking book that the first grade children could interact with as a whole class.

The IWB can be used throughout the storybook project. First, the students use the collaborative devices to brainstorm appropriate subjects and stories and the ideas are displayed on the IWB. Second, the students can work in pairs to produce their presentations. Third, to improve their presentations the students can share their projects with the entire class to get valuable feedback. Fourth, the students receive feedback from their first grade audience. This project is a valuable learning experience for not only the first graders who experience the interactions designed for them but for the 6th graders who are creating an interactive story. This authentic learning experience provides them with the practice they will need in the real world to collaborate, incorporate feedback, and present in front of a group.

What Students Like and Dislike about IWBs

Overall, the reason students seem to like the IWBs is its versatility. Upon close examination,

the user realizes it is a combination of numerous technologies: whiteboard, TV, video and DVD player, digital projector, texting device, and a personal PC with the ability to interact with the various aspects of the multimedia (Hall & Higgins, 2005).

Students seem to prefer the IWB over a traditional white board for several reasons. First, numerous resources are readily available for immediate access and use. For example, Internet sites that include games and simulations can be downloaded or accessed played on the IWB. Second, the graphics are clear, accurate, and realistic because users do not have to draw it yourself. Third, the students are motivated and engaged by the visual, auditory, and interactive aspects of the IWB. Students learn best when they are using their senses of seeing, hearing, and touching. The IWB provides an active learning environment for the students that stimulate all three of these senses simultaneously. This direct manipulation of the IWB can provide real world examples from the child's experience. Last, the students seem to enjoy the educational games and they commented it makes learning fun (Hall & Higgins, 2005).

On the other hand, there are several problems with the IWBs. With any technology it is frustrating when it crashes or freezes. This causes a disruption in the flow of the lesson while the technology is restarted. Many times the teacher may just use the plain whiteboard to finish the lesson. Another common problem was the need to recalibrate the board. If the board is not calibrated correctly, the text can be unreadable and the objects may not move correctly.

Besides the technological problems, students may not be able to see the board because of room conditions (sunlight on the board) or where they are physically located with respect to the board. Teachers or presenters need to be aware of the lighting conditions in the room and the location of the students with respect to the board to be assured that they can all see. The same can be said of the audio.

Assessment

When IWBs are implemented effectively using the vote response systems, text systems, tablet, or pens, the teachers said they felt more in control of the classroom activities because they can examine the students' work in progress during the lesson or activity. One of the features of the board allows for all previous material to be easily reviewed by a click of a button. By recalling previous screens, issues can be addressed and students' questions answered. In addition, many of the IWBs can be set to print mode and the lesson and explanations are scripted and recorded for later review. This feature is also useful for students who are absent. Although this feature was possible, it was used in only 4 out of the 21 lesson observed (Glover, Miller, Averis, & Door, 2007).

Assessments can be seamlessly integrated into the presentation or lesson so individual progress is monitored instantaneously. Teachers, trainers, or presenters can easily gauge the progress and retention of the individual participants so they can make adjusts to the content "on the fly'. In addition, the user can look at the results at a later date so it can used for grading and assessment or to make adjustment to the curriculum to meet the needs of the users. This continuous assessment, both formative and summative, can be tracked by the IWB software.

Another part of the assessment is the peer review process. Through peer review, users help each other understand and improve the quality of their work, thus providing formative assessment. For example, the users can share a draft of their project on the IWB. Since everyone in the room can see the project, the participants collaboratively problem-solve and this process facilitates knowledge sharing. The final product is enhanced because of collaborative problem solving. One of the authors teaches an instructional design class and the peer review process is an integral part of the design process. Many times the student will share an underdeveloped or vague idea and the students in the class ask questions and provide suggestions so the end result is a well developed project idea that the student can then develop further. It is important to provide several opportunities for peer review during the project development. Students frequently commented on how they learned so much from the peer review process and their project improved through the collaborative exchange of ideas.

Exemplary peer reviewed projects and lessons can be archived on a server to allow for further review. Through online access, these lessons and activities serve as readily available resource materials. Exemplary interactive lessons developed by the users can serve as models and online resources for other users. These interactive projects are also used in real-world applications such as simulations, games, and tutorials for schools and businesses.

Future

Aware of the need for technology implementation and integration in the classrooms of today and tomorrow, universities working with in-service and pre-service teachers are modeling the use of IWB systems (VanMetre, Larson, Pearce, & Lewis, 2008). IWB integration seems to create favorable conditions for enhanced content presentation thereby creating effective environments for learning. The effects on student motivation seem promising as well. However, the research as to whether the IWB has a positive impact on student learning and teacher effectiveness is ongoing. By allowing users to physically interact with the content on the board as well as revisit previous learning sessions electronically stored, the IWB seems to offer features, which when used appropriately, could contribute to effective conditions for learning.

Additionally, professional development must continue and ensure that the use of the IWB is beyond static whiteboard/chalkboard use into full implementation of multimodal delivery and student interaction. Interactive multimedia presentations posing need for audience input through the board, slate, and/or individual response systems will need to be developed and archived. The IWB may not be as useful for all content delivery, but for the most successful use in any area, the IWB will require substantially different content preparation from traditional lesson planning. Built in features in software and hardware can offer the teacher a variety of ways to incorporate interactivity. Exemplar lessons, activities, and other resources can be archived for later use with modifications for learner needs.

The IWB is not a "panacea for all ills'. The IWB alone cannot bring a classroom and its users into a twenty-first century visually stimulated environment (Glover, Miller, Averis, & Door, 2007). What the IWB can do is offer the users, through software and hardware, a pedagogical tool for improved participation in content delivery. Although the evidence indicates increased excitement and motivation in students while implementing the IWB, the novelty of the board has not yet worn off. Ongoing studies may confirm "It's not what you use it's how you use it" (Smith, Higgins, & Miller, 2005).

CONCLUSION

Access and availability of the board constitute one of the biggest issues in IWB implementation. Many schools have only a few IWB systems so faculty members are less likely to utilize the technology because they have to share the board and pre-plan for its checkout. For teachers to feel comfortable implementing IWBs, professional development should be an ongoing process. Technology support should be readily available and immediate so valuable instructional time is not lost while the teacher attempts to fix software and hardware issues. It is essential that professional development be provided to help faculty modify pedagogy to effectively implement the IWB.

For the IWB to be effectively implemented, it must be used beyond the projector and screen capability. The features which offer teacher and student interactivity must be utilized to realize the full potential of the IWB. Moving teachers from the *supported didactic* to the *enhanced interactivity* requires the continual implementation of the interactive tools provided by the IWB: individual response systems, tablets, slates, pens, and wands.

If appropriate to the lesson, the students, working individually or collaboratively, can receive immediate feedback on answers to content related questions. They can brainstorm ideas on projects using the response devices. They can all participate actively both with physical contact with the board as well as with the tablets and slates at their desks.

Students like the systems because they are readily available, they can access the internet to 'play' with games and simulations, they like the realistic nature of the graphics, and they are motivated by the interactive aspects of the board. This active learning environment uses senses of seeing, hearing, and touching.

Technological problems include crashes, freezes, and calibration problems. Without proper calibration, the text is not readable and the objects may not move correctly. Students may also have difficulty seeing the board because of room conditions such as glare and their physical location with respect to the board.

Using response systems, text systems, tablets, and pens, the teachers felt they were more in control of the classroom activities because they could examine the students' work in progress during the lesson or activity. With the capability to assess during the lesson, the teacher can make adjustments if students are struggling with concepts. The assessment system can also be used in peer review of project-based learning activities.

Interactive whiteboard technology promotes active engagement and interactive content delivery. With the implementation of the IWB still relatively new in the United States, there is a need for more extensive research to truly understand the impact of this technology.

REFERENCES

Glover, D., Miller, D., Averis, D., & Door, V. (2007). The evolution of an effective pedagogy for teachers using the interactive whiteboard in mathematics and moderns languages: An empirical analysis from the secondary sector. *Learning, Media and Technology, 32*(1), 5–20. doi:10.1080/17439880601141146

Greiffenhagen, C. (2002). *Out of the office into the school: Electonic for education.* Retrieved on August 20, 2008, from ftp://ftp.comlab.ox.ac.uk/pub/Documents/techreports/TR-16-00.pdf

Hall, I., & Higgins, S. (2005). Primary school students' perceptions of interactive whiteboards. *Journal of Computer Assisted Learning, 21*(2), 102–117. doi:10.1111/j.1365-2729.2005.00118.x

Knight, P., Pennant, J., & Piggott, J. (2005)... *The Power of the Interactive Whiteboard, 21*(2), 11–15.

O'Hanlon, C. (2007). The teacher becomes the student. *T.H.E. Journal, 34*(11), 20–21.

Philips, M. (2008). It makes teachers touchy. *Newsweek, 152*(12), 10.

Smith, F., Hardman, F., & Higgins, S. (2006, June). The impact of interactive whiteboards on teacher-pupil interaction in the national literacy and numeracy strategies. *British Educational Research Journal, 32*(3), 443–457. doi:10.1080/01411920600635452

Smith, H., Higgins, S., & Miller, J. (2005). Interactive whitheboards: Boon or bandwagon? A critical review of the literature. *Journal of Computer Assisted Learning, 21*(2), 91–101. doi:10.1111/j.1365-2729.2005.00117.x

Somekh, N., et al. (2006). *Making a difference with technology for learning: Evidence for college leaders.* Retrieved on August 20, 2008, from feandskills.becta.org.uk/download.cfm?resID=25958

VanMetre, S., Larson, L., Pearce, G., & Lewis, B. (2008). *Promethean activeclassroom: Integration for improving candidate academic performance.* Louisiana Board of Regents, Board of Regents Support Fund LEQSF (2008-10)-ENH-TR-38.

Wall, K., Higgins, S., & Smith, H. (2005). The visual helps me understand the complicated things: Pupil views of teaching and learning with interactive whiteboards. *British Journal of Educational Technology, 36*(5), 851–867. doi:10.1111/j.1467-8535.2005.00508.x

Chapter 6
Analysis of Interactions through a Web Annotation Tool in a Pre–University Mathematics Online Course

Núria Escudero-Viladoms
IES Pompeu Fabra, Spain

Teresa Sancho-Vinuesa
Universitat Oberta de Catalunya, Spain

ABSTRACT

We analyze the interactions produced through a Web annotations tool. This communication tool, usually employed as a collaborative tool or as a medium of artistic or social criticism, has been introduced in a mathematics course for online pre-engineering students. The objective of this innovation is to integrate the communication and the subject's contents and to check whether a better level of communication between students and professors improves the acquisition of basic mathematical competencies. As a result of this study, we put forward a model for the analysis of the online interaction, as well as a classification of students in relation to the use of the communication tool.

INTRODUCTION

Acquisition of competencies in Computer Science and in Telecommunication Engineering requires certain skills in handling mathematical concepts. Indeed, students have to master basic concepts and techniques of Algebra, Mathematical Analysis and Statistics. This situation is especially problematic when students are adults with professional experience, with not much time to study, with insufficient

prior knowledge in maths and studying at a distance. In fact, academic results are rather poor in this kind of subjects as Sancho-Vinuesa and Gras-Martí (in press) have shown for Mathematics I (Telecommunication Engineering) with basic contents in linear algebra and calculus. This is the context of the Universitat Oberta de Catalunya (Open University of Catalonia, UOC), where the present cases study has been carried out. We focus specifically on a course, *Introduction to Maths for Engineering* that has a twofold objective for the students: to acquire

DOI: 10.4018/978-1-60566-826-0.ch006

fundamental concepts, techniques and terminology in Algebra and Analysis, and to facilitate the practical use of these contents.

The pedagogical model at the UOC is based on a virtual classroom organized into four independent sections: planning, communication, resources and assessment (Sangrà, 2002). Thus, the teaching process is led through a work schedule, drawn up by teachers, that sets objectives, contents, didactical resources, methodology and the assessment system, and which is integrated with all the other subject matters in the syllabus. Indeed, deadlines for the delivery of exercises provide the rhythm for a process that has, as its main starring role, study materials and communication. Tutor-student interaction is currently performed through the virtual classroom forum.

Generally, students interact with study materials following the schedule and, when a doubt arises or when they want to make a comment or ask a question, they contact the teacher through their personal e-mail or the forum of the virtual classroom. The channels of communication with the rest of the students are the same. Therefore, the individual work of a student, based on a set of well-organized learning resources, is clearly separated from the dialogue space where they interact with fellow students and with the tutors. Our experience in virtual classrooms during 10 years shows that these interactions among members of the class when carrying out the proposed activities are needed. The tutor, on the one hand, provides guidance or hints, asks questions and clarifies concepts; on the other hand, students and tutors pose questions in the forum and suggest ways of solution. The interaction is carried out in an area separated from where the teaching material is displayed. The difficulty arises, then, of managing different messages related with the same content, and consequently the integration of the communicative dimension with the learning process is practically impossible under those circumstances.

The present case study is a contribution to try to remedy this situation. We contribute some relevant elements in analyzing the influence of technological advances in questions relating to the learning process of online students. Specifically, we analyze the influence of a tool for annotations to websites (DIIGO), which has been used to integrate communication and contents in our classes. In order to confirm that learning is supported using web technologies, the mode of communication is an important factor that must be considered, as pointed out by Han and Hill (2007). They note that this is one of the challenges in conducting research in theories related to collaborative learning. We look for possible improvements, due to the use of this communication tool, both in the perception of students about mathematics and in the students' self-confidence in their mathematics abilities.

With a Web annotation system, a user can add, modify or remove information from a Web resource without modifying the resource itself. Thus it can be thought of as a kind of social software tool that can be used to improve or adapt the contents of a web page; for instance, as a collaborative tool or as a medium for artistic or social criticism. In particular, the tool chosen for this study has not been created with an education purpose in mind.

Specifically, this web annotation tool enables us to write comments and raise questions in websites, which are shared by a group of people, so that anyone in the group can read these annotations and edit them or contribute comments. In order to be able to participate, the student must register as a DIIGO user and join the subject-matter group. Furthermore, one needs to download a specific tool bar for the web browser. The teacher has created a DIIGO tutorial for the maths students.

The screenshot in fig.1a shows an annotation at a certain point in the lecture notes and in fig.1b the annotation is fully displayed (for that purpose, one just places the pointer on the bal-

Figure 1. Screenshots of the material with annotations written with DIIGO

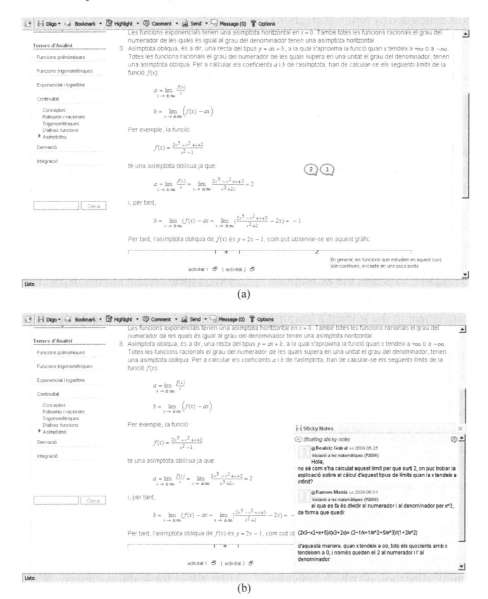

(a)

(b)

loon icon). Both screenshots show DIIGO's tool bar at the top.

The basic assumption of this research is that the integration of contents and communication spaces will lead to a significant improvement in the acquisition of basic mathematical competencies for pre-engineering students. There are two reasons for this expectation. On the one hand, it will allow the teacher to better follow up the student's learning process and, therefore, a better personalization of this process may be achieved. On the other hand, it should contribute to the increase in the student's confidence in his abilities in the mathematical handling of concepts and procedures. Maths contents pose communication difficulties to the students (mostly due to the specifity of the notation) and specific cognitive difficulties; both kinds of difficulties are augmented in an online context, since tutor-student communication is not instantaneous as concluded by Smith et al (2008). The use of DIIGO does not facilitate instant communication either, but minimizes this shortcoming by linking contents, questions and comments about the content materials. It is our assumption then this will help in establishing the necessary relationships among basic maths ideas that the students should master and, hence, consolidate the learning of concepts and procedures.

This chapter deals, therefore, with both research and innovation. Our research aims at defining a model for the analysis of the interactions facilitated by the communication tool used. Teaching innovation will then be a consequence, as long as the research validates the assumption that an improvement in communication can give rise to an improvement in the student's learning process.

The objectives of this chapter are twofold:

a) to present a model of the interactions, which allows us to analyze and assess which level and type of interactions are produced with the use of the communication tool proposed;
b) to draw up, through this analysis, a classification of the interaction profiles of the students.

Moreover, we also wish to establish which aspects have to be considered in the introduction of a new communication tool and which strategies are necessary in order to motivate its use, with a view to improving the learning process and overcoming the student's isolation in distance learning. Thus, in this research we use some critical variables related to learning in web-based learning environments described by Han and Hill (2007): group interaction processes, seamlessness of technology and pedagogical strategies.

BACKGROUND

The conceptual framework which supports this research is structured around four axes in relation to: the main analysis object, interaction (interaction axis); the website annotation tool and its use and impact in interaction (instrumental axis); the knowledge that annotations refers to (epistemological axis); and the virtual learning context where take place (situational axis).

In the interaction axis, we comment the interactions and its analysis in a distance learning context. In the instrumental axis, we present a framework for questions referring to the instrumentation of a website annotation tool. In the epistemological axis, aspects related to the mathematical content of the annotations are presented. Finally, in the situational axis, we briefly discuss the instructional inflexibility which occurs in distance and online learning.

Interaction Axis

The theory of interaction in distance learning is one of the frameworks of this study. According to Roblyer and Wiencke (2003): "research yields consistent indications that increased interaction in distance courses is associated with higher achievement and student satisfaction" (p.78). Furthermore, two positions are described in relation to the existence of technological resources that allow for learning: improvement according to Clark (quoted in Roblyer & Wiencke (2003)), no resources exist with unique characteristics that allow this improvement, and according to Kozma, the technologies can offer unique opportunities of quality learning as long as the procedures are well substantiated in the cognitive and social processes by means of which knowledge is constructed. One of the objectives of the present research is to contribute evidence towards an empirical verification of the arguments given by Kozma, in the specific context that we deal with. Roblyer and Wiencke (2003) also state that distance learning environments designed for the effective use of technology resources can offer unique opportunities to obtain the student's commitment and lead to gains in learning once this commitment is obtained. In this sense, it must be stressed that the tool investigated here is used in conjunction with several other technological resources (Java Applets, Wiris calculator, self-evaluation tests, video-recordings and Flash sequences). Roblyer and Wiencke (2003) also mention the three requirements that, according to Wagner, are necessary in order to explore the possibility of offering these opportunities to the students and in order to obtain by means of the interaction a useful structure that yields research techniques and designs for distance learning environments:

1) to obtain an operational definition of "interaction" based on relevant theory and research,

2) to design courses that will go further than just reproducing face-to-face methods and promote interaction, and

3) to perform an empirical evaluation of the interaction and measure the effect upon students' success.

The complex nature of the interaction in distance learning courses and the difficulty of designing the evaluation of the interaction process and, hence, of designing evaluation tools that allow us to build a solid theoretical framework, are pointed out by Roblyer and Wiencke (2003) as the reasons for the difficulties in going from theory to practice. There are, then, difficulties in developing practical guidelines to make the interaction concept measurable and useful to teaching and research staff. Taking into account these difficulties, they then study the characteristics contributing to the interaction and the factors influencing it;

these aspects will allow us to obtain measurable variables in the analysis of the data gathered with the present research.

Varsidas and McIsaac (quoted in Roblyer & Wiencke (2003)) establish relevant variables appearing in the interaction and they will be taken into account in the analysis that we propose. The variables are established with respect to the students (number of students in the classroom, quantity and kind of feedback given by the instructor to the students, experience in distance learning), with respect to the instructor (knowledge level, experience in group management, facilitation abilities), and with respect to the messages (characteristics of the feedback, message content). These variables will be taken into account in the analysis of the interaction data gathered in this study.

We have taken into account Bales' categories for the interaction analysis, namely, the Interaction Process Analysis (IPA); even though they were put forward in 1950, they have been applied and justified in recent studies of computer-mediated discussions (Fahy, 2005), where they have been considered as a useful tool to describe interaction processes in online groups. The IPA consists of twelve processes grouped according to four basic functions: positive socio-emotional reactions (to show solidarity, distention or agreement), responses in relation to assignments (to suggest, give opinions, or guide), questions regarding tasks (to ask for guidance, opinion or suggestions) and negative socio-emotional reactions (show disagreement, tension or antagonism).

Instrumental Axis

As we have stated in this research, a new communication tool has been introduced, which has been integrated in the online study material which includes contents, proposed activities, different learning resources, study guides and diverse complementary material. This experience has taken place in a specific context: students who hold a priori conceptions about curriculum content (since they have previously followed other courses) based on a traditional "paper and pencil" learning environment. In this context, some questions become of special relevance, like those regarding the instrumentation of the website annotation tool, the relationship between technical and conceptual learning, and the relationship between paper and pencil techniques and instrumental techniques.

A framework for the reflection about these questions is offered in the anthropological approach developed by Chevallard and in the publications about cognitive ergonomics by Rabardel, both detailed in Artigue (2002). Later on, Artigue (2004) also describes an instrumental approach derived from the analysis of questions involving the integration of computer environments in maths teaching. Furthermore, she develops a point of view about these questions which will also underlie the instrumental axis of the present investigation.

Just as Artigue (2002) indicates, the anthropological approach also has an institutional basis. She offers the viewpoint, shared with sociocultural approaches, that the mathematical objects are not absolute objects, but entities emerging from practices within given institutions. These practices or "praxeologies" are described with respect to three kinds of issues: with respect to tasks where the object fits, with respect to techniques used to solve these tasks, and with respect to a discourse that explains and justifies the techniques. Artigue (2002) remarks that advance in an institution's knowledge require the routinization of certain techniques and, hence, a weakening of the associated theoretical discourse occurs. In the present study, we will reflect upon the possibilities that the communication tool suggested affords, in order to reinforce the theoretical discourse. As Artigue (2004) remarks, the research by Chevallard and Bosch starts with the dialectics between what is ostensive (the various technological resources placed in the students' hands) and what is not ostensive (the mathematical objects). It is in this dialectics that we want to observe the potential of the communication tool that we have introduced.

The cognitive ergonomic research allows Artigue (2002) to reflect about the instrumentation processes. She points out that, for an individual, a given artifact - in our case, the new communication tool - does not have, in principle, an instrumental value. The artifact becomes an instrument through a genesis, that is, through the construction or the appropriation of social schemes. Artigue also argues that this process or instrumental genesis works in two directions; one directed towards the artifact, or "instrumentalization", and one directed towards the subject, or "instrumentation". The process of instrumentalization endows progressively the artifact with potentiality and transforms it for specific applications. The process of instrumentation leads the individual to the development or to the appropriation of the schemes of the instrumented action. In the present study, we wish to analyze these processes and the potentialities of the instrumented work.

The instrumental focus that is discussed in Artigue (2004) is the result of the first series of investigations, based on the framework that we have just presented. This research evidenced the contrast between the discourse sustained about the potentiality of the instruments introduced for learning mathematics, and the reality of their functioning in the observed students' classes. Likewise, they showed the unsuspected complexity of the instrumental genesis and the imbrication of the technical knowledge about the artifact and the mathematical knowledge. Furthermore, this technical knowledge is foreign to the official curriculum as it is spelled out in the traditional mathematical approach based on paper and pencil work. An important question is set forth, then: what is the real legitimacy of the computer technology; one should necessarily take into account this question in a piece of research of this kind.

Finally, Artigue (2004) explains how the epistemological approach helps them to rethink the relationships between the technical and the conceptual aspects. Their research aims at studying the modifications that may originate the introduction of computer tools in the link between the epistemic value of a technique (the value of the technique in relation to what it brings in order to understand the objects that participate) and its pragmatic value (the potentiality that it offers to produce results). In Artigue (2004) it is assumed that, in general, these computer tools (calculators and programs) tend to weaken the epistemic value and reinforce the pragmatic value, but it is shown how this reinforcement can also restore the epistemic value by focusing the use of the tool in a particular way. In this sense, Artigue (2004) claims that the research has to find ways of reinforcing the epistemic value of the techniques instrumented, with respect to the epistemic value already recognized for the techniques of paper and pencil. Within the framework of the present study, the tool is not a purely mathematical one and therefore it departs in a certain way from this approach; rather, the interest here is if the communication tool can help to reinforce the equilibrium between the two values of the technique, by favoring the discussion of questions about the techniques explained in the material and the technological resources that are used. So, this brings up the possibility of thinking about the communication tool that we are introducing as a means for this reinforcement, in a distance learning and online environment.

Epistemological Axis

Azcárate et al. (1996) state that the teaching of mathematics should be based upon the dialectic relationship between mathematics as an "instrument of knowledge" and as an "object of knowledge". In spite of differing in a local way in the initial approach, although not in the global approach, the cognitive processes involved in the learning of topics related to differential calculus discussed, in the work of Azcárate et al (1996), take special importance in the analysis of the interaction that we bring up in this study. In relation to the conceptions of the students about the concept of

derivative, it is important to consider the research done by Orton (quoted in Azcárate et al. (1996)), where students' errors are classified in three types: "structural errors", related with the concepts involved, "arbitrary errors", related with an arbitrary behavior of the student without taking the data of the problem into account, and "execution errors", produced in the handling of mathematical objects. Azcárate et al. (1996) present results in relation to the students' difficulty in using graphic representations, especially relevant in an online context as shown by Smith et al. (2008). This is an important factor in this research too, since in the web material and understanding and handling of applets with graphical representations are quite often required.

Situational Axis

From a situated learning point of view, "the construction of meaning is tied to a specific context" (Han & Hill, 2007, p.91). This is a virtual one in our study and we must focus on specific features of the context and their link with the learning process.

According to Barberà (2006), in a virtual learning context, a certain instructional inflexibility is produced, since, in spite of the flexibility with regard to timelines and location that characterize online studies, the teaching process results in an accumulation of tasks with fixed deadlines. This can affect the learning process and even impede it. However, we assume that the creation of a learning environment that integrates contents and communication should allow the qualitative return to the students' activity and should improve the follow-up and orientation of their learning process and, therefore, to overcome this inflexibility.

But from a sociocultural approach, the virtual learning context not only facilitates or impedes learning (van Oers, quoted in Forman (1996)), it modifies the activity setting – in the sense of Gallimore and Goldenberg (exposed in Forman) –. The scripts for conduct that govern participants' actions is one of the variables that determine an activity setting and the introduction of the communication tool in this virtual learning context modifies the scripts of the students from an independent task to an instructional conversation ("classroom discourse that permits the co-construction of meaning" defined by Tharp and Gallimore, quoted in Forman, 1996, p.118). In addition, the introduction of a communication tool also changes task demands, since students must develop communication skills.

ANALYSIS AND DISCUSSION

Population

The population of this study is the 88 students taking the introductory course on mathematics for Engineering at the UOC during the second semester of the academic year 2007-08. The tutor for this subject has collaborated actively in the research; he has used the tool for annotations in web pages in order to carry out a Continued Evaluation Test (CET), and he has promoted the use of the tool by posing questions to students and by solving students' doubts.

Students were advised that the annotations tool DIIGO would be introduced and, therefore, from the beginning, the tool was considered as an added resource for the subject; its use was reinforced through the CET of the module dealing with functions. Besides this open offer, some students were asked explicitly for their voluntary collaboration in the research through an opinion notebook where they expressed more precisely their appraisals about the introduction and use of the tool.

The typical profile of the student of this subject matter is that of an adult person with work responsibilities and often, as they indicate in some presentations in the classroom forum, with family responsibilities. In their presentations, some students claim that 10 to 15 years have elapsed since they studied mathematics and that they have an academic background only in professional training.

Methodological Approach

In order to analyze the interactions produced via the web-page annotations tool, a combined model is used which includes quantitative data (who interacts, how much and where) and qualitative data (how one interacts).

The quantitative approach allows the analyzing, on the one hand, the degree of interaction among the students and among them and the teacher; furthermore, one can analyze the study materials of each student and in what particular context is the interaction produced. Through this quantitative analysis, one intends to observe, mainly, who initiates the interaction, among whom it is produced and which aspects of the contents of the subject are the reason for, or accumulate, more interaction.

The qualitative approach of the model allows the investigating of the type of interaction that is produced, by analyzing qualitatively the contents of the annotations and also of the messages in the forum, where the students state their opinion publicly about the introduction of this new tool; attention has to be paid to the cognitive aspects but also to those emotional aspects that inform us, then, about the social function of the communications tool.

This variety of models of analysis, allows us to combine a macro level, in which all the students in the class are taken into account, and a micro level, in which the students that have used or have attempted to use the tool are taken into account. Thus, the macro vision allows us to broaden the context of the analysis since we account for those students who have given up the subject matter prior or after the introduction of the tool, and those that have not used it for the follow-up of the subject matter; with the micro vision one intends to observe the influence and incidence of the introduction of the tool not only in the interaction, but also in the learning process of these students.

Tools and Strategies

A preliminary study, performed during the first semester of the academic year 2007-08, allowed us to think about which data was relevant for the study. Students and tutor annotations are the main data, but we cannot forget the set of complementary data: the student profile (mainly in relation to interaction) and students and tutor appreciation about the website annotation tool. Being aware of the complexity of the data, all of them relevant in relation to the study, we propose an observational strategy and this is obviously through the virtual campus.

This kind of observation allows us to understand the context of the scenario and to uncover some information not directly given by the students. For instance, through the quantification of initial and replied forum messages, we can measure students' interaction predisposition and role assumed by them. It is worth noting that an advantadge of this type of observation is that all public interactions are registered and linked automatically. The observation set out allows the in-depth study of the virtual campus and its organization as an interaction context.

However, we have to take into account that we only have a text collection with some special constraints due to virtuality. On the one hand, we have no access to private students and tutor-students interaction, but this also happens in a face-to-face observation where students and teacher can share experience out of the observed class. On the other hand, this kind of observation does not allow us to see, in a physical sense, many aspects of non verbal communication. We try to glimpse some emotional aspects through the content analysis of interaction.

Observation is semi-structured and non participant. In order to motivate the use of the tool

when it was introduced, we proposed the tutor some annotations about math concepts in the web material. Even so, the observation is considered non participant because researchers did not interact with the students directly during their learning process.

For the annotations through the web-annotation tool, the main data in our study, two spreadsheets for data acquisition have been drawn up: one of them to collect annotations linked to the student who annote and another one to collect annotations interns of who and what are annoted. For the complementary data, a variety of tools are proposed: a spreadsheet to collect student profile and forum messages, and a student and tutor interview.

Interaction Analysis

The analysis of the interaction and, specifically, of the interaction profile of the students in relation to the annotations carried out (together with the information brought about by the complementary data) is carried out regarding three dimensions: instrumental dimension, interlocutive dimension and contents or thematic dimension. The consideration of these three dimensions is a consequence of the theoretical positioning regarding the instrumental axis, the interactive axis and the epistemological axis, respectively. In the instrumental dimension, the processes of instrumentation of the students are analyzed taking into account that the process of instrumental genesis is complex and that there can be a contrast between the discourse sustained about the potentiality of the tool and the observed reality. In the interlocutive dimension, the attention is focused on the interlocution, that is, in the emotional aspects and in the disposition of the student during the interlocution. Finally, in the thematic dimension the attention is centered on the mathematical contents of the annotations.

The analytical process starts by suggesting various aspects one should have to assess for each of these dimensions in relation to the process which, a priori, it is guessed that a student can follow in his interaction with the tool. Afterwards, five levels are established for each of the dimensions that have been specified for the analysis of the annotations. This classification in terms of dimensions leads us, finally, to a general classification of student interaction levels with the tool DIIGO.

In the **instrumental dimension**, the degree of instrumentalization is distinguished from the degree of instrumentation. In relation to the degree of instrumentalization, that is, of how the student progressively endows the artifact with potentiality, the analysis focuses the attention on the following aspects:

a) evidence that the student endows the tool with potentiality in relation to its influence on the process of learning from a pragmatic viewpoint, that is, as a means for the resolution of procedural doubts
b) evidence that the student endows the tool with a potential to give epistemic value to the techniques, that is, that he brings up the possibility of posing questions of a conceptual character
c) evidence that he endows the tool of potential in relation to a more personal aspect, namely, how it may propitiate an increase of self-confidence in the mathematical skills and an increase of commitment towards the subject (in a certain way, towards the teacher, the rest of the students and the institution)
d) evidence of the use of the tool for solving procedural and conceptual doubts, thereby approaching the attainment of an equilibrium among the values of the technique under study

And in relation to the degree of instrumentation, that is, of how the student appropriates himself or develops the schemes of the instrumentated action, the attention is focused on:

a) evidence of not using the tool with an appropriation of the potentialities as they have been made explicit or observed
b) evidence of the use of the tool in order to solve procedural doubts, without providing a reflection on the concepts that are characteristic of the subject under study
c) evidence that the student appropriates himself of the potentialities that have been made explicit or observed
d) evidence of a conscious use of the tool in self-benefit, in relation to acquiring confidence in the personal mathematical skills and to establish a conscious tie with the subject, the teacher and the rest of the students.

During the analysis, the model is outlined and finally in the instrumental dimension, three blocks are considered: procedural, conceptual and social. These blocks are interrelated and are attained in a gradual way as the tool is being interacted. The process followed by the student in interacting with the tool starts at a basic procedural level, at which the student intends to solve those more practical questions that worry him directly, and in a more immediate way, in his interaction with the study material.

Can anyone tell me where this 6 is coming from and why will the following square root not disappear?

Later on, once these difficulties are overcome, the student is worried about the understanding of the study material, and interrogates himself on the deeper aspects and, therefore, about conceptual considerations that allow him to go into greater depth in his study.

Hello, I do not know how this limit has been calculated in order to get 2 as an answer. Where can I find the explanation for this type of limits when x tends to infinity?

Finally, after a period of time centered in the students' activity with regards to learning, the student can become aware of being a member of a group, thereby not only using the tool in his own interest (a fact that can keep on going in the other phases of the process) but in aid of mutual benefit, taking into account the rest of the educational community and his possible contribution to the learning process of the rest of the students. Taking this process into consideration, the following levels of usage are established. Still, since one must admit that the development of this process is not a linear progression for all students in the way we have indicated; we have contrasted this rather qualitative appraisal with a quantitative appraisal that contemplates the possibility of irregularities in the process, showing also that these do not influence in a relevant way on the classification scheme.

In the **interlocutive dimension,** five aspects become important and have to be assessed during the analysis:

a) the type of communication
b) the role assumed in its intervention
c) to whom it is addressed
d) the structure of the annotation and
e) socioemotional aspects

Table 1. Levels of the instrumental dimension

Level 0	The degrees of instrumentalization and of instrumentation are nonexistent or rudimentary
Level 1	The process of instrumentalization and of instrumentation has been initiated in procedural aspects
Level 2	The process of instrumentalization and of instrumentation is found at a medium/high level in relation to the procedural aspects and at low/medium level in relation to conceptual aspects
Level 3	The process of instrumentalization and of instrumentation is found at a medium/high level in relation to the procedural and conceptual aspects, but at a low level in relation to social aspects
Level 4	The process of instrumentalization and of instrumentation is found at a high level in relation to the three aspects

As a result of the analysis, we have singled out characteristics of these aspects that allow one to establish levels for this dimension; these are shown in table 2.

With respect to the interlocutive dimension, and taking into account the diversity of variables that play a role, the quantitative assessment in establishing levels of usage becomes of special importance. We show in table 3 a qualitative gradation, contrasted with the quantitative scale, which allows one to get an idea about the gradation of the levels of interlocution.

In the **thematic dimension**, the contents of the annotations take significance. One should note that in the dimension of instrumentation and instrumentalization, reference has already been made to whether the doubts are of a procedural or conceptual kind. However, it is in this point where a more accurate analysis of these doubts is made, not only establishing if they are of one type or another, but analyzing fully the procedures and concepts that play a role, as well as the origin of those doubts.

Correspondingly, attention is focused on whether the students' annotations:

a) make a reference to possible errors, without arguing the error, but only expecting the confirmation of the teacher
b) are merely social
c) make a reference to possible errors and make an argument for the possible error
d) make a reference to procedural doubts whose origin are arbitrary errors, that is, they are a consequence of the students' arbitrary behavior, who did not take into account the data provided in the exercise, or the explanations provided in the study materials
e) make a reference to procedural doubts that have their origin in execution errors, that is, errors in the handling of the mathematical objects
f) make a reference to procedural doubts which originate in conceptual or structural errors,

Table 2. Characteristics of the aspects considered in the interlocutive dimension

Aspect	Name	Definition	Example
Type of communication	Vertical	One of the interlocutors has a higher position	*If there is a way of doing it,**couldyou**give me a hint?*
	Horizontal	Communication is produced between equals	*Is the question correct, or is there a mistake when talking of APPLICATION*
Role	Submissive	Shows a dependency on the interlocutor's part	*(...)**I wanted to ask**if the function in the example referenced in the question of activity 1 is the one in the on-line syllabus f(x)= 2x**? for I do not know if I am doing this correctly.**(...)*
	Dominant	Shows mastering over contents and leadership in the communication with the interlocutor	No intervention in this sense.
	Collaborator	Shows a willingness to participate in a discussion between equals	*To solve this indetermination, you**should**divide, in this case, numerator and denominator by x^.*
To whom it is addressed	Student	Addressed to classmates	*(...) I would thank**anyone**that sent me the solution to the fourth section of activity 1 (...)*
	Teacher	Addressed exclusively to the teacher	*I do not understand what**you mean**in section b*
	Everyone	Addressed generally to students and teacher	*Hello, I do not know how to calculate this limit to get 2,**where can I find**the explanation of this type of limits when x tends to infinity?*
	Adequated	Addressed to the interlocutor related to the kind of annotation that he makes	
Structure	Traditional	The annotation has a closed structure consisting of an introduction or presentation, a body and a farewell	***Hello,*** *And a way of calculating roots, or do we have to do it graphically?, because, I try reasoning and calculating it without the graph, but I cannot get it done ... If there is a way of doing it, you could give me a hint.* ***Thanks.***
	Alive	The annotation is direct and close to an oral communication	*I think the -29 should be a 29, because the sign is changed.*
	Alternative	The student does not maintain the same kind of structure for all the annotations he makes. He uses the tool, but not necessarily with a specific criterion.	
	Evolving	The student initially uses a traditional structure, but as he interacts with the tool, he uses a structure more directed to the contents.	
Socio-emotional aspects	Negative	Shows disagreement, rejection or tension	*(...)**I am not able**to find the correct determinant. (...)**Much as I keep checking,**I cannot find my mistake.(...)*
	Neutral	It does not manifest socioemotionally	*This derivative differs from the one in the table of derivatives of tanx=1/cos²x. How come?*
	Positive	Shows agreement, support or distension	No intervention in this sense

Table 3. Levels of interlocutive dimension

	Communication	Role	To whom it is addressed	Structure	Reactions
Level 0	Vertical	Submissive	Teacher	Traditional	Negative
Level 1	Vertical	Submissive	Students	Traditional	Negative
Level 2	Vertical	Submissive	Everyone	Alternative	Neutral
Level 3	Vertical	Dominant	Students	Evolving	Positive
Level 4	Horizontal	Collaborator	Adequated	Alive	Positive

that is, they are related to the concepts involved, or

g) make a reference to conceptual doubts, which derive from the material and occur after having reflected on it, without the need for a procedure that generates them.

In relation to this dimension, the various levels are established after assessing both the contents of the annotations and the variety of contents in the annotations, since this is also an indicator of the versatility in the use of the tool. We provide in the following a qualitative gradation that takes these two factors into account, and in which a heavier weight is given to the annotations carried out in relation to the study material rather than to the annotations concerning the CET; this is because the annotation to the CET are just circumstantial, as a consequence of the particular situation that arose at a key point during this investigation. Here also, like in the interlocutive dimension, the quantitative assessment is of special significance because, when properly weighed, it allows us to make a better classification of the different variables that come into play.

From this classification of the students' interaction profile in relation to the established dimensions, the global classification is obtained. This classification is made, directly, from an arithmetical average using equal weights:

Level of use of the tool = 1/3 (instrumental level + interlocutive level + thematic level)

The final level is established from the whole

part of the arithmetical average; we believe that, through using a truncated average, the assigned value is more robust. The decimal part of the value obtained will allow us to qualify the position of the student in the corresponding level.

This numeric solution can seem a priori a coarse measure, because it can lead us to situations such as: "the level in the use of the tool of a student with a level 0 in the instrumental dimension, a level 0 in the interlocutive dimension and a level 4 in the thematic dimension, is 1". But this kind of situation should not occur because of the link that exists among the three dimensions; if the aforementioned case would occur, one would probably have to reassess correctly the levels corresponding to each dimension.

In table 5, we establish, finally, a general classification of the students in relation to the use of the tool.

Next, we show the classification of the students who have carried out annotations and which have been analyzed in this research.

With this classification it can be clearly observed, without a need of entering into the details of the qualitative analysis, that all the students analyzed are situated in an intermediate or low level. This is mainly due to a low level on the thematic dimension; in spite of being linked with the rest of the dimensions, it is in the thematic dimension where it can be more clearly observed that the students have not exploited the possibilities of interaction that the tool potentially provides. The fact that all the students analyzed have a

Table 4. Levels of the thematic dimension

Level 0	Annotations with respect to technical problems with the tool
Level 1	Annotations to the CET
Level 2	Annotations to the CET plus annotations to the study material because of an errata, and procedural doubts due to arbitrary and/or execution errors
Level 3	Annotations to the CET, annotations to the study material related to errata and procedural doubts due to arbitrary and/or execution errors, and annotations with the purpose of relating with the rest of the participants
Level 4	Annotations to the CET, annotations in the study material due to errata and procedural doubts, and conceptual doubts and annotations with the purpose of relating with the rest of the participants

Table 5. Description of general levels of use of the tool

Level 0	Minimum level. The student does not use the tool.
Level 1	The student starts using the tool in a natural and spontaneous manner.
Level 2	The student starts to make a deeper use of the tool in certain aspects, and starts to incorporate it as an added element in his learning process.
Level 3	The student begins to analyze in greater depth the possibilities offered by the tool in relation to the interaction with the group and with his learning process.
Level 4	Maximum level of use of the tool. The student uses the tool regularly, and exploits all its possibilities.

Table 6. Level of use of those students that have been analyzed.

Student	Instrumental dimension	Interlocutive dimension	Thematic dimension	Global classification
A	Level 2	Level 3	Level 1	Level 2
B	Level 2	Level 2	Level 1	Level 1
C	Level 2	Level 2	Level 1	Level 1
D	Level 3	Level 3	Level 1	Level 2
E	Level 0	Level 2	Level 1	Level 1
F	Level 1	Level 2	Level 1	Level 1
G	Level 1	Level 2	Level 1	Level 1

level 1 in the thematic dimension shows that, in general, the annotations have referred to the CET and not to the contents of the study material for the subject. By taking the levels obtained by the analyzed students into account, it is concluded that the students have not used the tool as a resource for the subject. Therefore, their level of interaction has not increased and they have not taken advantage of the possible benefits that could derive from it.

If one checks the process followed by the students who have made annotations, and the opinions shown by the students through the forum or through the specific collaborations with this research, one notices a variety of factors that had an influence on the low or intermediate levels attained, and in the use or, rather, the lack of use of the tool. On the one hand, the profile of the students has been an important factor, not only in relation to the professional and family responsibilities already commented upon, but also in relation to the predisposition with respect to the interaction. It is

necessary to motivate students towards the interaction and to do it in several ways, since a given situation can induce a student to participate, but it produces the opposite effect in another one. Once we realized that there was a very low or null use of the tool during the first month of the experience, it was decided to force the use of the tool through the area of partial evaluation. In some cases, the rejection towards this decision has been so great that the possibility to use the tool has been blocked and, even more, in some cases, has resulted in a no-show of some students in the test. However, for other students, this imposition has been the initial point of interaction with the tool and they have later on continued to make a more in-depth study of the possibilities of the tool and benefiting themselves from it. Another clear motivation has been the request for collaboration in the research, thereby increasing the links with the teacher and, therefore, increasing the commitment towards the subject. But this motivation has also been a double-sided issue: some students felt an increased pressure and the contrary effect resulted. On the other hand, another of the determining factors has been the moment in which the tool was introduced. The fact that the tool was not introduced at the beginning of the course, at the same time as the rest of the resources, but a couple of weeks later, has led students to question the pedagogical legitimacy of the tool. Thus, they have questioned the need to learn to use a new tool when they are already immersed in learning the subject and, in some cases, with the added feeling of lack of time to understand the contents of the subject and to respond to its instructional structure. Finally, it is necessary to highlight another factor that has also influenced the assessment and the use of the rest of the technological resources, namely, the need to work online. Some students have been reluctant regarding the possibility of studying with the support of the computer and have manifested the need to work exclusively with "paper and pencil"; they have even requested the study material be available in this format. Some resistance appears, here, to a change in a traditional learning process that was already taken on board by the students in former educational stages, and which was probably deprived of any technological tool. They do not appreciate the advantages of a process enriched by a diversity of technological resources.

This chapter has outlined the aspects that should be considered in order to understand the situation that developed in introducing DIIGO, and to go into greater depth in the process followed by the students in the adaptation to a new form of communication. We have also analyzed the factors that influence this process, and have put forward an instrument for assessing the level of use of the tool. These considerations open new areas of research about the influence of interactions in the students' learning process in an online setting and, at the same time, to try and improve the learning process by means of interactions facilitated by the tool.

The degree of transferability of the results is high because we can apply them to other com-munication tools and to other subject matters. The assessment that is proposed with respect to the levels of interaction can apply to other communication tools, not necessarily integrated into the study material; it is possible to apply this analysis, for example to discussion forums and chats, among others. In this way, one could compare, for the same subject matter, the interactions produced through different forms of communication and, therefore, to appraise and to contrast their didactic efficiency. On the other hand, we can apply the results to any other science subject and even to any other subject matter in general. The distinction in the thematic dimension (the one that could be considered as more specific to the subject) has been kept at the level of evaluation and of study material and, concerning students' doubts, to conceptual and procedural questions. In non scientific subjects, one just needs to establish the procedures and concepts that the student has to learn.

CONCLUSION

In this section, the observations and assessments carried out throughout this chapter are discussed in terms of the theoretical framework discussed in the introduction. Therefore, the ideas that have been presented will follow the same structure: firstly, we shall offer some conclusions in relation to the interaction axis, next in relation to the instrumental axis, then on the epistemological axis and, finally, on the instructional axis. To finish off, we will summarize up to what point we have been able to reply to the research questions brought up initially.

In the theoretical framework, two standpoints were set forth: the first one, defended by Kozma (quoted in Roblyer & Wiencke (2003)), according to which the technologies can offer singular opportunities for learning as long as the instruction is well supported in the cognitive and social processes by which knowledge is produced; and the second one, defended by Roblyer and Wiencke (2003), according to which the technologies can also offer unique opportunities for achieving the students' commitment. In our research, although we have obtained only minor evidence of this influence on the students' learning and commitment, we have been able to ascertain that the technologies do not lead to the achievement of these opportunities in a spontaneous and immediate way; furthermore, as Wagner affirms, one of the requirements that hold special importance in a distance learning environment is the design of the courses and of the promotion of the interaction. Thus, it is not just a matter of merely reproducing face-to-face methods. One cannot establish a level of correspondence between the complexity and multiplicity of stimuli in a face to face environment and the complexity and multiplicity of stimuli in a virtual environment. A specific mediation is necessary in the promotion of the interaction that has to take into account different strategies and factors. One example is the moment of introduction of the tool, or the use of the evaluation but, especially, one has to take into account the different reactions that these strategies can provoke in students; it is necessary that these strategies are multiple in order to foresee the adequacy of this mediation to the different profiles of students, since these profiles are a priori unknown. The complexity of this mediation is part of the complex nature of the interaction that Roblyer and Wiencke (2003) pointed out as one of the difficulties in making the transition from theory to practice.

The third requirement which is necessary if we wish to achieve a useful structure with the interaction, so as to obtain research and design techniques for distance learning environments, as pointed out by Wagner, is the evaluation of the interaction. In this chapter, we have suggested a classification that allows the interaction to be evaluated, by taking three dimensions into account: the instrumental dimension (in relation to the tool from which the interaction is produced), the interlocutive dimension (in relation to the communication that is established in the interac-

tion) and the thematic dimension (in relation to the contents of the interaction).

With respect to the instrumental axis discussed in the theoretical framework, it started by considering the possibilities of the communication tool for reinforcing the theoretical discourse. After the analysis and observation of the processes followed by the students, it can be stated that the reinforcement of the theoretical discourse is at an advanced level in the process of instrumentation. Indeed, the student assumes initially the potential of the tool and uses it as a means of consolidating his learning process or to overcome the obstacles that keep showing up in his interaction with the study material.

In the reflection on the instrumental genesis, Artigue (2002) indicates that it works in two directions, instrumentation and instrumentalization. This genesis has been taken into account in the instrumental dimension of the classification of the students in relation to the interaction; besides, we have contemplated the relation between these two processes. On the other hand, Artigue also points out a contrast between the discourse sustained about the potentiality of the instrument and the reality of the observation of the follow-up of the subject matter. In our research, this contrast has been observed, for example, in students who keep a very positive discourse in relation to the tool but who do not carry out any annotation and, therefore, one would think that the discourse is exclusively motivated by a justification towards the teacher. In another sense, this contrast has also been observed in students who have used the tool to make annotations. In general, a poorer discourse concerning the potentiality of the tool is clearly seen in these students, in comparison to the use that they finally make of it. Artigue (2002) also points out the unsuspected complexity of the instrumental genesis, which in our research has been reflected in the multiple factors that have influenced on the incompleteness of the instrumental process. Finally, we wish to point out a question related to the pedagogical legitimacy of introducing technical knowledge which is alien to the official curriculum. In this sense, this question appears clearly in the students' opinions, but we believe that in order to assess this questioning, it is necessary to take into account the particular moment in which the tool was introduced in our experience, since, in general, within the framework of the UOC, the students assume that specific requirements about the installation of the tools and technological resources will be given at the beginning of each subject. Therefore, although a priori this would not necessarily have been a problem, it has become one due to the relatively late moment of the introduction of the tool, once the semester had begun.

What we concentrate our attention now is in the epistemological axis; it is necessary to highlight that in the proposed classification of the students, specifically in the thematic dimension, the classification of errors is generalized in relation to the concept of derivative that Orton suggested as detailed in Azcárate et al (1996). It has been observed how the procedural doubts brought up by the students have an origin mainly in an *execution* error, which are possibly those most immediately ascertainable by the student and the simplest ones to verbalize and solve. On the other hand, we wish to stress that the difficulty that Azcárate et al.(1996) pointed out in relation to the use of graphical representations is worsened when interactive graphs are used; this has been observed in the annotations and in the opinions of the students. Thus, it would be necessary to carry out a study in order to assess the confusion that can be generated in the students and the measures which would be necessary to take into account, in order to avoid this difficulty. In relation to the communication tool under study, it would be necessary to assess the possibilities that it can offer as a support to reflect about these difficulties with graphs and to exert a direct influence on the learning process.

Finally, in referring to the situational axis, it has been shown that the instructional inflex-ibility has consequences in the process of the students' learning and in their capacity to accept new elements, like the communication tool. This instructional inflexibility increases the pressure on the student, and provokes a tension which has turned out to be one of the factors that makes the introduction of the tool difficult.

Finally, we just wish to stress the fact that, in relation to the analysis of the interactions, we have suggested a classification of the interaction levels that can be produced with the use of the tool under study; we have also provided an analysis of the type of interactions that can be produced, as well as the causes of the type and level of interactions that take place.

FUTURE RESEARCH DIRECTIONS

The research lines suggested as a result of this work focus on the continuation of the experience that has been initiated, using the model of analysis proposed and the classification of the level of use of the tool to analyze the students' contribution and to establish a taxonomy of student's types of behavior. The analysis carried out should be broadened with the competence analysis and the situational analysis. With the competence analysis, one intends to investigate what influence the interaction has on students' learning and on the increase of self-confidence in their mathematical skills. With the situational analysis, we wish to analyze the didactic efficiency of the interactions among students and between students and teacher in the aforementioned context. Likewise, it is necessary to broaden the analysis of the interactions to include the teaching action, that it, to include the teacher's influence on the level of interaction of the students and the particularities of the teacher's annotations.

In order to be able to carry out this in-depth and to make a broader analysis of the study, we suggest that a number of aspects should be taken into account, that we have been breaking down throughout the discussion and the conclusions, and which can become key factors in the success of future experience:

- The moment when the communication tool is introduced. The best option is to introduce it before the students establish contact with the contents and at the same time that the rest of the tools and technology resources are introduced.
- A tool integrated with the learning setting. DIIGO is a commercial, external tool which is independent of the institution and not conceived as a pedagogical tool or as a mathematical communication tool. This fact has entailed some obstacles for the students. Therefore, it is necessary to take into account the introduction of a specific, internal tool which is integrated with the learning environment that the students use.
- The factors to provoke and to motivate the use of the tool. It is necessary to make an effort to offer a diversity of reasons for the use of the tool, and not only centered on the evaluation of the contents; motivations are necessary of a personal kind and of an epistemological nature. Thus, it will be good to make special care in showing the possibilities of the tool in relation to solving doubts, but also in relation to the possibility of reflecting about the concepts, and about the origin of the possible errors that have been made. Here, it is also important to take into account the possibility of breaking the isolation of the student in a distance learning environment with the promotion of the online learning mode. The potentialities of the tool in relation to solving specific doubts and, specially, procedural doubts, is quite natural and spontaneous in the students. For this reason, it is especially important to show all the other possibilities to the students. Indirectly, we wish to observe how the encouragement of online learning in relation to communication,

promotes the use of other technology resources that are offered to the students in the study material and which seem to be hardly used by them. To a large extent, students sustain learning conceptions strongly linked to a traditional and a technological face-to-face environment.

REFERENCES

Artigue, M. (2002). Learning mathematics in a CAS environment: The genesis of a reflection about instrumentation and the dialectics between technical and conceptual work. *International Journal of Computers for Mathematical Learning, 7*(3), 245–274. doi:10.1023/A:1022103903080

Artigue, M. (2004). Problemas y desafíos en educación matemática:¿qué nos ofrece hoy la didáctica de la matemática para afrontarlos? *Educación Matemática, 16*(3), 5–28.

Azcárate, C., et al. (1996). *Cálculo diferencial e integral.* Madrid, España: Editorial Síntesis, S.A.

Barberà, E. (2006). Aportaciones de la tecnología a la e-evaluación. *RED Revista de Educación a Distancia, monographic number VI.* Retrieved on January 15, 2009, from http://www.um.es/ead/red/M6

Fahy, P. J. (2006). Online and face-to-face group interaction processes compared using Bales'interaction process analysis (IPA). *European Journal of Open Distance and E-learning EURODL.*

Forman, E. (1996). Learning mathematics as participation in classroom practice: Implications of sociocultural theory for educational reform. In L. Steffe, P. Nesher, P. Cobb, G. Goldin & B. Greer (Eds.), *Theories of mathematical learning* (pp. 115–130). Mahwah, NJ: Lawrence Erlbaum Associates.

Han, S. Y., & Hill, J. R. (2007). Collaborate to learn, learn to collaborate: Examining the roles of context, community, and cognition in asynchronous discussion. *Journal of Educational Computing Research, 36*(1), 89–123. doi:10.2190/A138-6K63-7432-HL10

Roblyer, M. D., & Wiencke, W. R. (2003). Design and use of a rubric to assess and encourage interactive qualities in distances courses. *American Journal of Distance Education, 17*(2), 77–98. doi:10.1207/S15389286AJDE1702_2

Sancho-Vinuesa, T., & Gras-Martí, A. (in press). Case study: Teaching and learning (T&L) undergraduate mathematics in an online university. In W. Kinuthia & S. Marshall (Eds.), *Cases'n'places: Global cases in educational and performance technology.*

Sangrà, A. (2002). A new learning model for the information and knowledge society: The case of the UOC. *International Review of Research in Open and Distance Learning, 2*(2).

Smith, G. G., Torres-Ayala, A. T., & Heindel, A. J. (2008). Disciplinary differences in e-learning instructional design: The case of mathematics. *Journal of Distance Education, 22*(3), 63–88.

Chapter 7
Harnessing Web 2.0 for Context-Aware Learning:
The Impact of Social Tagging System on Knowledge Adaption

Wai-Tat Fu
University of Illinois at Urbana-Champaign, USA

Thomas Kannampallil
University of Illinois at Urbana-Champaign, USA

ABSTRACT

We present an empirical study investigating how interactions with a popular social tagging system, called del.icio.us, may directly impact knowledge adaptation through the processes of concept assimilation and accommodation. We observed 4 undergraduate students over a period of 8 weeks and found that the quality of social tags and distributions of information content directly impact the formation and enrichment of concept schemas. A formal model based on a distributed cognition framework provides a good fit to the students learning data, showing how learning occurs through the adaptive assimilation of concepts and categories of multiple users through the social tagging system. The results and the model have important implications on how Web 2.0 technologies can promote formal and informal learning through collaborative methods.

INTRODUCTION

The World Wide Web (WWW) gained extreme popularity during the late 1990s due to its simple architecture and design (Millard & Ross, 2006). The 1990s version of the WWW, now dubbed as Web 1.0 (O'Reilly, 2005), is characterized as "read-only" web. Web 1.0 efforts included content management systems, fixed directory structures and portals that used client-server architecture. In stark contrast, Web 2.0 is characterized by user-generated content (e.g., blogs, photos), communities of users (e.g., social networks), peer to peer networks (e.g., Napster), and content syndication (O'Reilly, 2005). While the exact definitions of Web 2.0 is open to debate, it is important to note that web applications have evolved into collaborative user-centered rich internet applications (RIA). The implication of this evolution is significant considering its possible

DOI: 10.4018/978-1-60566-826-0.ch007

impact in a variety of domains ranging from healthcare (Kaldoudi *et al.*, 2008), marketing (Parise & Guinan, 2008), e-Science (Fox *et al.*, 2007) and education (Ullrich *et al.*, 2008).

The traditional WWW has been a strong medium for development of the e-learning tradition. The use of traditional web as a teaching and learning medium has led to the development of traditional learning management systems (e.g., WebCT and Blackboard) and also more adaptive intelligent tutoring systems. But, research on the use of Web 2.0 technology for teaching and learning is limited (Ullrich et al., 2008). The features afforded by Web 2.0 are in line with educational theories such as constructivism, exploratory learning, and connectionism, making it extremely interesting instructors, learners and designers. Ferdig (Ferdig, 2007) describes four theoretical aspects of Web 2.0 that make it suitable for pedagogy. He argues that Web 2.0 technologies: (a) provide an environment for scaffolded learning (with teachers, peers or an intelligent system), (b) support collaboration, cooperation and shared work resulting in active student participation learning, and (c) provide constructivist learning environments by encouraging students to actively publish, revise and comment on others' content. Alternatively, (Ullrich et al., 2008) provide technical, social and cultural characteristics of Web 2.0 that make it useful for pedagogy. These include the support for individual creativity and exploratory behavior, usability aspects such as desktop-like interactions, technological aspects such as the use of light-weight architectures and easy modifications, and multiple modes of access (e.g., PC, mobile devices).

Though researchers have claimed the potential usefulness in using Web 2.0 technologies for educational purposes, there are very few studies that explore how Web 2.0 technologies can be effectively incorporated into the public education milieu. One possible reason could be relative newness of these technologies. But, it is interesting to note that several for-profit compa-

nies have strongly encouraged their employees to write blogs and develop internal wikis (Ajjan & Hartshorne, 2008). Another reason could be the instructors' lack of knowledge or interest in using these technologies or tools in the classroom. Ajjan and Hartshorne (Ajjan & Hartshorne, 2008) use a survey based study to investigate faculty interest in using Web 2.0 technologies in the classroom in a large public university. They found that faculty members are generally aware of the pedagogical benefits of using Web 2.0 technologies. But, more than half of the respondents did not plan to use any Web 2.0 technologies in their classrooms.

Researchers have explored the development and use of Web 2.0 technologies in a variety of domains and tools. One domain that has received attention for Web 2.0 technologies is e-Science projects. Pierce et al (Pierce *et al.*, 2008) developed outreach tools as a means of creating communities of like-minded researchers. This is an e-Science venture aimed at outreach activity of broadening the participation from minority institutions. Fox et al (Fox et al., 2007) examine the usefulness of tagging and social bookmarking for identifying and building keyword-based profiles that can be used for "collaborator match-making services". The system, called Minority Serving Institution-Cyber Infrastructure Empowerment Coalition (MSI-CIEC) incorporates online bookmarking and tagging for researchers. Mason and Rennie (Mason & Rennie, 2007) report on the development and use of a range of Web 2.0 technologies that supported the development of a community in Scotland. The social software helped in community interaction, ownership and pride about the local landscape and learning about the local tourist locations.

With respect to the use of Web 2.0 technologies for education, most research reports have focused on design and development of tools. Others have argued about the opportunities for using these tools (Alexander, 2006). Kaldoudi et al (Kaldoudi et al., 2008) describe a problem-based learning approach using wikis and blogs for supporting medical education. The authors contrast the lecture-based tradition in medical education with the active, exploratory learning approach that is afforded by Web 2.0 technologies. The authors describe a wiki-blog based system that supports collaboration among medical experts, support strong instructor presence, helped in continuous monitoring of student activities and provided tools for student inquiry. Takago et al. (Takago *et al.*, 2007) describe the ineffectiveness of their e-learning system designed for teaching engineering design. The original design was assembled from independent software components and provided static web content. The new Web 2.0 based re-design is based on analysis of students' learning activities and helps students publish revise and exchange information. It also helped instructors (and peers) track the progress of the students to give them constructive feedback. Synchronous Learning Environment with Web 2.0 (SLEW) is another application developed with AJAX technology. SLEW is a synchronous distance-learning application that supports dynamic interaction, knowledge sharing and interaction between teachers and learners (Lin *et al.*, 2007). SLEW uses Web 2.0 technology and YouTube API to develop instructional courses for distance learning.

Web 2.0 technologies also face several potential disadvantages. One of the more explored aspects is the challenges Web 2.0 technologies pose for security and privacy (e.g., (Ahern *et al.*, 2007); (Lam & Churchill, 2007)). Recent studies have shown that users are often not sure about the available privacy choices and often are not in a position to make well-informed decisions (Ahern et al., 2007). The openness of Web 2.0 systems is also another potential disadvantage for new users. Bhattacharya and Dron (Bhattacharya & Dron, 2007) discuss the challenges of effectively integrating Web 2.0 technologies for pedagogy. They organize the challenges into the following categories: technical challenges confronting the instructor and students, devising effective mechanisms for monitoring the students within

and outside the classroom, and learner assessment processes. The authors do not provide any insights about how to overcome these challenges.

The possibilities for using Web 2.0 technologies for pedagogy are endless. But as we can see from the literature, these technologies are still new and there is limited research on how they can be applied to improve context-aware learning. More empirical studies are required to evaluate the challenges in using Web 2.0 in the classroom or at home on a longer-term basis. In this chapter, we will focus on a popular Web 2.0 technology called social tagging. We will first briefly discuss its history and characteristics, followed by a description of an empirical study that investigates how social tagging systems may directly impact concept development. Finally, implications to long-term learning are discussed.

SOCIAL TAGGING SYSTEMS

Social tagging systems are major Web 2.0 technologies that have gained popularity in recent years. A popular social bookmarking web site is called del.icio.us (http://del.icio.us). Users register and personalize their own collection of bookmarks in their own page. Each bookmark is accompanied by a short description, or tags, of the contents of the site that the bookmark leads to. Users can also see the tags that other users create, search for bookmarks with certain tags, or browse the collection of bookmarks created by other users. Social bookmarking web sites therefore allow a new form of collaborative information discovery and sharing. Users can quickly set up a social bookmarking page for a topic of interest; learn from others who have similar interests, and discover new topics or subtopics and their connection to other users.

Alexander (Alexander, 2006) describes the increasing role of social bookmarking in pedagogical applications. He explains their importance in information search and discovery, acting as an "outboard memory", helping in finding collaborators with similar interests and self-reflection on patterns by evaluating one's own tag clusters. Additionally, it also provides interesting opportunities for evaluating student (or group) progress by tracking their bookmarks and tags. In addition to publicly available social bookmarking systems such as del.icio.us, specific applications have been developed to support user needs in different environments. Examples include the PennTags project (http://tags.library.upenn.edu/) and the Harvard H2O project (http://h2o.law.harvard.edu/index.jsp). The PennTags project helps online library users at University of Pennsylvania to tag and organize their favorite library resources. The H2O project at Harvard law school creates an online venue for communities to create and exchange ideas through online interaction and discourse.

One major reason why social tagging becomes popular is that people are becoming less satisfied with the Internet being used as a large information database, from which users can retrieve facts easily through powerful search engines. Instead, people are increasingly relying on the Internet to explore and comprehend information, and to share experiences and socialize among other users. The major difference is that Web 1.0 aims at deriving powerful algorithms to index massive amount of information, but Web 2.0 aims at deriving semantic structures among these information that are pertinent to real-world information tasks imposed to real users. For humans, this distinction is not particularly prominent because the human cognitive system naturally conjoins the two functions as we process information. As we will elaborate later, when a person learns to index a new object, such as when learning that a four-leg animal is a cat, the person tends to naturally encode contextual information and classify the object in certain mental categories. When the person encounters an object in the future that is known to be a cat, he or she can then infer only that it has four legs, but also that it meows, has fur, etc. The formation of these mental categories

therefore not only allows the cognitive system to capture the structure of the contextual information related to the object, but also allows the cognitive system to capture the similarities and differences across structures in the environment. This is arguably the process that humans can perform much better than computers, and the reason why Web 1.0 fails to satisfy the needs of users. We address this point later in the chapter.

Instead of relying on mental concepts and categories to exploit contextual information, search engines, on the other hand, often rely on automated indexing software to determine the information content of web pages. For example, software such as web crawlers will visit hyperlinks in multiple web sites on the Internet and develop a list of keywords that appear on each of the web pages to which these hyperlinks connect. Eventually, a large database consisting of a master list of these keywords is created. When a user enters a query in the search engine, the words in the query are compared with those in the database. The results of the search are all of the web sites that have been listed under the keywords in the database that match the query words, and the links to these web sites are returned in the order that is determined based on frequency of visits, certain usage histories in the past, location of keywords in the documents, number of other sites that link to each of these web sites, or other features that are believed to increase the likelihood that the information returned from the search engine will match the information goal of the user. Information accessed by this kind of indexed retrieval is often just an *ad hoc list*, with no internal organization at all. Therefore, the fundamental problem with this kind of simple indexing and retrieval is that it does not capture the natural structural relationship among these web sites based on their information content. Although many online systems do provide classification information such as subject headings in book-selling web sites such as amazon.com, or topics or directories links in search portals such as Yahoo.com, one has to keep in mind that these categories are created by the humans, presumably someone who believe these classification is general enough that they could help users to find information more efficiently. Search engines by themselves, are not very good at generating these classification. In other words, the major drawback of the simple indexing and retrieval in Web 1.0 is that it does not allow users to directly learn the context under which the information naturally appears, thus preventing users to develop the natural structural relationship and classification of information based on the informational structures that naturally exist in our environment.

Social tagging systems, on the other hand, allow collective indexing of the massive information space based on the subjective interpretation of the information in the web pages by different users. Human indexing not only allows better representation of semantics at the level that other humans can easily understand, it also allows multiple interpretations by people with different knowledge background and information needs. The major drawback, compared to automated indexing, is the lower speed of processing. However, this drawback seems to be well compensated by the massive volume of users as they provide metadata to the web sites that they find useful and are happy to share with others with similar interests. Indeed, results show that although users may have diverse backgrounds, the dynamics of tags are found to stabilize quickly as the number of users increases (Cattuto *et al.*, 2007; Golder & Huberman, 2006). This is perhaps one of the most fascinating aspects of social tagging as well as other Web 2.0 technologies, as demonstrated by the success of Wikipedia and other similar open-source projects.

With the increasing popularity of social tagging systems, many are hopeful that they can potentially promote learning about social events, beliefs, or concepts that go beyond knowledge acquired from textbooks or formal instructions in classrooms. Although many are hopeful that Web 2.0 technologies may provide a revolutionary way

of learning, some researchers question whether this kind of informal learning may only lead only to superficial knowledge acquisition – accumulation of bits and pieces of facts by collective indexing without necessarily developing the deep structural networks of knowledge acquired in formal learning environments. Indeed, most recent studies on social tagging systems have focused on user motivation for contributing to different web sites (Sen *et al.*, 2006)or aggregate usage patterns in specific web sites across a specific period of time (Cattuto et al., 2007; Golder & Huberman, 2006). To a certain extent, many of these studies have treated social tagging systems as a form of technology that provides more meaningful indexing of information than automated indexing by search engines. To our knowledge, no empirical study has been done to investigate how the interactions with social tagging systems may potentially influence higher-level cognitive structures and promote "real" learning beyond indexing of information. To illustrate this point, we will first review the ideas of distributed cognitive systems before we present our study that directly test how social tagging systems may directly influence learning.

Social Tagging Systems and Distributed Cognitive Systems

Social tagging systems are excellent examples of distributed cognitive systems (Fu, 2008; Hollan *et al.*, 2000; Hutchins, 1995; Zhang & Norman, 1994). In contrast to the traditional definition of cognition, a distributed cognitive system encompasses all flow of information among individuals and the resources in the environment. The idea is that when one examines the outcome from the distributed cognitive system, one cannot easily attribute the outcome to any isolated component of the system. In fact, the basic premise of a distributed cognition framework is that behavior arises out of the interactions of the components of the system. The functional unit of analysis of behavior in a distributed cognitive system should include all elements that bring themselves into coordination to accomplish some tasks, and any isolated analysis of its parts is insufficient to understand how the system works. A classic example is the demonstration of distributed memory systems in the cockpit by Hutchins (Hutchins, 1995), who showed that the encoding and retrieval of critical information by pilots rely on various displays inside the cockpit as much as individual memory. In addition, information from the external environment provides more than simply a cue to internal memory, but provides opportunities to reorganize the internal and external representations in the distributed cognitive system.

Under the distributed cognitive systems framework, the current analysis of social tagging systems will focus on the intricate interactions between internal and external representations of concepts, tags, and documents as a user is engaged in as they interact with the system. Figure 1 shows a notational diagram of this theoretical framework. Multiple users have their internal representations of the world, as they interact with the social tagging systems and consume information on different

web pages. These internal representations partially reflect the different background knowledge of different users, as well as differences in their information needs. These internal representations will influence how they interpret the information in different web pages, the tags created by others, as well as the tags they will create to associate with the web pages that they visit. To a certain extent, these internal representations are shared among others through the external representations (tags) of the information content of the web pages. It is not only the case that users may contribute tags to different web pages, but the interpretation of tags created by others may also influence their own internal representations as some forms of knowledge adaptation. The major characteristics of this distributed cognition framework is that: (1) both internal and external representations may influence the search and interpretation of the web document, and (2) the understanding and interpretation of the web document may influence both the internal (concepts) and external representations (tags).

Figure 1. A distributed knowledge representations framework in a social tagging system (reps = representations).

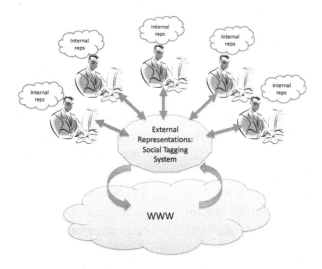

Tagging, Schemas, and Knowledge Adaptation

Researchers in cognitive science have proposed different representational structures to capture the properties of our general knowledge of objects around us, and one prominent representational structure is called a schema (Rumelhart & Ortony, 1976). Schemas represent our concepts of objects such as their attributes and their categorical relationship. For example, we know that houses have rooms, can be built of wood or stone, serve as human dwellings, and are a type of building. The importance of the category information is that it stores predictable information about instances of a category, such that when someone mentions a house we have a rough idea of the object being referred to. Note that schemas represent knowledge at an abstract level, in the sense that they encode what is generally true rather than what is true about specific instance.

One important property of schemas is that there are default values for certain schema attributes, which are presumably developed from our past experiences. This provides schemas with a useful inferential mechanism. Many studies have been conducted to confirm the psychological reality of schemas. For example, Brewer and Treyens (Brewer & Treyens, 1981) conducted a study in which participants were told that they were in an office. After a short period of time, participants were asked to recall objects in the office. Results showed the participants were much better at recalling objects that can typically be found in an office than those that are not. In addition, participants mistakenly recalled objects (such as books) that can typically found in an office, but were in fact not in the specific office that they were in. These studies show that when given a hint to what the object belongs to, people will utilize their existing knowledge to infer the other "hidden" attributes of the object.

As people interact with their environment and acquire more experiences their schemas may be modified to make sense, or used to make sense of the new experiences. This process of knowledge adaptation can be traced all the way back to the Piaget's (Piaget, 1975) developmental model of equilibration of cognitive structures in children. According to Piaget, there are at least two processes through which new experiences interact with existing schemas. When new experiences are modified to fit existing schemas the process is defined as assimilation. In contrast, accommodation is an adaptation process of knowledge acquisition that changes the schemas in order to fit the new experience, or the person creates an entirely new schema in order to accommodate new data that does not fit any of their existing schemas. Through the process of assimilation and accommodation, people can adapt to new experiences that they obtain from their interactions with others, such as when they discuss, share, or exchange information.

Consider the case when a user is browsing for information related to a broad topic of interest, such as when one is interested in knowing more about facts or events related to the independence of Kosovo. We called this kind of *exploratory learning* an ill-defined information task (as opposed to well-defined task in which a specific piece of information is needed such as looking for the address of a hotel, see Chin, Fu, & Kannampalil, 2009; Fu & Pirolli, 2007), in which one only has a rough idea about what they are looking for, and the information goal itself will be refined throughout the search process. During the search, social tags created by others can be utilized as useful cues to select and navigate to the documents pertaining to the topic of interest (Marchionini, 2006; White *et al.*, 2007). Through this process of *exploratory search-and-learn*, the user gains a better understanding of the topic through the enrichment of internal representations of concepts relevant to the topic (either assimilation or accommodation, or both). The user may then create their own tags for the web documents based on their own understanding as well as the existing social tags, and may choose to perform another cycle of exploratory searching and learning, refinement of concepts, and so on. *In other words, through iterative exploratory search-and-learn cycles, the interactions between internal concepts and external tags gradually lead to sharing and assimilation of conceptual structures as more and more people assign social tags to represent ideas or concepts that they extract from the massive amount of web documents.*

Applying the above framework of knowledge adaptation to social tagging, we have three specific predictions on how social tags may influence knowledge development. First, the ability to predict based on category membership is presumably the major utility of tags that are assigned to a bookmark. Tags invoke certain internal schemas of the user, and these schemas allow the user to predict what information is "hidden" in the web page that the bookmark leads to. It follows that the higher the "quality" of tags (in the sense that they allow better prediction of the underlying schemas), the higher the efficiency of the user in finding the right information. Second, given an information goal, when there are more high-quality tags that match the existing schemas of the user, the existing schemas of the user will be richer through the process of assimilation. Third, when information content is more diverse, more distinct schemas will be developed through the process of accommodation. We will formalize these processes in the next section.

A Formal Model of Social Tagging under the Distributed Cognition Framework

To formalize the analysis of social tagging, we will present a probabilistic model of exploratory learning behavior as users interact with a social tagging system. The formal model allows not only allows precise predictions on behavior, but also provides clear characterization of how different components and processes influence behavior. The model as-

sumes that people will naturally categorize web documents as they go through and comprehend them (with the tags helping by adding additional features), and *the reason why mental categories (schemas) are formed is that this is an adaptive response to the inherent structure of the stimuli from the external world to our minds that allow humans to predict features of new objects better.* Tags assigned to documents are just another set of features that allow us to predict the unobserved contents of the documents, and with the formation of mental categories, the tags will not only inform the user what they literally refer to, but also other unobserved features of the documents.

Assume that a user has a set of schemas S and a set of semantic topics T. The information goal is to predict whether topic T_j (some useful information) can be found by following a link with tags G, i.e., the user is trying to estimate this probability: $P(T_j|S,G_k)$ when deciding on links, which can be broken down into two components based on the distributed cognition framework. One component predicts the probability that a particular topic can be found in a given schema, and the second component predicts the probability that a given set of tags are associated with a given schema:

$$P(T_j \mid S,G) = \sum_m P(S_m \mid G)P(T_j \mid S_m)$$

(*Equation 1: Likelihood of finding topic T_j given schemas S, and tags G*)

In other words, to predict whether topic T_j can be found in a particular document, one can first estimate $P(S_m|G)$: the probability that the document with tags G belongs to a particular schema Sm. This estimate depends on how much the internal and external representations match each other: The higher the match, the better is the model able to predict to which categories the document belongs. It also provides a measure of the "quality" of tags, as it indicates how much the tags may help invoke the set of schemas in the user. The second estimate $P(T_j|S_m)$ is the probability that topic T_j can be found in schemas S_m. This estimate therefore depends on the relationship between the topics and the schema. The overall probability $P(T_j|S,G_k)$ can then be estimated by enumerating the product of these two probabilities over all mental categories.

Assimilation: Enrichment of Mental Categories

If we assume a set of schemas that people may have, one can first estimate the prior probabilities for each of these schemas, and calculate how likely a tag created by a user is created based on a particular schema by the Bayes theorem. Specifically, if $P(S_m)$ is the prior probability of schema S_m, and $P(G|S_m)$ is the conditional probability that tag G belongs to S_m, then we can obtain $P(S_m|G)$ by:

$$P(S_m \mid G) = \frac{P(S_m)P(G \mid S_m)}{\sum_m P(S_m)P(G \mid S_m)}$$

(*Equation 2: Probability that a document with a tag G is created from schema S_m*)

To estimate the prior probability, one can assume that there exists a prior probability for any two random objects (e.g., documents) to belong to the same schema in a particular (informational) ecology. The higher the value of this prior probability, the lower the likelihood that any two objects will belong to a new schema. For the current purpose, we assume that a prior probability that any two web documents belong to the same category for a particular information task. The prior probability therefore depends on the general structures of the information distribution and the information goal. For example, the top of Figure 2 shows a notational diagram of 5 topics (A, B, C, D, & E) in a given information space, and these topics have some levels of overlap in their information contents. Assume that for information task

Figure 2. Notational diagrams showing the original information space (top), and the information space for relevant topics for information task X (left) and Y (right). Each circle represents a topic.

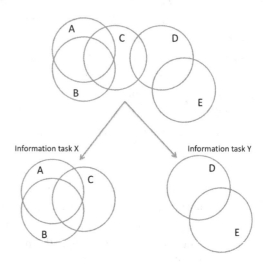

X, topics A, B, & C are relevant. The information space becomes highly overlapped (bottom left of Figure 2). However, for information task Y, topics D and E are relevant, and the information space contains topics that have low overlap. Therefore given the same information space, information task X will have a higher prior probability that any two relevant documents will belong to the same schema, but for information task Y, the same prior probability will be lower.

The conditional probability $P(G|S_m)$ can simply be estimated by the ratio of the number of members in schema S_m that contains G and the total number of members in G, i.e.,

$P(G|S_m)=n/n_m$

(*Equation 3: Probability that a tag belongs to mental category m*).

When the user is browsing different documents and their corresponding tags, estimates of how these tags may come from any of the existing schemas can be derived by calculating the value of $P(S_m|G)$ for each m. The schema that has the highest value of $P(S_m|G)$ can then be selected, and refined based on Equation 3. As more and more documents are processed, the new experiences will be assimilated with the existing schemas of the person and the existing set of schemas will be enriched through this process.

Accommodation: Formation of New Mental Category

It is possible that a person may encounter a new piece of information that does not fit into any of his or her existing schemas. In that case, the existing schemas need to be adjusted to accommodate for the new piece of information. This decision was based on the value of *max[P(S|G)]*, where G represents the contents and tags of the document and S represents the set of existing schemas, and the max operation is performed in the set S. Specifically, a new category will be created only if

$$P(R_{new}) > max[P(R|S)]$$

(*Equation 4: New mental category*)

i.e., the probability that the document belongs to a new category is larger than that for it to belong to any of the existing schemas. If this condition is met, a new schema will be created. The accommodation process therefore allows new schemas to be formed from new experiences.

Assigning Tags to a Bookmark of a Web Document

Given an existing tag G_k, the model will calculate the value of $P(G_k|S_m)$, where S_m is the category to which the current document is assigned according to Equation 3 & 4. The model will assign this tag G_k to this document only if

$$P(G_k|S_m) > \tau_{threshold}$$

(*Equation 5: Assigning an existing tag*)

Where $\tau_{threshold}$ is a free parameter to be estimated from the data. A new tag is created only if any of the tags associated with the documents in category S_m is larger than the maximum of $P(G|S_m)$ for all existing tags, i.e.,

$$P(G_{new}|S_m) > P(G_{max}|S_m)$$

(*Equation 6: Assign a new tag*)

Note the model does not predict which particular tags will be used, it only predicts how likely existing tags will or will not be used based on the relationship between the tags and the predicted mental categories formed.

EMPIRICAL STUDY

The main purpose of the empirical study is to test to what extent interactions with a social tagging system will directly impact knowledge adaptation. In addition, precise protocol data was collected to verify the predictions made by the model, which specifies both the assimilation and accommodation processes that underlie knowledge adaptation. A set of exploratory learning tasks was chosen. In all tasks, undergraduate students were given a rough description of the topic and gradually acquired knowledge about the topic through an iterative search-and-learn cycle. Students were told to imagine that they wanted to understand the given topic and to write a paper and give a talk on the given topic to a diverse audience. Two general topics were chosen: (1) "Find out relevant facts about the Independence of Kosovo" (IK task), and (2) "Find out relevant facts about Anti-aging" (AA task). These two tasks were chosen because the IK task referred to a specific event, and therefore information related to it tended to be more specific, and there were more Web sites containing multiple pieces of well-organized information relevant to the topic. The AA task, on the other hand, was more ambiguous and was related to many disjoint areas such as cosmetics, nutrition, or genetic engineering. Web sites relevant to the IK task have more overlapping concepts than those relevant to the AA task. The other characteristic is that because the AA task was more general, the tags tended to be more generic (such as "beauty", "health"); in contrast, for the IK task, tags tended to be more "semantically narrow" (such as "Kosovo"), and thus had higher cue validity than generic tags.

Participants

4 participants were recruited from the University of Illinois. Participants were undergraduate students and all had extensive experience with general information search and the del.icio.us Web site. Participants were randomly split and assigned to one of the tasks. From their self-report it was obvious that they were unfamiliar with the given topics. Participants were told that they should explore all relevant information to learn about the topic using either the search function in del.icio.us or any other Web search engines, and should create tags for Web pages they found relevant to the topic and store them in their own del.icio.us accounts. Participants were told that these tags should be created for two major purposes. First, to allow them to re-find the information quickly in the future; second, to help their colleagues to utilize the relevant information easily in the future for their search purposes.

Procedure

Each student performed the task for eight 30-minute sessions over a period of 8 weeks, with each session approximately one week apart. Students were told to think aloud during the task in each session. All verbal protocols and screen interac-

tions were captured using the screen recording software *Camtasia*. All tags created were recorded manually from their del.icio.us accounts after each session. Students were instructed to provide a verbal summary of every Web page they read before they created any tags for the page. They could then bookmark the web page and create tags for the page. After they finished reading a document, they could either search for new documents by initiating a new query or selecting an existing tag to browse documents tagged by others. This exploratory search-and-tag cycle continues until a session ended. All tags used and created during each session were extracted to keep track of changes in the shared external representations, and all verbal description on the Web pages were also extracted to keep track of changes in the internal representations during the exploratory search process. These tags and verbal descriptions were then input as contents of the document.

One week after the last session, participants were asked to come back to perform a sorting task. Participants were given printouts of all web pages that they read and bookmarked during the task, and were given the tags associated with the pages (either by themselves or other members in del.icio.us). They were then asked to "put together the web pages that go together on the basis of their information content into as many different groups as you'd like". The categories formed by the participants were then matched to those predicted by the assimilation and accommodation processes in the rational model.

RESULTS

Participants on average created 88.5 bookmarks (IK1=93, IK2=84) and 379.5 tags (IK1=392, IK2=367) for the IK task, and 58 bookmarks (AA1=52, AA2=64) and 245 tags (AA1=256, AA2=234) for the AA task. Participants in the IK task created more bookmarks and assigned more tags than those in the AA task, but the average number of tags per bookmark is about the same (4.3

tags per bookmark) for the two tasks. As expected, finding relevant information for the AA task is more difficult, as reflected by the fewer number of bookmarks created. Given that distribution of information was more disjoint in the AA task (e.g., there is little overlap of information between web sites on skin care and genetic engineering), the results were consistent with the assumption that the average rate of return of relevant information was lower for the AA task then the IK task.

Figure 3 shows the proportion of new tags created by the participants (left) and model (right). Perhaps the most interesting pattern was that even though participants assigned fewer tags, but the *proportions* of new tag creation over total number of tag assignment were higher in the AA task than in the IK task. This was consistent with the

lower rate of return of relevant information in the AA task, and this lower rate was likely caused by fact that the existing tags on del.icio.us was less informative for the AA task. Indeed, concepts extracted from the documents by the participants in the AA task were more often different from the existing tags than in the IK task, suggesting that the existing tags did not serve as good cues to information contained in the documents. The general trends and differences between the two tasks were closely matched by the model ($R^2=0.75$). Again, the major mismatches were found in the first sessions, where the model tended to under-predict the creation of new tags, especially for the IK task. A model that randomly assigns tags was created and compared to performance by humans and model. Chi-square tests show that both human and model

Figure 3. Proportions of new tags created over total number of tags assigned across the 8 sessions by the students (top) and models (bottom).

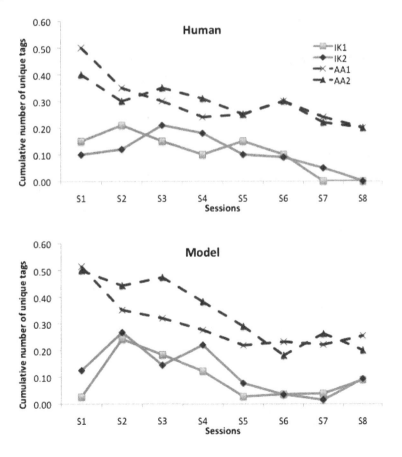

performance was significantly different from the chance model (p<0.01), showing that they are significantly above the chance level.

Formation of Mental Categories

One core assumption of the rational model was that the assignment of tags and the selection of links were both based on the set of mental categories formed from observing existing tags assigned to documents that they processed. It is therefore critical to verify that the set of mental categories formed by the model match those formed by the participants. To do this, correlations between the mental categories formed by the model and the participants were calculated by constructing "match" tables for each participant and model. Items that are in the same category will be given a value 1, otherwise a 0. For example, two possible categorization for the set {a,b,c,d,e} are {ab},{c,d},{e} and {a,b,c}, {d,e}. In that case, their correlation can be calculated as r=0.102 based on the match table.

The major determining variable for mental category formation in the model is the value of the coupling parameter, c (see Equation 6). This was set to 0.6 for the IK task and 0.3 for the AA task to best fit the data. Because the information distributions are more disjoint for the AA task, the value of the prior probability of P(S) was set to a higher value. Table 1 shows the number of categories formed by each participants and model, as well as their correlations. As predicted,

participants formed more categories in the AA task, reflecting the structures of the information sources. However, as shown earlier, participants in the AA task had lower rate of return in their information search, suggesting that they spent more time looking for relevant information. Although the number of categories formed was higher in the AA task, the quality of these categories (in terms of how much they help in finding information) was lower than those in the IK task (results shown next). The correlations between the participants and the models were high in both tasks, suggesting that the model roughly formed similar mental categories as participants, even though the inherent information structures were different between the two tasks.

DISCUSSION

From our knowledge, the current study is the first that shows social tagging systems not only can facilitate dissemination of information, but can also induce cognitive changes such as concept formation and knowledge assimilation. The current results also show that social tagging systems have the potential to facilitate not only collaborative indexing of the massive amount of information, but also as a means for social exchange of knowledge structures, and thus has the potential to promote formal or informal learning of diverse topics and the development of common schemas or understanding within or across different com-

Table 1. Number of categories formed by each participant and model, and the correlations of the partitions of the categories of the models and the students calculated using the match tables.

	#categories (Students)	#categories (Models)	Correlations of the partitions
IK1	6	6	0.71
IK2	5	6	0.68
AA1	12	13	0.59
AA2	10	11	0.67

munities. Given the direct impact on the development and refinement of mental schemas, it is not hard to imagine that social tagging systems could also impact collaborative activities that involve higher-level cognitive processing, such as problem solving, decision making, or creative designs. Indeed, many innovative ideas were generated by the sudden realization that knowledge structures in disjoint domains are relevant. It seems that we have only started to harness the potential of socio-technological systems, especially in the area of education.

The formal model was developed under the assumption that humans adapt their knowledge schemas through the assimilation and accommodation processes as they explore the Internet and comprehend knowledge extracted from web documents. The model, developed under the distributed cognition framework, was successful in providing good quantitative predictions on the emergent behavior of four different individuals across an extended period of time. The model shows how internal representations slowly assimilate to the external informational distribution through the processing and assignment of social tags, and how individuals create new tags based on their internal representations. The dynamic interactions between internal and external representations captured by the model has also highlighted the value of the distributed cognition framework, as they imply that isolated analysis of either the distributions of external tags or cognitive mechanisms of the user will unlikely lead to good characterizations of the dynamics that emerge from socio-technological systems.

The formal model also provides direct design guidelines for future social tagging systems. For example, the formal analysis of the current distributed cognitive system can be implemented as software tool that facilitates extraction and exchange of mental categories for different groups of people who have different expertise in different domains. Can tags, for example, be organized by mental categories extracted from experts in different fields in ways that facilitate knowledge

transfer? Will transfer or exchange of knowledge at the fact, concept, and category levels facilitate innovation because they encourage re-structuring of existing knowledge structures? The del.icio.us system in this study was a general-purpose social tagging system. The current results suggest that social tagging systems can be specialized for different purposes. For example, to facilitate context-aware learning, perhaps the systems can be combined with knowledge engineering software that extracts and classify knowledge according to top-down domain knowledge to facilitate knowledge adaptation.

REFERENCES

Ahern, S., Eckles, D., Good, N. S., King, S., Naaman, M., & Nair, R. (2007). Over-exposed? Privacy patterns and considerations in online and mobile photo sharing. *Proceedings of the SIGCHI Conference on Human Factors in Computing Systems*. San Jose, CA: ACM.

Ajjan, H., & Hartshorne, R. (2008). Investigating faculty decisions to adopt Web 2.0 technologies: Theory and empirical tests. *The Internet and Higher Education, 11*(2), 71–80. doi:10.1016/j. iheduc.2008.05.002

Alexander, B. (2006). Web 2.0: A new wave of innovation for teaching and learning? *Educause Review*.

Bhattacharya, M., & Dron, J. (2007). Cultivating the Web 2.0 jungle. *Seventh IEEE International Conference on Advanced Learning Technologies, ICALT 2007*.

Brewer, W. F., & Treyens, J. C. (1981). Role of schemata in memory for places. *Cognitive Psychology, 13*, 207–230. doi:10.1016/0010-0285(81)90008-6

Cattuto, C., Loreto, V., & Pietronero, L. (2007). Semiotic dynamics and collaborative tagging. *Proceedings of the National Academy of Sciences of the United States of America, 104,* 1461–1464. doi:10.1073/pnas.0610487104

Chin, J., Fu, W.-T., & Kannampalil, T. G. (2009). Adaptive information search: Age-dependent interactions between cognitive profiles and strategies. In *Proceedings of the ACM Conference on Computer-Human Interaction (CHI),* Boston, MA.

Ferdig, R. (2007). Examining social software in teacher education. *Journal of Technology and Teacher Education, 15*(1), 5–10.

Fox, G. C., Pierce, M. E., Mustacoglu, A. F., & Topcu, A. E. (2007). Web 2.0 for e-science environments. *Third International Conference on Semantics, Knowledge, and Grid.*

Fu, W.-T., & irolli, P. (2007). SNIF-ACT: A cognitive model of user navigation on the World Wide Web. *Human-Computer Interaction, 22,* 355–412.

Fu, W.-T. (2008). The microstructures of social tagging: A rational model. In *Proceedings of the ACM 2008 Conference on Computer Supported Cooperative Work (CSCW)* (pp. 229-238), San Diego, CA.

Golder, S. A., & Huberman, B. A. (2006). Usage patterns of collaborative tagging systems. *Journal of Information Science, 32*(2), 198–208. doi:10.1177/0165551506062337

Hollan, J., Hutchins, E., & Kirsh, D. (2000). Distributed cognition: Toward a new foundation for human-computer interaction research. *ACM Transactions on Computer-Human Interaction, 7*(2), 174–196. doi:10.1145/353485.353487

Hutchins, E. (1995). How a cockpit remembers its speeds. *Cognitive Science, 19,* 265–288.

Kaldoudi, E., Bamidis, P., Papaioakeim, M., & Vargemezis, V. (2008). Problem-based learning via Web 2.0 technologies. *21st IEEE International Symposium on Computer-Based Medical Systems, CBMS '08.*

Lam, S. K., & Churchill, E. (2007). The social Web: Global village or private cliques? *Proceedings of the 2007 Conference on Designing for User eXperiences.* Chicago, IL: ACM.

Lin, Y.-T., Chi, Y.-C., Chang, L.-C., Cheng, S.-C., & Huang, Y.-M. (2007). A Web 2.0 synchronous learning environment using ajax. *Ninth IEEE International Symposium on Multimedia 2007.*

Marchionini, G. (2006). Exploratory search: From finding to understanding. *Communications of the ACM, 49*(4), 41–46. doi:10.1145/1121949.1121979

Mason, R., & Rennie, F. (2007). Using Web 2.0 for learning in the community. *The Internet and Higher Education, 10*(3), 196–203. doi:10.1016/j.iheduc.2007.06.003

Millard, D. E., & Ross, M. (2006). Web 2.0: Hypertext by any other name? *Proceedings of the Seventeenth Conference on Hypertext and Hypermedia.* Odense, Denmark: ACM.

O'Reilly, T. (2005). What is Web 2.0: Design patterns and business models for the next generation of software. Retrieved on July 30, 2008, from http://www.oreillynet.com/pub/a/oreilly/tim/news/2005/09/30/what-is-web-20.html

Parise, S., & Guinan, P. J. (2008). Marketing using Web 2.0. *Proceedings of the 41st Hawaii International Conference on System Sciences.*

Piaget, J. (1975). *The equilibration of cognitive structures* (T. Brown, Trans.). Chicago, IL: The University of Chicago Press.

Pierce, M. E., Fox, G. C., Rosen, J., Maini, S., & Choi, J. Y. (2008). Social networking for scientists using tagging and shared bookmarks: A Web 2.0 application. *International Symposium on Collaborative Technologies and Systems*.

Rumelhart, D. E., & Ortony, A. (1976). *The representation of knowledge in memory*. La Jolla, CA: Center for Human Information Processing, Dept. of Psychology, University of California, San Diego.

Sen, S., Lam, S. K., Rashid, A. M., Cosley, D., Frankowski, D., & Osterhouse, J. (2006). Tagging, communities, vocabulary, evolution. [*th Anniversary Conference on Computer Supported Cooperative Work*. Banff, Alberta, Canada: ACM.]. *Proceedings of the*, *2006*, 20.

Takago, D., Matsuishi, M., Goto, H., & Sakamoto, M. (2007). Requirements for a Web 2.0 course management system of engineering education. *Ninth IEEE International Symposium onMultimedia, ISMW '07*.

Ullrich, C., Borau, K., Luo, H., Tan, X., Shen, L., & Shen, R. (2008). Why Web 2.0 is good for learning and for research: Principles and prototypes. *Proceeding of the 17th International Conference on World Wide Web*. Beijing, China: ACM.

White, R. W., Drucker, S. M., Marchionini, G., & Marti, H. M., & Schraefel, M. C. (2007). Exploratory search and hci: Designing and evaluating interfaces to support exploratory search interaction. *CHI '07 Extended Abstracts on Human Factors in Computing Systems*. San Jose, CA: ACM. `

Zhang, J., & Norman, D. (1994). Representations in distributed cognitive tasks. *Cognitive Science*, *18*, 87–122.

Chapter 8
ScreenPLAY:
An Interactive Video Learning Resource for At-Risk Teens

Evelyne Corcos
York University, Canada

Peter Paolucci
York University, Canada

ABSTRACT

This chapter explores the various facets of screenPLAY, an interactive video intervention for at-risk teens, which presents social skills in a medium that is both familiar and motivating to this age group. The chapter begins with a discussion of the pedagogical ideas that motivated the creation of screen-PLAY, from the necessity to move away from a skill-driven to a content-driven social-skill intervention, to promoting learning from experience, and then to the importance of clarifying learning objectives. In addition to the adoption of a constructivist perspective, a case is made for including cognitive and linguistic concomitants with social skill acquisition. A description is provided of how these additional two variables relate to behavior and the way they are integrated in the structure of the intervention. A cognitive skill is embedded in each of the eleven templates used to present content. Video clips displaying vignettes employing student actors are analyzed in a context that requires users to record their responses, thoughts, and observations in audio or text files that are uploaded to be accessed later by other users. The anonymity of both users and actors is protected, first, by the provision of an avatar to represent the user, and then, by having the video clips transformed into a comic book look. The technical details of the construction of this digital platform are provided, as well as a dialectic analyzing how the obstacles, encountered along the way, ultimately contributed to the overall innovative functionality. Future directions are examined in the context of screenPLAY's modular structure that allows the addition of content and functionality.

DOI: 10.4018/978-1-60566-826-0.ch008

INTRODUCTION

screenPLAY is a web-based assessment-intervention tool that was designed specifically to teach skills associated with the successful management of social situations. Developed with the intention of capitalizing on the many features of technology that teens find attractive, screenPLAY engages them through new media and interactive gaming technologies which generate the type of experience that appeals so much to their generation. Using imaging that emulates graphic novels, digital games, and animation-enhanced movies – key entertainments and touchstones for this demographic – screenPLAY is instantly intriguing to them because it presents their peers (adolescents of their own age) in familiar situations that resonate with their sense of the world. Thus, while engaged and at play, they are also learning and building the skills which will have the potential to change their lives in ways beneficial to themselves, their families, their educators, and society in general. Our intention is that screenPLAY should represent an opportunity for the convergence of learning and pop culture, the purpose being to access a previously unreachable demographic.

In the school context, at-risk adolescents typically under-perform while manifesting a range of antisocial behaviors including aggressiveness, violence, various types of addiction, and untreated emotional problems. Not surprisingly, when these students frequently find the school experience unrelated to their reality they consequently disconnect and choose to leave. Lacking, as a consequence, both literacy and the employment skills required for legitimate job seeking, some are attracted to criminal behavior; others, succumbing to addiction, mental illness, or the burdens of parenthood at a very young age, become integrated into the social welfare system, where public institutions sustain them.

The creation of screenPLAY was motivated initially by a desire to develop a tool that would serve both as assessment and as intervention in a social curriculum for at-risk youth. Rejecting the "wait until they fail" (Kaufman, 1999) model, such a tool was expected to benefit both students and teachers because social skills, unlike other curricula taught in a classroom, are addressed incidentally only as part of an unintended curriculum. Typically, when an inappropriate situation occurs, perhaps it motivates attention that might take the form of a discussion, a story, or a movie. Usually, however, compliance is encouraged with the use of mild punishment – time out, loss of privileges, being sent to the office, and other methods. screenPLAY, then, would not only help teachers to present these skills in a systematic manner but would also generate data about the typical ways in which at-risk youth, or youth in general, deal with the many social demands placed on them in their varied social and educational contexts. With the addition of this social perspective to the classroom environment, learning to deal with other people, finding appropriate ways to have one's personal needs met, and other such important proficiencies are addressed in a learning environment that is safe and wholesome.

The most central challenge in the social skills curriculum has involved the realization that no unique "scientifically based technology of behavior" exists (Kehle & Bray, 2004). On the other hand, many psychological theories abound, each with independent ways of explaining behavior; as a result, each promotes interventions consistent with the relevant interpretation. In educational settings, academic skills, such as literacy and numeracy, as well as subject-specific skills (e.g., science, history), have been studied and organized to generate pedagogical objectives. Social skills, however, have not; although an examination of social skills programs demonstrates that many are fashioned parallel to other academic curricula, they are skill-driven (Mathur & Rutherford, 1994) and as such, overlook that they are normally acquired implicitly, and usually target the behavior of young children. Finally, educators generally do not teach social skills explicitly (Kehle & Bray,

2004), although those who do typically rely on approaches involving "knowledge-telling", that is, having students learn the pre-set steps to conflict resolution, in a way similar, for example, to finding out how to divide with a two-digit divisor.

In order to circumvent this predicament, it was decided that screenPLAY should not be skill-driven, nor involve "knowledge-telling", but rather should be context-driven. Prosocial behavior is reliant on the appropriate application of skills essential to a specific situation: depending on the context, an individual uses a different language form when speaking to the "boss" or to a friend in an informal setting. Similarly, social appropriateness is determined in the same manner – assaulting a person is accepted in war and in self-defense situations but not in daily life.

When the focus is the context, two additional dimensions become relevant: social communication, an approach that teaches and offers practice in language (Pennebaker, Mehl, & Niederhoffer, 2003), and social cognition, in thinking involved in problem-solving, found naturally in many social contexts meaningful to youths. Another reason to shift from a skill-based framework is also required in order to address the lack of skill transfer that plagues many programs. If an individual engaged in an intervention is not capable of using the newly learned skills in everyday situations, the efficacy of the program is called into question. . It should be noted that transfer of learning is inherently difficult (O'Callaghan, Reitman, Northup, Hupp, & Murphy, 2003) because knowing does not imply the ability to integrate such knowledge in a behavioral repertoire. By addressing the linguistic and cognitive issues inherent in social skills, however, as well as constructing opportunities for transfer of learning, we have expected a greater likelihood of success. For example, many researchers (Sanger, Hux, & Riztman, 1999; Sanger, Coufal, Scheffler, & Searcey, 2003) identify pragmatic situations that address such as topics as: 'what is conversation?'; 'what stops conversation?'; 'the speaker's job' ; 'keeping a conversation

going'; 'providing adequate information during conversational exchanges'; 'the listener's job'; 'negotiating'; 'solving problems'; 'disagreeing effectively during conversations'; and 'expressing feelings'.

For any intervention to be effective, it must have the commitment and full engagement of the participants. In addition to creating a theoretically sound underlying structure for the content, it is necessary to insure that the content is both meaningful and motivating to the learner (Covington, 2000). Corcos (2003) argues that motivating a student to participate in an intentional learning activity requires a particular manipulation of the variables: meaningfulness—the identifiable level of personal relevance between the student and the content of the curriculum; difficulty—the level of difficulty found in concepts, vocabulary, and other elements; and novelty—the level of familiarity detectable in the presentation, content, and activities. As they are experienced in combination, the three levels will raise or decrease a student's motivation to engage in a particular learning activity.

screenPLAY, then, addresses meaningfulness by insuring that the content of all activities will be personally relevant to life-like situations. Second, to minimize frustration, the demands of each task are sequentially ordered from low to increasingly difficult levels (Corcos, 2003), with the user always having the choice to go back, examine the work of others, and re-do each task. In addition, for students with literacy difficulty, the multi-media platform insures that regardless of competence, every student has the option to participate. Anonymity of the student also works in favor of the reticent student.

An additional consideration for this age group is their fascination with gaming and technology. Other interventions (Carbonaro et al., 2008; Hartley, 2007; Hubal, Fishbein, Sheppard, Paschall, Eldreth, & Hyde, 2008; Smokowski & Hartung, 2003) take advantage of the fact that users not only enjoy playing computer games but are also motivated to pay attention to content presented in the new technologies, as well as learning through play and gaming (de Castell & Jenson, 2004). In the case of ScreenPLAY, we see technology as a feasible substitute for face-to-face options, because, despite realizing that they are interacting with a computer and not a person, students still behave as if they were encountering a human (Nass & Moon, 2000). For example, Nass & Moon (2000) discovered that a male voice employed to encourage the user is perceived as confident and friendly, while a female voice is found more preferable in conjunction with love and relationship topics. In addition, when the computer program is perceived as helpful, for example, when it provides hints, the user is likely to work harder, and, when a digital character appears to disclose personal information, the user is more likely to reciprocate. ScreenPLAY incorporates a novel web presentation of the content that includes cartoon-like animation, as well as sound clips, reminiscent of a game-like format. The user receives immediate feedback regarding performance and is awarded points for such action as: time on task, satisfactory completion of an activity, repetition of an activity when the student deems it is warranted by performance levels. .

In this chapter, we have, so far, provided the ideas and thoughts that motivated the creation of screenPLAY. These introductory concepts will be followed by sections discussing the psychological, linguistic, and cognitive factors underlying the intervention; also detailed will be the pedagogical framework and its relationship to the functionality of screenPLAY. The technological underpinnings, as well as the rationale behind the choices, will be explored. Finally, we will outline the research implications and future directions of this project.

Psychological Aspects

Poor social skills are known to be linked to depression (Segrin, 2000) and to other psychosocial problems (Segrin, 2001) such as learning disabilities (Elias, 2004), Attentional Deficit Hyperactivity Disorder (Ylvisaker & DeBonis, 2000), Conduct Disorders (Joffe, Dobson, Fine, Marriage, & al, 1990), Oppositional Defiant Disorder (Frankel & Feinberg, 2002; Matthys, Cuperus, & Van-Engeland, 1999), and delinquency (Kadish, Glaser, Calhoun, & Ginter, 2001; Palmer & Hollin, 1999; Sarris, Winefield, & Cooper, 2000). Of the many social skills interventions for reducing antisocial behavior, however, cognitive behavioral interventions fare the best (Losel & Beelmann, 2003) and demonstrate the highest level of success.

Of course, the problems of such youth are not a new phenomenon; over the years, a variety of theories have attempted to explain why these adolescents are not socialized into the middle class to become good citizens. Most of these explanations allude to biological, psychological, and sociological variables (Corcos, 2003), but in order to produce a psychological framework for ScreenPLAY, it was necessary to articulate the learning theory that would form its basis. Considering that children and adolescents acquire their social skills through the process of observation – by modeling the behavior of others (Bandura, 1997; Bandura, 2001) -- young persons may, by noticing, be able to ascertain which behavior is rewarded and which is punished. But simple observation does not provide access to the more salient information that is not observable – the metacognitive processes and the covert language that take place unnoticed. Without a focus on these two additional dimensions, transfer of knowledge from one situation to another (classroom, family) can lead to the creation of misconceptions. Consider this analogy: As a result of encountering arithmetic problems with unique answers, a student might erroneously conclude that a single right answer exists in all situations involving problem-solving. Likewise, because aggressive confrontation is helpful in dealing with a bully on the street, a young person might adopt this method to resolve all disagreements. Not to be forgotten are the mistaken attributions that stem from the egocentric perspectives of children and young persons; for example, the common youthful concept that punished behavior is synonymous with being disliked.

If the acquisition of social skill occurs by learning from experience, then it is possible to tap into Kolb's (1984) theory of Experiential Learning with its two principal ways of knowing: by direct experience – apprehension, the concrete knowing that is developed in the context of screenPLAY vignettes and by knowing about – comprehension, the abstract knowing that is the outcome of completing the cognitive activities. After all, it is through experience that individuals intentionally extract meaning from events, and ultimately will test their abstract assumptions (Atherton, 2002). The development of schemas of social constructs will continue to evolve and become more refined as more contexts are encountered.

We have adopted a social constructivist perspective (Karagiorgi & Symeou, 2005) for screenPLAY because, first and foremost, as described in the previous paragraphs, the designer must lay a foundation consisting of a deep understanding of the learning theory behind the intervention.

For the social constructivists, knowledge is viable not only personally, but also in social contexts (Tobin & Tippings, 1993), while reality is viewed as a constructive process embedded in socio-cultural practices (Duffy & Cunningham, 1996). Culture provides different types of tools to help us construct meaning. For example, language, the most frequent of these tools, is characterized by a dynamic process of interchange during which meanings are chosen. Our construction of meaning is grounded in the groups to which we belong through social interactions (von Glasersfeld, 1995; Willis, 1998). Correspondingly, learning that focuses exclusively on individual construction of knowledge is inadequate; our experiential world appears as a negotiation between individual and social knowledge, whose contributions have a dialectical relationship and cannot be meaningfully separated. (p.18)

Some additional considerations involve the idea that learning is a social and not just a private event. The learner acquires knowledge from the environment, often testing its validity by implementing it in social contexts, and then obtaining confirmation of its appropriateness from personally relevant groups. For this reason, we have included in screenPLAY a collaborative component that conveys both the thoughts and language of other users as a validation. Examining the anonymous responses made by other users will also serve as a form of reciprocal tutoring (Wong, Chan, Chou, Heh, & Tung, 2003).

The Linguistic Aspect

In the process of examining the social skills of at-risk youth, it is surprising to discover that a high percentage of youth exhibiting maladaptive behavior also demonstrate language difficulties (see Table 1 and 2). The same pattern is evident when comparing delinquent to non-delinquent youth. To date, however, social skills interventions have not directly targeted at-risk youths with language impairment or language difficulties, although some programs include pragmatic skills (Bourke, 2001). When examining delinquents, researchers (Davis, Sanger, & Morris-Friehe, 1991; Sanger et al., 1999; Sanger et al., 2003; Sanger et al., 2000; Spitzberg & Dillard, 2002) find that many in this group not only manifest language disabilities but also, frequently, have not received services to treat their problems (Sanger et al., 2000). Similar results are known to exist with youths referred for psychiatric difficulties (Cohen, Barwick, Horodezky, Vallance, & Im, 1998; Cohen, 2001; Cohen et al., 1998; Vallance, Im, & Cohen, 1999). In addition, children of low socio-economic status are shown, very early in their educational careers, to have very weak language skills, and to be less engaged than the average student in intentional learning (Rogoff, Paradise, Arauz, Correa-Chavez, & Angelillo,

2003), as well as to manifest more social problems (Qi & Kaiser, 2004). Of additional interest, when considering the problem of such youth, are the relationships among psychopathy, empathy, and communication (Soderstrom, 2003).

Whereas research has traditionally focused on risky behavior rather than person variables (McKay, 2003), a shift to examining aspects of the at-risk person highlights primarily biological variables and contextual situations. Important are the connections among language, cognition, and social behavior because these dictate the manner in which a person addresses the demands of a particular environment. After all, the relationship of linguistic skills to social behavior is compelling, if, as Halliday (Halliday, 1975) suggests, language development occurs in a social context:

Because all our linguistic acts as adults, are mediated by the ideational and interpersonal systems, which are the center of the language system we create for ourselves, every act is not only linguistic, a use of the potential of the language system, but social and cultural, an expression of who we are and what we gave value to.

It should not be forgotten that in social contexts, both verbal and non-verbal language play a central role by allowing individuals to communicate their intentions and feelings to others (Conger, Neppl, & Kim, 2003; Diener, Oishi, & Lucas, 2003; Eisenberg, 2000; Furlong & Smith, 1998) to understand and interpret events in various settings (Davis et al., 1991; de Montes, Semin, & Valencia, 2003); to negotiate with others for chosen things (Gobbo, C., & Chi, M., 1986; Hastie, 2001; Keysar, 2000; Keysar, Barr, Balin, & Brauner, 2000); to mediate

Table 1. Proportion with language impairment

Proportion with Language Impairment	Population	Previously Identified	Severity/Type of Behavior	Source
50%		no	Severe	(Gualtieru, Koriath, Van-Bourgondien, & Saleeby, 1983)
33%		no	Less severe	(N. J. Cohen, Davine, & Meloche-Kelly, 1989)
68%	Institutionalized delinquents	no	Communication disorders	(Taylor, 1969)
75% (Normal=66%) 50% -- 1.5 SD below the M	Deliquent vs. Nondelinquent	no	Informal test TOAL-2 Test of Adolescent Language	(Davis et al., 1991)

Table 2. Proportion of LI with psychiatric disorders

Proportion of LI with Psychiatric Disorders	Population	Previously Identified	Type of Disorder	Source
46%	Psychiatric outpatients	no	ADHD	(N. J. Cohen et al., 1998)
63%	7-14 yr. Psychiatric outpatients	no	ADHD	(N. Cohen et al., 2000)
66%	7-14 yr. Psychiatric outpatients N=380		Conduct Disorders	(N. J. Cohen et al., 1998)

when faced with problem solving (Bosley, 1998; McHugh, Barnes-Holmes, & Barnes-Holmes, 2004); albeit to develop their sense of self (Caire, Pliner, & Stoker, 1998; Caire, & Cosgrove, 1995; Ellemers, Spears, & Doosje, 2002). Furthermore, both aspects of language provide the protocols for engaging in interpersonal relationships with strangers, acquaintances, peers, and significant others (Coleman, Catan, & Dennison, 1997; Mathur & Rutherford, 1994; Mignault & Chaudhuri, 2003; Miller, 2001; Rutherford, 2004).

Overall, a general level of support exists for the idea that non-verbal and problematic behavior, exhibited by delinquents, is, to some extent, related to their inability to acquire age-appropriate speech and language skills (Carr & Durand, 1985). Conversely, children with Specific Language Impairment will continue to manifest the same behavior problems into their teenage years, depending on their levels of narrative retelling skills and expressive syntax (Botting, Faragher, Simkin, Knox, & Conti-Ramsden, 2001; Botting & Conti-Ramsden, 2008; Conti-Ramsden & Botting, 2004). In addition, certain types of language impairment may produce a range of behavioral difficulties (Goodyer, 2000); for example, comprehension problems were able to predict behavior ratings (Lindsay & Dockrell, 2000). Interestingly, studies of children with language/learning disabilities indicate the presence of pragmatic rather than knowledge deficits (Lapadat, 1991), semantic rather than syntactic errors (McCabe & Meller, 2004), and problems with interpretation of metaphors as well as oral expression (Vallance & Wintre, 1997). The ability to use covert language (Abbeduto, Short-Meyerson, Benson, & Dolish, 2004; Minowa, 1997) may be seen to impact on the ability to analyze challenging social situations and to arrive at a plan of action or comprehension (Callicott, 2003). Last of all, language ability may be implicated in various ways in the social expression of emotions, personal expectations, sense of self, and personal relationships (Sullivan & Ruffman, 2004).

Deriving meaning from non-verbal information plays an important role in social communication; for example, facial expressions (Schmidt & Cohn, 2001), behavioral mimicry (Patterson, 2003; Van Swol, 2003), laughter (Patterson, 2003), eye gaze (Adams & Kleck, 2005; Adams & Kleck, 2003; Kelly, 2001), pointing gestures (Kelly, 2001), and vocal features (Rockwell, 2000; Russell, Bachorowski, & Fernandez-Dols, 2003). When these non-verbal forms of language are analyzed, both the perception and the production of facial expressions are believed to represent cognitive processes with the involvement of subcortical and cortical areas (Erickson & Schulkinb, 2003). The interpretation of this non-verbal information impacts on social communication and behavior; included here would be, for example, such constructs as politeness (Laplante & Ambady, 2003), dominance (Mignault & Chaudhuri, 2003), social anxiety (McClure & Nowicki Jr, 2001; Mullins & Duke, 2004), cooperation and trustworthiness (Boone & Buck, 2003), truthfulness (Vrij, Akehurst, Soukara, & Bull, 2004). Interestingly, individuals who perceive themselves as capable of reading the minds of others are found to be capable of perceiving emotions in the faces and speech patterns of those others (Realo et al., 2003). All of these must be translated into a virtual environment that expresses these constructs and social codes.

The Cognitive Aspect

Inner speech is perceived as the vehicle for internalizing experience, executing complex tasks, planning, and problem solving (Vygotsky, 1978). Using inner speech – speaking in the mind's ear – promotes a reflective style, one that involves thinking before acting. Behavioral options, plans, and consequences are considered before committing to a course of action. Common in young children and many at-risk youth is the inverse -- an impulsive style where actions pre-empt any thinking or consideration. ScreenPLAY is designed to promote a reflective style.

A cognitive perspective also concerns itself with the information processing abilities of the student. If the student possesses an intact modality which can be used to produce learning, it should be promoted as a fundamental remedial strategy, especially in those students who exhibit a broad array of strengths and weaknesses. For example, recognizing a student's visual memory strengths as a means of improving weak language skills appears to be an appropriate instructional practice. The multi-media aspect of screenPLAY provides the option to learn through the student's strengths, to overcome the student's weaknesses, or to access both strategies (Corcos, 2003).

In screenPLAY, learning activities are presented in the form of games played in a framework of eleven templates. Because each template focuses on a specific cognitive skill, the user will play many games with varying content that will reinforce the same cognitive skill. In a manner similar to the one by which individuals develop semantic knowledge – through a variety of life experiences -- screenPLAY attempts to simulate the same process. Each game requires users to observe a video clip that highlights an interaction between characters in a specific situation and setting. In order to play, the user must be capable not only of understanding what is taking place but also of making judgments; for example in the template "Feelings—see and hear", the user must be able, for each character, to pinpoint the body language associated with a particular feeling.

Several templates display environments that require the identification of emotions, instances, (and non-instances) of classes of behavior, perspective-taking, and other types of social problem-solving. This platform, especially created for presenting cartoon-like video clips of social situations, offers a game-like environment in which teens choose potential options for resolving the social problems; then, using video, sound, or text, participants provide reasons for their choices -- an important

feature for promoting language and cognitive skills. A searchable database allows students to request the voting record of other students, along with their verbal rationales, in order to examine social standards, not, however, to promote right/wrong answers. At all times, the identity of students is protected by a cartoon filter that makes video images unidentifiable; in addition, avatars are used to represent the participant. Not only do the avatars themselves provide both privacy and a public identity (nerds, athletes, gender-ambivalence), but each avatar has a range of seven different emotions (neutral. anger, disgust, fear, happiness, surprise, grief). Administrators (teachers) can track student progress by monitoring the activity and progress of any given student's avatar.

In the first template "Instance or not", users are asked to view a video clip and decide whether it exemplifies a certain dominant behavior. The objective here is to develop the user's receptive vocabulary by presenting the names of dominant behaviors and their respective definitions. Such knowledge would be useful in other activities. For example, in the template "What happened", the user is required to describe the events in a situation; it is hoped that the vocabulary recently acquired in the previous template will assist the user with this new cognitive demand.

In more thoroughly examining the demands of the first template, "Instance or not", (see Figure 1), we previously stated that the user is asked to make judgments about examples and non-instances of particular social concepts (politeness, bullying behavior, honesty, etc.). When the user chooses this template, a video clip plays, while an audio file asks "Is this an example of polite behavior?" The user is offered two options: the "Yes" and "No" buttons. The higher order cognitive activity appears in the next requirement. The user is asked to justify the choice, by audio recording an answer that is tagged to the avatar chosen earlier to represent the user. At this point, the user has access to a definition providing information about polite behavior (See Figure 2) which can be consulted. To encourage checking and reinforcing the definition, the words are later used in a Scramble game played for points.

Once a rationale is provided for the answer chosen, the user may request to see how other users have voted. This data is displayed in graph form. The next step provides the audio recordings of rationales generated by other users to justify their decisions. Three audio files are available, each represented by an avatar. The user is then asked to make a judgment about which of the four justifications is more effective; three belong to other users, one belongs to the originator. By dragging and dropping the avatars in boxes, rank ordered from most effective to least effective, the user employs higher order skills. The final step in this sequence involves a prompt to add or change responses if necessary.

The learning level is enhanced when a "lightning round", is played for points; this is included for additional motivation, practice, and overlearning. The template's difficulty can be increased by making aspects of the video clip more subtle (three levels of difficulty – low, medium, and high – are assigned to each video clip) or by increasing task demands (See "What happened?" template). As always, the user may replay the clip many times and choose whether questions are in text or in audio. The exposure of students to both receptive and expressive language is met by this format. The final screen also displays and records the score. Points are awarded for time-on-task, number of models consulted, and other behaviors. Always, the student may re-do the activity.

Two supplementary activities are included in most templates: one to cement vocabulary, the other to promote transfer of learning. As mentioned earlier, in the process of encouraging vocabulary development, the Scramble game displays anagrams of words taken from the definitions of target behavior. Because of the memory process called priming (Tulving & Schacter, 1990), anagram solutions are completed faster by users who have consulted the definitions. This opportunity to earn

Figure 1. The "Instance or Not" template

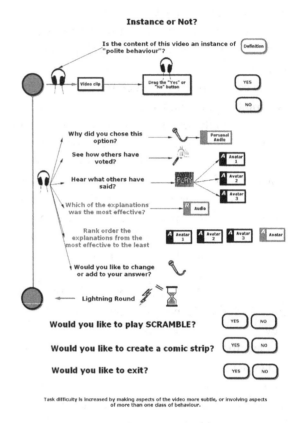

Figure 2. Definition screen for polite behavior and scramble game. The student is encouraged to read the definition of the behaviour addressed in the scenario.

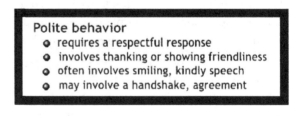

And then words

bonus points intensifies the experience, contributes to the game-like atmosphere, and encourages participation in activities that might otherwise be overlooked by the user. Transfer of learning is the objective of the comic strip, an aspect that is strengthened when users are required to produce a situation associated with the target behavior, derived either from a personal experience or from a newly created one. Users have the choice of characters, contexts – they can choose from a set of backdrops, and text bubbles.

The template "What happened?" (See Figure 3) has a similar structure to the first. It is our intention to insure a level of familiarity in the structure of templates in order to obtain a rapid learning curve regarding task variables between templates. A proper amount of task familiarity is required to maintain motivation. In this template, the levels of difficulty are more visible. For the easy and medium levels of difficulty, users watch a video clip and then choose from three options the best description of the events. In the "difficult level" no options are provided and users are asked to record their own description. Because options are provided in the first two levels, users are given models for the type of response that is required; it is hoped this knowledge will be incorporated when their own descriptions are required.

In teaching students to understand and interpret events in various settings (Davis et al., 1991; de Montes et al., 2003), templates such as "What happened?" and "Choose a title" develop the cognitive skills of comprehension, as well as synthesis (Bloom, 1974) respectively. For example in "Choose a Title," the student must identify the common thread linking observed events. After seeing a clip and three optional titles, the student drags and drops the best one. As with other templates, elements become complex, more options are added, and, finally, in this one, instead of choosing from a set of options, the user now must generate a personally created title.

Because both verbal and non-verbal language play a central role in allowing individuals to

Figure 3. "What happened?" template

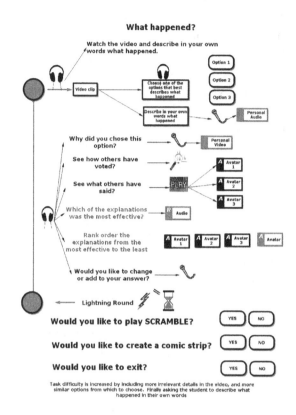

communicate intentions and feelings (Conger et al., 2003; Diener et al., 2003; Eisenberg, 2000; Furlong & Smith, 1998), two templates have been created: "Feelings" and "Feelings – Hear, See"; the former asks the student to associate affective observations with verbal labels, while "Feelings – Hear, See" targets recognition of non-verbal aspects of emotions. "Feelings" requires the student to watch a video clip and to choose the element that best describes the emotion(s) expressed by the character. To increase difficulty, more complex emotions appear and more subtle labels will be added: e.g., jealousy vs. envy. Then the student is asked to identify the character's feelings. The template "Feelings – Hear, See" asks which visual and auditory markers indicate the character's emotions. The question is asked, for example, "What did you see and hear that indicates anger?" As difficulty increases, more subtle non-verbal details are added, while the options require more probing judgments and the student is required to use personal language to list the cues indicating emotions.

A relationship between causality and language (Mohan & van Naerssen, 1997) is explored in the games "Cause and Effect" and "Reading between the Lines." In addition to being asked to isolate the contingencies that bind events, students are also encouraged to make inferences (Penn & Povinelli, 2007). "Cause and Effect" initially pinpoints the consequence of the action in a video clip. At first, when options are offered, the user may choose the one that represents the most realistic consequence. Later, complexity is added with more similar nuanced choices, along with a requirement to describe the appropriate consequence. "Reading between the Lines" elicits examination of information and then observation of character interaction, asking whether friends, acquaintances, or foes are involved; perhaps a verbal threat has been made although it is not stated.

Two other templates, "Problem Solving" and "Perspective taking", encourage users to learn to negotiate with others for chosen things (Gobbo, C.,& Chi, M., 1986; Hastie, 2001; Keysar et al., 2000; Keysar, 2000), to mediate when faced with a problem (Bosley, 1998; McHugh et al., 2004), and to adopt the perspective of another person (McHugh et al., 2004; Soderstrom, 2003). In the game "Problem Solving", video clips of situations requiring win-win solutions for all parties are presented. Users select a clip from a set and then later must explain the most appropriate solution. The template "Perspective Taking" presents a video biography, requiring the user to imitate the character and complete the game by role-playing that individual. At first, a closed set of options is provided; then the student produces a personal response.

After the mastery of the cognitive skills highlighted in the templates, the final one, "Direct your own video", requires the integration of all the previous skills, and, in keeping with Bloom's

(1974) concept of application, this one is the true test of the user's knowledge acquisition.

The learning that takes place is expected to be both iterative and incremental, with exercises increasing in complexity and subtlety as the student's exposure to the resource increases. Just as important, users are in control of when and how quickly they advance through the material. This intervention, then, uses a web-based education format to promote learning from experience (Kolb, 1984; Aggarwal, 2003), and one that empowers students with choice and timing.

INTERVENTIONS USING IT

In exploring the various social skills interventions using technology as a medium, it is evident that there is no unifying educational theory of technology (de Castell, Bryson, & Jenson, 2002). Such a theory would not only guide the integration of educational goals into new technologies but would, in the schools, also promote the use of software that is educationally-driven rather than technology-driven.

We did not find an initiative that addresses all the issues undertaken by screenPLAY. Several programs have piqued our interest, however, because they focus on issues that we believe are important. For example, the use of a game platform to promote both social and cognitive factors is found in Phoenix Quest (Young & Upitis, 1999) and STARstreams obtains positive outcomes when students are asked to view videos of social conflict and then use on-line discussion (Goldsworthy, Schwartz, Barab, & Landa, 2007). There are many differences, however. For instance, Phoenix Quest, in teaching Math and Science, provides a body of knowledge that is not as personal as screenPLAY's experiential basis. STARstreams, which is closer to screenPLAY's intentions, does not allow for an older demographic -- it deals with grades 5 and 6 -- and contains less interactivity, while lacking the incremental and iterative dimensions.

Although many interventions target Autistic users (see Robins, Dickerson, Stribling, & Dautenhahn, 2004), we found Bishop's (2003) PARLE system interesting because, with the intention of helping users to comprehend and define emotions, as well as to communicate with peers, it uses cell phones to allow individuals with Autistic Spectrum Disorder (ASD) to interpret dialogue, prosody – tone of the utterance, and facial expressions. After all, ASD users represent the extreme of the social-skills distribution on a continuum of social impairment. This general direction seems to us to be a fruitful one.

Hartley (2007) examines technology in five teaching situations: direct instruction, adjunct instruction, facilitating the skills of learning, facilitating social skills, and widening learners' horizons, as well as in five different contexts: primary schools, secondary schools, higher education, special education, and out of school. With reference to direct instruction, computer-based instruction yields better results than traditional methods in Mathematics and Sciences, but negative effects for literacy activities, with the most pronounced benefits to younger children and students with special needs. Examining adjunct (blended) instruction reveals that where the technology and teacher work together collaboratively, advantages occur when the technology is in-line with and supportive of teacher instruction. This is consistent with our conviction that ScreenPLAY should be offered to teachers willing to integrate it into their curricula. Although users would have a certain amount of independence to complete activities, when teachers are able to adopt the roles of mentor and facilitator, they will elicit greater student engagement along with transfer of learning, if content from screenPLAY is discussed and applied in the classroom.

Hartley's (2007) review of social skills and new technology indicates a primary focus dealing with collaborative learning because the role of the classroom is justified as part of what is being addressed: "As Philip Jackson (1968) pointed out long ago, pupils in classrooms have to learn to deal with problems arising from overcrowding, different sources of power, pupil–pupil and pupil–teacher relationships, and success and failure."

Other researchers have recognized that because many users enjoy playing computer games, they are motivated to pay attention to the content presented in the new technologies, as well as to learning through play and gaming (de Castell & Jenson, 2004), and to acquire cognitive and literacy skills (Gee, 2003) . For example, Carbonaro et al. (2008) created ScriptEase (www.cs.ualberta.ca/~script/), a tool to be used in conjunction with commercial ones that allows students to create interactive games' stories and to make the reader an active participant in the story. There is no doubt that the work of Carbonaro et al. (2008) supports the constructivist perspective by differentiating between "players of games", which is the user role in most games, and "builders or designer of games", the role they promote in their learning tool.

Fenstermacher et al. (2006) explore the social skills of students with attention and hyperactive disorders. Recognizing that these students manifest skill deficits, their intervention consists of computer-facilitated direct instruction activities focusing on seven identified sub-skills of problem solving determined *a priori*. Using videos depicting real-world situations, these skills are presented by a peer actor who also models problem-solving situations. This is followed by instruction using an approach recommended in *The Tough Kid Social Skills Book* (Sheridan, 1995) -- chalk and chalkboard, narrated voice-over, television. The effectiveness of their intervention is assessed by observing video-recorded role-play activities involving the student in similar situations. The same process is repeated for each problem-solving sub-skill which consists of body basics – eye contact, maintaining appropriate distance, body posture, and voice; waiting for a good time to start problem solving; demonstrating self-control; recognizing the problem; generating at least one alternative; generating a second alternative if the first one does not pan out; ending an interaction. Most interesting is the operational definition of these sub-skills.

Smokowski (2003) discusses the various techniques employed by social workers in behavioral intervention with school children. These include simulations such as improvisation, role-playing, psychodrama, and behavioral rehearsal, which are used to develop and bolster specific skills, as well as considering and rehearsing a variety of responses in the context of a safe environment. New technologies have been applied to these interventions to produce computer-simulation and virtual-reality applications. Smokowski (2003) concludes that whereas computer simulations are most commonly applied in the commercial gaming industry to deliver entertainment, they have not been applied to acquiring prosocial skills even though users are very motivated to try them.

A more technologically sophisticated intervention is described by Hubal et al. (2008) who discuss the use of Embodied Conversational Agents (ECAs). These consist of virtual characters, displayed on a video monitor, who are capable of engaging a user in conversation. Such an application incorporates: a language processor which accepts spoken, typed, or other input from the user and maps it to an underlying semantic representation; a behavior and planning engine which accepts semantic content and other information, and guides ECA behavior using cognitive, social, linguistic, physiological, planning, and other models; and a visualizer which displays the ECA performing gesture, movement, and speech actions. Although the authors endorse social-skills simulations, role playing, and ECA simulations as effective, they believe that ECAs have the additional advantage of creating a safe environment for the users.

In terms of structure, their first study (Hubal et al., 2008) has many features that overlap with screenPLAY. The decision-making and social competence of high-risk adolescents is evaluated by focusing on skills associated with emotional control, information seeking, expressing one's own preferences, negotiation and willingness to compromise, and using non-provocative language. Structured interviews are provided to evaluate baseline skill levels and then users are shown a video "Workin' It Out" designed to train negotiation and conflict-resolution skills. Vignettes are created for the purpose of evaluating what users would do in challenging situations; for example, in a vignette about stolen goods, the user is asked to put a bag in his/her locker. The response to the request is evaluated on the basis of various behavioral dimensions – seeking information, denying the request, verbalizing feelings, and other possibilities.

Relevant to our intervention, these authors have discovered that users find pre-recorded speech much more acceptable than any currently available speech synthesizer; the more realistic the ECA, the better the user interaction; any speech disruptions by the ECA interfere with the flow of conversation; a spoken rather than typed interface increases the realism and believability of the dialogue. Hubal et al. (2008) conclude that future ECAs should respond to the user's tone and body language in order to produce advantages over video or still images, therefore encouraging more engagement. We were inspired by their use of ECA and will consider this application in future directions of screenPLAY.

ACCESS, PERMISSIONS AND BASIC FUNCTIONALITY

screenPLAY has a generalized public area open to everyone (http://screenplay.glendon.yorku.ca/) but, beyond this promotional page, there are three levels of secured access for administrators, users, and guests. Guest-level access allows outsiders to view the main features of screenPLAY without seeing anything that would reveal the users' identity, and with yet-to-be-determined features that would remain hidden for security and privacy reasons.

This third level is yet to be implemented.

Administrators create, modify, and delete user accounts. They also create scenarios by uploading pre-edited and processed video clips, and they design and input specific questions relevant to the video clips, as well as contextually appropriate (rubric) for the relevant eleven templates. This input is gathered through Flash and then passed to the database via XML.

Administrators can also monitor and therefore analyze user activities such as time-on-task, frequency of use, frequency of viewing repetitions, frequency and quality of inter-user reactions, and so on. In addition, they can also design the mapping of multi-media content to a database of context-sensitive keywords, a mapping that is able to define the search logic in the resource. Because the database behind screenPLAY is a combination of XML and MySQL, all data, including all multimedia, are mapped to flat ASCII labels and keywords to allow the processing and locating of information to happen very quickly. Future functionality will allow teachers to oversee the creation and uploading of new video scenarios and activity templates; but, for the time being, this administrator capability is reserved for project investigators.

The administrator's uploading or previewing of video and audio clips is accomplished through Flash (.SWF); the .SWF file is embedded in a PHP page, which, in turn, logs the session, connects to the database, retrieves any required data, launches the appropriate .SWF file, and then passes any required information -- for example, the administrator and scenario identification -- to the .SWF file, either through an encoded-URL query string or via FlashVars.

The second level of access permission is for the user. Users must first request a screenPLAY account, by providing personal information, and then select an avatar and an emotion to their liking – perhaps one that corresponds best to their sense of self. The system (database) then encodes the user's choice of avatar that will be recalled upon login; next it encodes the user information—name, gender, age, school affiliation, etc.—, and, subsequently, it will organize and manage the video and audio file information associated with the user; concurrently, it will encode data about user access and interaction with the scenario clips. The "request account" page is an embedded Flash application. Once the user has filled in the required information, Flash posts this data to a

Figure 4. An example of an avatar and its range of emotions Avatars are also found in the three-panel, drag-and-drop comic strip creation tool. Upon the completion of an activity, a user is asked to create a comic strip related to the social issue that was encountered. All of the avatars are available for this purpose including the individual's own (see Figure 5).

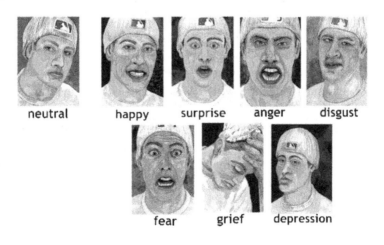

Figure 5. The comic strip creator

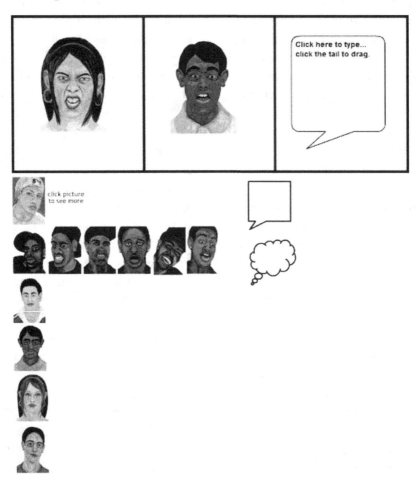

PHP page where it is processed and then emailed to screenPLAY's administrator. In this way, a non-registered user has no direct access to the screenPLAY database, security being an essential component of the project. Currently, permissions are approved by the administrator, but, in future, a "manager level" access may allow teachers to replicate this process for their own students. Our reservation recognizes that such a feature will increase access to user private information by others and, therefore, expand the number of security risks involved in protecting privacy.

Currently, a set of six avatars drawn by a graphic artist to represent a series of teen stereotypes -- jock, nerd, gender-ambivalent male, gender-ambivalent female, and others -- is available to users with the expectation that more will become available as the project unfolds. For each avatar, seven different emotions are available -- neutral, anger, disgust, fear, happiness, surprise and grief., as well as a "neutral" or non-emotional expression (see Figure 4).

Although user identification and data about personal profile are mapped to avatar choice, subsequently only the avatar choice is represented on the system. This allows all sensitive information about the user to be stored in a secured location. It is true that the set of avatars is at present limited, and as a result, multiple users will undoubtedly select the same avatar. It is also possible that users who have an avatar choice in common may establish an affinity to each other although their real identities are confidential. Nevertheless, users may change their avatar at any point, but such modifications are recorded and included in the analysis of a user's progress.

Regarding the protection of data mentioned earlier, instead of Flash, PHP is used for the login page to validate user identification in the server's database. With PHP, although the actual code is not available to the browser, the results of the code's operation are. While Flash could have been used to create a comparable login, it is less secure because Flash's compiled .SWF files can be captured/cached via the browser and decompiled using reverse engineering techniques (.SWF decompilers).

Last, the actual mapping (a LOOKUP table) of real user names to avatars, is stored on a computer that is not connected to the Internet; thus, the analysis of data is secure from potential Internet intruders, leaving only local flashpoints (physical access to the storage room or the machine itself) as possible security and privacy threats.

Once logged in, users choose and then view short video clips ("scenarios"), interacting with those clips by answering questions, playing skill-testing games, and recording responses; they upload this data so that it can be stored in the database to be accessed later by other users. The system also organizes and manages relationships between groups and users, analyzes the user-input information, and stores designing scenario steps, as well as the user's interactions with these scenarios. As a result, users are able to observe their gaming history.

It is important to note that user-created responses are posted only after acceptance by an administrator. This step is necessary to ensure that the content being posted follows the ethical guidelines of the site; for example, it should avert pornographic material being posted on the site. Subsequently, other users will have access to permitted responses because these will be permanently entered in the database. Although users cannot delete personal responses once those have

been uploaded, they can supplement earlier responses by adding or qualifying their opinions.

The Technical Perspective

In technical management, we encountered unexpected difficulties which resulted from the interplay between structural constraints inherent in the project's intentions and the hoped-for learning outcomes. The technologies that would produce, deliver, store, present, and interpret the content brought action upon the content itself, which, in turn, then acted on the technologies. In addressing these challenges, the producers encountered a dialectic synergy that allowed the project to grow in unexpected but welcome ways. For example, video-recorded responses were first considered but were dismissed when it became clear that they could not be uploaded and processed instantaneously with the comic book effect that would protect user identity. Instead, the use of avatars and audio files was integrated. Other such technological limitations forced a creative re-thinking of content, again, with desirable effects, and these, in turn, forced new and creative side steps. In the following pages, this dialectic, as well as a fuller description of ScreenPLAY's technical functionality, is examined.

From the outset, screenPLAY has been expected to approximate, if not fully embrace, "sexy media," or, those interfaces and technologies like Facebook™ and Youtube™ that have, for some time now, either "eclipsed" or challenged TV network popularity (Fox News, 2006). Although we were striving to make the interface familiar, Nielsen (1990, 1994) indicates that a heuristic should strive for the "match between system and the real world. The system should speak the users' language, with words, phrases and concepts familiar to the user, rather than system-oriented terms. Follow real-world conventions, making information appear in a natural and logical order" [to the particular users]. All along, screenPLAY has been motivated by two premises: first, that the target population is also expected, to some degree, to exhibit literacy problems, and second, that the social content of the intervention is best addressed through learning from experience – at risk-teens should need to encounter, to engage, and to internalize socially appropriate behaviors. We usually expected to blur any separation between learning and entertainment, thereby effectively reaching these kinds of at-risk teens.

Because mashups like Facebook™ and Youtube™ enable the creation, uploading, storage, and transmission of video clips within hours, and in some cases, even within minutes, users expect short waiting times. The speeding up front-end ease of use requires, however, a sizeable investment of resources in back-end, server-side support. Distinct from the resources available for the creation of commercial products, the human, technological, and financial ones available for educational development are considerably smaller. In sum, the process of monitoring, managing, and responding to this resource discrepancy became a focal point in the project's development, one which ultimately generated many positive benefits.

Servers, Network Matters, and Scenario Creations

Users view short video clips, interact with those clips, record their own responses in audio or text format, and then upload this data to be stored in the database for later access by all users. Administrators (project staff), create and manage scenarios and upload audio instructions. A database table has been created for each of the template types, and, as a result, there is a unique template identification assigned and reserved in the database. The reason for assigning the template identification at the start of the scenario building process – instead of at its completion -- rests on the procedure of uploading immediately all audio files into one directory. Therefore, these need to be prefixed with the template and administration identification, as well as with the scenario type,

in order to prevent the overwriting of previous audio files that may have the same name (e.g., question1.mp3, instruction.mp3).

Given that original projections called for as many as fifty simultaneous users, a major consideration is the robustness of the bandwidth. Many contributing variables exist to make bandwidth a complex issue; for example such factors as CPU processing time, DNS resolution, intranet, ISP traffic, Internet traffic. In this instance, we are interested only in what our server provides to the Internet because we recognize that general Internet traffic, the client's ISP, local access methods, and individual machines (CPU-Ram) are beyond our control. Accordingly, we are interested only in the quality and robustness of what is served to the WWW.

screenPLAY is housed in virtual servers (Schick, 2006) provided by our academic institution, York University, Glendon Campus. The equipment consists of three virtual servers on a single box (Sun) and, using Sun Microsystems' StorageTek, our in-house technical support team has set up a storage area network (SAN) by consolidating "13 servers onto five Sun Fire X4100 servers running VMware virtualization software." Our server has been installed with Flash 9 server-side software and FTP access for the WWW content. PHP 5.2.2 and MySQL 5.0.37; charset UTF-8 Unicode (utf8) and local host via TCP/IP have also been installed with Protocol version 10. Because we require streaming and video-uploading capability for videos, we have been assigned 5 gigs of storage, a unique URL, multiple and synchronous anonymous FTP uploading (only certain file types that are specifically video types -- .wmv, .qt, etc.), and email accounts with a fully functioning email server.

Initial concerns about hard drive storage space never materialized, but other issues around the processing of video became evident. Although the infrastructure accommodated storage, there was not enough processing power to handle video uploads as well as the video processing (rosterization) that would be required.

The major challenge has involved the process-ing of video images in order to disguise the faces of the teen actors in the scenario videos. We need a process that disguises the faces of the actors but also provides enough clarity so that facial expressions, even nuanced ones, may be noticed and decoded by users. After many unsuccessful attempts, we have settled on the appearance of characters seen in Charles Schwaab commercials that appear on Television and are found on You-tube; however, we wanted the effect to be more intense and dramatic. The technique is generally called "filtering", and, with the help of our student film editors, a unique brand of filters has been developed to treat screenPLAY video clips. This effect has accomplished the animated cartoon-like quality that we initially tried to achieve. The process of finding the right tool has been arduous because we needed an effect both easy to produce and cost effective. Once again, circumventing a technical problem has led to a new element in the resource: we have been able to disguise student faces and produce an exciting effect that also speaks directly to this generation of teens in a way that is meaningful to them.

The production of the effect requires a batch process in Photoshop that applies several special-effects filters at once to a single frame; it then executes a global processing of all the frames in the clip; clips are then exported and specially converted into web-ready formats (see Figure 6). The scenarios are video files recorded in one long clip from a two-camera shoot and then edited into small, discrete, fifteen-second chunks. They are then named uniquely and labeled (tagged with content keywords). Next, using *Final Cut Pro*, video clips are exported one at a time as image sequences in targa file format, with a frame rate of 29.97 fps. Then, with the use of *Photoshop*, a combination of filters is applied to a single image from each clip (the first frame), and then a batch process is executed so that filters are applied, globally, to the remaining images in the clip. It generally takes about eight minutes for every 15

Figure 6. The rotoscoping effect

seconds of footage, but this varies, depending on the length and specific content of each clip and the processing power of the editing computer. Subsequently, the image sequence is opened in QuickTime and then re-saved as a self-contained .mov file. The process is repeated for each of the clips.

A fifteen-second clip can take up to several hours to process (depending on how much data is in the file), and there is no easy way to automate the processing on the server side once a file is uploaded. This means that while the technique of processing these videos serves two purposes at once, we have had to forego our original intention to allow users (the at-risk teens themselves), with the help of their teachers, to design, create, and upload their own scenarios. We have resolved the problem by creating all video content and processing it before it is uploaded to the database.

To minimize the time required to manually process the video, a second server (Mac Pro) with two 3.0 GHz processors, 16GB memory, and a 1 TB drive for memory was purchased. For graphics, we added 4 x ATI Radeon HD 2600 XT 256MB along with the following peripherals: 20' flat panel screen, a 16x optical drive, an Apple mighty mouse, and English keyboard, Final Cut Express 4.0. A backup drive (also 1 TB) and RAID were added.

The filtering of video images has provided a graphic novel "look", but took hours instead of minutes to be processed on a normal server. Rotoscoping, therefore, is a visualization effect that enhances the immediacy and effect of the teen-user experience, but it also created a technical problem because of the insufficient processing power to manage the video clips. Before we added further processing power to solve the processing problem, it became apparent that a screen capture of the rotoscoped video might work as an avatar as well as a protector of user privacy. At the same time, we were also exploring the idea of using artist-rendered sketches of different faces as a substitute for rotoscoping normal video clips.

When these two lines of thought were conflated, it became apparent that artist-drawn sketches could be animated just as easily a single-frame screen captures from rosterized video, and both could be effectively used as ECAs. These insights have led to the design of the comic book drag-and-drop tool that allows teen users to imagine and create positive behavioral scenarios; it also has led to the double use of avatars, first to protect user privacy, and, second, to visually enhance thought and feeling -- powerful versions of emoticons.

FLASH and PHP

The adoption of Flash in the front end was an easy decision to make, since Youtube and Facebook (among many others) employ it as an intermediary tool for passing variables (data and parameters) to and from a database. Flash easily allows for animations; not only does it accommodate user interactivity, but it is remarkably adept and powerful at interacting with databases, especially open-source ones like PHP. Flash libraries can also expedite design features; the plethora of such resources, already developed, is widely known and used across the Internet (see http://www.needscripts.com/Resource/41422. html, for example). Some of these are free or cost only a few dollars, making their access easy and economical when the functionality they offer is needed. For academic research and development, PHP and its open source support libraries are ideal. In other instances, for example the drag-and-drop functions in the comic-strip builder, it was more advantageous to develop the functionality in-house. Lastly, Flash was adopted because it also offsets (somewhat) the bandwidth issues needed for up and downloading of video clips.

Flash has presented a few challenges as well. First, its comprehensive catalogue of authoring tools, objects, properties, methods, components, features, and its own programming script (i.e., ActionScript, available in versions 1.0, 2.0, and 3.0) is difficult to master. As a result, time and effort were needed to train in the use of Actionscript and other parts of Flash, with the result that our requirements pushed our young programmers to their limits. Such challenges extended the project's time-on-task and its duration, putting us behind in the meeting of our milestones; on the other hand, our student workers gained considerable and valuable work-world experience. More importantly, because our young programmers were still close enough in age to share visual culture and interface semiotics with our target users, much of the time lost in searching for technical solutions and debugging errors was restored to us when we saw how quickly our programmers could build interfaces that resemble state-of-the art, popular Mashups. Our programmers and senior Psychology student workers have had relatively little difficulty in creating and positioning interface functions as well as in using color palettes appropriate -- to our intended users.

Feedback from Users

Preliminary feedback was obtained from users (N=34, 18 girls, and 16 boys) attending a high school in an urban area. In the context of the *Instance or Not* template, fifteen- and sixteen-year old students were shown 12 scenarios. Following their participation in the activities, they were asked to complete a questionnaire that explored various aspects of their experience.

In addition to beta-testing, we were interested in obtaining feedback about screenPLAY using Leung's (2003) contextual framework for constructing an effective computer-based learning program. In this framework, Leung pinpoints four aspects to be addressed and incorporated: topic selection, authenticity, complexity, and multiple perspectives. The first challenge, topic selection, relates initially to the subject area chosen for the learning program and then to the appropriateness of its integration in computer-based formats. screenPLAY has been developed as a web-based intervention because, upon examining how social

skills are naturally acquired, the producers found it evident that technology was able to simulate a similar process—the promotion of learning by experience. Providing users with pseudo social experiences through the presentation of scenarios, promotes the development of schemas in semantic memory, as well as presenting specific cognitive skills inherent in each of the templates.

About the importance of acquiring social skills, users overwhelming agreed (91.2%) that it was important for teens to improve their social skills while 64.7% ranked these skills as central to doing well in life. When asked whether screenPLAY is a suitable way for teens to learn about social skills, 41.2% agreed but 44.1% gave a neutral response. Perhaps users having only a brief opportunity to explore all of the many features in screenPLAY did not have an opportunity to make a definitive judgment.

Nevertheless, screenPLAY has very methodically attempted to meet the challenge of authenticity, Leung's (2003) second aspect, by using real student actors from high school drama classes. Moreover, while the actors were given situations and guidelines to follow, they had no prepared scripts, thereby enabling them to engage in less-than-perfect improvisation in order to create a more realistic, cinéma-vérité effect, superior to a formal too-perfect presentation. Further, not only did we intentionally promote cultural and racial diversity in the video clips, we encouraged actors to use street language (natural speech) authentic to teen situations.

In user responses to the realistic scenarios, they were decisive (61.8%) about the belief that video clips were close to real-life situations. Interestingly, 88.3% agreed that teen actors should be used and 58.9% felt that the actors sometimes reminded them of real people they knew. In addition, 41.2% of user-respondents felt that the language employed was similar to the way they would talk with their friends.

Many users commented on the authenticity of the acting. They made comments such as "Make the actors more believable"; "Have the teens less scripted so it looks they are actually in a situation"; Actors didn't look that into it, that's why I think it wasn't as good as it shoud've been"; "Have better actors that show more emotion to different situation". As a result, it will be important in the creation of subsequent scenarios not only to select more skilled actors, but to encourage them to be more convincing to a teen audience. What needs to be determined with more precision is the extent to which acting and content/theme interact to produce a convincing authenticity. The complexity of this parameter will require more attention, especially since authenticity lies somewhere between a subjective perception and a tangible and calculated relevance that was hypothesized by the resource designers and our teenage actors.

"Chunkifying" content has been daunting because it is so labor intensive; however, the modularity of our intervention structures allows for continuous and specialized content development, customized for particular teen sub-groups. In this instance, 50% of students agreed that screenPLAY presents a variety of social topics.

Leung (2003) describes his third aspect—complexity—as the degree to which the activities reflect real-life situations and therefore challenge the learner. screenPLAY has been structured to lead the user from a basic (obvious) to a difficult (nuanced) level of illustration by varying the cognitive and linguistic demands of activities. Although there are built-in functions to scaffold the learning of social situations, the intention is to allow the user, ultimately, to transfer skills to the real-life situations that are part of personal experience. Participant-users generally judged the difficulty level of the activities to be appropriate, and, more importantly, 58.8% felt that flexible choices, separate approaches for everyone's learning needs (41.1%), and different learning styles (47.1%) were provided.

Lastly, Leung (2003) insists that computer-based learning should offer the learner multiple perspectives rather than a single way of doing things. By surrounding the user with a variety of contexts in which to make judgments, and allowing each one access to the thoughts and explanations provided by other participants, screenPLAY is expected readily to satisfy this aspect. Despite the limited exposure to activities experienced by the user group, 47% agreed that screenPLAY makes students more reflective, causes them to be more able to think in a new way about real world situations (55.9%), encourages users to provide reasons for their answers (64.7%), and, most interestingly, demonstrates that there is more than a single solution to deal helpfully with each social situation (61.7%).

We were pleased to see that 41.2% felt that they learned something new by doing the screenPLAY exercises, 55.9% enjoyed listening to what others thought about the situations, and 44.1% learned something on the basis of the comments of others. Finally, 35.3% claimed to have a deeper understanding of their fellow teens and of their points of view, and 38.2% would tell their friends about screenPLAY although the same proportion remained neutral. We are hoping, once their have access to all the functions contained in screen-PLAY, that a greater number of users will be convinced of its utility.

The purpose of seeking feedback from users, employing a restricted demonstration of screen-PLAY allowed us to obtain promising initial results that will guide subsequent development. We will remain cautious, however, until more information is gleaned from a larger sample and until we can allow users to experience more of the available functions.

FUTURE DIRECTIONS

The architecture of the screenPLAY platform is designed to be modular in order to accommodate new functions, new templates, and new content. We began with the development of a shallow prototype that imported only one format of video, one format of audio (mp3), and two formats of text (ASCII and MS Word). Limited to two templates, it was capable of monitoring only time-on-task, Nine more templates were added, as well as the ability to track every step of the user's interaction with the system and the facility to record points awarded to users for engaging in additional tasks.

The avatar and comic strip features grew out of responses to specific technological obstacles. Unable to locate financially affordable software that would cartoon-ize user input and scenario creation, we solved the problem by filming student actors, subsequently adding avatars, first to establish user identity and then to protect all identities. It will be necessary to add new avatars, particularly a black female because such an idenity was requested several times in the focus group; next will be to the animation of the avatars, as well as synchronization of lip- and mouth-movement with audio instructions and feedback. As we have greater ethnic and racial diversity in our avatars than in our teen actors, during our projected expansion of both these parameters, we are predicting that the evaluation of the authenticity and relevance of the scenarios will improve immeasurably.

Content development remains a persistent challenge because we are creating a curriculum from research findings where none at present exists. In addition, we are relying on the skills of the schools' drama students who are attempting to address the subject perceptions of students at risk. The dilemma exists because, by the time actors have acquired enough experience to express very nuanced kinds of behaviors and attitudes required for higher-order thinking and processing activities, they are old enough to be recognized as "other" or "non-teen" by our target audience. In part, our planned comic-strip creation function will allow alienated users to express their anxieties and ideas clearly enough to give us hints about how to re-organize and re-direct our actors. We also hypothesize that the addition of new actors -- whose racial and ethnic backgrounds more closely reflect the users' own—should help to

overcome the limits of student acting abilities. Additionally, we might be able to employ student feedback to coach our current actors in ways that are helpful, but without pressuring them into "being" something (or someone) that does not feel authentic to them. If it turns out that content or location (setting) are also obstacles (some student testers indicated they wanted sports-based situations or scenes set outside the school), we can certainly create more scenarios to accommodate these suggestions.

Inspired by the work of Hubal et al. (2008), ECAs (Embodied Conversational Agents) in the context of screenPLAY can be used as mediators and tutorial leaders who question users about their choices and rationales, prompt them to explain further, and engage them in dialectic and questioning. Such an adjunct would advance both the linguistic and the cognitive objectives of screenPLAY, while increasing user engagement.

screenPLAY readily lends itself to synergetic alliances with other leading-edge research and development, most notably based in Taiwan, including the three-dimensional spatial mapping of avatars in chat rooms (Park, Ji, et al, 2008) and the use of a context aware interactive robot to monitor student attention spans regarding online activities (Wu et al., 2008). The former will assist greatly in our analysis of user-activity data and the latter will indicate much about the attention spans of our users, and by implication, the appropriateness of the design of our activities and our interface. The pursuit of such partnerships is both necessary and desirable.

screenPLAY will continue to be beta-tested in secondary school classrooms, not only to refine its functionality, but, more importantly, to begin the process of evaluating its assessment and intervention utilities. Research data and feedback from users will be employed to enlarge the content library in order to include issues relevant to specific groups, for example, bicultural issues, violence in schools, and other elements.

Information obtained from user performance

on the various templates will provide insight into the relationship of cognitive and linguistic factors associated with social skill performance.

CONCLUSION

Adopting a constructivist perspective, screen-PLAY has incorporated many features for the purpose of engaging a teen population in examining and exploring the social situations that challenge their lives, ones which, when inappropriately resolved, often provide obstacles instead of meeting their needs.

We are confident that the theoretical basis and design of screenPLAY will be well received by both teachers and students. Meanwhile, we continue to rely on upcoming research data from its implementation, projecting it to guide further development.

ACKNOWLEDGMENT

This project was funded by two Image, Text, Sound, and Technology grants from the Social Science and Research Council. The authors are grateful to the team of individuals who continue to work on this project: database programmer Shirley Hu; flash and web programmer, Boze Zekan; York student, Fiona Dyshniku of Glendon's Psychology Department, working on the videos and their content; York Fine Arts student, Samantha Shute, on the production of the videos; content editor, Nancy Vichert, and graphic artist, Fiona Macdonald; in addition, with the financial assistance of the RAY and Work and Study programs, students, Javeria Arshad and Mohammad Affan Jalal, who participated in the research of content and the collection and analysis of data; as well as student videographers who assisted in the filming of video clips. We would like to thank Luc Mallet, systems administrator, who has contributed his expertise in connection with the new VM server initiative on the Glendon campus of York University, in Toronto, Ontario, Canada.

REFERENCES

Abbeduto, L., Short-Meyerson, K., Benson, G., & Dolish, J. (2004). Relationship between theory of mind and language ability in children and adolescents with intellectual disability. *Journal of Intellectual Disability Research, 48*(2), 150–159. doi:10.1111/j.1365-2788.2004.00524.x

Adams, R., B., & Kleck, R. E. (2003). Perceived gaze direction and the processing of facial displays of emotion. *Psychological Science, 14*(6), 644–647. doi:10.1046/j.0956-7976.2003. psci_1479.x

Adams, R. B., & Kleck, R. E. (2005). Effects of direct and averted gaze on the perception of facially communicated emotion. *Emotions, 5*(1), 3–11. doi:10.1037/1528-3542.5.1.3

Aggarwal, A. (2003). *Web-based education: Learning from experience*. Hershey, PA: IGI Global.

Assor, A., Kaplan, H., & Roth, G. (2002). Choice is good, but relevance is excellent: Autonomy-enhancing and suppressing teacher behaviors predicting students' engagement in schoolwork. *The British Journal of Educational Psychology, 72*(2), 261–278. doi:10.1348/000709902158883

Atherton, J. S. (2002). *Learning and teaching: Learning from experience* [online]. Retrieved on September 26, 2004, from the http://www.dmu. ac.uk/~jamesa/learning/experien.htm

Bandura, A. (1997). *Self-efficacy: The exercise of control*. New York: W.H. Freeman.

Bandura, A. (2001). Social cognitive theory: An agentic perspective. *Annual Review of Psychology, 52*(1), 1–26. doi:10.1146/annurev.psych.52.1.1

Bishop, J. (2003). The Internet for educating individuals with social impairments. *Journal of Computer Assisted Learning*, *19*(4), 546–556. doi:10.1046/j.0266-4909.2003.00057.x

Bloom, B. (1974). *Taxonomy of educational objectives: The classification of educational goals.* New York: D. McKay.

Boone, R. T., & Buck, R. (2003). Emotional expressivity and trustworthiness: The role of nonverbal behavior in the evolution of cooperation. *Journal of Nonverbal Behavior*, *27*(3), 163–182. doi:10.1023/A:1025341931128

Bosley, M. E. (1998). An analysis of language maturity, verbal aggression, argumentativeness, and propensity toward violence in middle school adolescents. *Dissertation Abstracts International Section A: Humanities and Social Sciences, 58*(10A), 3773.

Botting, N., & Conti-Ramsden, G. (2008). The role of language, social cognition, and social skill in the functional social outcomes of young adolescents with and without a history of SLI. *The British Journal of Developmental Psychology*, *26*(2), 281–300. doi:10.1348/026151007X235891

Botting, N., Faragher, B., Simkin, Z., Knox, E., & Conti-Ramsden, G. (2001). Predicting pathways of specific language impairment: What differentiates good and poor outcome? *Journal of Child Psychology and Psychiatry, and Allied Disciplines*, *42*(8), 1013–1020. doi:10.1111/1469-7610.00799

Bourke, M. L. (2001). Social problem-solving skills training for incarcerated offenders: A treatment manual. *Behavior Modification*, *25*(2), 163–188. doi:10.1177/0145445501252001

Caire, J., Pliner, P., & Stoker, S. C. (1998). An expert-novice approach to assessing implicit models of the self. In A. Colby, J. James & D. Hart (Eds.), *Competence and character through life.* Chicago: The University of Chicago Press.

Caire, J. B., & Cosgrove, S. M. (1995). An expert-novice approach to self. *Behavior Therapist*, *18*, 137–140.

Callicott, K. J. (2003). Effects of self-talk on academic engagement and academic responding. *Behavioral Disorders*, *29*(1), 48–64.

Carbonaro, M., Cutumisu, M., Duff, H., Gillis, S., Onuczko, C., & Siegel, J. (2008). Interactive story authoring: A viable form of creative expression for the classroom. *Computers & Education*, *51*(2), 687–707. doi:10.1016/j.compedu.2007.07.007

Carr, E. G., & Durand, V. M. (1985). Reducing behavior problems through functional communication training. *Journal of Applied Behavior Analysis*, *18*(2), 111–126. doi:10.1901/jaba.1985.18-111

Cohen, N., Vallance, D. D., Barwick, M., Im, N., Menna, R., & Horodezky, N. B. (2000). The interface between ADHD and language impairment: An examination of language, achievement, and cognitive processing. *Journal of Child Psychology and Psychiatry, and Allied Disciplines*, *41*(3), 353–362. doi:10.1111/1469-7610.00619

Cohen, N. J. (2001). *Language impairment and psychopathology in infants, children, and adolescents.* Thousand Oaks, CA: Sage Publications, Inc.

Cohen, N. J., Barwick, M. A., Horodezky, N. B., Vallance, D. D., & Im, N. (1998). Language, achievement, and cognitive processing in psychiatrically disturbed children with previously identified and unsuspected language impairments. *Journal of Child Psychology and Psychiatry, and Allied Disciplines*, *39*(6), 865–877. doi:10.1111/1469-7610.00387

Cohen, N. J., Davine, M., & Meloche-Kelly, M. (1989). Prevalence of unsuspected language disorders in a child psychiatric population. *Journal of the American Academy of Child and Adolescent Psychiatry, 28*(1), 107(5)-112.

Cohen, N. J., Menna, R., Vallance, D. D., Barwick, M. A., Im, N., & Horodezky, N. B. (1998). Language, social cognitive processing, and behavioral characteristics of psychiatrically disturbed children with previously identified and unsuspected language impairments. *Journal of Child Psychology and Psychiatry, and Allied Disciplines, 39*(6), 853–864. doi:10.1017/S0021963098002789

Coleman, J., Catan, L., & Dennison, C. (1997). You're the last person I'd talk to. In S. Tucker & J. Roche (Eds.), *Youth in society: Contemporary theory, policy, and practice* (pp. 227-234). Thousand Oaks, CA: Sage Publications, Inc.

Conger, R. D., Neppl, T., & Kim, K. J. (2003). Angry and aggressive behavior across three generations: A prospective, longitudinal study of parents and children. *Journal of Abnormal Child Psychology, 31*(2), 143–160. doi:10.1023/A:1022570107457

Conti-Ramsden, G., & Botting, N. (2004). Social difficulties and victimization in children with SLI at 11 years of age. *Journal of Speech, Language, and Hearing Research: JSLHR, 47*(1), 147–162. doi:10.1044/1092-4388(2004/013)

Corcos, E. (2003). *Teaching children and adolescents with behavioral difficulties: An educational approach.* Toronto, Canada: Tigress Publications.

Covington, M. V. (2000). Goal theory, motivation, and school achievement: An integrative review. *Annual Review of Psychology, 51*(1Journal Article), 171-200.

Davis, A. D., Sanger, D. D., & Morris-Friehe, M. (1991). Language skills of delinquent and nondelinquent adolescent males. *Journal of Communication Disorders, 24*(4), 251–266. doi:10.1016/0021-9924(91)90001-Y

de Castell, S., Bryson, M., & Jenson, J. (2002). Object lessons: Towards an educational theory of technology. *First Monday, 7*(1), 1–18.

de Castell, S., & Jenson, J. (2004). Paying attention to attention: New economies for learning. *Educational Theory, 54*(4), 381–397. doi:10.1111/j.0013-2004.2004.00026.x

de Montes, L. G., Semin, G. R., & Valencia, J. F. (2003). Communication patterns in interdependent relationships. *Journal of Language and Social Psychology, 22*(3), 259–281. doi:10.1177/0261927X03255381

Diener, E., Oishi, S., & Lucas, R. E. (2003). Personality, culture, and subjective well-being: Emotional and cognitive evaluations of life. *Annual Review of Psychology, 54*(1), 403–425. doi:10.1146/annurev.psych.54.101601.145056

Eisenberg, N. (2000). Emotion, regulation, and moral development. *Annual Review of Psychology, 51*(1), 665–697. doi:10.1146/annurev.psych.51.1.665

Elias, M. J. (2004). The connection between social-emotional learning and learning disabilities: Implications for intervention. *Learning Disability Quarterly, 27*(1), 53–63. doi:10.2307/1593632

Ellemers, N., Spears, R., & Doosje, B. (2002). Self and social identity. *Annual Review of Psychology, 53*(1), 161–186. doi:10.1146/annurev.psych.53.100901.135228

Erickson, K., & Schulkinb, J. (2003). Facial expressions of emotion: A cognitive neuroscience perspective. *Brain and Cognition, 52*, 52–60. doi:10.1016/S0278-2626(03)00008-3

Fenstermacher, K., Olympia, D., & Sheridan, S. M. (2006). Effectiveness of a computer-facilitated interactive social skills training program for boys with attention deficit hyperactivity disorder. *School Psychology Quarterly, 21*(2), 197–224. doi:10.1521/scpq.2006.21.2.197

Fox News. (2006). *YouTube popularity eclipses, and influences, fall TV season.* Retrieved on August 20, 2008, from http://www.foxnews.com/story/0,2933,209022,00.html

Frankel, F., & Feinberg, D. (2002). Social problems associated with ADHD vs. ODD in children referred for friendship problems. *Child Psychiatry and Human Development, 33*(2), 125–146. doi:10.1023/A:1020730224907

Furlong, M. J., & Smith, D. C. (1998). Raging Rick to tranquil Tom: An empirically based multidimensional anger typology for adolescent males. *Psychology in the Schools, 35*(3), 229–245. doi:10.1002/(SICI)1520-6807(199807)35:3<229::AID-PITS4>3.0.CO;2-I

Gee, J. P. (2003). *What video games have to teach us about learning and literacy.* New York: Palgrave MacMillan.

Gobbo, C., & Chi, M. (1986). How knowledge is structured and used by experts and novice children. *Cognitive Development, 1,* 221–237. doi:10.1016/S0885-2014(86)80002-8

Goldsworthy, R., Schwartz, N., Barab, S., & Landa, A. (2007). Evaluation of a collaborative multimedia conflict resolution curriculum. *Educational Technology Research and Development, 55*(6), 597–625. doi:10.1007/s11423-006-9006-5

Goodyer, I. (2000). Language difficulties and psychopathology. In D. Bishop & L. Leonard (Eds.), *Speech and language impairment in children* (pp. 227-244). Hove, UK: Psychology Press.

Gualtieru, C. T., Koriath, U., Van Bourgondien, M., & Saleeby, N. (1983). Language disorders in children referred for psychiatric-services. *Journal of the American Academy of Child and Adolescent Psychiatry, 22*(2), 165–171.

Halliday, M. A. K. (1975). *Learning how to mean: Explorations in the development of language.* London: Edward Arnold (Publishers) Ltd.

Hartley, J. (2007). Teaching, learning, and new technology: A review for teachers. *British Journal of Educational Technology, 38*(1), 42–62. doi:10.1111/j.1467-8535.2006.00634.x

Hastie, R. (2001). Problems for judgment and decision making. *Annual Review of Psychology, 52*(1), 653–683. doi:10.1146/annurev.psych.52.1.653

Hubal, R. C., Fishbein, D. H., Sheppard, M. S., Paschall, M. J., Eldreth, D. L., & Hyde, C. T. (2008). How do varied populations interact with embodied conversational agents? Findings from inner-city adolescents and prisoners. *Computers in Human Behavior, 24*(3), 1104–1138. doi:10.1016/j.chb.2007.03.010

Joffe, R. D., Dobson, K. S., Fine, S., & Marriage, K. (1990). Social problem-solving in depressed, conduct-disordered, and normal adolescents. *Journal of Abnormal Child Psychology, 18*(5), 565–575. doi:10.1007/BF00911108

Kadish, T. E., Glaser, B. A., Calhoun, G. B., & Ginter, E. J. (2001). Identifying the developmental strengths of juvenile offenders: Assessing four life-skills dimensions. *Journal of Addictions & Offender Counseling, 21*(2), 85–95.

Karagiorgi, Y., & Symeou, L. (2005). Translating constructivism into instructional design: Potential and limitations. *Educational Technology & Society, 8*(1), 17–27.

Kaufman, J. M. (1999). How we prevent the prevention of emotional and behavior disorders. *Exceptional Children, 65*(4), 448–468.

Kehle, T. J., & Bray, M. A. (2004). Commentary: Current perspectives on school-based behavioral interventions: Science and reality of the classroom. *School Psychology Review, 33*(3), 417–420.

Kelly, S. D. (2001). Broadening the units of analysis in communication: Speech and nonverbal behaviors in pragmatic comprehension. *Journal of Child Language, 28*, 325–349.

Keysar, B. (2000). The illusory transparency of intention: Does June understand what Mark means because he means it? *Discourse Processes, 29*(2), 161–172. doi:10.1207/S15326950dp2902_4

Keysar, B., Barr, D. J., Balin, J. A., & Brauner, J. S. (2000). Taking perspective in conversation: The role of mutual knowledge in comprehension. *Psychological Science, 11*(1), 32–38. doi:10.1111/1467-9280.00211

Kolb, D. A. (1984). *Experiential learning: Experience as the source of learning and development.* Englewood Cliffs, NJ: Prentice-Hall.

Lapadat, J. C. (1991). Pragmatic language skills of students with language and/or learning disabilities: A quantitative synthesis. *Journal of Learning Disabilities, 24*(3), 147–158. doi:10.1177/002221949102400303

Laplante, D., & Ambady, N. (2003). On how things are said: Voice tone, voice intensity, verbal content, and perceptions of politeness. *Journal of Language and Social Psychology, 22*(4), 434–441. doi:10.1177/0261927X03258084

Leung, A. C. K. (2003). Contextual issues in the construction of computer-based learning programs. *Journal of Computer Assisted Learning, 19*(4), 501–516. doi:10.1046/j.0266-4909.2003.00053.x

Lindsay, G., & Dockrell, J. (2000). The behavior and self esteem of children with specific speech and language difficulties. *The British Journal of Educational Psychology, 70*, 583–601. doi:10.1348/000709900158317

Losel, F., & Beelmann, A. (2003). Effects of child skills training in preventing antisocial behavior: A systematic review of randomized evaluations. *The Annals of the American Academy of Political and Social Science, 587*(1), 84–109. doi:10.1177/0002716202250793

Mathur, S. R., & Rutherford, R. B. (1994). Teaching conversational social skills to delinquent youth. *Behavioral Disorders, 19*(4), 294–305.

Matthys, W., Cuperus, J. M., & Van-Engeland, H. (1999). Deficient social problem-solving in boys with ODD/CD, with ADHD, and with both disorders. *Journal of the American Academy of Child and Adolescent Psychiatry, 38*(3), 311–321. doi:10.1097/00004583-199903000-00019

McCabe, P. C., & Meller, P. J. (2004). The relationship between language and social competence: How language impairment affects social growth. *Psychology in the Schools, 41*(3), 313–321. doi:10.1002/pits.10161

McClure, E. B., & Nowicki, S. Jr. (2001). Associations between social anxiety and nonverbal processing skill in preadolescent boys and girls. *Journal of Nonverbal Behavior, 25*(1), 3–19. doi:10.1023/A:1006753006870

McHugh, L., Barnes-Holmes, Y., & Barnes-Holmes, D. (2004). Perspective-taking as relational responding: A developmental profile. *The Psychological Record, 54*(1), 115–144.

McKay, S. (2003). Adolescent risk behaviors and communication research: Current directions. *Journal of Language and Social Psychology, 22*(1), 74–82. doi:10.1177/0261927X02250058

Mignault, A., & Chaudhuri, A. (2003). The many faces of a neutral face: Head tilt and perception of dominance and emotion. *Journal of Nonverbal Behavior, 27*(2), 111–132. doi:10.1023/A:1023914509763

Miller, D. T. (2001). Disrespect and the experience of injustice. *Annual Review of Psychology, 52*(1Journal Article), 527-553.

Minowa, N. (1997). Lack of words, lack of control: Relationship between language proficiency and frequency of aggressive behavior. *Dissertation Abstracts International: Section B: The Sciences & Engineering, 58*(5-B), 2691.

Mohan, B., & van Naerssen, M. (1997). Understanding cause-effect: Learning through language. *Forum, 35*(4), 22–40.

Mullins, D. T., & Duke, M. P. (2004). Effects of social anxiety on nonverbal accuracy and response time I: Facial expressions. *Journal of Nonverbal Behavior, 28*(1), 3–33. doi:10.1023/B:JONB.0000017865.24656.98

Nass, C., & Moon, Y. (2000). Machines and mindlessness: Social responses to computers. *The Journal of Social Issues, 56*(1), 81–103. doi:10.1111/0022-4537.00153

Nielsen, J. (1994). Heuristic evaluation. In J. Nielsen & R. L. Mack (Eds.), *Usability inspection methods*. New York: John Wiley & Sons.

Nielsen, J., & Molich, R. (1990). Heuristic evaluation of user interfaces. *SIGCHI Conference on Human Factors in Computing Systems: Empowering People* (pp. 249-256) Seattle, WA.

O'Callaghan, P. M., Reitman, D., Northup, J., Hupp, S. D. A., & Murphy, M. A. (2003). Promoting social skills generalization with ADHD-diagnosed children in a sports setting. *Behavior Therapy, 34*(3), 313–330. doi:10.1016/S0005-7894(03)80003-5

Palmer, E. J., & Hollin, C. R. (1999). Social competence and sociomoral reasoning in young offenders. *Applied Cognitive Psychology, 13*(1), 79–87. doi:10.1002/(SICI)1099-0720(199902)13:1<79::AID-ACP613>3.0.CO;2-Q

Park, S., Ji, S., et al. (2008). A new 3-dimensional comic chat environment for online game avatars. *Proceedings from the Second IEEE International Conference on Digital Game and Intelligent Toy Enhanced Learning* (pp. 18-22) Banff, Canada.

Patterson, M. L. (2003). Commentary evolution and nonverbal behavior: Functions and mediating processes. *Journal of Nonverbal Behavior, 27*(3), 201–207. doi:10.1023/A:1025346132037

Penn, D. C., & Povinelli, D. J. (2007). Causal cognition in human and nonhuman animals: A comparative, critical review. *Annual Review of Psychology, 58*, 97–118. doi:10.1146/annurev.psych.58.110405.085555

Pennebaker, J. W., Mehl, M. R., & Niederhoffer, K. G. (2003). Psychological aspects of natural language use: Our words, our selves. *Annual Review of Psychology, 54*(1), 547–577. doi:10.1146/annurev.psych.54.101601.145041

Qi, C. H., & Kaiser, A. P. (2004). Problem behaviors of low-income children with language delays: An observation study. *Journal of Speech, Language, and Hearing Research: JSLHR, 47*(3), 595–610. doi:10.1044/1092-4388(2004/046)

Realo, A., Allik, J., Nolvak, A., Valk, R., Ruus, T., & Schmidt, M. (2003). Mindreading ability: Beliefs and performance. *Journal of Research in Personality, 37*(5), 420–445. doi:10.1016/S0092-6566(03)00021-7

Robins, B., Dickerson, P., Stribling, P., & Dautenhahn, K. (2004). Robot-mediated joint attention children with autism: A case study in robot-human interaction. *Interaction Studies: Social Behaviour and Communication in Biological and Artificial Systems, 5*(2), 161–198. doi:10.1075/is.5.2.02rob

Rockwell, P. (2000). Lower, slower, louder: Vocal cues of sarcasm. *Journal of Psycholinguistic Research, 29*(5), 483–495. doi:10.1023/A:1005120109296

Rogoff, B., Paradise, R., Arauz, R. M., Correa-Chavez, M., & Angelillo, C. (2003). Firsthand learning through intent participation. *Annual Review of Psychology, 54*(1), 175–203. doi:10.1146/annurev.psych.54.101601.145118

Russell, J. A., Bachorowski, J. A., & Fernandez-Dols, J. M. (2003). Facial and vocal expressions of emotion. *Annual Review of Psychology, 54*(1), 329–349. doi:10.1146/annurev.psych.54.101601.145102

Rutherford, M. D. (2004). The effect of social role on theory of mind reasoning. *The British Journal of Psychology, 95*, 91–103. doi:10.1348/000712604322779488

Sanger, D., Coufal, K. L., Scheffler, M., & Searcey, R. (2003). Implications of the personal perceptions of incarcerated adolescents concerning their own communicative competence. *Communication Disorders Quarterly, 24*(2), 64–77. doi:10.1177/15257401030240020301

Sanger, D., Hux, K., & Riztman, M. (1999). Female juvenile delinquents' pragmatic awareness of conversational interactions. *Journal of Communication Disorders, 32*, 281–295. doi:10.1016/S0021-9924(99)00003-9

Sanger, D., Scheffler, M., Drake, B., Hilgert, K., Creswell, J. W., & Hansen, D. J. (2000). Maltreated female delinquents speak about their communication behaviors. *Communication Disorders Quarterly, 21*(3), 176–187. doi:10.1177/152574010002100306

Sarris, A., Winefield, H. R., & Cooper, C. (2000). Behavior problems in adolescence: A comparison of juvenile offenders and adolescents referred to a mental health service. *Australian Journal of Psychology, 52*(1), 17–22. doi:10.1080/00049530008255362

Schick, S. (2006). Glendon puts end to server nightmare. *Computing Canada, 32*(15), 1–2.

Schmidt, K. L., & Cohn, J. F. (2001). Human facial expressions as adaptations: Evolutionary questions in facial expression research. *Yearbook of Physical Anthropology, 44*, 3–24. doi:10.1002/ajpa.20001

Segrin, C. (2000). Social skills deficits associated with depression. *Clinical Psychology Review, 20*(3), 379–403. doi:10.1016/S0272-7358(98)00104-4

Segrin, C. (2001). Social skills and negative life events: Testing the deficit stress generation hypothesis. *Current Psychology: Developmental, Learning, Personality, Social, 20*(1), 19–35. doi:10.1007/s12144-001-1001-8

Sheridan, S. M. (1995). *The tough kid social skills book.* Longmont, CO: Sopris West.

Smokowski, P. R., & Hartung, K. (2003). Computer simulation and virtual reality: Enhancing the practice of school social work. *Journal of Technology in Human Services, 21*(1-2), 5–30. doi:10.1300/J017v21n01_02

Soderstrom, H. (2003). Psychopathy as a disorder of empathy. *European Child & Adolescent Psychiatry, 12*(5), 249–252. doi:10.1007/s00787-003-0338-y

Spitzberg, B. H., & Dillard, J. P. (2002). Social skills and communication. In R. W. Preiss, & M. Allen (Eds.), *Interpersonal communication research: Advances through meta-analysis* (pp. 89-107). Mahwah, NJ: Lawrence Erlbaum Associates, Publishers.

Sullivan, S., & Ruffman, T. (2004). Social understanding: How does it fare with advancing years? *The British Journal of Psychology, 95*, 1–18. doi:10.1348/000712604322779424

Taylor, J. S. (1969). *The communicative abilities of juvenile delinquents: A descriptive study.* Unpublished doctoral dissertation, The University of Missouri, Kansas City, MO.

Tulving, E., & Schacter, D. L. (1990). Priming and human memory systems. *Science*, *247*(4940), 301–306. doi:10.1126/science.2296719

Vallance, D. D., Im, N., & Cohen, N. J. (1999). Discourse deficits associated with psychiatric disorders and with language impairments in children. *Journal of Child Psychology and Psychiatry, and Allied Disciplines*, *40*(5), 693–704. doi:10.1111/1469-7610.00486

Vallance, D. D., & Wintre, M. G. (1997). Discourse processes underlying social competence in children with language learning disabilities. *Development and Psychopathology*, *9*(1), 95–108. doi:10.1017/S0954579497001089

Van Swol, L. M. (2003). The effects of nonverbal mirroring on perceived persuasiveness, agreement with an imitator, and reciprocity in a group discussion. *Communication Research*, *30*(4), 461–480. doi:10.1177/0093650203253318

Vrij, A., Akehurst, L., Soukara, S., & Bull, R. (2004). Detecting deceit via analysis of verbal and nonverbal behavior in children and adults. *Human Communication Research*, *30*(1), 8–41. doi:10.1111/j.1468-2958.2004.tb00723.x

Vygotsky, L. S. (1978). *Mind in society: The development of higher psychological processes*. Cambridge, MA: Harvard University Press. Published originally in Russian in 1930.

Wong, W. K., Chan, T. W., Chou, C. Y., Heh, J. S., & Tung, S. H. (2003). Reciprocal tutoring using cognitive tools. *Journal of Computer Assisted Learning*, *19*(4), 416–428. doi:10.1046/j.0266-4909.2003.00046.x

Wu, E. Hsiao-Kuang, Wu, Hubert, Chi-Yu, et al. (2008). A context aware interactive robot educational platform. *Proceedings from the Second IEEE International Conference on Digital Game and Intelligent Toy Enhanced Learning* (pp. 205-206) Banff, Canada.

Ylvisaker, M., & DeBonis, D. (2000). Executive function impairment in adolescence: TBI and ADHD. *Topics in Language Disorders*, *20*(2), 29–57.

Young, J., & Upitis, R. (1999). The microworld of phoenix quest: Social and cognitive considerations. *Education and Information Technologies*, *4*(4), 391–408. doi:10.1023/A:1009600528811

Section 3
Educational Social Software:
The Teacher Perspective

Chapter 9
The e-Tutor in Learning 2.0 Scenarios:
Profile, Professional Empowerment, and New Roles

Mario Rotta
University of Florence, Italy

ABSTRACT

With this contribution, we briefly explain how both the e-Tutor role and competencies have changed since the beginning of the debate about this essential e-Learning human resource. Until now, what set of professional functions were requested to be a good e-Tutor? What training policies must be identified to give an answer to the needs of e-Tutors for them to be able to interact effectively in e-Learning scenarios oriented to sharing knowledge and social networking?

INTRODUCTION

The professional profile of the e-Tutor has been completely changed since the beginning of the debate about e-Learning. In the period 1993-1997, according to fundamental contributions by authors as Mason (1992), Berge & Collins (1995) or Rowntree (1995), the e-Tutor (more frequently called "e-moderator") has been described as an expert in mediated communication by e-mail, forums or chat. This approach concerns the "vision" of e-Learning in those years, initially considered as an opportunity to activate peer-to-peer communication and share thoughts on content: that model requires moderators with technical and communication skills, to avoid the risk of ineffectiveness due to poor experience of e-learners in the use of computer and network tools. However, the real evolution started when research and applications began to inquire the close relationship between the e-Tutor role and the development of more complex e-Learning models. This contribution is entirely focused on the profile of the e-Tutor from this point of view. The e-Tutor is now one of the most important professional profiles in e-Learning, as emphasized by researchers and stakeholders: we briefly explain how the e-Tutor's relevance has grown in the last few years and how his role has been defined as a profession. Then, we try to analyze how the e-Tutor's role in e-Learning scenarios will change in the next few

DOI: 10.4018/978-1-60566-826-0.ch009

Figure 1. The relationships between the role of the e-Tutors, learning goals and various instructional approaches.

	Instructor-centred models	Learner-centred models	Learning team-centred models	Network-oriented models
Open and flexible learning goals				*Evolutions of the role of the e-tutor*
Beahaviour-oriented learning goals			• e-tutor as "moderator"	
Skills-oriented learning goals		• e-tutor as "facilitator"		
Content-oriented learning goals	• e-tutor as "instructor"			

∧
Learning goals

Learning models
and course's ------>
approaches

Instructor-centred models	Learner-centred models	Learning team-centred models	*Network-oriented models*
Content & support approach	Wrap around approach	Integrated or collaborative approach	

years, in terms of functions to be performed, skills to be improved, and training policies to be planned. Probably, we can already imagine a "next generation" of e-Tutors, based on a lot of issues coming from the 2.0 scenarios: but, firstly, we have to understand the background of the e-Tutor's professional profile, and all the possible directions of future evolutions.

1. BACKGROUND: THE e-TUTOR AS AN e-LEARNING PROFESSIONAL: A BRIEF HISTORY

Especially between 1997 and 2000, the research (Calvani & Rotta, 2000; Cornelius & Higgison, 2000; Collison & al., 2000; Salmon, 2000) focused on more complex frameworks to define e-Learning: both researchers and practitioners defined or experimented e-Learning as a wide range of opportunities to change educational strategies. So, in that period, the e-Tutor was involved not only in moderating online communication but also in a lot of other tasks, such as facilitating learners in time management or content understanding, motivating students, supporting technical problems, organizing the virtual learning environment. The main framework (accepted in Italy for many years), according to scenarios described by Mason and Kaye (1992), reinforced by Rowntree (1995), and re-visited in Italy by Trentin (1999), Calvani and Rotta (2000), identified three main "levels" of e-tutoring, matching the main goals of different learning processes and the more referred models of online courses. Thus, referring to the profile of the e-Tutor, firstly we considered the *Instructor*, more involved in supporting content, and content and support models of courses, then the *Facilitator*, more focused on facilitating the learning process in learner-centred, and in the so called wrap-around courses, and, finally, the *Moderator*, more oriented towards the management of conferencing and social interactions between learners with a key-role in all courses based on collaborative approach. All the relationships between e-tutoring and instructional approaches were represented in a framework (Fig.1), in which we can easily identify all the possible evolutions of the e-Tutor's role.

This framework is an essential passage in the history of e-Tutoring studies. At first, the e-Tutor appeared as a complex professional role, to be described identifying a complete profile of competencies. Moreover, the focus on moderating as a specific role in learning-team oriented models of courses led to a deeper inquiry into the set of skills to be used by an e-Tutor in supporting collaborative learning strategies or social interactions, an important step for further evolutions. Finally, such a broad profile made the starting up of a initial discussion on training policies for e-Tutors easier.

1.1. The "Functions" of the Professional e-Tutor

But these scenarios have been changing again in last four or five years. The emergence of learning strategies based on the informal or social approach (use of blogs and wikis in education; social tagging to share knowledge; social networking to improve skills) and the development of e-Learning frameworks more oriented to explore different ways to approach teaching and learning online in universities, schools, corporate or public companies and other scenarios emphasized the need for a more articulated description of the role of e-Tutors. Almost in European vision, the research (Denis & al., 2003; Rotta & Ranieri, 2005) describes the e-Tutor as an expert skilled in a wide set of "functions" he could use in supporting or managing online courses, according to the specific context, and the complexity of the more and more dynamic instructional strategies set in e-Learning projects. The original model by Denis (2003) identifies 11 main functions to set up an "ideal" e-Tutor.

The *Content Facilitator* (function 1) is the e-Tutor when he is helping the students in understanding content with a specific focus on a subject. The *Metacognition Facilitator* (function 2) helps the students to be motivated and empowers theirs capabilities and their awareness of cognitive process, according to Flavell (1979) and other frameworks. The *Process Facilitator* (function 3) helps the students in setting up their learning strategies, suggesting useful solutions for managing time, tasks and goals, and supporting them in effective use of the virtual environment. The *Advisor* (or *Counsellor*, function 4) guides students in selecting courses or educational resources linked to their learning needs, according to the goals defined by a learning organization. The *Assessor* (function 5) assesses the knowledge acquired by the students in a course, but also evaluates the effectiveness of the learning process by monitoring it. The *Technologist* or "technical supporter" (function 6) supports students in using platforms, virtual learning environments and other communication tools to be integrated in a course. The *Resource Provider* (function 7) searches and selects the content to be integrated in the learning process from the Internet (especially in digital libraries, open archives or educational knowledge bases), according to specific needs or in answer to "just in case" or "just in time" student requests; he performs a role similar to the so-called professional information broker, but, in this case focused on educational resources. The *Manager* (or *Administrator*, function 8) helps the students in the management of course planning but can also manage the learning environment suggesting a better organization of content and a more sustainable timing; this function is also similar (as we will see) to the so-called "educational manager". The *Designer* (function 9) collaborates with Instructional Designers in the development of more effective educational resources; he also tests learning objects to be delivered in a course, and suggests learning strategies he can support better by giving the ID of all the elements to identify the best solution. The *Co-learner* (function 10) supports the students flanking them as a peer, so he may have a positive impact on motivation and on emotional implications of e-Learning. Finally, the *Researcher* (function 11) is able to reflect on his own experience, publishing studies about tutoring strategies and writing reports, guidelines and best practices.

1.2. Possible Evolutions of the e-Tutor's Profile

Despite the accurate articulation by Denis, and although similar suggestions are coming forward more and more from practitioners (Clark, 2006), clearly it appears that no e-Tutor (even a professional one with a lot of experience) can be skilled in all the functions identified in the Denis framework: the myth of the "complete" e-Tutor, according to Gardner (2000), does not match with the rising complexity of e-Learning solutions in Web 2.0 scenarios and future developments. Indeed, the same functional framework seems to be unfinished, and it cannot offer a real answer to new issues coming from the field, as the development of the informal approach to learning processes or the social networking as a way to improve the sharing of knowledge in complex organizations. Paradoxically, we need more functions to describe the e-Tutor, even if they are already too many to describe one acknowledged professional profile, and related training policies.

The problem to be solved has two aspects which need to be considered: on the one hand, it involves the search for a more accurate way to highlight all competencies, skills and capabilities really needed by an e-Tutor 2.0 (or simply by a more complex e-Tutor than the one we have observed in action until recently), in the ongoing evolution of e-Learning scenarios. On the other hand, it is closely related to the strategies that, both in a regional, as well as in a European perspective, are still being sought (or developed) for standards in the certification or training programs for e-Tutors. The question is: how we can consolidate the key-role of the e-Tutor in e-Learning as the ultimate challenge to offer a global answer to the scenarios of Life Long Learning, continuous adult education, and other educational perspectives?

2. THE ULTIMATE SETTING OF THE e-TUTOR'S PROFILE: RESEARCH, NOTES FROM THE FIELD AND THE STATE OF THE ART

2.1. The e-Tutor in some European Frameworks

In Europe, we usually consider UK projects and research as that which makes the most indepth inquiry about e-Tutor's roles and skills. The UK background in this specific area has been determined by the wide experience of Universities and Corporate Bodies, the high number of publications and contributions (Salmon, 2000; 2002; OTIS Research Group, and many others) and, lastly, the strategic interest of the government in ICT. Despite such attention to the e-Tutor profile (and even considering the number of absolutely effective applications that exist), UK research does not seem to explore the full opportunity to define a radically innovative vision of the e-Tutor in action. The UK e-Tutor is certainly a professional, but his profile is closely linked to the "e-Moderator" set of skills: above all, he is still an expert in Computer Mediated Communication and a facilitator of peer-to-peer interactions between students, with a special expertise in asynchronous team working (due to the large interest in shared and collaborative courses). A similar framework has been applied to the Training Foundation certificates: usually they identify a profile called e-Tutor, described by a basic set of skills in communication and educational technology; and an upgraded profile, called e-Teacher, described as a Subject Matter Expert able to support learners in content studying, and also capable of setting up and driving online synchronous lectures. Actually, the difference (or the similarity) between an e-Tutor profile which comes from content expertise or develops from the practice of online communication is a core problem. Meanwhile, the debate continues: since 2006, a European project called ISEeT (*Implementing Standards for European eTutor Training*) compares different regional strategies in setting up the e-Tutor profile and in defining related training policies. The UK contribution to the project focuses on e-tutoring skills for Life Long Learning "reflecting differing views of e-Learning practice, from online facilitation of learning groups through to definition as in any electronic intervention, not necessarily online, or web-enabled" and "reflecting different ideas on etutor roles: eFacilitator, eMentor, eTutor, eDeveloper, eTrainer". But other perspectives are emerging: in some countries in which e-Learning is not yet so wide-spread (e.g., Greece, Austria), the core competencies of the e-Tutor are still identified with technical expertise and the ability to manage platforms, to design simple learning objects, and to support their delivery. In countries with more background (e.g., Finland), the focus is on the training of trainers, with specific attention to the difference in learning needs of the different e-Tutors involved in educational programs based on a wide range of objectives. A similar approach - a sort of de-regulation of the profile, due to the evidence of the close relationship between the various functions of e-Tutors and the educational contexts - seems to be being followed in Germany, while, from the French perspective, a consolidated debate and research (Jacquinot, 2002; Rodet, 2008) highlights the metacognitive role of the e-Tutor, focusing especially on psychological skills.

2.2. The Professional e-Tutor in Italian Perspective

Although less known, a consistent contribution to the same focus comes from advanced Italian research on e-Tutor profile and skills. A two-year investigation sponsored by AIF (the *Italian Association of Trainers*) and supported by many stakeholders (universities, the *Italian*

e-Learning Society (SIeL), as well as public and private organizations) identified the e-Tutor as the first certified e-Learning professional in Italy (Panini, 2005), with the exception of a mandatory quality auditing procedure for an "online tutor" profile set up by CEPAS in 2004 according to the ISO standards for professional trainers. The AIF certification program starts begins with a precise description of the e-Tutor as one of the most important stakeholders in e-Learning scenarios. In defining the profile, skills and training policies, the research team builds on the theoretical framework of Denis (2004) and compares it with other models (Kemshal-Bell, 2001), as well as considering the Training Foundation quality assurance initiative. It also focuses on the relationship between e-Tutor skills and the learning experience as a complex process. Moreover, two new important features are introduced.

The primary innovation is in the articulation of the certification program. It envisages a double-level opportunity for professional e-Tutors. Thus, an e-Tutor can firstly request a "basic" certificate, called simply *e-Tutor*. To obtain this level, he must demonstrate expertise in complete set of skills usually associated with e-tutoring: advanced communication and relational skills, some technical capabilities, pedagogical expertise, educational and methodological competencies, strategic abilities in organizing collaborative groups of students and in facilitating the learning process from different perspectives. Despite its definition as "basic", this first level profile is very similar to the full e-Tutor as described in international research in the period 2002-2004. However, in the AIF framework a second level of certification is also envisaged; this focuses on three special sets of skills which are related to different contexts and to the evolution of the e-Learning marketplace. Thus, a *basic-level e-Tutor* can request an "advanced" certification as a "*Content Expert*", an "*Educational Manager*" and "*Community Facilitator*".

2.2.1. The e-Tutor as a Content Expert

The "*Content Expert*" is not *simply* a Subject Matter Expert (as defined in management studies or even in Instructional Design), neither is he an e-Teacher as defined in Training Foundation programs: he is an e-Tutor with an indepth expertise in facilitating students in relation to a defined content (Lentell, 2003), capable of sharing an epistemological vision of the subject-matter and in designing learning strategies closely associated with the content itself. We argue that this advanced profile could be a way to certificate many e-Tutors working in universities who are usually involved in content support. At the same time, we can also identify here an opportunity for all those e-Tutors who want to strengthen their learning design competencies and their ability to apply effective learning strategies to a specific field.

2.2.2. The e-Tutor as an Educational Manager

The "*Educational Manager*" (in Italian "*manager didattico*", a profile usually associated with universities and/or complex organizations, even in a more traditional role) is an expert in managing the virtual learning environment from a methodological perspective, but above all, he is an "evaluator" of the whole learning process. He gives assurance about the quality of a course, focusing on the interaction between participants and the related tasks. In fact, he coordinates the e-Tutors, testing the accessibility and the usability of the planned e-tivities (and suggesting improvements if necessary) and empowers the e-Tutors as a permanent "community of practice" inside the training provider context. Thus, this profile links directly to several developments: he could be the basis for a new key-role in the so called "learning organization" (i.e. an evolution of the roles referred to in educational change manage-

ment or to the quality control), as the first step towards exploring the value of teams of e-Tutors as "human capital" (Daniel, 2003; Rotta & Ranieri, 2005). In a word, the "Educational Manager" is also an advanced e-Tutor whose goal is to achieve optimal performance in a learning process, in terms of effectiveness and quality. To achieve this objective, he makes use of complex knowledge and skills i.e., from team-working to human resource empowerment, and usability to quality standards for e-Learning.

2.2.3. The e-Tutor as a Community Facilitator

Finally, the "*Community Facilitator*" encompasses the main profile of the e-Tutor ready for the challenge of Web 2.0 and related instances. He has been described as a professional who is able to start up a virtual learning community, such as in traditional scenarios (i.e. the activation of small communities of learners in collaborative courses, as does the e-Moderator in the 5-stage model by Salmon), or in experiences based on a more informal approach, focusing on the engagement of members in various kinds of social networks (communities of practice, professional communities, alumni groups and other). This advanced e-Tutor must develop a set of core skills to be used in his more relevant actions; these skills include: programming and acting specific strategies to support the motivation of the participants to the life cycle of collaborative groups and communities, organizing them and suggesting solutions useful to improve their performances; activating and moderating all groups and communities working online for educational proposals; driving learners to activate social networks beyond the formal conclusion of a course so they can increase their knowledge sharing resources and expertise with each other.

2.3. The New Functions of the e-Tutor in a Learning 2.0 Perspective

The AIF framework, as it is, is clearly more complete than other international programs. But the real innovation is not in the more complex articulation of the e-Tutor's profile. Rather, it is in a parallel inquiry into how to extend the Denis "functional" scheme to the specific competencies to be used by the e-Tutor in the growing marketplace of e-Learning 2.0, according to Wiley & Edwards (2002), Downes (2006b) and Bonaiuti (2006). So, in relation to the certified profile of the *"Community Facilitator"*, we have added other 3 "functions" to the 11 described by Denis, all closely oriented toward a new definition of the role of the e-Tutor.

2.3.1. The e-Tutor as a Community Manager

First, we define the e-Tutor as a general purpose *"community manager"*: this function requires advanced communication skills and capabilities in building working groups, activating and planning communities of learners (Rosenberg, 2001), facilitating the start up of communities of practice (Brown & Duguid, 2000), addressing all the participants as to their own and to shared goals, organizing the virtual collaborative working environment and, above all, motivating learners in effectively sharing knowledge and social interaction (Mason & Weller, 2000; Salmon, 2002). If we apply a perspective which comes from andragogy as well as from metacognition studies, we can also argue that the e-Tutor performs this community management function every time he tries to drive a group of learners toward a more independent level of social interaction.

2.3.2. The e-Tutor as a Coach

Then we identify the *"e-Coach"* function (in Italian it is like an*"allenatore"* in sport activities, or a *"master"*, if we refer to a game rule's expert) as an evolution of the community management abilities, more focused on supporting individuals in improving their performances in a collaborative group, in a virtual community or in a more complex social network (Biolghini, 2001). The e-Tutor as "e-Coach" must also support learners in educational role-games or in a lot of other active and collaborative learning strategies - such as Problem-Based Learning or Project-Based Learning - in which factors such as time management, team working, problem solving and knowledge of rules are extremely important (Rotta, 2007). In an extended interpretation of the meaning, this function can be associated also with the role of an e-Tutor when he is coordinating a team of e-Tutors with less experience.

2.3.3. The e-Tutor as a Mentor

Finally, we describe the e-Tutor as an *"e-Mentor"* (otherwise called *"supporter"*, as in Thorpe, 2002; but see also: Milne, 2005). This function identifies a set of skills to be used in supporting various kinds of complex social interactions (i.e. social tagging and social bookmarking, such as knowledge sharing strategies in communities of practices); these skills are activated in the planning of sustainable support services for life long learners. But the core of this function is in the mentoring paradigm itself: can an e-Tutor act as a strategic mediator between the objectives of a formal learning experience and all the outcomes the learner might reach increasing his own knowledge in a continuous education perspective? We think he can do so, even it might not be easy. Actually, even in some contexts (i.e. Anglo American universities) the practice of personal training seems to be wide-spread, we need more effective and global models, to give also an answer

Table 1. tTe e-Tutor's role from a "functional" perspective and the relevance of skills related to different functions.

Functions of the e-Tutor [A] Primary skills [B] Secondary skills	Technical skills	Content expertise	Instructional / educational skills	Management skills	Communication skills
Content facilitator		[A]	[A]	[B]	[B]
Metacognition facilitator		[B]	[A]	[B]	[A]
Process facilitator		[B]	[A]	[A]	[B]
Advisor / counsellor		[A]	[B]	[A]	[B]
Assessor	[B]	[A]	[A]	[B]	
Technical supporter	[A]			[B]	
Resource provider	[B]	[A]	[B]	[A]	
Educational manager	[B]		[B]	[A]	[A]
Designer	[A]	[B]	[A]		[B]
Co-learner	[B]	[B]	[A]		[A]
Researcher		[B]	[A]	[B]	[A]
Community manager		[B]	[B]	[A]	[A]
e-Coach		[B]	[A]	[A]	[B]
e-Mentor		[A]	[A]	[B]	[B]

to the need of sustainability in a process in which the boundary between the right of the learner to be supported in a lifelong learning process and the related commitment of the e-Tutor does not appear to be so clear.

2.4. The Professional e-Tutor: Functions and Related Skills

After this indepth investigation, we can summarize an extended framework to describe the e-Tutor's role with 14 main functions and related primary and secondary skill areas to be developed to improve the ability of the e-Tutor in every function he might perform (Table 1).

Although it is clear that the more skills are improved, the better the e-Tutor performance is achieved, this synthesis could be useful in planning training policies for e-Tutors. Moreover, it reports an acknowledged view of the complete e-Tutor role, as it has been defined by the research and by the applications in the field in last 5 years. But, are

we sure that such a framework could give an effective answer to issues such as the intense growth of context-aware learning, social networking and collaborative human interaction in both formal and informal e-learning strategies, or thinking of the issues associated with the charming "liquid" metaphor of the networked present suggested by authors like Zygmunt Bauman (2000)?

3. TOWARD AN INTEGRATED FRAMEWORK FOR THE PROFILE AND THE ROLE OF A "NEXT GENERATION" OF e-TUTORS

New research has a double objective: explore possible new "features" to set up a "next generation" e-Tutor, more updated than the profile encoded in learning organizations or international standards, and, at the same time, focus on a more simple framework to describe the e-Tutor's role. Even the functional description just explained could be a good outcome after years and years of theoretical debate and practical applications. The e-Tutor profile must be re-thought, because the e-Learning scenarios are quickly changing, toward a more complex set of instructional tools and educational strategies need to get ready to learn effectively in a full Knowledge Society.

3.1. The "e-Knowledge" Scenario: Definitions and Implications

Firstly, we focus on the conceptual definition of "*e-Knowledge*" (as a wider scenario than e-Learning) and. more in detail with regard to the profile of the so-called "*e-knower*", as an evolution of the profile of the e-learner, or "*virtual student*" (Palloff & Pratt, 2003). In his innovative contribution, Siemens (2006) shows us how the Web 2.0 is deeply changing the relationship between personal learning needs and knowledge resources and how working in the "knowledge ecology" will be important. The same themes were touched on in a lot of other studies and papers (Anderson, 2007; Downes, 2006a; Rotta, in press). The core concept of all these thoughts is the revolutionary reversing from a learning paradigm based on the role of the e-Tutor as a primary driver between learners and knowledge resources to an absolutely learner-centred perspective, in which every e-learner (or better, every e-knower) has almost complete control in a dynamic personal environment oriented to organizing information, learning and knowing (Downes, 2006b), and the e-Tutor (as with other professionals) focuses his action on a mere personalized "scaffolding" strategy. In this way, to identity the new role of the e-Tutors in their interactions with learners we must firstly ask ourselves what it really means to be a good e-knower today (Pettenati & Cigognini, 2007). Comparing literature and reflecting on these assets, we can identify a set of emerging attitudes and skills to be developed:

- **Searching:** The ability to use search-engines effectively and define search strategies to discover specific online resources (Johnson & Magusin, 2005);
- **Knowledge hunting:** The ability to explore the Internet browsing the resources from a serendipitous perspective and the ability to retrieve the information needed even if it is hidden in the so-called deep web;
- **Critical thinking:** The ability to compare knowledge resources for a better problem setting or to share them in a collaborative environment (Gokhale, 1995), and the ability to select the most appropriate ones for a subject-matter or for an objective, with particular attention to factors like accuracy, quality and coverage;
- **Self-mentoring:** The ability to address the learning process to outcomes connected with specific needs and to build new knowledge on prior knowledge, including the ability to improve performance in problem solving (Reisslein & al., 2007);
- **Self-evaluating:** The ability to analyze and evaluate how we are building new knowledge (even by self-assessment), to adjust the learning process and integrate it with other resources if necessary;
- **Managing knowledge:** The skills involved in organizing a personal information environment (Frand & Hixon, 1999; Gambles, 2001) or a knowledge base linked to learning needs and goals;
- **Interacting effectively:** The advanced communication skills useful to interact with knowledge providers, experts, colleagues and other learners, and the skill to do it both in peer-to-peer environments and in structured ones;
- **Connecting and networking:** The ability to participate actively to social networks, discussion groups, learning communities and communities of practice, including the

ability to contribute to the "architecture" of participation (Anderson, 2007);

- **Re-mediating:** The ability to decode the multiple languages of the Internet (Bolter & Grusin, 1999) and the skill to communicate and interact by using different media;
- **Envisioning:** According to various frameworks (Horn, 1998; Tufte, 1990), the ability to represent knowledge through images and diagrams (as in concept mapping, information mapping or other knowledge visualization models), and the ability to read and understand visual knowledge.

This list may, obviously, be incomplete, but it can represent a good starting point for a deep tracking of the evolution of the e-Tutor profile. We have to ask ourselves how many e-knowers really possess these abilities or are already so skilled. Probably, there is an unaccepted and unexplored gap between the opportunities of the Web 2.0 as a learning and knowing scenario, and the reality: e-knowers are not so ready to earn all the advantages of a self-centred perspective if we abandon them, even the optimists (as in the so called O'Reilly paradigm) would firmly believe in the "wisdom of the crowd", otherwise read as a power to be harnessed (Anderson, 2007).

3.2. The Role of the e-Tutor in Scaffolding the "e-Knower"

In fact, in integrated and personal environments e-knowers need to be more supported than in traditional ones, since the new ones are more open and complex. So, the relevance of the e-Tutor's role will grow, although the e-Tutor's profile will radically change. The first change concerns the role of e-Tutors in helping e-knowers to consolidate the attitudes and the abilities requested by the emerging scenario, as suggested above. This may involve the empowerment of some well identified e-Tutor functions, and the encoding of new functions to be added to the Denis theoretical framework and related extensions. The functions to be improved seem to be almost the "*process facilitator*", the "*advisor/counsellor*", the "*resource provider*" (see also Johnson & Magusin, 2005), the "*co-learner*" and the "*e-Coach*", as we can summarize in a table (Table 2).

We can observe that the process-oriented functions will probably become more and more important than the content-oriented. Second, despite the previously discussed relevance of the metacognitive actions (Rotta & Ranieri, 2005), we can argue that the emerging areas in which the e-Tutors will have to improve their skills will

Table 2. The emerging skills to be improved as e-learners or e-knowers and the related primary and secondary functions requested to the e-Tutors.

e-learner or e-knower skill to be improved and supported	Primary e-tutoring function to be applied to the improvement of e-learners and e-knowers	Other e-tutoring functions useful to reach the goal
☐ searching	resource provider	process facilitator
☐ knowledge hunting	resource provider	metacognition facilitator
☐ critical thinking	co-learner	resource provider
☐ self-mentoring	process facilitator	e-Coach, e-Mentor
☐ self-evaluating	advisor/counsellor	metacognition facilitator
☐ managing knowledge	resource provider	process facilitator
☐ interacting effectively	process facilitator	e-Coach, e-Mentor
☐ connecting and networking	e-Coach	community manager
☐ re-mediating	process facilitator	co-learner, designer
☐ envisioning	metacognition facilitator	designer

be above all *counselling, information brokering* and *management*. This is a very important step for future training policies: indeed, if the counselling skills seem to be closely connected to the e-Tutor's basic training in most of the frameworks (Rotta & Ranieri, 2005), only in few courses for e-Tutors have information brokering and management been usually considered as relevant items.

3.3. New "Functions" for Advanced e-Tutoring

In this way we could also re-think the functional framework for the e-Tutor's profile, adjusting some definitions or adding new functions more oriented to these scaffolding needs. For example, it appears easy to add a function we could call "*motivator*", widely described as a soft set of skills to improve the need of e-learners and e-knowers to be driven in their user-centred and process-oriented experience (according to several studies which focus on the relevance of motivational role of the e-Tutor, e.g. OTIS research or the ISEeT framework). We could also imagine more sophisticated functions not yet explored by the researchers, according to a lot of adult education frameworks on problem-based learning (i.e. Wood & al., 1976; Hay & Schmuck, 1993), peer-to-peer and self-assessed educational strategies (Bandura, 1997):

- the "*media educator*": a function to be used in supporting envisioning and re-mediating needs of e-knowers, but also a well studied instructional role to help learners in understanding multimedia communication and the specific languages of new media;
- the "*discrete connector*": a specific extension of the community manager skills, focused on the back-end actions needed to drive e-knowers in a more effective self-evaluation of their own networking and communicating capabilities;
- the "*serendipitous fellow*": an advanced co-learning function integrated with

information brokering skills, applied to the e-knowers' need to explore non-conventional resources on the Web and to improve their discovery learning skills;

- the "*problem setter*": a specific and well explored function to be used in problem-based and problem-solving educational strategies, i.e. the educational role of the e-Tutor when he is helping a student to identify and compare resources and points of view to solve a simple problem (e.g., in a web quest) or more and more complex problems, such as case-study solution searching.

3.4. The Conceptual Framework of Integrated Personal Learning Environments

But is this speculative inquiry really useful? It might only help us to built a too complicated theoretical framework (up to 19 main functions at the moment!), with little possibility of being applied. So, we have to evaluate other hypotheses, focusing on the more relevant e-Tutor actions in emerging scenarios or, better, on a more accurate inquiry into the relationship between *learners* and *learning* in the upcoming lifelong education. This is probably the way to plan our experimental strategy for the next years.

The primary argument to be explored is the concept of "*Integrated Personal Learning Environment*" (IPLE), still not very studied except in Mobile Learning frameworks (Corlett & al., 2005). An IPLE can be described as a dynamic answer to the lifelong learning needs of every *e-knower* who is aware enough (or motivated by the context, i.e. if he is a professional with less time to spend, or an adult with just-in-time or just-in-case needs) to learn usually following a three-way integrated strategy: a *formal* approach, an *informal* approach and a *social* approach. We can explain instantly the whole framework in a visual concept (Fig.2).

Figure 2. A visual synthesis of an integrated personal learning environment framework.

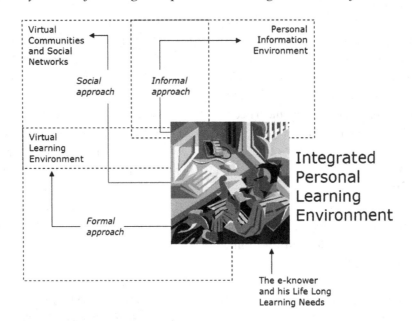

In the *formal* approach, the e-knower searches for an answer to his needs in the e-Learning marketplace, enrolling on a number of courses delivered by universities, government, public companies, corporate bodies or other providers. His learning experience could be individual or collaborative, or even partly social: but probably all the instructional strategies the learner will encounter in the courses he decided to enrol in will be based on a formal-driven model, in which, usually, learning is assessed, courses are time-scheduled, process is managed by a Virtual Learning Environment (i.e. an e-Learning platform) and content is well structured, selected or produced by the learning provider.

In the *informal* approach e-knowers search and download from the Internet distributed educational resources to learn from, following their needs and organizing the selected resources according to their goals. It is usually an individual approach, but it can evolve easily towards a social one, i.e. when e-knowers share their bookmarks or tags with other e-knowers by interacting in environments like Connotea, De.lic.ious or Think Tag, often useful

as organizers for the resources selected. Moreover, the informal approach is self-assessed and unrecognized, but it represents a good opportunity to learn using a time-independent strategy and the usual and necessary integration of every personal lifelong learning policy, even if it involves a lot of self-motivation.

In the *social* approach e-knowers learn by sharing with other e-knowers expertise, problems and solutions or simply questions and answers: they interact in networks built starting with a topic, a goal, a professional need or a cultural trend. They communicate using specific integrated environments, which are now more and more the hybrid result of the evolution of VLEs. According to consolidated studies and suggestions by researchers (Palloff & Pratt, 1999), we can identify many different kinds of communities and networks (e.g., communities of interest, communities of practice, professional social networks), each with its own process-oriented strategy. Thus, it is difficult to describe this approach as a uniform model. We can only say that, from the learner's point of view, it is a typical collaborative and interactive approach,

Figure 3. The core actions of the e-Tutor in supporting the e-knowers in an integrated personal learning environment.

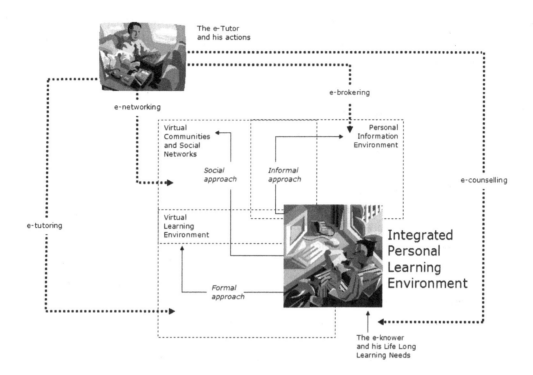

often de-structured and usually self-assessed, but not so time-independent as it seems.

3.5. The Role of the e-Tutor in Integrated Personal Learning Environments

It's clear that the e-knowers cannot gain real advantages by integrating all these approaches without an effective support and a goal-oriented scaffold. In reality, most e-Tutors are involved only in the formal area, supporting courses, assessing learning or driving e-tivities. Thus, we have to complete the framework strategically directing e-Tutors toward a more integrated scaffolding. First, we can allocate e-Tutors in all the areas of the integrated environment, focusing on the roles he can interpret in such a scenario. In this way, the conceptual framework appears

to be almost complete, so we can easily track the e-Tutor's *core actions* with reference to the different areas in which the e-knowers interact (Fig.3). In this way we can identify a new vision of the e-Tutor's strategic role from a perspective we could dare to call "learning[3]" (beyond the learning 2.0 paradigm).

3.5.1. The e-Counselling Role

The primary action to be considered as essential is *e-counselling*: the e-knowers must be supported and advised to identify all their learning needs and find an integrated solution using a blending of formal, informal and social approaches. So the e-Tutor will help them to do this, focusing on problem setting, gap analysis, problem solving, monitoring and evaluation. The main function of the e-Tutor in this activity is quite that of the "educational manager", but a lot of new skills will have to be developed, especially those which refer to problem setting, evaluation of learning processes and systemic approach (useful in suggesting integrated solutions to the e-knowers, considering their expectations and the possible outcomes).

3.5.2. The Strictly e-Tutoring Role

The strictly *e-tutoring* action in the formal approach area is more similar to the "traditional" role of the e-Tutor which has been widely analyzed by the literature and explained above. This activity is very important in all its functions, which usually include the content, the process and the metacognition facilitator. But, from a wider perspective *e-tutoring* is also helping the e-knowers to set up and organize their learning environments according to their personalized needs. Thus, the e-Tutors need to improve management skills, instructional skills and specific attitudes for working with the constant flexibility requested to "adapt" the courses selected by the e-knowers, i.e. integrating the standardized format usually set by the providers, scheduling and managing alternative learning activities.

3.5.3. The e-Brokering Function

The *e-brokering* role is quite innovative: the core function related to this role is the "resource provider", according to its extended definition (see table 2). But the specialist e-Tutors involved in this area will also have to improve technical skills to work effectively with personal information environments (including the capability to program intelligent agents for data mining); he will have to develop strong skills in knowledge management and semantic approach to web resources, including working with multi-lingual thesauri, ontologies and information mapping tools. Certainly, e-knowers will also need to be supported in surviving to emerging 2.0 information

overload (Rotta, 2008) and in locating effective and quality-confirmed resources. Therefore, this action area will probably soon evolve toward a new professional profile (Johnson & Magusin, 2005), with the double-skills found in both educational strategies and a librarian's background.

3.5.4. The e-Networking Funtions

Finally, the *e-networking* actions, even they might seem to be referred to a primary set of consolidated skills, are radically different from those expected in a traditional e-moderator's role in communities and social networks. The social approach of the e-knowers in their integrated learning environments can in fact only be flanked by the discrete touch of a specialist e-Tutor, but not directly driven (because of the nature of social networking 2.0 itself, and because of the self-regulated organization of professional communities or communities of practice). Thus, the core functions of the e-Tutors in this area cannot be so related to mediated communication or conferencing *inside* communities and networks, but rather to the "e-coaching" and the "e-mentoring" roles toward e-knowers. As an *e-networker*, the e-Tutor is an independent third part who moves between the e-knowers and the networks in which they are interested or involved. He helps the e-knowers in selecting the more goal-oriented approach toward their learning (or professional) needs; drawing the architectures of their active participation; motivating them to share expertise, information, problems and more, so they can gather useful resources and construct new knowledge. Perhaps this is a very difficult role to perform, and it is also difficult to limit it in a solid framework. However, as we will see, it could be partially solved by integrating the actions of the *e-counselling*, *e-brokering* and *e-tutoring*.

4. APPLICATIONS: AN ASSISTED LEARNING STRATEGY FOR LIFELONG LEARNERS SUPPORTED BY A NEXT GENERATION OF e-TUTORS

Most of this framework has been adopted by E-Form (one of the most important Italian consortia of universities and other stakeholders) to activate a support service for lifelong learners called PAL (*Personal Assisted Learning*). As in other countries, also in Italy there is a growing debate on how e-Learning could be integrated effectively in lifelong learning policies (Calvani et. al., 2008; De Vita, 2007; Federici & Ragone, 2008). Universities and professionals, as well as public companies, are trying to find a uniform framework to apply some principles shared in a European perspective (e.g. the acknowledgement of learning credits and the emphasis on e-portfolios), and make e-Learning a sustainable alternative way to vocational training. So, with reference to emerging trends, the PAL service starts from the process of knowing from the e-knower perspective, in order to find the best answer to lifelong learning needs in an integrated and personal learning environment, scaffolded with a coordinated range of parallel actions carried out by a team of e-Tutors interpreting respectively the roles of the *e-counsellor*, the *e-broker*, and *e-tutor* in the strict sense of the term.

4.1. The Learning Process and the Actions of the e-Tutor

Usually, in this application every professional e-Tutor chooses and interprets only one of the possible roles, according to skills, expertise and attitudes. But the roles may be interchanged without negative impacts on the framework, if all the actions of the e-Tutor are transparent toward the e-knower, whose primary and direct interactions (beyond the ones he performs with educational resources, colleagues or other par-

ticipants in courses, groups or networks in which he is involved by chance) are those he performs with the *e-tutoring* role, since, in most cases, the *e-counselling* and the *e-brokering* is interpreted as acting indirectly on the process and on the environment. The whole process can be described at least in ten main steps (Table 3).

As we can see, the role of the e-Tutors in this application is far beyond the traditional functions. Moreover, we have to consider that, in such a model, the extended meaning of "resource" exceeds the educational materials we can find in distributed digital libraries, open archives or learning objects repositories, and includes both courses delivered by different providers, goal-oriented communities and other context-aware learning environments, in which specific and context-oriented e-Tutors can interact with the e-knowers. Thus, the e-Tutors involved in a service like PAL are not only working on a more open and wide scaffolding framework, but they are also exploring a dynamically changing meta-role, to be performed by improving skills. Now the immediate question is: how many e-Tutors are really ready for this challenge?

5. TOWARD THE FUTURE: ADVANCED TRAINING POLICIES FOR A NEXT GENERATION OF e-TUTORS

The issue involves another question: how can we become good e-Tutors in near future? For many years teachers or trainers learned to be e-Tutors in two typical ways: they attended formal courses, usually on computer mediated communication, e-Learning theories, virtual identity and instructional strategies; and, directly, by doing hands-on, supporting individuals or moderating groups of learners, often without a suitable background to do so. In fact, in the past, most e-Tutors improvised: they learned especially from experience and practice,

Table 3. The role and the core actions of the e-Tutors in an integrated and personalized learning process.

The e-knower	The integrated personal learning process according to the e-knower's perspective	The role and the actions of the e-Tutor		
		As e-Counsellor	As e-Broker	As e-Tutor
Explains his learning needs or knowing wishes	**Searching and selecting educational resources, courses and networks**	*Suggesting topics and resources to be selected*	*Searching and selecting educational resources*	*Testing the selected resources*
	↓			
Chooses resources, enrols in courses, becomes a member of networks	**Building an Integrated Personal Learning Environment with selected resources, courses or networks**	*Calculating the value of resources in CFU (learning credits) and assigning resources according to number of credits to be acquired*	*Organizing a shared knowledge base (KB), by referencing and tagging all the selected resources*	*Organizing the IPLE of each e-knower according to suggestions of the e-counsellor and extracting resources from the KB*
	↓			
Works on resources, attends the courses, participates in networks	**Activating the IPLE and starting the learning process according to a more formal, informal or social approach**	*Scaffolding in social approach area, helping the e-knower to interact effectively with networks*	*Scaffolding in informal approach area, helping the e-knower to build his own dynamic Personal Information Environment (PIE)*	*Scheduling the delivery of all the resources assigned and scaffolding the e-knower as a process facilitator*
	↓			
Self-evaluates progress toward the goals related to needs	**Monitoring the learning process**	*Suggesting integrative e-tivities*	*Tagging assigned resources by relevance according to self-evaluation of the e-knower*	*Monitoring the process applying different formats to formal, informal and social approach*
	↓			
Performs integrative e-tivites	**Integrating the learning process with personalized e-tivities**	*Evaluating the progress according to credits to be assessed*	*Suggesting useful resources to plan integrative e-tivities*	*Planning and delivering integrative e-tivities and scaffolding the e-knower as a metacognition facilitator*
	↓			
Enriches knowledge acquired with integrative resources	**Delivering integrative educational resources**	*Assigning integrative resources*	*Integrating the KB with other resources*	*Scaffolding the e-knower as a content facilitator*
	↓			
Performs assessment tests	**Assessing knowledge**	*Evaluating the results of assessments*	*Organizing a KB for the assessments to be re-used or shared*	*Planning and delivering assessments*
	↓			
Self-evaluates the outcomes and highlights other possible learning needs	**Evaluating knowledge and acknowledging learning credits**	*Registering the results on the e-Portfolio and acknowledging credits*	*Verifying the format of e-Portfolio entries*	*Writing a final report on the objectives reached and outcomes related*

by trying to apply their often useless theoretical framework and their unsystematic expertise to changing scenarios and different contexts.

5.1. European Training Policies for the e-Tutor Professional Profile

The same *European Core Curriculum for e-Tutors in Vocational Education and Training* (VET) defined within the ISEeT project is still founded on 5 traditional modules:

- Facilitating, supporting, and promoting learning online
- E-learning theory in practice
- Using technology in e-learning
- E-learning and course design
- Assessment and e-learning

These modules, as wrote in the ISEeT project, "can be extended using optional modules according to national needs". But it appears clearly that, although the content of the courses might be quality-oriented, such a standard cannot cover the complex range of skills requested to be a "real" e-Tutor.

Based on new research and on the frameworks and the applications explained above, we are now identifying other strategies for more effective "next generation" e-Tutor training policies. This is a role which is evolving toward a more and more complex articulation of needs especially for a real professional training. The most effective instructional strategy to achieve that is probably a *blended* solution consisting of formal courses or modules (but based on case-studies and problem solving tasks), informal learning, non-formal apprenticeship in-the-field supported by an expert e-Tutor (in a mentoring role), and continuous education, which also sustains the development of professional communities (such as the business-oriented American *e-tutor.com*, or the Italian *etutorcommunity.org*) as opportunities for sharing

knowledge and expertise in a social approach and social interaction between colleagues.

5.1. A Framework for the Vocational Training of the "Next Generation" e-Tutors

Various frameworks (Denis, 2003; Kemshal-Bell, 2001; Salmon, 2000) and specific studies on e-Tutor improvement with a comparative analysis of many quality-oriented experiences (Rotta & Ranieri, 2005), agree on a well-structured 7 steptraining strategy:

1. *Activation.* A non-formal step in which the applicant e-Tutor can activate prior knowledge by self-assessment and self-evaluation, so as to verify the requirements necessary and the skills possessed to become professionals. The step could be integrated using informal resources about e-Learning theories, educational strategies or other content about scenarios in which the e-Tutor will possibly be involved.

2. *Problem setting and critical thinking.* A formal problem-based module which focuses on samples and case-studies. The applicant e-Tutor observes many typical situations which need to be solved and gives feedback to the learner or applies other support strategies, and evaluates different solutions to the problem set. Though usually collaborative, the module can be integrated with individual formal assignments on computer mediated communication.

3. *Building and reinforcing knowledge.* The core formal module in which most of the content could be delivered to applicant e-Tutors. The typical content could be the same as that described in the ISEeT *European Core Curriculum for e-Tutors in Vocational Education and Training*, or in other formal frameworks, adding, if necessary, other

context-related content together with both individual and collaborative assignments. However, the step must also be integrated with a laboratory on e-Tutor skills, both to assess the progress of the training and to make the applicant e-Tutors more conscious of their professional development.

4. *Modelling and planning strategies.* A formal and partly non-formal module, similar to the so-called "application" step in some post-constructivist frameworks (e.g., Merrill, 2002; Salmon, 2002), or to the problem solving approach in problem-based learning models. The applicant e-Tutor begins to apply both the theoretical and the practical knowledge acquired during the previous steps, trying to plan in detail a complete e-tutoring strategy to be executed in a specific context or scenario (either a real or a simulated one), which includes templates for core-actions or feedback messages and the scheduling of e-tivities. The step could be partly collaborative, and could be integrated with informal educational resources useful in reinforcing specific skills, such as project management, information brokering, or web writing.

5. *Simulations.* A formal and partly non-formal step in which part of the e-tivities or other instructional strategies planned by the applicant e-Tutor in the previous module will be simulated to verify their sustainability and effectiveness. Simulations will be driven by an expert and, in part, reviewed peer-to-peer. Also specific e-tutoring operating areas (e.g., moderating synchronous interactions in a virtual chat room, using shared whiteboards, and/or other networked educational software) will be simulated, so that e-Tutor basic training can be considered complete.

6. *Professional training by apprenticeship.* A step (similar to a formal stage) for the improvement of the skills of applicant e-Tutors, so that they can really become professionals.

During a 3-6 month period each apprentice e-Tutor works with a "master" (an expert e-Tutor as a mentor) in one or more real courses or educational projects, in a co-tutoring role, partly moderating and supporting the learners directly thanks to the suggestions of the "master", and partly monitoring the process and reflecting on how the "master" himself is solving problems and performing effective e-tutoring strategies.

7. *Continuous vocational training.* The final step to improve e-tutoring skills using a social approach focused on active participation in both general purpose virtual communities of e-Tutors and specific communities of practice (e.g. the social networks activated to coordinate the action of a group of e-Tutors involved in an educational project, as in Giannini & al., 2005).

Most of the e-Tutor training programs are generally limited to step 3 or, sometimes, to steps ranging from 1 to 4, according to more innovative instructional models or more specific needs (e.g. a master degree on e-tutoring). Simulations (step 5) are rarely scheduled in courses for e-Tutors, probably because they are a difficult educational strategy to implement and perform. Professional and continuous training are opportunities which still need to be explored.

CONCLUSION

An initial concrete application of the whole framework explained above is close to being applied as a pre-requirement for professional e-Tutors performing their role within the *Personal Assisted Learning* (PAL) project of E-Form, and as a development of the AIF (*Italian Association of Trainers*) quality certification strategy. The innovative training program is called *e-Tutor UP* and will initially be delivered in Italian, and then in other European languages. In these ready-to-go training program simulations, problem-based approach are greatly improved, and the final two steps of the strategy will be based on a virtual training "playground" in which e-Tutors are coached by senior e-Tutors and share questions while they are waiting to play an active role in one or more phases of the e-learning projects and/or courses which need support. The participation of the e-Tutors in professional communities or other social networks will be acknowledged in learning credits, by evaluating the quality of social interactions and the measurable improvement in skills, according to self-assessed grids defined by the coaches.

However, even vocational training policies for e-Tutors will be greatly improved in the next few years. The most important question is if this will be enough. As explained above, the e-Tutor role is difficult to define precisely. Moreover, the e-learning scenario is changing quickly, and a growing range of communication technologies and educational software will be considered in implementing learning projects. For example, the e-Tutor Project by JISC (Joint Information Systems Committee) states that "the potential to develop and deliver education and training on-line using ubiquitous technologies, social networking and open source software, and freely available on-line resources" is yet to be explored as a matter of e-tutoring. The consequence of such an evolution is the need for e-Tutors expert in executing more and more specific functions and ready to adapt to more and more complex instructional strategies. Thus, in the near future, the "general purpose" e-Tutors will probably be unable to perform a relevant role and will disappear quickly as a professional profile. However, the same "next generation" e-Tutors (i.e. the professionals defined by the functional extended framework) might not be a definitive solution to the fluid situations which can be identified in innovative learning and knowing environments, especially those related to the use of social software and social networks in education or training.

The next question is, how can we describe the e-Tutor profile related to these scenarios? Many other questions need to be answered. Can the ability to interact as a proactive e-Tutor in social environments oriented toward educational goals really be decoded in terms of functions and related skills? How will the e-Tutor role change with the impossibility to decode non-formal and informal learning processes as an accurate sequence of steps to be supported by e-tivities as in structured online courses? And how can the e-Tutor interact effectively in open social environments which are highly focused on the peer-to-peer relationship between participants? There are two views in relation to these and other related themes. The first, according to authors such as Wiley & Edwards (2002) or Siemens (2006), considers learning-oriented social networks usually as decentralized and self-organized environments; consequently, in this knowledge-based *connective* hypothesis, the relevance of strictly e-tutoring decreases, and the e-Tutor's role focuses on an improvement in soft communication, interaction and knowledge sharing between learners. On the contrary, the second perspective, according to research on *e-moderating*, seems to be more interested in exploring the increasing role of educators and trainers in "bridging" between learners, learning needs, learning goals and learning strategies, especially when communities or groups of learners interact in open social environments. From this point of view, the more a learning environment is open and social-oriented, the more it must to be moderated by professional e-Tutors engaged in a discrete but effectiveness-oriented support strategy. However, both perspectives are converging on the primary need of a *human touch* in learner care and in supporting online social interactions, so we can say that the debate on e-tutoring competencies will grow.

The core of this debate is an *agenda* for the search for a new paradigm of the e-Tutor's role: as we tried to explain, the main issues in such an agenda can be considered as the outline of

Figure 4. A new framework: the main directions of the e-tutoring area.

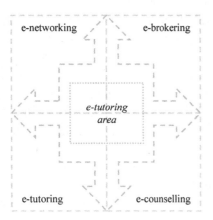

a dynamic new framework (Fig.4) in which e-tutoring appears as an open "area" extending in 4 main directions: e-counselling, e-brokering, e-networking and e-tutoring in a common sense approach (i.e., e-moderating).

This framework could be read in two ways: it can identify the issues necessary to explore the complex skills and the whole definition of a complete professional e-Tutor who is able to perform all the functions related to the different areas; or, it might suggest that in the future we will have to consider e-tutoring as a sort of "mashup" of 4 different specific (and partly innovative) roles to be integrated into developing e-learning projects or knowledge-building strategies, each of which is to be performed by different specialists. Both options can be evaluated as effective, although the second seems to be a better solution for advanced scenarios (i.e. complex organizations), and for most e-learning projects oriented toward community-based or social-based solutions, or interested in social software and social environments. In these visions, the complexity of interactions between participants and the range of educational instances grows. Thus, acting as an e-Tutor in every area of this extended vision can involve a more and more specific set of functions, and the need of specialists in e-counselling, e-brokering, e-networking, or

e-tutoring instead of a full performer, even if the solution and the balance between different options must be evaluated on each occasion.

Till now, we have also been asking how we might extract from such an extended framework some guidelines for training policies for e-Tutors in a lifelong learning perspective. As mentioned above, the most important issues to be explored are continuous training and the professional empowerment of e-Tutors. We have many courses for e-tutoring throughout Europe (even if most of them do not consider the "next generation" profile of the e-Tutor), but we have only a few opportunities to maintain and improve e-tutoring skills as scheduled in some regional quality certification frameworks. The way to do this may be the development of professional communities for e-Tutors as opportunities to share problems, knowledge and best practices, so that we might integrate strategies to help e-Tutors to overcome the gaps in policies for the evaluation of e-tutor skills shortages, as in other professional areas.

English Text Reviewed by Elisabeth Guerin

REFERENCES

Anderson, P. (2007). What is Web 2.0? Ideas, technologies, and implications for education. *JISC, Technology & Standards Watch*. Retrieved on August 14, 2008, from http://www.jisc.ac.uk/media/documents/techwatch/tsw0701b.pdf

Atwell, G. (2007). E-portfolio: The DNA of the personal learning environment? *Journal of E-Learning and Knowledge Society*.

Bandura, A. (1997). *Self-efficacy: The exercise of control*. New York: W. H. Freeman.

Barker, P. (2002). On being an online tutor. *Innovations in Education and Teaching International*, *39*(1), 3–13. doi:10.1080/13558000110097082

Bauman, Z. (2000). *Liquid modernity*. Cambridge, MA: Polity Press.

Berge, Z. L., & Collins, M. P. (Eds.). (1995). Computer mediated communication and the online classroom (Vols. 1-3). Cresskill, NJ: Hampton Press.

Biolghini, D. (Ed.). (2001). *Comunità in rete e Net learning. Innovazione dei sistemi organizzativi e processi di apprendimento nelle comunità virtuali.* Milano: Etas.

Bolter, J., & Grusin, R. (1999). *Remediation. Understanding new media.* Cambridge, MA: The MIT Press.

Bonaiuti, G. (Ed.). (2006). *E-learning 2.0. Il futuro dell'apprendimento in rete tra formale e informale.* Trento: Erickson.

Brown, J. S., & Duguid, P. (2000). *The social life of information.* Cambridge, MA: Harvard Business School Press.

Calvani, A., Bonaiuti, G., & Fini, A. (2008). Lifelong learning: What role for e-learning 2.0. *Journal of e-Learning and Knowledge Society, 4*(1), 2008. Retrieved from http://www.je-lks.it/en/08_01/06Metcalv_enl.pdf

Calvani, A., & Rotta, M. (2000). *Fare formazione in Internet.* Trento: Erickson.

Canzi, A., Folcio, A., Dilani, M., Radice, S., Santangelo, E., & Zanoni, E. (2004, May 10-12). *Da tutor-facilitatore a tutor-instructional designer: Evoluzione del ruolo in contesti di blended learning, in AICA (Ed.), Didamatica 2004.* Ferrara.

Clark, D. (2006). *E-tutoring.* EPIC, White Papers. Retrieved on August 14, 2008, from http://www.epic.co.uk/content/resources/white_papers/pdf_versions/Delivery/Epic_White_Paper_E_tutoring.pdf

Collison, G., Elbaum, B., Haavind, S., & Tinker, R. (2000). *Facilitating online learning. Effective strategies for moderators.* Madison, WI: Atwood Publishing.

Corlett, D., Chan, T., Ting, J., & Sharples, M. (2005). Interactive logbook: A mobile portfolio and personal development planning tool. In *M-Learn 2005 Proceedings.* Cape Town, M-Learn. Retrieved from http://www.mlearn.org.za/CD/papers/Corlett.pdf

Cornelius, S., & Higgison, C. (2000). *Online tutoring e-book.* OTIS Research Group, Online Tutoring Skills Project. Retrieved on August 14, 2008, from http://otis.scotcit.ac.uk/onlinebook/

Daniel, B., Schwier, R. A., & McCalla, G. (2003). Social capital in virtual learning communities and distributed communities of practice. *Canadian Journal of Learning and Technology, 29*(3), 2003.

De Vita, A. (2007). *L'e-learning nella formazione professionale. Strategie, modelli e metodi.* Trento: Erickson.

DeKerckhove, D. (Ed.). (2003). *La conquista del tempo. Società e democrazia nell'era della rete.* Roma: Editori Riuniti.

Denis, B. (2003). Quels rôles et quelle formation pour les tuteurs intervenant dans des dispositifs de formation à distance? *Distances et savoirs, 1*(1), 2003.

Denis, B., Watland, P., Pirotte, S., & Verday, N. (2004). Roles and competencies of the e-tutor. In *NCL2004.* Retrieved from http://www.shef.ac.uk/ncl2004/Proceedings/Symposium

Downes, S. (2006a). Learning networks and connective knowledge. Retrieved on August 14, 2008, from http://it.coe.uga.edu/itforum/upcoming.html

Downes, S. (2006b). Web 2.0, e-learning 2.0, and personal learning environments. Retrieved on August 14, 2008, from http://www.downes.ca/files/nutn2006.ppt

Federici, G., & Ragone, G. (2008). University and lifelong learning in Italy: Policies and higher education, and training systems integration. *Journal of e-Learning and Knowledge Society, 4*(1). Retrieved from http://www.je-lks.it/en/08_01/03Metfed_en1.pdf

Flavell, J. H. (1979). Metacognition and cognitive monitoring: A new area of cognitive-developmental inquiry. *The American Psychologist, 34*(10), 906–911. doi:10.1037/0003-066X.34.10.906

Frand, J., & Hixon, C. (1999). Personal knowledge management: Who, what, why, when, where, how? Berkeley, UCLA. Retrieved on August 14, 2008, from http://www.anderson.ucla.edu/faculty/jason.frand/researcher/speeches/PKM.htm

Gambles, A. (2001, March). The headline personal information environment. *D-LIB Magazine*. Retrieved from http://www.dlib.org/dlib/march01/gambles/03gambles.html

Gardner, H. (2000). The complete tutor. *Technos: Quarterly for Education and Technology, 9*, 3.

Giannini, L., Nati, B., Pettinari, E., & Rotta, M. (2005, May 12-14). FAD: Didattica dell'italiano. Riflessioni tra contenuto e relazione nel progetto di formazione in rete Giunti Scuola. In AICA (Ed.), *Didamatica 2005*. Potenza.

Gokhale, A. A. (1995). Collaborative learning enhances critical thinking. *Journal of Technology Education, 7*(1). Retrieved from http://scholar.lib.vt.edu/ejournals/JTE/jte-v7n1/gokhale.jte-v7n1.html

Hay, J. A., & Schmuck, M. F. (l993). *Problem-based learning: Development and analysis of a tutor evaluation form for use in small-group problem-based learning*. Paper presented at the Annual Meeting of the American Educational Research Association.

Hermans, B. (1998). Desperately seeking: Helping hands and human touch. *First Monday, Peer Reviewed Journal on the Internet, 3*, 11. Retrieved from http://www.firstmonday.dk/issues/issue3_11/hermans/index.html

Horn, R. E. (1998). *Visual language: Global communication for the 21ˢᵗ century*. Beainbridge Island, WA: Macro Vu.

Jacquinot, G. (2002). Absence et présence dans la médiation pédagogique ou comment faire circuler les signes de la présence. In *Pratiquer les TICE, former les enseignants et les formateurs à de nouveaux usages* (pp. 103-113). Bruxelles, De Boeck.

Johnson, K., & Magusin, E. (2005). *Exploring the digital library. A guide for online teaching and learning*. San Francisco, CA: Jossey Bass.

Kanuka, H., Jugdev, K., Heller, B., & West, D. (2006). *The rise of the telecommuter and the fall of community: False promise*. Edmonton, Canada: Athabasca University. Retrieved from http://auspace.athabascau.ca:8080/dspace/handle/2149/1074

Kemshal-Bell, G. (2001). *The online teacher. Final report prepared for the Project Steering Committee of the VET Teachers and Online Learning Project*. ITAM ESD TAFENSW International Centre for VET Teaching and Learning. Retrieved on August 14, 2008, from http://cyberteacher.onestop.net/final%20report.pdf

Lentell, H. (2003). The importance of the tutor in open and distance learning. In A. Tait & R. Mills (Eds.), *Rethinking learner support in distance education* (pp. 64-76). London: Routledge.

Lesser, E. (Ed.). (2000). *Knowledge and social capital: Foundations and applications*. Boston: Butterworth-Heinemann.

Mangione, G. R., Cigognini, M. E., & Pettenati, M. C. (2007, July 4-6). Favorire l'uso critico creativo ed etico della rete nella gestione personale della conoscenza. In Sie-L Società italiana di e-Learning (Ed.), *E-Learning fra formale e informale*. Macerata, Università di Macerata.

Mason, R. D., & Kaye, A. R. (1992). *Collaborative learning through computer conferencing*. Berlin: Springler Verlag.

Mason, R. D., & Weller, M. (2000). Factors affecting students' satisfaction on a Web course. *Australian Journal of Educational Technology, 16*(2), 173–200.

Merrill, M. D. (2002). First principles of instruction. *Educational Technology Research and Development, 50*(3), 43–59. doi:10.1007/BF02505024

Milne, C. S. (2005, January). E-learning: Personal computing. How can mentoring or coaching by email help learners get more out of e-learning? *IT Training*. Retrieved from http://www.train-net.co.uk/news/full_news.cfm?ID=4676

Palloff, R., & Pratt, K. (1999). *Building learning communities in cyberspace*. San Francisco, CA: Jossey Bass.

Palloff, R., & Pratt, K. (2003). *The virtual student. A profile and guide to working with online learners*. San Francisco, CA: Jossey Bass.

Panini, S. (2005). Certificazione AIF del tutor e-learning: Metodo e stato dei lavori. *FOR. Rivista per la Formazione*, 63.

Pettenati, M. C., & Cigognini, M. E. (2007, July-September). Social networking theories and tools to support connectivist learning activities. [IJWLTT]. *International Journal of Web-Based Learning and Teaching Technologies, 2*(3), 39–57.

Reisslein, J., Sullivan, H., & Reisslein, M. (2007, January). Learner achievement and attitudes under different paces of transitioning to independent problem solving. *Journal of Engineering Education*. Retrieved from http://findarticles.com/p/articles/mi_qa3886/is_200701/ai_n18706112

Rodet, J. (2008). Tuteur à distance, entre function et métier. Retrieved on August 14, 2008, from http://jacques.rodet.free.fr/intjrci.pdf

Rosenberg, M. J. (2001). *E-learning: Strategies for delivering knowledge in the digital age*. New York: McGraw-Hill.

Rotta, M. (2007). Il project based learning nella scuola: Implicazioni, prospettive e criticità. *Journal of e-Learning and Knowledge Society, 3*(1), 75-84.

Rotta, M. (in press). Learning³: Gli scenari dell'innovazione nelle strategie per la costruzione della cittadinanza digitale e della conoscenza in rete. In Istituto Pedagogico di Bolzano (Ed.), *Sviluppo delle competenze per una cittadinanza digitale attiva e responsabile*. Dobbiaco, 10-13 luglio 2008.

Rotta, M. (2008). La conoscenza proibita ovvero la società del sovraccarico informativo. In P. Capitani & M. Rotta (Eds.), *Comunicare diversamente: Gli scenari della comunicazione e lo spazio dell'informazione*. Roma: Garamond.

Rotta, M., & Ranieri, M. (2005). *E-tutor: Identità e competenze*. Trento: Erickson.

Rowntree, D. (1995). Teaching and learning online. A correspondence education for the 21st century? *British Journal of Educational Technology, 26*(3), 205–215. doi:10.1111/j.1467-8535.1995.tb00342.x

Salmon, G. (2000). E-*moderating, the key to teaching and learning online*. London: Kogan Page.

Salmon, G. (2002). *E-tivities, the key to active online learning*. London: Kogan Page.

Siemens, G. (2006). *Knowing knowledge*. Complexive Inc., Knowing Knowledge. Retrieved on August 14, 2008, from http://www.knowing-knowledge.com/book.php

Thorpe, M. (2002). Rethinking learner support: The challenge of online learning. *Open Learning, 17*(2), 105–120.

Trentin, G. (1999). *Telematica e formazione a distanza, il caso Polaris*. Milano: Franco Angeli.

Trentin, G. (2008). *La sostenibilità didattico-formativa dell'e-learning. Social networking e apprendimento attivo*. Milano: Franco Angeli.

Tufte, E. (1990). *Envisiong information*. Cheshire: Graphics Press.

Wiley, D., & Edwards, E. (2002). Online self-organizing social systems: The decentralized future of online learning. OER Commons. Retrieved on August 14, 2008, from http://www.oercommons.org/matters/online-self-organizing-social-systems-the-decentralized-future-of-online-Learning

Wood, D., Bruner, J., & Ross, G. (1976). The role of tutoring in problem solving. *Journal of Child Psychology and Psychiatry, and Allied Disciplines, 17*, 89–100. doi:10.1111/j.1469-7610.1976.tb00381.x

Chapter 10
Entering the Virtual Teachers' Lounge:
Social Connectedness among Professional Educators in Virtual Environments

Randall Dunn
Liberty University, USA

ABSTRACT

As communication and connection are essential instruments for professional educators, this chapter seeks to examine the effectiveness of an online "virtual teacher's lounge" in the framework of offline communities. Essentially, an online discussion forum for educators is evaluated for the purpose of determining whether the forum provides a "space" conducive for the development of a community of professional educators as benchmarked against an understanding of offline community formation and existence. The foundational works of Ferdinand Tonnies, James Coleman, and Ray Oldenburg are used to develop 12 characteristics of community—as understood in the context of social communities. The study finds that online communities closely resemble offline communities in structure and interaction, but only for select participants. The participants observed demonstrating or facilitating the characteristics of community comprise around 10% of the total number of users participating in the analyzed discussions.

INTRODUCTION

As globalization continues to bring more individuals to computer-medicated communication (CMC) of interaction as found in the phenomenon of the Internet, the education community must continue to embrace the technologies that exist to better address social, pedagogical, and professional needs. The United Kingdom has looked to technologies as cornerstones of recent educational reforms (Selwyn, 2006). It is only reasonable for the educational community, speaking in general terms here, to purposefully explore the latest technological innovations as possible means of assisting in communication for the purposes of professional development, collaborative support in pedagogical and social contexts, and for the discovery and connections of important content expertise. These tools can prove to be the connecting points between education professionals on opposite sides of the globe and around the literal

DOI: 10.4018/978-1-60566-826-0.ch010

corner. The challenge is to properly determine the most important and effective methods to allow educators the opportunity to effectively use resources and time to best meet the needs and demands of the 21st century.

This chapter examines significant developments in the specific context of the communication needs of professional educators as met by naturally-forming virtual environments. The primary question asked is whether virtual environments can serve the social needs of educators – essentially becoming virtual teacher's lounges, or more generally educational "third places" (see Oldenburg, 1991). This question is addressed through a primarily qualitative study, examining a single naturally forming educational community in an online environment.

The included background section creates a framework in which to evaluate an online discussion forum and its efficacy as a social community of professional educators. This chapter will review the sub-questions of the research –12 characteristics – in terms of analytical findings and synthetical conclusions. Conversational analysis and general observational techniques are employed to accomplish this study's goals. Further analysis of context illuminates other areas of interest as part of this study's execution.

BACKGROUND

The true nature of community promotes copious debate; or specifically, debate centers on whether community exists today as it once did, whether it will ever exist as it once did, and whether community has dynamically evolved and has therefore adopted a new meaning (Bauman, 2001; Putnam, 2000).

As the 1998 edition of the Dictionary of Sociology notes, "the concept of community concerns a particularly constituted set of social relationships based on something which the participants have in common — usually a common sense of identity" (Marshall, 1998). Identity is an important com-

ponent of the formation of and participation in community. The perception of self, the subsequent behavior, and the juxtaposition of self with others all are vital concepts to understanding community (Bauman, 2003; Turkle, 1995). Community really can be considered a relationship between identity and the formed relationships with that identity.

George Hillery notes in Definitions of Community: Areas of Agreement in Rural Sociology (1955), "there is one element, however, which can be found in all of the concepts . . . all of the definitions deal with people. Beyond this common basis, there is no agreement" (Marshall, 1998). So communities are built upon relationships among individuals, aside from specific interests, geographical proximity, or necessity. None of these elements are present in agreed-upon definitions. This is particularly important for the pursuit of an understanding of computer-medicated communication (CMC)-based community formation.

Offering a different perspective, Zygmunt Bauman (2001) argues that the sense of community depends upon a community not knowing it is a community. This community must evolve "naturally" and not be artificially manufactured. Once realization occurs, then community is no longer pliable and that real community becomes something entirely different (Bauman, 2001, pp. 10-13). Grossman et al. actually attempted to fabricate such a community in an urban educational environment (2001). However, forced construction does not a community make.

Turning to an analysis of community, Bauman separates communities into two basic types: aesthetic and ethical. Aesthetic communities are formed as temporary, often based on an "idol." Membership in these communities remains noncommittal. Ethical communities, on the other hand, are communities that are based on rules, allowing members to experience security, safety, and certainty (Bauman, 2001, pp. 59-73), thus creating stronger ties.

Marshall's (1998) focus is on the distinction between community and society, which is important in this discussion. This distinction is made through sociological terms, coined by Ferdinand Tönnies in 1893, Gemeinschaft and Gesellschaft (Harris, 2001). The former denotes community — focusing on relationships based on family and close face-to-face ties. Elements in such a community are an attachment to place, concern over ascribed social status, and elements of homogeneity. Gesellschaft refers to society and general association, denoting the concepts of urbanism, industrial life, mobility, heterogeneity, and impersonality (Marshall, 1998).

For the purpose of this discussion, this study looks at communities as self-forming informal units of interaction – of the more ethical community type as Bauman defines them – where individuals have social connections on multiple levels in a stable and securely established conduit of communication. This can be best summed up by Ray Oldenburg's description of the "Third Place." This is the pub house, the bar, the bowling alley, the church meeting hall, or any place where informal relationships are continually reinforced. The Third Place exists outside of family and work (the first and second places, respectively). And for the purpose of this discussion, the Third Place can actually not be an actual place at all.

Oldenburg, in the *Great Good Place* (1997), describes the problem of place in America as manifesting in "a sorely deficient informal public life." He argues that America must revitalize its informal connections — dubbed "The Third Place" — a generic designation for a great variety of public places that host the regular, voluntary, informal, and happily anticipated gatherings of individuals beyond the realms of home and work." This Third Place is community, the informal connection among individuals on personal common interests and issues. Home and work are the first two "places," according to Oldenburg. These first two places remain a large factor of a person's identity. The existence of the Third Place is in decline (Oldenburg, 1997).

Oldenburg describes the Third Place as having the following elements: escape/ time-out from daily duties, neutral ground, "leveler," conversation, accessibility/accommodation, regulars, low profile, playful mood, and a home away from home. These aspects are implied to be unique to the third place. Oldenburg sums up that "(t)hird places that render the best and fullest services are those to which one may go alone at almost any time of the day or evening with assurances that acquaintances will be there" (Oldenburg, 1997). The Third Place is the home away from home (and away from work) – the place where people know they are accepted, feel comfortable, and interact informally with those they care about.

Another relatively recent concept in the realm of community, and relevant to this study, is the concept of Social Capital, focusing on beneficial relationships (mutual and singular).

Social capital has been defined as "features of social organization such as networks, norms and social trust that facilitate co-ordination and co-operation for mutual benefit" (Putnam, 1995). As individuals and as groups, people desire interaction with one another for specific benefits, whether these benefits are economic, social, political, cultural, psychological, physical, or even educational.

The actual formation of the social capital theory arose out of a need to reconcile the differing approaches of economists and social theorists with regard to individual motivation – one explaining it in terms of gain and the other in terms of complying with norms (Coleman, 1988; Bourdieu, 1983). A theory was necessary to demonstrate the effects both social expectations and individualistic drive have on an individual's choices and actions (Coleman, 1988).

The informal third place becomes very important in light of social capital. The benefits are not merely confined to Putnam's list of characteristics (escapism, neutrality, playfulness, conversational, community-feel, etc.), but rather may directly rely upon more social advancement-related reasons. People need interaction that indirectly or directly has positive effects on their development. They gather valuable tools, form valuable relationships, and establish long-lasting relationships to their benefit.

Talja Blokland found that those socially less advantaged could glean much from the "urban elite," provided there exists "informal rather than institutional relationships" and that success depends on "specific characteristics of reciprocity and mutuality of neighborhood networks across race and class" (Blokland, 2002).

This is a challenging time concerning informal connectedness. Putnam sees the great influence of the Baby Boomer generation as changing the way people interact in American society. There is a debate of which came first: the decline in community and subsequent use of technology or the use of technology in lieu of more traditional means of connecting with others. This issue has a great effect on this paper as the question arises as to whether people can experience connectedness — the macher/formal or schmoozer/ informal types as Putnam describes — in a seemingly disconnected environment (Putnam, 2000). However, as Lerner notes and Oldenburg reiterates, there still exists a "Problem of Place in America" where the small town (informal) cannot be revitalized, so a new community structure must evolve to take on integrated community needs in the "quest for community" (Lerner, 1957).

This research has established concepts surrounding community, community formations and the relationship to a third place (as defined by Oldenburg) and social capital (as defined by Putnam and Campbell). This study now turns to Etienne Wenger's Communities of Practice.

In the last two decades, Wenger (with the help of Jean Lave) developed a theory set exploring the concepts of learning and organizations and their convergence. He rooted this theory-set in a concept called communities of practice. In short, these particular communities contain "members (who) regularly engage in sharing and learning, based on their common interests" (Lesser &

Storck, 2001). The theory's application travels from the commercial/ business world to the world of education as it looks at learning as a social process (with deep roots in John Dewey). Community members seek to learn from social groups in addition to collectively developing the social rules for engagement as pertaining to practice among its membership.

Grossman et al. (2001) looked at the semi-natural formation of an educators' community in a secondary school among history and English teachers. This project sought to put these groups of teachers together to accomplish two primary activities in the context of professional development: the development of pedagogical practice and of professional content knowledge in view of the two disciplines. While seeing some success in the discussions that developed, the researchers noted that the discovery of constructed professional communities saw less success than was initially anticipated. Merely providing time and resources does not meet the basic needs of community formation among professional educators. There is a mysterious element, very social or intellectual in nature that addresses this gap in effective formation.

The classical examination of social learning theories includes primarily face-to-face communication methods as the necessary component. More recently, a re-examination of this theory set has allowed for the discussion to expand to include other media such as e-mail and discussion forums. In fact, not only do these technologies provide a means to grow communities of practice but these media can actually be the primary facilitation for the development of entities (Lesser & Storck, 2001).

Regardless of medium or method, the initial development and further cultivation of communities of practice are directly related to the exchange of social capital. Members exchange social capital in the form of trust, mutual obligation, and language. Through structural (connections between members), relational (connections among networking processes), and cognitive (shared context and codification of meaning and processes) dimensions, communities of practice evolve.

This is the primary benefit of an examination of communities of practice: to examine as how a group of teachers develop methods and means to improve their practice as teachers (Wenger, 1998). In the context of informal social exchanges, researchers can use the relational dimension as discussed above to further solidify discussions on social capital and Oldenburg's work. The above is provided to develop a framework for teacher communities, but the use of the communities of practice model (or the work of Grossman) is primarily devoted to exploration of professional communities as they develop the practice pertinent to them. This research explores the nature of the social exchanges of participants in communication avenues and whether these exchanges support the construct being applied of communities (yes, professionally labeled but social in nature).

Concerns have arisen over the direction of community (see Bauman, 2003, and Giddens, 2002, for discussions on negative aspects of the globalization of community) with the advent of the Internet. The Informational Revolution is here (see Putnam, 2000). So how effective can virtual environments be in helping to establish or progress community?

Manuel Castells (1996) notes that the technological innovations that brought into being the Internet and virtual networking were conceived to solve a problem concerning connecting individuals. Suddenly, the world is connected and geographic boundaries are no longer impeding the formation of global communities.

Virtual communities as Castells defines them are "like Howard Rheingold('s) self-defined electronic network of interactive communication organized around a shared interest or purpose, although sometimes communication becomes the goal in itself." He notes that virtual communities may be formalized systems (like Bulletin Board System (BBS) or hosted conferences) or

be spontaneously formed. In either case, the communities are ephemeral from the point of view of the participants —where users can move in and out as necessary. Virtual community participants are described as either transitory or electronic "homesteaders" (Castells, 1996; Ward, 2002),

What is unusual about CMC in general, and virtual communities specifically, is there exists a many-to-many relationship (Castells, 1996). This provides for many touch points for interests and individualism. It also makes it difficult to account for the many different informal virtual communities in existence as individuals can pass casually from one informal community to another without completely attaching.

Howard Rheingold, like Hammon (1998), has suggested that virtual interactions and relations overlap in to the real/physical lives of those participating. Face-to-face meetings were common among Rheingold's compatriots in the 1980s, spending their evenings sharing information and experiences in online environments and some weekends gathering for picnics to see who actually was the individual behind the virtual identity (Rheingold, 1994).

Some studies show that more than half of participants in newsgroup discussions not only begin long-lasting relationships in online environments but also continue off-line relationships with these online friends. Other avenues of communication are employed (postal service and telephone), and over time these develop into long-lasting personal relationships. Social bonds become redefined. Thomsen et al. sums up that newsgroup relationships "typically serve as catalysts for long-term and meaningful relationships" (1998).

Furthermore, evidence demonstrates that physical co-presence is not necessary for "intimate quality interactions" (Thomsen et al., 1998). As he also notes — as do Steven Jones (1998), Ray Oldenburg (1997) and Howard Rheingold (1993) —the various CMC technologies "have sprung out of the need to re-create this sense of community that participants join and become involved with the express purpose of re-establishing social bonds.". Suddenly virtual communities become Oldenburg's "Third Place," where bonding relationships can be established through the exchange of informal social capital.

The cyber-community becomes the connection to the real world for the Web-surfer. As Steve Jones surmises, Internet users have strong attachments online (1998, p. 5), thus it is a real experience. As Markham (1998) notes, "All experiences are considered real so therefore virtual is a misnomer." The gravest of subjects becomes a real exploration using online community tools to interact with other real participants through virtual communication lines.

Research on virtual communities in the context of professional educators has been limited. This is likely due to the fact that the world of virtual communities is completely reliant upon the only recently birthed CMC modes, such as the Internet. Obviously, because it is recently formed, there is a small window of time for exploration.

Selwyn (2000) provides one such exploration into the world of teacher-based virtual communities. This study examined the SENCo community (a communication group of Special Educational Needs Coordinators for schools in the United Kingdom). As a result of the government's push for the use of "virtual communities" as part of its educational reform practices, the researchers began to question if these virtual communication avenues truly accomplished the goal of connecting educators in communities from geographically disparate locations. The format of these communications followed what has been called discussion forums but also can be called e-mail list-servs (or e-mail groups that get archived in online environments).

Selwyn (2000) found that participants certainly did exchange in three of the four communication purposes (information exchange, empathetic exchanges, virtual respite), but the deep connectedness of community (the fourth) was not as prevalent. One more note here in this study

is the emergence of some 24 participants who essentially became the hard-core users. These participants contributed some 50 percent of the message analyzed.

A distinction in this community formation is the imposition of the creation of community (as in Grossman's study above) by external forces as opposed to the natural evolution of community.

As discussed earlier, Coleman, Oldenburg, and Tonnies provide the foundation of what is understood about social communities (close-knit, naturally forming, and homogenous). An understanding of online communities can be found in works by Howard Rheingold, Steve Jones, Sherry Turkle, Robin Hammon, Stephen Doheny-Farina, Nathaline Bowker. Wenger's work moves toward understanding the formation of professional communities, but his work focuses on how communities of professionals share meanings so as to articulate, develop, and refine processes and knowledge to assist in practice. Selwyn attempted to look at the viability of these communities in the context of government-identified educational groups (identified with a job function), but does not see the arrival of communities online in that form or under those conditions. What is missing here is an understanding of teacher social communities and specifically teacher social communities online.

Taking these findings, one may synthesize a full picture of the potential of educator communities in online environments. Research notes communities are naturally forming, often informal, social groups. These groups are built on conduits of communication and social connections. Norms for behavior are established as part of a collaborative process, where individuals agree through negotiation on proper processes for group functioning. Participants gain membership – and thus are enveloped into the system of trust – in the group. Community is strengthened by the participation and efficiencies developed.

The development of understanding as related to problems, the contributive nature of participants, characteristics of movements of information, the development of tools, and professional language features all are uniquely identified in the communities of practice theory set (Wenger, 1998). The study here looks at the social exchange features of Coleman, Tonnies and primarily Oldenburg. These comprise the main drives of design for the study as the informal social and non-professional purposes of community formation of these (and primarily Oldenburg) present the type of community attempting to be analyzed/ identified.

This synthesis of understanding of community is the foundation for proceeding in this study, where in the section following, the study investigates online interactions for efficacy of community.

RESEARCHING ONLINE COMMUNITIES

The research, undertaken as part of this project, works to answer the question of whether online social communities created and maintained among professional educators constitute an informal community as earlier defined.

This is the construction of the design of this project: a positivist approach employed in a simple research question accompanied by interpretations/ analysis of the gathered textual data for attaching deeper meanings to the associations. Simply put, the analysis of unsolicited textual submissions proves to be too complicated for a simple quantitative mode of enquiry. A more inductive approach is necessary for such meaning-rich data that employs analysis of numerical representations of social phenomena (Kuikin & Muill, 2001).

To determine the nature of exchanges among professional educators in virtual spaces, these exchanges must be analyzed in light of a model for an off-line, informal community. The study uses Ray Oldenburg's descriptors of the *Third Place*, Ferdinand Tönnies' *Gemeinschaft*, and the discussion of social capital as the basis of this benchmark off-line community (and thus the

impetus for the identified categorizations to be used in the study). These together form the necessary picture of informal community: close-knit, supportive, mutually beneficial, and connected. Deliberately excluded from this group is Wenger's notions of community in the context of professional communities. These chosen sets used for constructing a model for interpretation comprise an image of exchanges of the purely informal variety for the purposes of social interactions, not for the development of professional practices.

In order to gauge the community existence in this project, the study employs the 12 community characteristics gleaned from the works of Oldenburg, Coleman, and Tönnies, to create the following questions and guide conclusions.

- Is the virtual space a location for participant escapism?
- Does the locale provide an area of neutral ground for all participants?
- Do all members have equal access to participation?
- Does conversational-style communication dominate the environment's discussion patterns?
- Are there "regulars" in this environment?
- Is there evidence of playfulness in this virtual space?
- Does this place act as a "home away from home" for the membership?
- Is there an obvious attachment to place among the place's membership?
- Is there evidence of a concern over ascribed social status among the place's membership?
- Are there elements of homogeneity – via beliefs, interests, or backgrounds – among the space's membership?
- Does the "community" exert self-regulation? Is there evidence of a contract (explicit or understood) for membership governing behavior and participation?

- Is there evidence of an exchange of ideas for the development of individuals?

These questions then are transformed into the coding-based categories for examining the relationships and the interactions contained within the chosen community.

To answer the outlying question of what types of exchanges occur in virtual communities of professional educators, the study selected an online teacher community (primarily consisting of a cost-free discussion board area so as to remove boundaries of limited access). A particular weekday was selected, and every electronic discussion (and preceding discussions with the same attached date) active on that particular weekday was then gleaned for analysis. In essence, a random sample of discussions was then used for answering the basic questions posed as part of this study. The participants in this online community are primarily educational professionals or para-professionals.

The sheer volume of the available discussions led to the consideration of limiting the analysis. However, all discussions were included, with the one exception of limiting very long threads to no more than 100 posts. This limited the ability to analyze previous discussions, but many of these proved to be the "game-like" discussions and appear to not have impacted the study.

The other limitation to note here is elaborated upon and developed further later. This relates to the notion of what has been categorized as the "regular user." The limitation of this study identifies a group of users in such a category, but the number identified here and its relevance does not speak to the actual occurrence of "regular-ness" in quantifiable terms. In other words, the 30 identified "regular users" do not speak to how many users are actually represented by this group. In some respects, this is an intrinsically focused number and categorization so as to identify further characteristics and understandings of those more identifiable as regulars in an online forum.

In consideration of the above, this study's primary approach for data collection and analysis are now described.

All discussions posted to or created within the 24- hour period (12 a.m. EST to 12 a.m. EST of the following day) are saved as text files. Some of the actual discussions contain multiple pages (possibly as many as 30 pages). If so, then all discussion posts within the most recent 100 posts are gathered. On average, some 10 topics are "active" (i.e., have been active on any given day) per a forum. The resulting discussion threads from the 25 discussion forums were imported into QSR International's NVivo 7's software interface for organization and analysis. At this point, the coding of the data proceeds.

The following categorizations provide the guiding aspects for the coding of the data gleaned from the forums (based on the guiding theoretical discussion questions as noted above): participant escapism, neutral ground, equal access to participation, conversational as dominant style, "regulars," playfulness, home away from home, membership attachment to place, social status a concern?, homogeneity (as in identified perceived like-ness in areas of interest, professional or vocational identification, ethnic affiliation), self-regulation/ contracts, and idea exchange for individual development.

The number of occurrences and the level of adherence to these concepts are examined. Further in this phase, the additional peripheral statistics are gathered to develop contextual understandings of the posters. Finally, additional information on posting policies, FAQs and other Web site provided information on the forums are gathered to use toward answering the questions posed. This document review is used to complement the interpretation of the gathered data from participation.

All data gathered is used to form an analysis of the actual interactions contained within these randomly selected in the study. Primarily, the method of analysis involved the specific examination of these discussion threads in isolation and the collection of additional peripheral information as related to the governance and structure of the forum and general data on users.

PARTICIPANTS AND PLACE

Below is a provided background of both nature of the "place" where these discussions occurred and the participants in this study.

The forums pre-created, as repositories for organizing potential discussions, can be divided into three primary types: those as related to professional needs, those as related to social needs, and those as related to the management of the discussion forum itself. For example, the forum has established sub-areas for each broad level of education (elementary, secondary, etc), for types of activities (classroom penpals, postcard exchanges, behavior management, etc.), and for specialty areas (like Montessori education, special education, pre-service teachers). The other areas range from exam preparation to general game and chatting sub-forums. Some of these areas remained quite professionally focused (like the exams area) while others were exclusively non-professional (like games and chitchat). Others oscillated between these two general characterizations depending on the specific subject/ topic.

The greatest number of active threads took place in the TeacherChat forums on the day of collection (comprising discussions geared toward social and professional needs). What is misleading here is that we arrive at this conclusion because of an accounting of the amount of threads active, not the actual amount posted in each thread. This point is revisited and further elaborated upon below. Regardless, we can draw some conclusions.

The highest number of active discussions occurred in the Elementary Education sub-forum of the TeacherChat Forums (with 16). The next highest number of active discussions in a sub-forum

appeared in the New Teacher Sub-Forum of the TeacherChat Special Interest Forums. Following closely behind are the Games and the ChitChat sub-sub-forums (both of the TeacherChat Forums/ Teacher TimeOut Sub-Forums) and the Teacher TimeOut Sub-Forum main area itself. These discussions will be examined in more detail below. The ChitChat area proves to be the most active area during the discussion analysis period.

These users are primarily participating in discussions about a specific professional need (like Elementary Education) or they bear participating in social engagements (like ChitChat and Games). This very differentiation – a divide between the professional and the social - becomes a hallmark of the analysis of this forum *world* in the following sections.

As the nature of this study remains quite observational where interaction is intentionally minimal, all data illustrative of the participating users' backgrounds is gathered from public sources, primarily from the users' member profiles. Here, the location, the age, the overall posting record, and the particular vocational (or personal in some cases) interest of the poster (with some other background details) can be gleaned. With the exception of the posting history, all details remain optional for the forum members, thus only a sampling can be provided of the types of users posting to this forum. The count of non-responders is included with each demographic below. This sampling still remains illustrative and enlightening.

Out of the 301 users who participated in the discussions, around 86% of the users listed a location (a specific state, a province, or a country). Primarily users reside in the USA, with Canada and Australia representing much smaller segments. Within the United States, California clearly is the most common origination point for users (with 22% of the total United States-based users living their offline lives here). Other states with relatively high counts of participants include Florida, Michigan, New York, New Jersey, and Texas.

The next piece of data involves age of the participants. This piece of data is not used to draw specific conclusions, as there are some issues with this piece. First, users may not be honest about their ages when listing this in a public forum. Next, the users who reported ages may be more inclined to do so as these users may be more representative of the younger segment of the user group. With these caveats, reported ages are examined. The users who chose to include a birth date in their profiles comprise 22% of all users, with users including birth date in their profiles tending to be younger (with those aged 30 and below comprising 71% of the total). The oldest recorded was 66 while the youngest was 20.

Next, an understanding of vocational and professional pursuits or personal interests can be quite helpful in understanding the users posting to this forum. The data gathering process identified 50 different types of professions or affiliations. Several users noted in-between affiliations (4th/5th grade, for example). Even with these in-between affiliations, a clear pattern emerges. The first, second, and third grade teachers (not counting in-betweens) comprise 18% of the overall user group. Also interesting to note, 22 (or 7%) of the users identified themselves as students (or college students in teacher education programs).

Elementary Education rises to be the most identified profession. This is corroborated through an examination of the actual postings and active discussions (discussed below and above respectively).

With general understandings of the place and the participants, the below sections detail the analysis and synthesis of this research undertaken and the constructed broad categories of results:

- The Participant Divide: Regulars and Non-Regulars
- Regulars and the Role of Expert: Professional Assistance
- Regulars and the Online Playground: Social Interaction

The Participant Divide: Regulars and Non-Regulars

This research discovered a distinct divide between two groups of individuals: the Regulars and the Non-Regulars. The question of "regulars" really relies on the notion that there exist those who frequent and feel attachment and affection for this "place" — enough to participate in the discussion, enough to be present more than a few times, enough to move from a new member to a prodigal member to a fully engaged member (Oldenburg, 1997).

A small portion of the posting community was responsible for a large portion of the actual posts analyzed. This aspect is a reinforcement of Selwyn's findings (2000). The selected group (a group of 30) became the identified "regulars." These regulars (as coded by the schema "Regular_(number)") acted as experts, asked questions of one another, enjoyed each other's company during reflections, during hard times and stressful situations, and through silly and nearly meaningless conversations. These regulars embraced new and relatively unknown members graciously.

While this might seem to be an obvious conclusion, the questions surrounding this could multiply. Before we assume many conclusions, we must be skeptical and honest about this particular study. The very restrictive nature of this study – in initial and natural structure and the specific employment of methodological approaches in research design and execution, limits our generalization of findings. This study has identified that there is clearly a separation between regular and non-regular, but it cannot be so easily relied upon quantifiably as reported. Keeping this limitation in mind, we can draw some tentative conclusions – to be explored in other studies employing other approaches.

Posting rates overall proved high in this group of regulars – both in the posts in the analyzed documents and in the overall posting rates in each of the regulars' board histories. Additionally, two of the essential components of becoming a regular are to establish trust and to act decent. These 30 live up to this set of standards (Oldenburg, 1997).

The challenge in this question is that 30 users became regulars in this virtual space. Two hundred eighty one did not. The specific numbers can be held in suspect but the actual comparison should be accepted. The types of discussions in which these two groups participated are illustrative of the needs being met for each. The regulars participated heavily in light discussions while the non-regulars did not and chose rather to participate in those discussions that proved serious and focused often on professional questions and issues. This is further elaborated upon in other questions below.

Further reflections should be made, referring back to Soukup's criticisms, of whether the actual nature of these interactions (among Regulars) can be considered along line with off-line interactions. Would the nature of the actual discussion forum actually impact the results of these interactions? In addition, would these take place in MOOs, MUDs, MMPORGs, etc as noted by Soukup? What role does the nature of this forum (asynchronous, textual posting) play in the development of these interactions between Regulars? In short, would these Regulars still be the same type of "Regular" we see here and how would the environment impact that? This impact could only be gauged by revisiting this study in other technological settings (in Second Life for example).

Another note to make here is the further unknown group that participates in this forum to some extent: that of the lurker. This individual explores content – presumably personal and professional – potentially to answer not only questions (like in the case of licensure questions, issues on behavior management or on the organization of instruction) but also to merely enjoy the conversations (in a potentially a voyeuristic way) of the participants. Can this group – the great unknown – be considered part of the "community?" Is their undefined benefit making them any less as compared to their Regular comrades? Do they feel that they are part? Moreover, potentially, could we even

say that some Regulars actually could function in this role

Regulars and the Role of Expert: Professional Assistance

Social status as a component of Tonnies' Gemeinschaft (Marshall, 1998) plays a large role in this discussion. The complexities have yet to be revealed, but the different approaches are clearly discernable. Users enjoy visual and textual notations of status in the community (based on chosen identities, expressions of professional affiliation, and posting counts). Further, some of the regulars (and even some of the non-regulars) gain notoriety in their various roles – such as a math expert, an expert on certification issues, etc. This is status and this provides identity in a world where identity is often masked.

With a large number of participants (generally speaking in terms of the life-time of the forum) never exiting "new member" status, the question arises again – what pushes one user to leave the group of thousands of nearly unknown users with monikers to users with reputations in a group of elite posters? And what pushes the lurker to a new member status?

Tonnies' Gemeinschaft (Marshall, 1998) again provides direction useful in this analysis. This group of users and this virtual space provide opportunity for users of like interests, backgrounds, or identities to congregate and share. This is the nature and often the primary purpose of online discussion forums – and this forum proves to be no different.

The affiliations of a professional nature clearly point to like mindedness in interests. The elementary contingent (self-identified in profile creation in the forum) is notable among the groups with others trailing close behind. Further, the structure of the forums themselves attracts members to specific areas for specific query types (or general discussion types). With discussions ranging from similar interests in math, music, and fashion trends to similar jobs, teaching practices, and geographic locations to level in pursuing certification, and stage in applying for a teaching job, the level of homogeneity is clear. The data confirms that the users share similar interests and congregate according to these. The similar backgrounds are often identifiable through profiles.

What would prove interesting is an exploration of the level of connected-ness (to place or to one another) experienced by these various types of homogeneity. Our understanding of community in general dictates assumptions of homogeneity. How these homogenous identities play in virtual worlds may change that further. The simple existence of these types of relationships was observed in this context.

Further in this context of professional identity enters the concept of idea exchange. The exchange of ideas (and its presence in a community) deals directly with the concept of Social Capital (Coleman, 1988). The users primarily use this forum for exchanging ideas – ideas for classroom management, ideas for projects, lessons and activities, ideas for gaining employment, ideas for studying for exams, or ideas for a nonsensical game or notion. These are all exchanges that others benefit from in one way or another.

The presence of some experts, the regulars self-identifying in these roles, provides a basis for providing the exchange of ideas. The notion that the receiver then becomes the giver is not easily discernable in this data, as the scope of analysis is limited to a specific set of discussions and time frame for many of the discussions. The four primary types of exchanges noted in the analysis include teacher practice assistance, teacher application assistance, personal advice, and teacher certification assistance. The obvious exchange for benefit exists in this environment. The true nature of the exchanges and their adherence to the understanding of social capital needs more study.

Regulars and the Online Playground: Social Interaction

While Oldenburg's Third Place has no place for "serious conversation" (Oldenburg, 1997), the online teacher community embraces such conversation. Many of the discussions center on serious questions of a personal, professional, or even pedagogical nature. This does not mean that the playful discussions do not exist; they are merely relegated to their own home in a forum entitled the Teacher TimeOut Sub-Forum.

This area is set aside for the casual discussions of light-hearted remembrances of years past, word and get-to-know-you games escapist in nature, and general social discussions that enter the realm of laughter as participants play games of who would be kicked out if this were a reality television show. The playfulness of discussions is present, just often contained in where it is meant to be. This is an interesting natural separation – and almost naturally occurring phenomena in online discussions. This discussion forum takes time to be sure that participants know what can be posted where. Some of these understandings are explicit and some are implicit. This actually can be likened to Social Learning Theory and in the Community of Practice construct as those participating – and the more they participate – develop and build understandings of where it is appropriate to discuss X and where it not appropriate to do Y.

Oldenburg's Third Place (1997) experienced a feeling of a "home away from home" – espousing the gift of regeneration, at-easeness, and hints of possessiveness from its occupants. One of the most important roles this forum plays is that of a means for teachers to come together to regenerate. Many of the teachers (or educationally-minded participants) seek others to share frustrations and joy, but also to escape (as discussed above) and to recuperate. Discussions seeking a result of regeneration included personal issues, disappointment with students, and frustrations with parents and the profession in general. Participants note that they cannot find the answers and comfort in their workplaces that they can find in the virtual space of this forum.

These participants are at ease possibly simply because they remain anonymous. However, to be sure, these regulars also know one another and must take comfort in identity and status on the forum. These participants joined as members of this board, and they return as they find the answers they need or meet the needs they have. This is their forum and they found it.

The regulars (the 30 heavy posters) comprise a group who fit into Tonnies' Gemeinschaft (Marshall, 1998) — one where they feel an attachment to this virtual space. They have developed an identity here (and it is interesting to note that this identity is in terms of actually who they present themselves to be and how they see themselves apart from presentation in the context of the virtual space). These 30 posters return (many daily) to the forum to gain the answers they seek or the comfort they need (or maybe just because it is fun). The unrepresented group here is the vast number of people that register and post a few times or less and never return. The attachment does not appear to exist for them. They gain the answer they need and move on, possibly to never return. The difference between these two types of users proves to be the interesting question that needs to be explored.

Regardless, the regulars – the ones who return to this home away from home – possess this virtual space as theirs. What has not been clearly examined in the nature of membership in this group in the context of personal identity. This can only be determined by getting behind the screen instead of interpreting discussions. There would need to be more examination of the nature of this community formed as an exclusive community of an inclusive one.

This notion of identification and attachment with place is more definitively identified as such as compared to Selwyn's work (2000) that found little evidence of attachment to place. The differ-

ence between these two studies appears to be in motivation. In Selwyn's examination, the users were provided space with a very specific set of content to be explored and shared (very professional in nature and following a mind-set of a community of practice – sharing practice, etc) whereas this community studied is completely naturally forming and the ideas and topics have developed form the users participating. More work is needed here.

The non-regulars, the vast majority of the users in the study, obviously do not attach in the same way as the regulars identified. This is a crucial finding – these regulars have entered a different phase of interaction in this virtual environment.

In conclusion, how does this analysis answer the research question posed:

The research, undertaken as part of this project, works to answer the question of whether online communities created and maintained among professional educators constitute a community, as we understand them in the context of off-line communities.

Using the benchmarks as formed from the literature reviewed for this project, the analysis points to a complex answer. While this community of users strongly feels an attachment to place, self-regulates through informal contracts, exchanges ideas for the benefit of the individual, are homogenous in interest, have the opportunity to express social status in the context of the environment, play (at times), converse and escape the realities of the world in a neutral environment; they do this if they have moved to a status of regular (or near-regular). The challenge is in the statistic: 83% of all of the forum users have posted less than five times. This is sobering statistics that demonstrates a large number of users exist who definitively do not feel a connection in this environment. Is this environment a community for virtual members? Yes – but only for some.

The basic construction of online discussion forums for professional educators contain two primary targets of content – the discussions centered on issues of a professional nature and those discussions centered on a personal/ social nature. While the discussions themselves are organized as such, the people participating in these and moving from one to the other behave and interact in different ways according to the discussion content.

In those discussions centered on content of a professional nature – those that focus on certification issues and questions, on job applications and hiring questions and advice, on level-specific teaching methods and approaches, and on general pedagogical and professional issues – the participants contributed in very professional ways. The process here involved the query/ problem stated, the contributions of those in positions of authority on the subject (or even those that empathized) and a synthesis (or confluence of ideas) to form a best approach for the participant/initial poster. Many of these discussions proved shorter in nature, very focused, and many of those who were frequent posters acted as the subject matter experts.

In contrast, those discussions focused on more social interactions – those that focused on game-like discussions, on personal issues and celebrations, on funny stories, on past reflections, and on home life and its trials and fun – proved more interactive (as to the types of interactions), more long-lasting, containing higher levels of participation, and the presence of those that are more participatory in the forums as a whole.

These two types of interactions constitute the gamut of types of discussions on these boards. The question remains: Do these types of discussions (the process, the content, and the outcomes) effectively create environments of community for those who participate?

FUTURE RESEARCH DIRECTIONS

This study (as Selwyn's before) serves well as a frame of reference for other studies on the efficacy of community for professional educators. Selwyn's work relied heavily on government-created communities whereas this study worked with communities that arose naturally among the participants (at least one).

Further studies should examine the actual nature of these "regulars" and why they moved from the new status to member (and beyond). What is the mysterious factor that pushed the social experience from casual participant/ lurker to "regular?" Additional research into the motivations and needs of these users would prove useful in understanding the potential use of online environments for teacher interaction and community-building. Working on illuminating more details on who these participants really are and what skills they have acquired and what lives they lead would greatly expand the understanding of this mysterious factor. Specifically, more should be done on following users – if possible – through these phases of online existence. In addition, work and examination in areas of professional identification and personal and social identification as juxtaposed with this notion of "regular user" should be worked into future research in this area.

This study sought to understand informal social exchanges, but in the process found the professional development potential for such online environments (pedagogically and subject-specific). This area could be further explored as its potential for addressing the time issue and the definitive need for professional development for today's educators is undeniable. Important here is the understanding of potential policy implications – can we develop effective online professional development modules AND online avenues for professional communities (as envisioned in the Selwyn study). If so, do our notion of Regular user and our eventual understanding of the nature of the Regular user's evolution as an online persona have an impact in this venture design and implementation?

In addition, how does the impact of these lurkers – the silent observers – change the way this community should be considered? Do we then conceptualize the nature of community based on what is present (surface-level) and what is potentially possible based von assumed lurkers? Does the presumptive presence of these lurkers have implicit impacts on the types of participation or the level of personal (or professional) interactions in these environments? In addition, of course, does the actual venue of the technology have an impact here?

Other questions arise concerning the true nature of the exchange of social capital among these educators online and if the differences exist between non-regulars and regulars. Additional research in the nature of the discussions – i.e., more of a topical analysis going much further than the scope of this paper – would also bring to light an understanding of these communities.

Much works needs to be done here. This study has pointed to an unknown gap between those who participate and those who do not. This phenomenon could result in real impact on how we design and develop online communities (or online spaces for interaction) for professional educators.

CONCLUSION

This chapter, at its core, examined the development of understanding of virtual communities (based on understandings of off-line communities), established benchmarks for analysis, examined an existing community for adherence to benchmarks, and used conclusive results to further the discussion of the reality of, the importance of, and the benefits of virtual communities in the professional educational sector. This has been an untouched area heretofore and is ripe for the examination.

Upon analysis of the gathered conversational data, this study initially concludes that a select few individuals self-identifying as professional educators form communities of users in online environments much in the same fashion as off-line communities. This conclusion is based on the existence of a body of individuals (identified as "regulars" and numbering 30) who exemplify the general nature of the sought-after characteristics of informal, social off-line communities.

The limitations of this research and the restrictions on collection and data types make this a tentative conclusion that needs further solidification through other modes of data analysis. This formulation of a community appears to be anomalous as compared to the entire body of potential and registered users. Admittedly, an unknown lingers in this discussion that bears heavy weight upon the conclusions – the 30 identified regulars represent a larger body of individuals and that number is not known. The individual purposes and the self-established meanings and significances of these individuals' participation in this community was not established in this study, but would be an obvious next step for understanding the nature of the transformation persons experience in moving from casual disconnected participant to fully participating and involved member of an online community.

REFERENCES

Blokland, T. (2002). Neighbourhood social capital: Does an urban gentry help? Some stories of defining shared interests, collective action, and mutual support. *Sociological Research Online*, 7(3).

Bourdieu, P. (1983). The forms of capital [originally published as Ökonomisches Kapital, kulturelles Kapital, soziales Kapital]. In R. Kreckel (Ed.), *Soziale Ungleichheiten (Soziale Welt, Sonderheft 2)* (pp. 183-198). Goettingen: Otto Schartz & Co.

Bowker, N. I. (2001). Understanding online communities through multiple methodologies combined under a postmodern research endeavour. *Forum Qualitative Sozialforschung/Forum: Qualitative Social Research.*

Castells, M. (1996). *The rise of the network society* (Vol. 1). Oxford: Blackwell Publishers.

Coleman, J. (1988). Social capital in the creation of human capital. *American Journal of Sociology, 94,* S95–S120. doi:10.1086/228943

Doheny-Farina, S. (1996). *The wired neighborhood.* New Haven: Yale University Press.

Fukuyama, F. (1999). *Social capital and civil society.* Paper presented at the IMF Conference on Second Generation Reforms. Retrieved on April 10, 2005, from http://www.imf.org/external/pubs/ft/seminar/1999/reforms/fukuyama.htm

Gordon, M. (Ed.). (1998). *A dictionary of sociology.* New York: Oxford University Press.

Hamman, R. (1998). *The online/offline dichotomy: Debunking some myths about AOL users and the effects of their being online upon offline friendships and offline community.* University of Liverpool, Liverpool.

Jones, S. (Ed.). (1998). *Cybersociety 2.0: Revisiting computer-mediated communication and community.* London: SAGE Publications.

Lerner, M. (1957). *America as a civilization: Life and thought in the United States today.* New York: Simon & Schuster.

Marshall, C., & Rossman, G. (1999). *Designing qualitative research.* London: Sage Publications.

Oldenburg, R. (1997). *The great good place: Cafes, coffee shops, community centers, beauty parlors, general stores, bars, hangouts, and how they get you through the day.* New York: Marlowe & Company.

Putnam, R. (2000). *Bowling alone: The collapse and revival of American community.* New York: Simon & Schuster.

Rheingold, H. (1993). *The virtual community: Homesteading on the electronic frontier.* New York: Addison-Wesley Publishing Company.

Selwyn, N. (2000). Creating a "connected" community? Teachers' use of an electronic discussion group [electronic version]. *Teachers College Record, 102*(4), 750–778. doi:10.1111/0161-4681.00076

Soukup, C. (2006). Computer-mediated communication as a virtual third place: Building Oldenburg's great good places on the World Wide Web. *New Media & Society, 8*(3), 421–440. doi:10.1177/1461444806061953

Tonnies, F. (2001). *Tonnies: Community and civil society.* New York: Cambridge University Press.

Turkle, S. (1996). Virtuality and its discontents: Searching for community in cyberspace. *The American Prospect, 7*(24).

Ward, K. J. (1999). The cyber-ethnographic (re) construction of two feminist online communities. *Sociological Research Online, 12.*

Wenger, E. (1998). *Communities of practice: Learning, meaning, and identity.* New York: Cambridge University Press.

KEY TERMS AND DEFINITIONS

CMC: Computer-Mediated Communication

Third Place: The informal aspect of community, as identified Ray Oldenburg, not related to concepts of Home and Work (the first two places)

Newsgroup: A communication venue found in CMC where users can post messages related to actual news and general information of interest.

Regulars: In the context of this study, the users who posted most frequently, numbering about 10% of the total analyzed posters

Non-Regulars: In the context of this study, these are the other 90% of users who posted in this forum who did not post frequently

Section 4
Educational Social Software Applicability and Evaluation

Chapter 11

From Theory to Practice:
Communities of Practice across the Canadian Public Service

Hope Seidman
Canada School of Public Service, Canada

Andrea Mamers
Canada School of Public Service, Canada

Bev Mitelman
Canada School of Public Service, Canada

Mariève Gauthier
Canada School of Public Service, Canada

ABSTRACT

As the average age of Canada's public servant inches toward 50, it is expected that between 30-40% of the government's key knowledge workers will retire in the next five years. Consequently, the government is challenged with attracting and retaining new employees and ensuring that all public servants have the necessary skills and knowledge to do their jobs well. Since formal learning does not alone prepare employees to perform in complex work environments, the federal Public Service is implementing informal learning strategies to facilitate knowledge creation and exchange and to manage tacit knowledge. This chapter describes how technology-supported communities of practice are being employed across Canada with the support of the Canada School of Public Service. The strategic context, challenges, lessons learned, and vision for the future are also discussed.

INTRODUCTION

"Communities of practice are groups of people who share a concern or a passion for something they do and learn how to do it better as they interact regularly". (Wenger, 1998, p. 11)

DOI: 10.4018/978-1-60566-826-0.ch011

The purpose of this chapter is to describe how the Canada School of Public Service is supporting the development and implementation of Communities of Practice (CoPs) across the Public Service and how these communities are providing added value to various government organizations. Consequently, this chapter will provide a guide for theory to practice with examples of the design, development, implementation and evaluation of technology-supported CoPs. Related to the goals of this book, the following chapter is further aimed at demonstrating how the specific context of Canada's Public Service plays a key role in the design and implementation of collaborative technologies and social learning approaches.

Specifically, authors will discuss how CoPs contribute to the challenge of capturing and storing knowledge and how they stimulate interaction among colleagues to improve upon performance in the workplace. The chapter will also address key challenges, lessons learned and the future vision of social learning technologies in the Public Service.

PUBLIC SERVICE OF CANADA

The second largest country in the world, Canada is composed of 10 provinces and 3 territories that stretch from the Atlantic Ocean in the east to the Pacific Ocean in the west. Northern Canada reaches into the Arctic Circle, while southern Canada stretches below the northern points of the United States. Canada has one of the lowest population densities in the world, with a population of almost 33 million (Statistics Canada, 2008). Canada's two official languages are English and French and the nation's capital is located in Ottawa, Ontario.

With approximately 260 000 Canadians employed in 392 departments, agencies and sub-agencies, the Public Service of Canada is the country's largest employer. Like many organizations, the Public Service must address a significant demographic challenge. In particular, over half of its employees are over the age of 45 and the Public Service must renew its workforce in the strongest labour market in over 35 years (Dutil & Reid, 2007). Consequently, the government is challenged with attracting and retaining new employees and ensuring that all public servants

have the necessary skills and knowledge to effectively perform their jobs.

Public Service Renewal is the ongoing and deliberate process of ensuring the Public Service can continue to serve Canadians with professionalism, integrity and excellence. Public Service Renewal is about ensuring that all public servants have the support and tools they need to deliver results to Canadians. Recruitment is a top priority in the context of an aging and retiring population as well as orientation and training of new employees to the organization (Lynch, 2008).

Related to this process of renewal is the government's Policy on Learning, Training and Development (Treasury Board of Canada Secretariat, 2006) which was created to ensure that the Public Service is equipped to meet the challenges of the 21st century. Specifically, the objectives of this policy are to:

- help build a skilled, well-trained and professional workforce;
- strengthen organizational leadership; and
- adopt leading-edge management practices to encourage innovation and continuous improvements in performance.

CANADA SCHOOL OF PUBLIC SERVICE

As the common learning service provider for the federal government, the Canada School of Public Service (also referred to as the Canada School) serves the learning and leadership needs of public servants across Canada. Headquartered in Ottawa, the Canada School employs approximately 800 dedicated professionals that are geographically dispersed across six regions. Operating in a bilingual and diverse environment, the Canada School directly supports Public Service Renewal by: (a) fostering a common sense of purpose, values and traditions in the Public Service; (b) helping public servants gain the knowledge, skills and competencies they need to do their jobs effectively; and (c) assisting deputy heads in meeting the learning needs of their organization.

A recent internal publication highlighted the importance of managing organizational knowledge effectively (Stoyko & Fang, 2007). In addition to retirements, internal restructuring, employee mobility and increased use of contracts with external organizations are also having an impact on retaining organization memory. While renewal efforts are needed in the Public Service to attract and retain highly qualified employees, renewal presents new challenges for the Canada School to ensure that public servants are able to perform in their current job, and take on the challenges of the next job in a dynamic, bilingual environment.

Consequently, the Canada School is faced with considerable costs associated with developing, delivering and maintaining formal training across the country in its two official languages. For example, it is tasked with training a significant number of new employees. As of March, 2008 at least 4000 post-secondary graduates were offered appointments to indeterminate positions (Lynch, 2008). These geographically dispersed individuals are required to take an "Orientation to the Public Service" course within their first six months of employment. For all of its employees, the government must also support long-term succession planning and provide the right people, with the right skills to meet changing needs across the organization.

Classroom training has been the dominant method of delivery within the Canada School. Courses are offered in subject areas such as language training, leadership, information management, human resource management, procurement and mandatory courses for first-time managers in the Public Service. The Canada School, however, recognizes that formal training programs serve many purposes, but are often limited in their capacity to continuously develop expertise and required knowledge in rapidly changing contexts.

Informal learning approaches and flexible delivery in the workplace are playing an increasingly important role within organizations (Carnevale, Gainer, & Villet, 1990; Cross, 2007; Eraut, 2000; Lave & Wenger, 1991; Smith, 2003). Accordingly, the Canada School began taking an interest in blended learning methods and social and informal learning approaches such as virtual communities. Additionally, the Canada School has developed an online campus with over 350 e-learning products and is using other technologies such as webcasts, podcasts, wikis and interactive internet-based video to increase access, improve flexibility and to enrich the learning experience of public servants.

CENTRE OF EXPERTISE IN COMMUNITIES OF PRACTICE

The Canada School, especially the Quebec region, has been involved with CoPs for over ten years. In 2006, the Centre of Expertise in Communities of Practice was launched to support the work of the Canada School in this area. Located in Montreal, Quebec, the Centre's main goal is to use social learning and technology-enhanced approaches to learning and knowledge transfer to help support Public Service Renewal and the Policy on Learning, Training and Development. Specifically, the Centre's mandate is to favour the development and implementation of CoPs and to promote social learning approaches within the Public Service. The team is made up of highly specialized experts, with the majority of its members holding Master's and Doctoral Degrees in Educational Technology. Since 2006, the Centre has supported the development of 55 virtual CoPs for public servants across Canada using social media technologies. These communities are situated in the wider strategic context of Public Service Renewal by:

- integrating technology into learning, networking and knowledge transfer which helps to attract and retain younger employees and leverage the wealth of information and ideas of all its workers (DiGiammarino & Trudeau, 2008);

- educating public servants on the value of CoPs and how to maximize the potential of this approach; and
- bridging the time and space gap for public servants to help bring people together, network with one another, share best practices and capture knowledge interdepartmentally.

The Centre operates on a cost-recovery basis with the goal of covering its costs associated with user licenses and human resources devoted to internal projects. To clarify, "clients" are groups of federal public servants who are employed within the government's 392 departments, agencies and sub-agencies. As such, these government organizations or inter-departmental communities are charged community start-up fees for consulting services, needs assessments, administration of the technology platform (e.g., setting up user accounts, customizing the user interface), training and formative evaluations. They also cover the cost of platform licenses and technical support for each community member. In some cases, members belong to more than one community, but pay one annual fee. Clients may also choose to buy supplemental services such as in-depth evaluations or hire one of the Centre's full-time Learning Advisors to act as a community facilitator.

In sum, the Centre's role is to offer consulting services and expertise to help build and maintain virtual communities within the federal Public Service. It offers comprehensive support for the technological platform and additional services such as presentations on social collaboration approaches and technologies. Finally, the Centre provides assistance in the design and implementation of other collaborative tools such as wikis and web conferencing. Regardless of technology, the Centre uses a similar process model and project management approach for each project.

Theoretical Framework

The work carried out by the Centre is grounded in theory and guided by best practices related to CoPs. Specifically, the Centre operates within a constructivist paradigm grounding its work in socio-cultural theories (Brown, Collins & Duguid, 1989; Lave & Wenger, 1991; Vygotsky, 1978; Wenger, 1988). In particular, situated learning and legitimate peripheral participation emphasize how peer interaction and apprenticeships are important ways to facilitate individual cognitive growth and knowledge acquisition (Lave & Wenger, 1991).

While social learning is an age-old practice, CoPs have gained popularity in recent years. Lave and Wenger (1991) coined the term "communities of practice" while exploring the concepts of situated learning and legitimate peripheral participation. More recently, Wenger (1998) defined CoPs as "groups of people who share a concern or a passion for something they do and learn how to do it better as they interact regularly". (p. 11)

Lave and Wenger (1991) explored learning as participation in a social world and described how people learn better in social settings and through social interaction. Knowledge otherwise remains unused if taught in contexts that separate knowing from doing. Situated learning is particularly relevant to "learning on the job" or cognitive apprenticeships (Brown et al., 1989; Lave & Wenger, 1991). As apprentices, learners have strong goals and motivation; through engagement in practice, they develop a more global view of the enterprise. Most of the learning is done on the job while working for a mentor who helps the apprentice learn the trade through activity and social interaction. Apprentices enter the culture of practice that allows them to witness practitioners solving problems and carrying out authentic tasks in real-life situations (Brown et al., 1989). Apprenticeships are an exemplary case of legitimate peripheral participation. New members participate at first from the periphery. Over time, they become more engaged in the culture and move toward the community's core to eventually assume the role of expert (Wenger, 1998).

The common theme among social learning theorists is the emphasis placed on social learning, knowledge sharing and interacting with people. CoPs provide a forum in which a group of individuals are united with the common goal to learn from one another and share best practices.

Technology has influenced the way in which we communicate, interact and learn. Traditionally, CoPs were thought to be geographically bound. In the past, we belonged to communities in the vicinity of our homes, workplace and recreational arena. With the influence of the Internet, geographical barriers have been bridged and members can meet in a virtual space to exchange ideas. At their core, traditional and virtual communities are similar in purpose. Virtual communities, however, provide a supplemental form of communication and interaction among members.

According to Johnson (2001), engaging in a virtual CoP enhances the learning environment since the learning that evolves from these communities is collaborative, in which the collective knowledge of the community is greater than individual knowledge. CoPs encompass this concept in that they establish a networked environment where improved learning can occur (Wenger, McDermott, & Snyder, 2002) using synchronous and asynchronous communication tools (Gannon-Leary & Fontainha, 2007).

The Centre's conceptual framework presents the CoP as a learning methodology that actively supports learners in an open context. Members of a CoP engage with one another and collaborate for many different purposes, including learning, accessing expertise and networking. That said, the foundational characteristic of a CoP is that members have a commitment to learning, solving problems and collaborating with one another.

Common characteristics can be found across all communities, regardless of context. Each community gives rise to insights and solutions that would not come about individually. This idea relates to the concept of synergy, where the whole is greater than the sum of its parts.

Therefore, implementing virtual CoPs across the federal Government has the potential of having positive affects on training and learning. For example, CoPs facilitate the exchange and opportunity to learn when and where public servants want. In addition, CoPs help employees to work in association with other practitioners to innovate in their field of expertise and benefit from the collective knowledge of public servants nationally. This allows for both explicit and tacit knowledge to be captured and stored from which others can learn, reducing the need to re-invent the wheel. More importantly, a CoP reduces an individual's feelings of isolation by providing opportunities to work with others and to negotiate meaning, learning and identity within the community (Wenger, 1998).

How We Do It: Process Model

Overview

The services offered by the Centre cater to a variety of client needs. The literature suggests that CoPs are not static or stable entities nor can they be mandated by management. Instead, management can support and facilitate the spontaneous emergence of communities or social networks (Ardichvili, Page & Wentling, 2003; Brown & Duguid, 2001). Accordingly, the Centre typically works with pre-existing communities that function in a face-to-face context. These communities contact the Centre to inquire about obtaining a virtual space to complement their current approaches. The Centre takes a hands-on approach, in which Learning Advisors walk clients through each step of developing a virtual community and provide a wide range of services from needs assessments through to evaluations. Regardless of client needs, the Centre is equipped to offer customized packages. It is important to note that once a community is up and running, members typically manage and facilitate their own community with ongoing support from the Centre. In cases where communities are significant in size, some clients take advantage of a Centre's Learning Advisor on a continuous basis to facilitate and coordinate their community.

The Centre's design and development approach is based on sound methodology, to facilitate the process of establishing and facilitating successful communities that will achieve the stated goals and objectives of its members. The Centre's process model is a three-phase, iterative approach that is grounded in expert advice from the field (e.g., Saint-Onge & Wallace, 2003) and based upon the Centre's experience. Three key phases are as follows:

1.   establish communities;
2.   grow communities; and
3.   expand communities.

The focus of the Centre's work is on helping clients establish communities. Consequently, the following section will focus on describing the development of communities and will provide a brief overview of how the Centre helps to support growth and expansion.

Establishing Communities

In this phase, the project is defined, components of the community are established and the community is launched. First, the client is offered a customized work plan that details each step of the process and associated deadlines. Consequently, a Steering Committee of core community members is formed and roles and responsibilities for the project are discussed. For example, a Sponsor is typically a manager or executive who values and supports the community by providing resources and by acting as a "champion" for the community. Sponsors also clear barriers and participate in milestone reviews. Additionally, the Steering Committee acts as an internal advisory board that takes on a leadership role. For instance, they draft procedures, decide upon membership and content and encourage community development. The Facilitator or Coordinator is often a community member who provides leadership, focus, stimulation for group interaction, support, team building, manages conflicts and responds to member feedback. The Centre's role is typically characterized by offering expertise and guidance on the development and implementation of CoPs, project management as well as technical advice and support for the community.

Once roles are clarified, a needs assessment is conducted with members of the Steering Committee or with the entire community. The main goal at this stage is to specify purpose, content, governance structure and membership of the community. Most importantly, the context of the community is defined along with goals and objectives that are explicitly linked to broader organizational goals and within the strategic context of the department. In other words, a shared understanding of purpose and expectations is created and the value of this initiative is highlighted.

After the needs have been analyzed, the Centre provides recommendations on how to proceed, including deliverables and resource requirements for the community. In addition, policies are established such as a policy on language, community mission statement, conflict resolution procedures and processes for sharing and storing knowledge. Next, the Centre guides the Steering Committee through the process of developing a customized interface and structure for the virtual space. A beta version is then opened online where the client has an opportunity to experience the space for the first time. Modifications to design and structure of the site are made until the client is satisfied. Implementation, training and communication strategies are also developed at this time.

Launching the community is carried out after members have been identified, the platform has been customized and tested, the site has been populated with some content and the client has signed off on deliverables. Members typically assemble for one day in a face-to-face context. The workshop generally entails a presentation on the value the CoP approach, clarification on the purpose and goals of the specific community and basic training on how to use the tool. While schedules may vary, design and implementation of the virtual community could take as little as 4-6 weeks.

To reiterate, the Centre typically works with pre-existing communities that wish to supplement their face-to-face meetings with online activities such as ongoing discussions and sharing of best practices. These communities differ from "work groups" or "project teams" in that CoPs are oriented toward knowledge sharing or collective problem solving around a common area of practice. Typically, they are not product-oriented nor do they have specific deadlines. The structured *process* of establishing virtual communities takes into account the context and purpose of its members in order to help ensure success (Saint-Onge & Wallace, 2003). Communities, however, constantly evolve and react to changing environments to support members' shifting contexts, needs and work-related activities. Noteworthy of mention is that clients are always reminded that community development is based on a process and that technology is merely a tool to support and facilitate current ways of working and interacting.

Growing and Expanding Communities

During these two phases, the community moves beyond the initial stages and establishes itself as a viable community through various activities. Members fill out their profiles, the Facilitator plays a key role in helping sustain and strengthen the community, members become more comfort-

able with the tool and refinements may be made to policies, rules of engagement and membership criteria. Reflection and feedback to improve the community are typically carried out at this time. This leads to recommendations to expand and improve upon the community and determine next steps. For example, after several months, a community may decide to create smaller sub-communities or open up their closed membership to other individuals with whom they can exchange and learn.

Ongoing Support

The Centre offers ongoing coaching opportunities and comprehensive support for communities. First, support includes training on the benefits of implementing CoPs, community objectives, technical training on how to use the tool and facilitation training for Facilitators of communities. Face-to-face or virtual training (using synchronous communication tools) is offered. Second, paper-based user guides and online training modules are included in the training package to complement the training. Third, the Centre has also created a community specifically designed to offer resources and facilitate exchange between Facilitators across communities of the portal. Finally, the Centre offers a dedicated, toll-free support line to all users. One of the Centre's Learning Advisors will walk a member through any technical difficulties or questions about the tool.

Community Types within the Public Service

Within an organization, CoPs can remain informal or they can be much more structured, with a well-defined mandate, member acceptance criteria and purpose. Moreover, the purpose of each community varies and is likely to evolve over time. Based upon experience and consistent with the literature, four types of virtual communities have emerged within the Public Service:

- community of practitioners;
- community of interest;
- community of learning; and
- the strategic community.

While there is overlap among these categories, communities typically revolve around one theme. For example, many communities are strategic in nature but focus on learning and performance on the job. As previously mentioned, the Centre mainly provides consulting services and support to closed virtual communities. Learning Advisors are not typically involved in community activities. Consequently, the following examples are not intended to be extended case studies of private communities. Instead, more general examples within the Public Service are provided.

Community of Practitioners

A community of practitioners is a place that allows practitioners, specialists, experts or leaders in the same field to develop, communicate, share information and innovate in their area of expertise. One such community is an interdepartmental community for human resource directors. Members of the community share information regarding different topics related to human resources, collectively solve problems and share expertise. In addition, community members share best practices and useful documents with one another. Currently this CoP has 29 members.

Community of Interest

A community of interest is a place where participants from various spheres exchange their knowledge and learn from others regarding an interest they have in common. One example in the Public Service is the National Learning Community, in which the topic of interest is learning and professional development. This community is open to all public servants who are members of the Centre's virtual CoP portal. Members cut across many government departments and include individuals at entry-level to executive positions. New employees, experienced public servants, specialists in many different fields as well as experts in learning can connect, share and learn from each other regardless of individual community membership. Facilitated by one of the Centre's Learning Advisors, the National Learning Community includes information and resources such as "site of the week", a list of upcoming events and external links related to learning and professional development. There is also a section dedicated to research and development of technology-supported learning. Most importantly, members can add their own resources and knowledge objects, post blogs and contribute to discussion threads.

Community of Learning

When members produce and exchange knowledge regarding a specific subject in order to develop new skills, they form a community of learning. This type of community is learner-centred and typically employs a blended approach to training. Communities of this type can be ad hoc or ongoing. For example, the government's central service provider for Canadian citizens has incorporated a virtual CoP into its leadership and management program. The course includes five phases over an 18-month period. The community serves both managers and team leaders, and provides them with online courses to learn more in depth about topics taught in face-to-face sessions. One key theme is mental wellness and workplace well-being. This course focuses on providing community members with the opportunity to reflect on ways to reduce stress in the workplace. Currently this CoP has around 500 members that is co-facilitated by two of the Centre's Learning Advisors.

Strategic Community

A strategic community enables an organization to pool knowledge and to attain strategic and organizational objectives. In particular, this community makes it possible to have a more complete picture of all facets of the organization, to make this information available, in whole or in part, to all employees. The approach helps to move quickly from the idea of a project to its implementation, to create a feeling of belonging in the organization, to reduce the effect of isolation for remote collaborators and to create a culture of knowledge specific to the organization. For example, during the transition towards a new delivery model for language training services, the Canada School chose to implement a community for Language Training professionals across Canada. This ongoing project is part of the strategy to support the organization's objectives in helping its employees to better understand the changes they are facing and elements of the new model. As well, this community helps its members develop new competencies related to new job requirements. Currently, the CoP supports 37 members.

Other examples include communities for executive and administrative assistants, knowledge exchange on issues surrounding public health and policy, and intensive leadership development programs designed for aspiring executives in Canada's Public Service.

COLLABORATIVE TECHNOLOGIES

Common Platform

Technology has given birth to a new set of tools that foster collaboration. This section will describe the technological platform, tools and features used to support social learning, collaboration, problem solving, sharing best practices, archiving and retrieving knowledge within the Public Service.

Virtual communities developed by the Centre reside on a common platform. While many commercial tools were evaluated before selecting the current platform, the tool was adopted for the following key reasons:

- features specifically designed to support CoPs;
- ability to accommodate English, French and bilingual communities;
- ability to customize look and feel to meet government requirements and customize visual elements for individual communities (e.g., community banner and homepage);
- security features; and
- Canadian-based company with excellent customer support.

For example, there are many well-known tools available (e.g., Facebook, Google Groups) but they are not specifically designed to support many types of community activities simultaneously (e.g., content management and social networking and collaboration). They also have limited security features. Nonetheless, the Centre is constantly evaluating technology options and is open to using other platforms as long as they meet government standards and client needs. A common platform for all communities allows the Centre to build expertise and offer continuous support for the specific tool and create links between communities. All members access their community through the CoP portal. The portal page offers information about the Centre, CoP approaches and technical support. It also includes a link to the National Learning Community that serves all 2400 members.

Key Features

The common platform used by the Centre supports community activities such as knowledge management, content management, social networking and collaboration. Locating experts, sharing tacit knowledge and best practices, and searching a variety of knowledge objects (e.g., members, blogs, documents, websites, discussions, images) are some of the features aimed at meeting multiple objectives.

Information and knowledge management. Knowledge management is an important function within a CoP (Allee, 2000; Saint-Onge & Wallace, 2003). Members can share documents and information with one another and organize this knowledge in a comprehensive and retrievable way. Forms, procedures, best practices and various other resources (e.g., websites, blogs, and announcements) can be tagged or classified and retrieved through a search engine. Members can retain knowledge in ways that are unlike databases or manuals because the tasks and processes respond to local circumstances and preserve tacit aspects of knowledge (Wenger, 1998). Learning from the experience of others and avoiding the duplication of efforts are key benefits.

Within the platform, members can upload and share document files, annotate, comment and discuss content. Updating content and version control are also features of the system. Alternatively, individuals often share best practices, documents and relevant information via telephone, email and in face-to-face meetings. This information is not typically documented or shared with a wider audience.

The tool also allows users to link and share objects across communities. If members have permission, they can access knowledge objects in other communities. In the process of creating a CoP, an unintentional boundary is established through membership and non-membership. Outsiders only have access to the community's resources by becoming a member. For this reason it is likely that an individual is a member of several CoPs at the same time. These individuals are known as boundary members. Participants observe knowledge develop within the boundaries of one community and determine its applicability within the boundaries of another community. They post what they think might be of importance between different communities and serve as the contact person should questions arise or clarification be required. This cross-pollination creates value for both the community members and the organization since it makes resources available, shares different perspectives and aligns effort (Wenger, 1998).

To facilitate connections between communities and members, a searchable member directory as well as a descriptive list of all communities are available to everyone in the portal. In addition, several activities have been designed by the Centre in order to facilitate links between communities. For example, a community member can contact the Centre to find out if other CoPs exist with similar interests as their own. In addition, a community can decide to spotlight their CoP in the National Learning Community. Presenting the community at the national level is a great way to publicize what the community is about and to advertise that community members would like to establish links with other communities that have similar interests.

Communication and collaboration tools. Asynchronous discussion tools are a large component of the platform and include features such as discussion boards and email distribution lists. Members discuss and share relevant information, offer one another support for problems encountered and create common artifacts related to their area of practice. Many communities choose to organize their discussions by major themes such as staffing procedures, resources for teaching, course readings and best practices but each page in the system includes a "start a discussion" option. In addition, wiki-style pages allow members to collaborate on documents in order to create collective artifacts and to innovate. Members can edit, update, and save a page, provided they have permission to do so.

Locating and sharing expertise. One of the main advantages of virtual CoPs is the ability to find answers to questions or problems or to locate tacit knowledge around a particular practice. The platform is built around this concept of connectivity since learning is an inherently social activity (Vygotsky, 1978). Specifically, members are encouraged to fill out their "business card" or member profile in order to inform other members about how they can be contacted, their roles and responsibilities, areas of expertise, education, credentials and general interests. Members are also encouraged to post a picture, in order to personalize the virtual space. All business cards can be viewed by any member of the portal and are not community-specific.

In addition, the tool lists recent contributions (e.g., resources posted, discussions) and the participant's community memberships. This feature links members to content, providing a more robust picture of the member's expertise from which others can benefit. Members of the CoP portal have access to thousands of other members within the portal, regardless of department or geographical location. Related to profiles, is a member directory that can be searched by community or the entire portal. This allows members to locate others with expertise across communities and government departments.

Other tools include a shared calendar, meetings and announcements, page subscriptions, editorial control and access privileges, bookmarking pages of interest, participation statistics and bilingual capabilities.

RESULTS

Evaluation of Communities

Quantitative data collected over the last few years indicate rapid growth in the number of community participants as well as opportunities to continuously share experiences, knowledge and skills. For instance, in 2005, the Canada School began with two virtual CoPs. Since then, the Centre of Expertise in Communities of Practice has supported the development of approximately 55 CoPs and includes more than 2400 members and 32 000 learning objects that can be accessed online at any time.

While the number of participants, communities and shared learning objects may be indicators of

success, continued demand for services from a variety of government departments and invitations to speak at internal conferences are equally important. Additionally, value is demonstrated by the number of members who renew their membership every year. Demand for the Centre's services continues to grow through word of mouth as well as through promotional initiatives such as conference presentations and marketing material.

In addition, anecdotal evidence suggests that the Centre's clients recognize the value of expertise provided and community members are continuously participating in communities to improve on-the-job performance:

Our community of practice has come to be an integral part of our workday, and as the project progresses, it will undoubtedly become an even larger environment geared towards social learning and on-the-job training. My colleagues and I discuss common [language training] issues and concerns, and by posting our solutions in the community, we hope that others will benefit from our experiences (Jane Newton, personal communication, December 20, 2007).

…My idea was to provide teachers in departments with the support that they needed to do their jobs well and a focal point so that although away from the main campus, they would continue to feel connected to the organization. The site provides a vast variety of material…

[teachers] have used it extensively and have contributed their own material for the use of other teachers. The site continues to grow and develop and we look forward to continued growth… (Leonard Courage, personal communication, January 8, 2008).

…through it we are able to share information, links, and business-related documentation quickly, safely, and effectively. It also provides a sense of teamwork and focus for individual participants that fosters greater interaction and exchange, and a sense of building something larger than yourself with others who share the same passion (Piero Narducci, personal communication, April 11, 2008).

Evaluation Strategy

Regardless of the evaluation method used, community builders agree that ongoing evaluation is an important part of building a successful community and that there is no single effective method for evaluating a virtual community (Allen, Ure & Evans, 2003). Continuous monitoring is also essential to determine if the community is meeting its specific objectives and to identify areas for improvement. Consequently, the Centre has developed a large-scale evaluation strategy that includes two key options: a) standard evaluation; and b) customized evaluation. Currently, the strategy is in its initial stages of implementation and as a consequence, evaluation data will not be presented. Instead, the following section will focus on providing a description of the evaluation strategy and its related components.

Standard evaluation. The standard evaluation consists of a survey with pre-determined questions that address concerns about CoPs. Closed and open-ended questions are based on general indicators of success found in the literature (e.g., Gannon-Leary & Fontainha, 2007; St-Onge & Wallace, 2003) such as opportunities for exchange and collaboration, access to expertise, perceived value of the community and whether or not it is meeting its intended goals. In addition, the survey has a designated area for short stories and anecdotal evidence of a member's individual experience with their community. The platform also generates a number of usage statistics to assess participation rates within the community. Results from the survey and analysis of usage statistics are then summarized in a report and presented to the community Sponsor with recommendations for future action. The goal is to eventually aggregate data from all communities in order to provide an overall picture of CoPs across the Public Service.

Customized evaluation. The customized evaluation is created with a specific community in mind. In collaboration with the client, specific research questions and the most appropriate methods of inquiry are selected. This resource-intensive evaluation uses various methods and sources and is suitable for those seeking a more in-depth and focused assessment

Indicators of Success It is important to identify indicators of success to determine what must be evaluated. Each community has objectives when it is initiated; therefore, the goal of the evaluation is to determine if the CoP succeeded at meeting its stated objectives. Table 1 includes a general list and brief description of community success factors. It should be noted that each community must define its own standards of success. For example, determining what constitutes adequate participation rates will vary from community to community.

Methods

Triangulation refers to an approach to data analysis that synthesizes data from multiple sources. By examining information collected from different methods, the chance of obtaining biased data that exists in a single study is reduced (Fraenkel & Wallen, 1996). In addition, multiple views enhance the understanding of a phenomenon. Therefore, focus groups, interviews, surveys, community observations and participant statistics are used to determine how well communities are meeting specific objectives.

Survey. The Centre has created a question bank to facilitate the custom design of surveys that are tailored to meet the needs of a specific community. Survey design is a collaborative effort between the Centre and the client. The collection of questions consists of both closed and open-ended questions that are typically delivered online. In addition, there is also a standard survey available for com-

Table 1. Indicators of successful communities

Indicators	Description
Learning and knowledge	CoP has led to enhanced skills, increased knowledge, conceptual change or improved performance on the job.
Achievement of objectives	CoP is successful at meeting its stated objectives.
Content	Content populating the CoP is meeting the needs of community members (e.g., relevant, organized, aligned with objectives).
Problem solving	Participating in the CoP is helping members solve work-related problems.
Sense of community	Members feel a sense of community and identity within the community.
Collaboration	Members are sharing information and expertise to accomplish work-related tasks.
Access to expertise	Members have adequate access to expertise within the community.
Design and layout of the tool	CoP tool is meeting the needs of the community (e.g., design, usability, navigation, features support community activities).
Facilitator	Facilitator is meeting the needs of the CoP and its members (e.g., leadership, focus, stimulation for group interaction, support, conflict resolution, member feedback).
Support	Technical support and training provided by the Centre is meeting the needs of community members.
Overall satisfaction	Members are satisfied overall and perceive there is value to participating in the CoP.
Participation	Participation rates are satisfactory and reasons for participation and non-participation are identified.
Knowledge management	Searching, accessing and archiving information is effective and efficient.

munities who opt for a more simple evaluation. This broad survey includes approximately 20 questions on items such as member perceptions of opportunities to collaborate with colleagues, access to expertise, relevance and organization of content, community support and facilitation, areas for improvement and overall satisfaction with the CoP and the technological platform.

Interview. Interview protocols and sample questions have been designed to facilitate the design and implementation of interviews. With the client, objectives of the interview, specific questions and members to be interviewed are identified. In addition to community members, the client might for example, choose to collect data from managers or the community Sponsor. Specifically, interviews may be conducted to identify members' perceived learning outcomes or to elicit a manager's perspective on the community's impact on job performance.

Focus groups. Protocols and sample questions have been designed in order to facilitate the design

and implementation of conducting focus groups. For instance, a focus group would be best suited to answer questions that determine if a community is collaborating or if there is a sense of community among members. Focus groups are typically conducted in person but can also be performed via teleconference or videoconference.

Usage statistics. Usage statistics are used to track how often members are using the CoP. For example, the Centre can collect information such as number of members contributing to the CoP, number of page views and number of new accounts. This data is automatically generated by the CoP platform. Communities must define in advance what they consider to be benchmarks for success, since standards of achievement are specific to each community.

Short stories and anecdotal evidence. Feedback in the form of anecdotes, stories or testimonials from community members provides rich, descriptive information about how the community has benefited them. Using content analysis methods

(Weber, 1990), the Centre classifies textual information by reducing it to more relevant, manageable bits of data using a set of procedures. This form of analysis helps to make sense of feedback and testimonials. If requested by the client, content analysis is also used to directly observe and analyze content residing in the virtual CoP.

Timing of the Evaluation

The life cycle of a CoP is always variable. Therefore, the traditional notion of formative and summative evaluations is difficult to apply. Instead, evaluations are implemented when it is deemed most appropriate to answer specific questions. For instance, after three months it is appropriate to conduct an informal evaluation of user satisfaction, adequacy of technical support or to identify areas for improvement. However, questions related to impact of the community on job performance or shifts in collaborative culture should be conducted after a minimum of one year.

Current Challenges and Lessons Learned

Previous sections have noted key benefits to implementing virtual CoPs into the workplace. However, CoPs continue to face several key challenges. Some of these challenges include: a) adherence to the process model; b) sustaining active participation in communities c) willingness to share and exchange knowledge and information; and d) use of technology.

The first challenge is related to the process model. The literature outlines an ideal approach for building communities but it is not always practical or feasible to implement in all contexts. The Centre has encountered several instances where operational requirements and other constraints such as time, budget and human resources have called for modifications in the process. For example, some clients focus on technology. They want to move quickly through the process or in

an unstructured manner without clearly defining structural elements such as the vision, mission, objectives and content of the community. These clients are later dissatisfied with participation rates. In these instances, the Centre goes back to the beginning and walks the client through the initial stages of community design to fill in the gaps. It has become abundantly clear that when phases are omitted or elements are carried out prematurely, it has a negative impact on community development.

Other clients have budgetary and time constraints that prevent them from taking advantage of the Centre's full training package. In order to support these projects, the Centre offers training at a distance using synchronous communication tools. In addition, the Centre provides a variety of ''training capsules''. These 15 to 30 minute "refresher" sessions are presented during a community's scheduled face-to-face meeting. Topics vary depending on community needs and cover technical aspects including: a) How to participate in asynchronous discussions; b) reviewing the role of members; c) revisiting the vision and mission statement; d) discussing techniques on how to increase participation; and e) various ways to welcome new members. In addition to assisting clients with budgetary and time constraints, this approach is also intended to help communities that have not been intentionally implemented by an organization for strategic purposes (Wenger, 1998). Rather, they started as committees whose members wanted to work in a more collaborative way by integrating a virtual component into their community. It should be noted that these spontaneous CoPs are some of the most active ones supported by the Centre.

Additionally, operational requirements sometimes take priority over learning needs. In one community for managers, the Centre was informed that future members would be in a five-day, face-to-face meeting and the client wanted to take this opportunity to ''launch'' the community. They also requested that users be trained on the tool at this time. This greatly affected the project because none of the structural elements (e.g., mission, purpose, content) had been put into place. Despite the fact that the community space had little to offer at this time, the training was conducted. Once again, success of the community was compromised and the client had to revisit earlier phases of the process model.

On one hand, the Centre has learned to be flexible and adapt the model in order to meet specific needs of clients. On the other hand, an important lesson learned is that the process model helps to ensure the success of communities. Developing the structural elements and informing members of them are key factors of success. It is also important to remind clients that virtual communities are not static websites and that the focus should be on its members. The tool is simply intended to support community objectives and activities. Striking a balance between clients' needs and the implementation of a reliable model is critical.

The second challenge is related to participation. Consistent with the literature, many public servants find that in a busy workplace, it is difficult to allocate time for CoP participation and sustain high levels of participation (Allen et al, 2003; Stoyko, 2002). Experts suggest that members should be allotted time to work in and contribute to communities since participation is crucial to success. Moreover, it is recommended that participation be subsumed into natural work processes and members be recognized for their contributions. Consequently, the Centre advises clients to build the tool around their current activities and integrate the virtual community into their face-to-face meetings. For example, meetings should include the community as an item on the agenda. Topics of discussion could revolve around ways to integrate the approach into members' daily tasks or ways to include new members into the community. Another idea offered is to include community participation into a member's annual Learning Plan and objectives for the year. In this case, members would be recognized for their efforts.

Communities require commitment. Members must be convinced that working collaboratively through communities will bring higher capabilities and performance than not participating (Saint-Onge & Wallace, 2003). It should also be clear that participating in a community is a different way of working and a shift in how work time is spent, not an additional burden on time and work responsibilities. The Centre communicates these points in the first stages of development and implementation but they should be re-enforced by the community's Sponsor and Facilitator over time.

The third key challenge appears to be members' willingness to share knowledge and information. Building trust is vital for information and knowledge exchange and is essential to develop a true sense of community among members. In the virtual environment, identities can remain hidden and members of the community may not be comfortable sharing information (Gannon-Leary & Fontainha, 2007). Since trust primarily develops through face-to-face interactions, the Centre typically incorporates face-to-face workshops to launch the community and further suggests that communities have additional face-to-face meetings over time to re-connect and establish relationships among members.

This challenge is closely related to resistance to change. When an organization or individuals are used to certain methods, change can make employees uncomfortable and uneasy. A good change management strategy can help change people's mindset, and therefore, make the value of communities clearer. Constant changes within the community also require a certain openness. Consequently, the Centre offers continuous professional support to client organizations, after the launch of the community. This is a challenging situation for members since constant change means constant adaptation. Members are informed from the start that they should expect changes that reflect community needs. For example, modifications could be made to the homepage, links added or new tools integrated into the community (e.g., chat, videoconferences).

Finally, every tool has its limitations and the current platform is no exception. While the tool was tested prior to implementation, the Centre is aware of some criticism related to the platform's usability. On the other hand, members who have been trained and have regularly interacted with the tool, do not find it difficult to use. Some strategies the Centre is using to overcome difficulties related to the tool, include manipulating the interface to make it easier to navigate, supplying personalized technical support and a implementing a variety of training and documentation strategies. Alternative tools are continually being explored

Contribution to Knowledge

In the workplace context, the implementation and evaluation of informal learning strategies and social learning technologies to support them are relatively new. While this chapter merely offers an overview of Public Service initiatives supported by the Canada School, many organizations world-wide are facing similar challenges and could benefit from descriptive cases of what others are doing, how they are doing it, successful practices and lessons learned. Specific to the aims of this book, this chapter has attempted to demonstrate how various learning methods, technology, community activities and evaluations are interconnected and take into account the specific workplace context and objectives of the Canadian Public Service. Hopefully, the literature will continue to thrive in this area in order to stimulate dialogue between large organizations struggling to preserve corporate memory and implement cost-effective and efficient approaches to training and professional development.

THE FUTURE OF SOCIAL LEARNING APPROACHES IN THE CANADIAN PUBLIC SERVICE

Given the desire of the Clerk of the Privy Council "to establish benchmarks and share best practices" and "to develop modern electronic platforms for online learning, networking and sharing best practices across the Public Service" (Lynch, 2007), it is reasonable to expect that the demand for virtual communities will increase exponentially. In 2008, the Centre experienced tremendous growth (from five employees to ten) as a result of the growing demand for services. This growth and continued interest in social learning approaches are positive indicators for the future of virtual CoPs in the Public Service.

That said, futurists not only use past trends to predict future direction, but also consider a number of other social, economical and technological markers. No doubt, these important drivers will play a role in the future of social learning approaches in the Canadian Public Service.

Influence of Social Trends

On the heels of a significant wave of public servant retirements, the Public Service is implementing strategies to recruit and train new talent. This renewal effort will undoubtedly bring rise to the most versatile workforce the Canadian Public Service has ever seen. This next generation of workers (those in their early twenties today), are higher educated, more technologically savvy, and heavily reliant on their extended personal networks they have built and nurtured using web-based technologies. This group of workers is likely to push for the continued implementation of virtual CoPs in the Public Service as they are accustomed to social learning approaches, computer-mediated communication and virtual networking. In fact, this generation of workers will likely demand a working environment that embraces the approaches and flexibility they integrate into their daily routines. Access to informal learning, networked environments and open-mindedness to new advancements in technology will become key markers in employee satisfaction. The organization must continue to advance in these areas, with the implementation of virtual CoPs being only one example, if it wishes to remain a viable work environment in an already competitive labour market.

Influence of Economical Trends

Accountability and performance management are key themes in the Public Service today. With tighter budgets and a wave of incoming new public servants needing training, the Canada School must look for more cost-effective and efficient ways to meet employee development targets. At the same time, the sharp rise in gas prices is being felt around the world. Clearly, the freedom to travel for meetings, conferences and learning activities has been affected, especially in Canada, where public servants work from coast to coast in a country that spans more than three million square miles.

As a result, the organization needs to evaluate and adopt new measures for communication, training, employee development and organizational performance. The implementation of virtual CoPs offers one attractive option to bring large groups of people together in a virtual space, hence eliminating the need for frequent travel. Integration of other synchronous tools such as videoconferencing and chat into a community space also helps to enhance the quality of communication and member exchanges, without adding much cost. In sum, the underlying models of mentorship and apprenticeship within a community are becoming more and more attractive in this growing reality that Canadian departments are facing.

Influence of Technological Trends

Technological advancements in today's world are hard to keep up with - new virtual platforms, personal devices and Web 2.0 tools come to market daily. Clearly, the next wave of inventions will impact how, when and why we choose to connect with one another. The Web is just a launching point for a future that will undoubtedly network thousands of communities and millions of members together worldwide. Integrated platforms will become more popular and people will move away from their laptops in favour of PDAs, cell phones and possibly even car-based computers.

The line between work and private life will continue to become increasingly blurred as technology will continue to close the gap between space and time, and people will continue to strive for equilibrium in their work-life balance. Introduction of such technological advancements changes the playing field. The work day of "nine-to-five" no longer exists. More employees work at a distance. New management models need to be considered for off-site teams. Managers in the next 10 years will need to recognize both the strengths and weaknesses of these trends in the workplace. Successful managers will be those that adapt to these changes, tackle related challenges and encourage employees to take advantage of the benefits.

THE COMING YEARS

Given the driving forces described above, the Centre for Expertise in Communities of Practice is well positioned to offer a solution to the growing demand for informal, social learning in the Canadian Public Service. Strategically, the Centre is working towards two main objectives in the coming years: (a) implementation of a government-wide CoP platform whereby every public servant has access; and (b) cross-pollination of the more than 50 closed communities already existing today into a linked and open forum to allow for knowledge transfer across functional groups and strategic communities. On a broader level, the vision is to integrate communities into the Canada School's standard products and services in order to build upon and add value to what is currently being offered.

These goals are ambitious and require extensive thought on how to best leverage technology to potentially connect more than 260 000 public servants into one forum. Certainly, it is expected that issues of information privacy, intellectual property, copyright and ownership of content will become hot topics of discussion over the coming years. However, the Canada School is committed to using innovation to support learning needs of today's and tomorrow's Public Service.

REFERENCES

Allee, V. (2000). Knowledge networks and communities of practice. *OD Practitioner . Journal of the Organizational Development Network, 32*(4).

Allen, S., Ure, D., & Evans, S. (2003). *Virtual communities of practice as learning networks.* Provo, UT: Brigham Young University Instructional Psychology and Technology.

Ardichvili, A., Page, V., & Wentling, T. (2003). Motivation and barriers to participation in virtual knowledge sharing teams. *Journal of Knowledge Management, 7*(1), 64–77. doi:10.1108/13673270310463626

Brown, J. S., Collins, A., & Duguid, P. (1989). Situated cognition and the culture of learning. *Educational Researcher, 18*(1), 32–42.

Brown, J. S., & Duguid, P. (2001). Knowledge and organization: A social-practice perspective. *Organization Science, 12*(2), 198–213. doi:10.1287/orsc.12.2.198.10116

Carnevale, A. P., Gainer, L. J., & Villet, J. (1990). Training in America. San Francisco: Jossey-Bass.

Cross, J. (2007). Informal learning: Rediscovering the natural pathways that inspire innovation and performance. San Francisco: John Wiley & Sons, Inc.

DiGiammarino, F., & Trudeau, L. (2008). Virtual networks: An opportunity for government. *Public Management, 37*(1), 5–11.

Dutil, P., & Reid, T. (2007). Time for a new networked public service. *Policy Options, 28*(1), 80–84.

Eraut, M. (2000). Non-formal learning, implicit learning, and tacit knowledge in professional work. *The British Journal of Educational Psychology, 70*(1), 113–136. doi:10.1348/000709900158001

Fraenkel, J. R., & Wallen, N. E. (1996). *How to design and evaluate research in education,* 3rd ed. New York: McGraw-Hill Inc.

Gannon-Leary, P., & Fontainha, E. (2007). Communities of practice and virtual learning communities: Benefits, barriers, and success factors. *E-learning Papers, 5*(1), 1887–1542.

Johnson, C. M. (2001). A survey of current research on online communities of practice. *The Internet and Higher Education, 4*(1), 45–60. doi:10.1016/S1096-7516(01)00047-1

Lave, J., & Wenger, E. (1991). *Situated learning: Legitimate peripheral participation.* Cambridge: Cambridge University Press.

Lynch, K. G. (2007). Fourteenth annual report to the Prime Minister on the Public Service of Canada. Retrieved on July 31, 2008, from http://www.pco- bcp.gc.ca/index.asp?lang=eng&page=information&sub=publications&doc=ar-ra/15-2008/rpt_e.htm

Lynch, K. G. (2008). Fifteenth annual report to the Prime Minister on the Public Service of Canada. Retrieved on July 31, 2008, from http://www. pco- bcp.gc.ca/index.asp?lang=eng&page=infor mation&sub=publications&doc=ar-ra/15- 2008/ rpt_e.htm

Saint-Onge, H., & Wallace, D. (2003). Leveraging communities of practice. Burlington, MA: Butterworth Heinemann.

Smith, P. J. (2003). Workplace learning and flexible delivery. *Review of Educational Research*, *73*(1), 53–88. doi:10.3102/00346543073001053

Statistics Canada. (2008, April 3). *Canada at a glance. Statistics Canada catalogue no. 12-581-XPE*. Ottawa. Retrieved on July 29, 2008, from http://www.statcan.ca/english/freepub/12-581-XIE/12-581-XIE2007001.pdf

Stoyko, P. (2002). *Communities of practice: Lessons learned from the research literature and public service experience*. Strategic Research and Planning Branch, Canadian Centre for Management Development.

Stoyko, P., & Fang, Y. (2007). *Lost & found: A smart-practice guide to managing organization memory*. Canada School of Public Service Action-Research Roundtable on Organizational Memory. Retrieved on July 31, 2008, from http://www.csps-efpc.gc.ca/Research/publications/html/p137/1_e.html

Treasury Board of Canada Secretariat. (2006). *Policy on learning, training, and development*. Retrieved on July 31, 2008, from http://www.tbs-sct.gc.ca/pol/doc-eng.aspx?id=12405&section=text

Vygotsky, L. S. (1978). Mind in society: The development of higher psychological processes. Cambridge, MA: Harvard University Press.

Weber, R. P. (1990). *Basic content analysis, 2nd ed*. London: Sage Publications.

Wenger, E. (1998). Communities of practice: Learning, meaning, and identity. Cambridge, MA: Cambridge University Press.

Wenger, E., McDermott, R., & Snyder, W. M. (2002). *Cultivating communities of practice: A guide to managing knowledge*. Boston, MA: Harvard Business School Press.

ADDITIONAL READING

Block, P. (2008). *Community: The structure of belonging*. San Francisco: Berrett-Koehler Publishers, Inc.

Bransford, J. D., Brown, A. L., & Cocking, R. R. (2000). *How people learn: Brain, mind, experience, and school* (expanded edition). Washington, D.C.: National Academy Press.

Dewey, J. (1933). *How we think*. Boston: DC Heath.

Kimble, C., Hildreth, P., & Bourdon, I. (2008). *Communities of practice: Creating learning environments for educators*. Charlotte, NC: Information Age Publishing, Inc.

Li, C., & Bernoff, J. (2008). Groundswell: Winning in a world transformed by social technologies. MA: Forrester Research, Inc.

Schilit, B., Adams, N., & Want, R. (1994). Context-aware computing applications. *IEEE Workshop on Mobile Computing Systems and Applications (WMCSA'94)*, Santa Cruz, CA (pp. 89-101).

Shirky, C. (2008). *Here comes everybody: The power of organizing without organization*. London: Penguin Group, Inc.

Tapscott, D., & Williams, A. D. (2008). *Wikinomics: How mass collaboration changes everything*. New York: Penguin Group, Inc.

Chapter 12
Web 2.0 and Collaborative Learning in Higher Education

Anna Escofet
Universitat de Barcelona, Spain

Marta Marimon
Universitat de Vic, Spain

ABSTRACT

The dissemination of university knowledge has been traditionally based on lectures to students organised in homogenous groups. The advantages of this method are that it can give a unified vision of content, guaranteeing equal access to knowledge for all students. The 21ˢᵗ century university must combine its learning and teaching methods and incorporate different strategies and educative resources, as well as seeking to advance individual learning and promote collaborative work. The relevance of Web 2.0 is clear in this university learning context as it enables collaborative work to be carried out using ICT. In this chapter, we will deal with the different possible uses of social software in university teaching. We will show that the proper use of Web 2.0 tools can favour collaborative learning and promote new ways of teaching and learning.

NEW LEARNING FORMS AT UNIVERSITY: COLLABORATIVE LEARNING IN THE NETWORK

University teaching has been traditionally focused on large group organisation. At one extreme this has meant grouping together students who learn in the same way at the same time and has brought with it a kind of teaching in which the group is considered homogenous, where the teacher has acquired a role in imparting the content in a unidirectional way and which has leant heavily on memorisation and the posterior verbalisation of what has been committed to memory rather than encouraging other aspects more related to the understanding of meaning.

Despite the fact that it has been shown that large group organisation of this type is not always an efficient system –given that not all students start form the same level or have the same needs–, the arrival in the halls of the ideas developed by authors such as Décroly, Cousinet, Freinet or Freire, defending the positive aspects which can be achieved by

DOI: 10.4018/978-1-60566-826-0.ch112

interaction among equals, has been neither easy nor homogenous. In spite of that, however, the present day university, with the adoption of the constructivist learning and teaching model, where the student constructs their own knowledge in an interactive process where the teacher acts as a mediator between student and content, allows us to consider group learning, making it possible for the students themselves to be the mediators in a collaborative way in their learning process.

This kind of organisation of learning has been studied by different authors to show its potential. Jonhson and Jonhson (1991) attribute different basic aspects, amongst those which mention the favouring of positive interdependence, individual responsibility in tasks, the development of inter-personal and small-group exchange skills and the awareness of belonging to a group. Monereo and Durán (2001) indicate that interaction among equals can have a positive effect on aspects such as socialisation, the acquisition of social skills, aggression control, the relativisation of points of view and an increase in the aspiration and academic performance. Onrubia (2003) highlights the fact that students can become tutors to their peers and instigate their development thanks to the contrast between different points of view facing specific tasks that need to be solved working in collabo-ration, the need to express their point of view quite explicitly and the obligation to coordinate roles, the interventions to help each other and mutual control of the work. Harasim et al. (2000) highlight that collaboration has motivational and intellectual advantages: on a part, to work in col-laboration introduces multiple perspectives about a same question; on the other hand, the learning nets allow a global and intercultural collaboration, which can help to fostering mutual respect, con-fidence and the capacity to work together. Adell and Sales (1999), affirm that the collaborative learning can be a good strategy to help students to being self-sufficient and to contribute to the collective construction of knowledge, since it favors the democracy and the solidarity on the

group and the autonomy in the organization of the student's learning

Crook (1998) indicates that these studies on collaborative learning underlines the cognitive advantages that stem from the most intimate exchanges that take place when students work together. According to the author, the problem consists of discovering how the discourse is mobilized to the service of the creation of a joint reference, in seeing how there is in use what has been created as platform for new explorations and in seeing how there can perform more or less favorable the material conditions of resolution of problems to the efforts to obtain this mutuality.

In this process of joint construction of knowl-edge, the eruption of Information Communication and Technology –with computers initially and now Internet– has also been crucial as regards collaborative learning. In a well-known article, Salomon, Perkins and Globerson (1992) draw a distinction between the types of research centred on the educative use of computers. They make a distinction between the analysis of the effects *with* the technology and the analysis of effects *of* the technology. In the first case, the effects with the technology, the emphasis is placed on everything that the student can achieve with the help of the computer; in the second, the effects of the tech-nology, they point out how the student changes their way of thinking thanks to the computer, in other words, their cognitive changes.

As suggested by Kolodner and Guzdial (1996) it is quite clearly necessary to apply this distinc-tion to the analysis of the possibilities of ICT in collaborative learning.

In the case of the effects with the technology, we need to centre our focus on the organisational aspects, on the possibilities of improving collab-orative learning situations, and in describing the activities and social grouping which increase the collaboration.

Regarding the effects of the technology, we need to look at the possible changes of the students, at both an individual and group level, after the collaborative experience. Different investigations (Slavin, 1990; Natasi and Clements, 1991) have shown the benefits that collaborative learning has on individuals, in relation to the academic benefits and also the cognitive benefits in groups of differing ages and socio-economic composition, and also different academic disciplines. Regarding Álvarez et al. (2005), these benefits of the computer supported collaborative learning express two important ideas:

- The idea about learning in collaborative way, with other, in group. The student is in interaction with the other ones, sharing goals and distributing responsibilities to themselves as desirable forms of learning.
- The emphasis in the role of the computer as an element of mediation, giving support to the process and favoring the processes of interaction and of joint solution of the problems.

The fundamental question is related with the way of contributing the resources necessary for the construction of a shared knowledge object, that is to say, or, in other words, to the way that ICT can mediate some forms of activity which create communities of shared knowledge (Crook, 1998)

All this can be encapsulated in these lines: the incorporation of ICT into university teaching brings advantages not only as regards the teaching, but also the learning process itself. And when the teaching/learning relations are based on a collaborative focus, then the social dimension becomes crucially important.

This relevance of the social dimension is a characteristic of the so-called Web 2.0[1], which moves the centre of control to the users themselves, where they communicate, produce and publish their opinions, products, experiences and know-how in a global manner, conforming to what has been called collective intelligence (Levy, 2004).

Web 2.0 is based on the possibility of using software with very simplified and friendly interfaces, which helps to explain the high number of Web users and their active participation. The spaces Web 2.0 can offer are so rich in possibilities and content, and use synchronic and asynchronic communication tools (from the more traditional such as messaging, forums and chats to more recent ones such as group video conferencing, MySpace or Facebook); management tools (calendars, agendas, ...); publishing and diffusion tools (PhotoLog, YouTube, Flickr, WordPress, Blogger). In short, the potential of Web 2.0 lies in the creation of integrated environments which can facilitate knowledge exchange, collaboration and the creation of social networks.

Various studies have shown the possibilities offered by the Web and the effect of the appearance of Web 2.0, principally due to its great educational potential. Prominent among those is the Horizon Report (2008) which identifies the challenges which educational organisations will need to face, reflecting the implications of the new practises and technologies in all areas of our lives, which modify our way of communicating and accessing information:

- Significant changes in teaching, teaching staff, creative expression and learning, which has generated a need for innovation and leadership at all academic levels.
- Higher education is faced with a growing expectation in services offered, content and audiovisual documents for personal and mobile devices.
- The renewed emphasis on collaborative learning is pushing the educational community to develop new forms of interaction and assessment.
- The academic world is faced with the need to provide formal instruction in computer, visual and technological literacy, and also creating valuable content with current tools.

The Horizon Report identifies the significant tendencies which affect teaching and learning environments and creative expression:

- The growing use of Web 2.0 and social networks –combined with collective intelligence and massive amateur production– is changing teaching practices in a gradual yet inexorable way.
- The way in which we work, collaborate and communicate is evolving as frontiers are becoming more flexible and globalisation is increasing.
- The access to content, and its transportability, is increasing as we are using smaller and more powerful means.
- The gap between the students and the teachers' perceptions of technology is still increasing.

And finally, the Horizon report highlights six emerging technologies or practices which will probably be in general use in educational institutions in the short, medium and long term:

1. Tools and software for recording, editing and sharing short video clips as a means of personal communication, such as the mobile phone used to record videos, pocket cameras, online tools for making and editing video clips (FixMyMovie, http://www.fixmymovie.com), video sites (YouTube, Google Video, Viddler o Blip.tv), sites with systems for instant reception of data by Webcam (UStream, http://www.ustream.tv), services to produce programmes collaborating with other producers and broadcasting live (Mogulus, http://www.mogulus.com), or services which allow us to construct social networks around their broadcasts (Stickam, http://www.stickam.com). All these tools and software have allowed us to reduce almost completely the production costs and distribution of videos, which has a considerable

effect on its use in educational situations. Teachers can use all kind of devices to incorporate video into the classroom. The students are able to access a wide range of online educational video content, be they small fragments on specific themes or whole conferences. Academic tasks can also be carried out which consist in elaborating video projects about subjects of interest or develop a digital history as a way of investigating and developing ideas and transmitting their knowledge in a visual way that goes beyond the walls of the lecture hall.

2. Tools for online collaboration. Thanks to a series of complementary developments in Web infrastructures, the social network tools, Web applications and collaborating work spaces, which have eliminated the limitations imposed by distance, the collaboration in projects with people geographically far apart and also among students form different campuses, have been improving to the extent that it has now become something habitual and inexpensive in online collaboration. One of these areas of development has tools which allows us to share and collaborate in the creation of content in an integrated way in its basic functions, with Web applications such as Zoho Office (http://www.zoho.com) or Google Docs (http://docs.google.com), which provide us with standard ICT office packets without the need to buy or install any kind of software. Another area of development is in work spaces for collaboration online, which allow us to create meeting points where a group of people can work together, share resources or information and even establish social relations, with for instance social networks like Ning (http://www.ning.com) or Facebook (http://www.facebook.com). The main potential in the educational environment is that it allows us to configure spaces for work in virtual collaboration where we can share

ideas and interests, work in joint projects and collectively monitor progress. Teachers can evaluate students' work while it is being developed, being able to leave comments on these same documents. Students can collaborate with other students in an asynchronic way and access study materials from any computer. These tools can also be used to install a personal portfolio, where the student can show their work in any format and incorporate multimedia content in their work.

3. Broadband, with ever increasing services for mobile and wifi networks. The services provided by mobile phones have increased enormously: today we can connect from any place with email, Web search engines, photos and videos, documents, searches and shops etc. Students who carry out field work can use their mobile phones to take notes and photos and send them straight to the course blog, or even access material when they have no access to a computer, or, combining social networks, collaborate from anywhere. In short, mobile phones are a portable tool which allows us to exploit all the potential of the Internet and all our social connections.

4. Mashups or hybrid Web applications where data from different sources may be combined in one single tool. These are applications which collect data online, such as a collection of video and music clips, and which organise and show these in the way the author desires. An example of this kind of tool is the Google Mashup Editor (http://code.google.com/gme/). An interesting educational practice which allows this tool to be used is geotagging, where you add geographical metadata like latitude, longitude or toponyms to images, Web sites and other media, in a way that we can mark information in the real world landscape. As these tools are being used by teachers and in learning, teachers can create mashups to illustrate

concepts and students can include these in their projects and work. These applications will change the way in which we visualise data, in such a way that we will be able to unite large amounts of data to perceive new conclusions or relations.

5. Applications for collective intelligence, such as blogs or Wikis. This term is used to designate the ingrained knowledge in societies or large groups of individuals, who are widely distributed, for the simple reason that thousands of active users enlarge, modify, revise and update them continually. The information is not organised in a conventional way, which allows us to create and exploit in multiple and different levels. In the teaching and learning environment, these sources of collective intelligence give us excellent opportunities to practise the construction of knowledge, which is what will concern us in the following lines.

6. Operative social systems, which allow the organisation of networks directed at people and not at content. An example is Facebook or MySpace, which provide a context to allow people to self define themselves, in an attempt to be able to interpret and evaluate the depth of their social connections. The diverse pilot projects are applications which unite information and services based on a contact. The problem is that the information we have available concerning the friends of our friends is still superficial and often more related to personal interests than professional activity. Besides, the social network systems are not conscious of the connections which we have not explicitly explained to them and very often there is little difference between a profound and a superficial relation. The fact of putting people and relations in the centre of informational space will have a great influence at all levels in the academic world. The way we relate information and knowledge, the way we investigate and

evaluate credibility, the way teachers and students interact together and the way in which students become professionals in their chosen disciplines, is going to change.

The diverse applications of these technologies have profound implications on education and the way teachers view the teaching and learning processes. Owen, Grant, Sayers and Facer (2006) analyse the interest of these technologies focusing on the interrelation between two key elements: one the one hand, the technological dimension, characterised by the continual progress made, more and more focused on the possibility of creating user communities where you share resources, collaborate and construct knowledge –social software–; and on the other hand, the educational dimension, with a growing need to provide help to the students not only to acquire information and knowledge, but also to develop resources and skills which will allow them to provide the answer to the social and technical changes in our society and carry on learning throughout their lives. In short, the most interesting aspect of these technologies is how they mediate the collaborative learning processes and pedagogical design.

Anyhow, it is necessary to stress that some critical voices have started hearing in relation to the web 2.0 and its educational uses. Most of them are centered on the following problems (Cambra, 2008):

- Equitation of experts and supporters, since each person is empowered for exercising tasks formerly trusting to experts. In the educational area this is especially remarkable, since on-line learning converts the students into creators of contents.
- Cultural impoverishment as a consequence of the former point.
- Equitation of knowledge with opinion, since the qualified and non qualified voices are equaled in the generation of knowledge.

- Loss of the power of the individual in the face of the collective power, since it is presupposed that the "collective intelligence" is superior and can manage to replace the individual.

Without obviate the weak notable points, the educational uses of Web 2.0 are potentially high in university teaching.

To do this, in the first place, we need to emphasis that we are starting form the premise that any learning process implies the development of the capabilities of different senses: on the one hand, the student must become an expert in the application of methods, concepts and theories; and on the other hand, the student is immersed in a socialisation process as a member of a group. In this sense, we conceive learning as a fundamental social experience, emphasising its interpersonal dimension. The students acquire the necessary elements to gain knowledge through the interaction with their colleagues, teachers and material. This social learning component implies learning with other and from other people.

In second place, it is important to highlight the importance of the mediating elements in the learning process. In this sense, the cognitive activity is not limited to simple repertoires of mental processes, limited and intimate, but also takes into consideration the effect of "exterior" resources on the person, which act as mediating elements; in fact, the learning is considered as a guided appropriation of mediating elements. In this way, the cognitive acquisitions are situated, in the sense of being linked to learning contexts, and contextualised in some type of social activity.

Finally, we need to highlight the profound social nature of cognition, in two senses: the mediating elements are created and evolve in a socio-cultural setting, and these mediating elements are found habitually in the course of our interchanges with other people.

We will now describe in more detail some of the emerging technologies and practices for facilitating and improving collective sharing and generation of Web based knowledge. In order to do this we need to distinguish between what are called collaborative digital tools on the Web and methodologies based on learning objects online (Wiley, 2002), understood as *"curricular units digitally supported which can integrate in distinct curricular contexts supporting training programmes with distinct objectives and target users "*.

COLLABORATIVE RESOURCES FOR WEB 2.0

Among these collaborative tools based in the Web are the Wikis, the Weblogs and the forums.

Wikis

This is a type of Web which is developed in a collaborative way by a group of users, and can be easily edited by any user. The Wiki systems allow us to create interconnected documents quickly by group collaboration, whose members can add new pages or edit existing pages. The best known example of Wiki technology is Wikipedia, an open, free access encyclopedia, administered by the non-profit making foundation Wikimedia, in which anyone can contribute.

One of the main inconveniences of this technology is the fact that users can, unintentionally or not, delete articles in Wiki. But in spite of the serious problem this represents, the solution can be found by the very own users of Wiki who are able to correct mistakes and rectify rapidly. Thus, the present tendency of Wiki users is to register as contributors, which often acts as a safeguard to bad or irresponsible use of this technology. Furthermore, one of the main characteristics of Wiki is that you can always recover any text written by other people which has been modified or deleted, as it has a record of changes.

In the educational environment, this technology allows us to consider constructivist ideas, as it is a tool for students to explore and construct their own content and to create their own meaning. According to Cych (2006), a Wiki environment differs from the traditional environment in that it encourages both the teachers and the students to learn together: *"knowledge is no longer transmitted from one to the other, but each person shares a part of what they know to construct a whole – in effect another form of peer-to-peer constructivist learning"*.

Some teachers are beginning to use Wiki to back up educational projects which promote the interchange of ideas and collaborative writing. Baggetun (2006) presents some examples which implicate different forms of collaboration in education through Wiki:

a) *Wikis as libraries for projects.* This is the case of those Wikis which at first facilitate a shared space to create projects, and then remain once the course is finished. The new students can use this library to get ideas, whilst the old students can keep them up to date, establishing a learning exchange.

b) *Interclass Wikis.* In this kind of Wikis, the students create an open content which can be used and inspected by anyone with the particularity that the access is not open, but restricted to the class students by a password. The results of one course are passed on to the following course, so that they can carry on working with it and updating and adding to it with new material.

c) *Wikis in educational institutions.* The idea is that the students themselves use and add content to the Web site, as an opportunity to contribute and be involved in spaces with local information.

Other uses of Wikis as shown by Mader (2006) are:

- Creating simple Web pages. Given the simplicity of creation, the student can concentrate on writing content, and not so much on receiving training in order to be able to publish something on the Internet.
- Developing peer-reviewed projects. Given the simplicity of writing, reviewing and posting tasks related to projects, the educator and classmates can follow the progress of written work developed in the Wiki, and provide retro-feedback with suggestions for improvements, continually and not just at the end of the process.
- Group creation. Improve on the previous group collaboration. Wiki brings together members of a group in the same space to construct the document in the same Wiki, with immediate and equal access for all members of the group.
- Monitoring projects. Members of a group can see the evolution of a document or group project, and follow the investigation being carried out; one member can see the resources that another member has used or consulted as the Wikis allow you to have pages for the group document and individual pages for each member of the group where they can store consulted sources and rough written drafts.
- Data collection. As it is easy to edit, the Wiki can be very useful for collecting data of a group of students.
- Presentations: Although not designed for this task, there are individual initiatives which have used the Wiki format to make presentations on specific topics.

These and other examples show us some of the possible uses of Wikis in education, in the way that they allow innovative forms of collaboration.

Weblogs

Weblogs or blogs are Web sites which compile articles chronologically from one or more authors, with the most recent appearing first. They usually collect daily, links, news and opinions with an informal and subjective style. The readers can add comments to any article and the author can respond. The Weblogs which are used for educational purposes or in educational environments are called edublogs.

Weblogs are a means of collective communication which promote the creation and the consumption of original and true information, through personal and social reflection on themes of individuals, groups and humanity. In the educational environment, they have a highly motivational character. They therefore need to strengthen the analysis, reflection and at the same time share experiences, knowledge and content, in such a way that the student can go on creating a collective learning entity, while developing their postings, and taking control of their own learning process.

Given their potential, Weblogs are becoming an extremely useful tool for educational use, as they are easy to use and cost hardly anything to publish periodically on the Internet. Gewerc (2005) highlights three advantages for using Weblogs in the educational environment:

- The tools for creating and publishing Weblogs are simple to use and one can learn very quickly how to use them.
- The design of Weblogs with predefined layouts makes it easy to use graphic design, which allows the students to concentrate more on the content and communication process.
- Weblogs offer a series of functions such as commentaries, trackback, file systems, internal search engines and permanent individual links of published material which adds an extra value to the production of content online.

According to the author, Weblogs combine effectively different traditional Internet resources: they can be used as search engines, with specific links recommended; they seem like mail with their informal style; you can join discussion forums as the readers participate and comment; and they offer the possibility to create texts, publish them and debate them with other people. This interactive and participative capacity is probably what distinguishes this Web modality from all other virtual offers.

As stated by Cych (2006), the use of blogs in education is more advanced in the United States, but it is still relatively new as a means of teaching and learning. More recently, multimedia variations of blogs have started to appear which can be particularly interesting in education such as: Podcast −a blog where articles are sound files recorded by the author−, Videoblog or Vlog −blog in video format−, Moblogs or mobileblogs −blogs with photos sent by mobile telephone to specialised Web sites−.

Forums

The forum, also known as the opinion or discussion forum, is a Web application which facilitates discussions and opinions online among users who wish to exchange ideas and points of view on diverse topics established in an asynchronic way, and form a kind of common interest community. The discussions are usually moderated by a coordinator or motivator, who usually present the theme and stimulate participation. All users' interventions are registered either chronologically or using a tree or nest diagram which makes it easy to follow the participants' interventions.

The educational potential of this application in university learning lies in the possibility of creating a participation structure among students which promotes the joint construction of knowledge based on a central theme. The teacher takes the role of moderator of the discussion and the educational interventions, while the student takes on the role of actively providing ideas, information etc. Harasim et al. (2000) propose some techniques that the teacher should bear in mind in order to develop the potential of the forums in university education:

a) *Change the relation between teachers, students and the learning content.* The construction of knowledge through the Web should be centred on the student with a different role for the teacher, more a helper-observer than the person in charge of giving lessons. Consequently, the emphasis is on collaborative learning and on the students' own intellectual process, which is responsible to a great extent for the students learning.

b) *Prepare the stage.* At the beginning of the activity, the teacher has to create a pleasant and inviting environment to attract the students into immediate active participation, by giving them clear instructions and support in order to build up their confidence and help them feel secure. The teacher must establish very clearly the kind of participation expected, give instructions to the participants, encourage them to answer amongst themselves, and stimulate a regular, active and considered participation.

c) *Supervise and stimulate participation.* Supervising that all the students have commenced the activity and carry on doing so throughout the whole process is essential for the student's progress, and to help those who have fallen behind or disconnected so that they may take part once again.

d) *Close the discussion, promoting metacognition and assessing the results.*

These techniques can contribute to helping the construction of knowledge through the forum becoming a satisfactory and enriching social and intellectual experience for all those who take part. Onrubia (2005) adds that the teaching through the Web has a necessary component of "carrying out work together" between teacher and student: only in this way can a sensitive and contingent intervention be achieved which will really help the student to go even further with the content than would be possible with an individual interaction.

METHODOLOGIES BASED ON LEARNING OBJECTS

Among the methodologies[2] based on learning objects are WebQuest, MiniQuest and Treasure Hunt (or Scavenger Hunt or Knowledge Hunt), with their common and consensual psycho-pedagogical methodology which establish them as a formula for guaranteeing said objectives. As stated by Esteban and Zapata (2008), the design of these educational digital applications should be controlled by criteria or orientations which guarantee the requirements of quality derived form the principles and theories of learning and metacognition in general, and define the cognitive singularity of said learning objects, marked by a learning environment and appropriate style or styles.

WebQuest

This is a learning methodology which allows you to incorporate the Internet at any educational level, in a constructivist framework and as a cooperative work. It was created by Bernie Dodge, educational technology teacher at San Diego State University, who defines it in the following way: "*A WebQuest is an inquiry-oriented activity in which some or all of the information that learners interact with comes from resources on the internet, optionally supplemented with videoconferencing*" (Dodge, 1995). As stated by Adell (2004), "*a WebQuest is a kind of pedagogical activity based on constructivist concepts of teaching and learning, which is based on group work techniques in projects and research as basic teaching/learning activities*". It works in a simple way: the students organise

themselves in small groups and are assigned a different role for each one to carry out along with a task. To do this they need to follow a well planned and structured process prepared by the teacher, in which they will need to carry out a series of activities which will lead them to the elaboration of a final product. These activities are based on information which can be obtained on the Internet by links which appear on the actual WebQuest, and which the teacher has previously selected as resources to facilitate carrying out activities. The students will need to carry out various actions such as reading, analysing and synthesising the information, to be able at a later stage to process, manipulate and organise it in line with the proposed task completion and learning objectives. Furthermore, the students will know beforehand the assessment criteria for the activity based on the known evaluation rubric, in which the process along with the product will be assessed, using a series of criteria graded up to excellence.

In order to develop all these potentialities, the design of a WebQuest must be based on a structure which contains the following fundamentals: introduction, where the activity is presented in a motivating way through a challenge or discovery; task, where what the student has to do is described, in other words what the end product will be; process, where how the task is to be carried out is clearly detailed –types of grouping, roles to take, intermediate stages ...–, and where a link to the Web resources required to construct the final product; evaluation, where it is made explicitly clear using a rubric, how they will be assessed and under which criteria; conclusion, to reflect on the work and collaborative experience of the student, such as the result achieved, bearing in mind the learning objectives. Furthermore, it is important that it contains other complementary sections such as: cover, with the name of the WebQuest, the author, date created and educational level aimed at; credits, where references used in the WebQuest are included along with possible collaborations; and didactic guide, with useful information for other

Table 1. Merrill Principles and WebQuest characteristics (Source: Quintana and Higueras, 2007)

Merrill Principles	Characteristics of WebQuests
Problems: the student has to be implicated in solving problems and situations in the real world.	Task: linked to reality with real application content. Needs to be contextualised, relevant and as real as possible.
Activation: activation of knowledge and previous relevant experience of the students, as a base for learning new knowledge and skills.	Process: what the student knows and knows what to do.
Demonstration: demonstrate exactly what has to be learned.	Task: describe the final product that the student needs to produce, not only conceptually but materially.
Application: the student has to use and apply their new skills and knowledge.	Task: the creation of content by the student, elaborating material and frequent public presentations.
Integration: the student integrates the new skills and knowledge into their world.	Task: linked to reality with real application content. Has to be contextualised, relevant and as real as possible.

Source: Quintana and Higueras (2007)

teachers who also wish to use the WebQuest, such as objectives, content, methodological aspects, bibliography, complementary activities, etc. This last part is fundamental in guaranteeing the sharing of resources among teachers on the Web.

Quintana and Higueras (2007) review the fundamentals of WebQuests, as methodological changes and the effect these have on teachers, not only in the planning stages –based on the specific WebQuest structure commented on previously– but also on roles carried out by the teacher and the learner –in a didactic approach focused on the development of the personal and professional competences of the student–. The relation established between the most distinctive characteristics of the WebQuests and the Merrill principles (2002), are especially interesting in order to be able to assess its effectiveness: (See Table 1)

Merrill PrinciplesCharacteristics of Web-QuestsProblems: the student has to be implicated in solving problems and situations in the real world.Task: linked to reality with real application content. Needs to be contextualised, relevant and as real as possible.Activation: activation of knowledge and previous relevant experience of the students, as a base for learning new knowledge and skills. Process: what the student knows and knows what to do. Demonstration: demonstrate exactly what has to be learned. Task: describe the final product that the student needs to produce,

not only conceptually but materially. Application: the student has to use and apply their new skills and knowledge. Task: the creation of content by the student, elaborating material and frequent public presentations. Integration: the student integrates the new skills and knowledge into their world. Task: linked to reality with real application content. Has to be contextualised, relevant and as real as possible.

The official and fundamental site for WebQuest can be found at http://Webquest.org/, where you can access various examples in Search for WebQuests, at http://Webquest.org/search/. Other examples of the use of WebQuest in university teaching and other educational levels can be found at the site Best WebQuests by Tom March at http://bestWebquests.com/. Quintana and Higueras (2007) have also compiled various links with collections of WebQuest, which show its viability in the university environment.

MiniQuest

Faced with the great development in Internet of WebQuest, MiniQuest, an abbreviated form of such a search activity on the Web, has much less of a presence. Nevertheless, we believe that it is a very flexible methodology and can be incredibly useful if its design responds to principles of knowledge building and collaborative development.

A MiniQuest is a learning activity based on a guided information search on the Internet. They are online instruction models designed by teachers for their students and promote critical thought and the construction of knowledge. They are inspired in the WebQuest concept and require only three steps, to overcome the limits of time and effort needed by WebQuest design. They can be built by teachers experienced in Internet use in just three or four hours. The students can do them completely in one class. They can be used by teachers who do not have a lot of time or who are just starting out creating and applying Webquest.

We can distinguish three types of MiniQuest:

- Discovery. These are done at the beginning of a unit with the aim of presenting it to the student.
- Exploration. These are done during a unit, with the aim of learning the necessary content to be able to understand a concept in particular or complete a learning objective.
- Culmination. These are done at the end of a unit. These Miniquests sometimes need to use information obtained in carrying out another type of MiniQuest or by other traditional educational methods. The students who work on these have a "knowledge base" because they are able to respond to questions much more profound or complex which have as a final result the MiniQuest. These questions are known as essential questions.

The structure of a MiniQuest:

- Setting. Present an initial situation through which the student can get themselves ready to be able to carry out the task. Put the students in a real role. Establish, as well, the essential question (formulated implicitly or explicitly) that the students need to answer.
- Task. Present the work to be developed. Although it is not obligatory, it is advisable

to formulate questions so that the student is aware exactly where to direct their investigations in order to answer the essential question (it is also possible to consider an activity based on fictitious identities or roles, following the principles laid down by Dodge for the WebQuest.). It needs to be well structured because the activity has to be completed in one or two class periods. Direct the students to specific Web sites (resources) which contain the information necessary to solve the questions in such a way that the acquisition of the "basic material" can be done in the established time and efficiently.

- Product. In this section we will try to offer a more detailed description of the work required to be carried out in order to answer the essential question posed. The students need to show understanding, which needs to be checked by the teacher through some means of evaluation of the product. The students have to develop a new way of looking at the problem. If the creation of knowledge is not promoted, then the activity becomes simply a worksheet online and not what it should be, a research activity. The product also needs to be real and reflect adequately the role assigned to the student.

Treasure Hunt, Scavenger Hunt or Knowledge Hunt

A Treasure Hunt is a kind of very simple pedagogical activity which consists of a series of questions and a list of Web page addresses where the answers can be found or inferred. These types of activities include a "big question" at the end, which requires the students to integrate the knowledge acquired during the process.

Adell (2003) proposes an interesting alternative for high level students, which is, instead of resolving them, to prepare themselves their

Table 2. Principles of online collaboration (Source: Garrison, 2006)

	Teaching presence		
	Design	**Facilitation**	**Instruction**
Social presence	Establish a climate of confidence and pertinence which supports the interaction and creates a community of investigation	Sustain the community through group cohesion	Develop collaborative relations and give support to students so that they can assume an increasing responsibility in their learning
Cognitive presence	Establish a critical reflection and discussion which supports investigation	Foment and support progression in investigation in order to solve the task	Ensure resolution and metacognitive development

Source: Garrison (2006)

own "treasure hunts" adopting the role of teachers. The hunts can be prepared in a group and then, each group can solve the hunt set by other teams. In this case and according to the author, the criteria for evaluating the hunt must include the representativeness, pertinence or relevance of the questions to the theme in question and to the available resources.

IMPLICATIONS OF WEB 2.0 IN THE DESIGN OF COLLABORATIVE LEARNING ENVIRONMENTS

Design environments of collaborative learning in Web 2.0 needs to find the balance between the social interaction means directed at the cognitive processes –the educational dimension of the social interaction – and the medium of social interaction addressed at the underlying socioeconomic processes in the group dynamic – the social dimension of social interaction.

As regards the educational dimension of the social interaction, Dillenbourg (2006) states that the different points of view in the social interaction bring about the socio-cognitive conflict. According to the author, for this conflict to be resolved, from the reformulation to the explanation, we need to understand the other perspective, which will lead us to a richer and shared understanding of the field of knowledge.

Concerning the social dimension of the social interaction, Kreijns, Kirschner, Jochems and Van Buuren (2005) consider that it is a fundamental factor which affects the collaboration, the group dynamic and its consolidation, as it favours social relations which allow an affective structure to be established, a social cohesion and a sense of community. In the author's words, these are the attributes of a solid social space, in which the open community can benefit the collaborative activities and the relevant information exchange.

Looking for this balance in the interaction, Garrison (2006) suggests that in the design of a collaborative learning process of constructivist character we need to consider the integration of the social presence and the cognitive presence in this process. In this way, the author affirms that the social presence reflects the ability to connect with members of the community of learners at a personal level, while the cognitive presence is the process of constructing meaning which is produced during the collaborative activity. These two elements go along with a third basic element, the presence of teaching, which allows us to structure and give support to the educational process, so that it can become a significant and interesting learning experience. In this way, there are three categories in the teaching presence –design, facilitation and instruction–, which identify a series of principles and directives from the ICT collaboration, as can be seen in the following table: (See Table 2)

Table 3.

Learning sequence phases	Analysis and exploration of problem	Articulation of the solution	Reflection on results and experiences
Learning activities	Start of investigation Analysis of related cases Consultation of information sources Use of cognitive tools	Development of proposals Use of cognitive tools Project diary	Establishing reflection practice Individual and group reflection
Support technology	Data bases Links Simulators E-mails Forums …	Conceptual maps Wiki Chat Blog Forums …	Conceptual maps Wiki Blog …

It is in the intersection of these three elements that a stimulating context is created, which can facilitate critical discourse and reflection in constructing meaning, and gives meaning to a community of educational objectives achieving a constructivist and collaborative learning experience.

A good model of collaborative learning practice are the so-called authentic activities. The authentic activities should be based on projects, problems or cases and the students must be able to tackle, analyse and finally resolve them. To do this, and taking the project/problem/case as the centre of the learning activity, the learning environment mediated by technologies has to offer support and contextual support to the student. The social support is articulated through conversation and collaboration tools (forums, Wikis, chats,…) which allow the students to share–with the teacher and also all their equals–their ideas and interpretations, negotiate them and organise themselves in groups. The contextual support (databases, Web page links, …) is based on information sources, cognitive tools and other resources. The information sources allow us to develop an understanding of the relevant principles and concepts, the cognitive tools facilitate the representation of the problem, its knowledge and can automate certain simple tasks and other resources – such as related cases, designed projects or solved problems – describe

solutions to previous similar problems, which allows the students to design their own solution.

The following table (based on Benett, 2004) summarizes the sequence of such a learning activity: (See Table 3)

In short, the social software Web 2.0 allows users to communicate, publish and collaborate with diverse technologies and practices, which have profound implications in the academic world, especially in higher education. It is inherently social software, with its benefits fundamentally based on collaboration. In spite of the limitations related to the fact that the technologies will not produce educational innovative practices if they do not adapt in an opportune way, its value in education is clear: emerging practices based on these technologies allow us to configure learning and practice communities, where the people linked by a fixed affinity can interact and interchange ideas. In this way students have the chance to participate in global learning communities, way beyond their geographical or social community, exceeding limitations of age, prior knowledge or gender. Thus, the discussion forums are explicit attempts of social software to create construction and knowledge communities, and the Weblogs or Wikis show the benefits that can be obtained form participating in digital communities.

REFERENCES

Adell, J. (2003). *Internet en el aula: A la caza del tesoro* [online]. *Edutec, Revista Electrónica de Tecnología Educativa, 16.* Retrieved from http://edutec.rediris.es/Revelec2/revelec16/adell.htm

Adell, J., & Sales, A. (1999). *El profesor online: Elementos para la definición de un nuevo rol docente* [en línia]. Retrieved on November 16, 2005, from http://tecnologiaedu.us.es/edutec/paginas/105.html

Álvarez, I., Ayuste, A., Gros, B., Guerra, V., & Romañá, T. (2005). Construir conocimiento con soporte tecnológico para un aprendizaje colaborativo [en línia]. *Revista Iberoamericana de Educación* (ISSN: 1681-5653). Retrieved on April 2, 2006, from http://www.rieoei.org/deloslectores/1058alvarez.pdf

Baggetun, R. (2006). Emergent Web practices and new educational opportunities [online]. *TELOS, Cuadernos de Comunicación e Innovación, 67.* Retrieved from http://www.campusred.net/telos/articulocuaderno.asp?idarticulo=9&rev=67

Bennet, A. (2004). Supporting collaborative project teams using computer-based technologies. In T. Roberts (Ed.), *Online collaborative learning: Theory and practice.* London: Information Science Publishing.

Cambra, T. (2008). El Web 2.0 com a distòpia en la recent Internet [online]. *Digithum, 10.* UOC. Retrieved from http://www.uoc.edu/digithum/10/dt/cat/cambra.pdf

Crook, C. (1998). *Ordenadores y aprendizaje colaborativo.* Madrid: Morata.

Cych, L. (2006). *Social networks. Emerging technologies for learning.* British Educational Communications and Technology Agency (Becta) ICT Research.

Dillenbourg, P. (2006). The solo/duo gap. *Computers in Human Behavior, 22*(1), 155–159. doi:10.1016/j.chb.2005.05.001

Dodge, B. (1995). *Some thoughts about Webquests.* [online]. Retrieved from http://webquest.sdsu.edu/about_webquests.html

Esteban, M., & Zapata, M. (2008). Estrategias de aprendizaje y e-learning. Un apunte para la fundamentación del diseño educativo en los entornos virtuales de aprendizaje. Consideraciones para la reflexión y el debate. Introducción al estudio de las estrategias y estilos de aprendizaje [online]. *Revista de Educación a Distancia, 19.* Retrieved from http://www.um.es/ead/red/19

Garrison, D. R. (2006). Online collaboration principles. *Journal of Asynchronous Learning Networks, 10*(1), 25–34.

Gewerc, A. (2005). El uso de weblogs en la docencia universitaria [online]. *Revista Latinoamericana de Tecnología Educativa, 4*(1). Retrieved from http://campusvirtual.unex.es/cala/editio/index.php

Harasim, L., Roxanne, S., Turoff, M., & Teles, L. (2000). *Redes de aprendizaje. Guía para la enseñanza y el aprendizaje en red.* Barcelona: Gedisa Editorial.

Johnson, R. T., & Johnson, D. W. (1991). *Joining together.* Boston: Ally et Bacon.

Kolodner, J., & Guzdial, M. (1996). Effects with and of CSCL: Tracking learning in a new paradigm. In T. Koschmann (Ed.), *CSCL: Theory and practice of an emerging paradigm.* New Jersey: Lawrence Erlbaum Associates.

Kreijns, K., Kirschner, P. A., Jochems, W., & Van Buuren, H. (2005). Measuring perceived sociability of computer-supported collaborative learning environments. *Computers & Education.*

Levy, P. (2004). *L'Intelligence collective. Pour une anthropologie du cyberespace.* Paris: La Découverte.

Mader, S. (2006). Ways to use wiki in education [online]. *Using Wiki in Education*. Retrieved from http://www.wikiineducation.com/display/ikiw/Ways+to+use+wiki+in+education

Merrill, M. D. (2002). First principles of instruction [online]. *Educational Technology, Research, and Development, 50*(3), 43-59. Retrieved from http://id2.usu.edu/Papers/5FirstPrinciples.PDF

Monereo, C., & Duran, D. (2001). *Entramats. Mètodes d'aprenentatge cooperatiu i collaboratiu*. Barcelona: Edebé.

Nastasi, B., & Clements, D. (1991). Research on cooperative learning: Implications for practice. *School Psychology Review, 20*, 110–131.

New Media Consortium. (2008). *2008 horizon report*. [online]. Retrieved from http://connect.educause.edu/Library/ELI/2008HorizonReport/45926

Onrubia, J. (2003). Las aulas como comunidades de aprendizaje: Una propuesta de enseñanza basada en la interacción, la cooperación, y el trabajo en equipo. *Cooperación Educativa Kikiriki, 68*, 37–46.

Onrubia, J. (2005). Aprender y enseñar en entornos virtuales: Actividad conjunta, ayuda pedagógica, y construcción del conocimiento [online]. *Revista de Educación a Distancia, n II*. Retrieved from http://www.um.es/ead/red/M2/conferencia_onrubia.pdf

Owen, M., Grant, L., Sayers, S., & Facer, K. (2006). *Social software and learning* [online]. Opening Education, Futurelab. Retrieved from http://www.futurelab.org.uk/resources/publications_reports_articles/opening_education_reports/Opening_Education_Report199

Quintana, J., & Higueras, E. (2007). *Les Webquests, una metodologia d'aprenentatge cooperatiu, basada en l'accés, el maneig i l'ús d'informació de la Xarxa*. ICE de la Universitat de Barcelona: Quaderns de Docència Universitària, 11.

Salomon, G., Perkins, D. N., & Globerson, T. (1992). Coparticipando en el conocimiento. La ampliación de la inteligencia humana con las tecnologías inteligentes. *Comunicación. Lenguaje y Educación, 13*, 6–22.

Slavin, R. (1990). *Cooperative learning. Theory, research, and practice*. New Jersey: Prentice Hall, Inc.

Wiley, D. A. (2002). *Connecting learning objects to instructional design theory: A definition, a metaphor, and a taxonomy. The instructional use of learning objects*. Bloomington, IN: Agency for Instructional Technology.

ENDNOTES

[1] The concept of *web 2.0* was conceived for Tim O'Reilly1 in 2003. «What is Web 2.0», O'Reilly Media, Inc. <http://www.oreillynet.com/pub/a/oreilly/tim/news/2005/09/30/what-is-web-20.html>

[2] Although the three methodologies were created in the Web 1.0, they assume all their pedagogic potential within the framework of Web 2.0 when they integrate the use of technologies based into the collective intelligence.

Chapter 13

Publishing with Friends:
Exploring Social Networks to Support Photo Publishing Practices

Paula Roush
London South Bank University, UK

Ruth Brown
London South Bank University, UK

ABSTRACT

Publishing with friends is the account of an action research cycle in which a print-on-demand Web site, Lulu.com, became a classroom for second and third year digital photography students to publish their photobooks. Building on the earlier use of a blogging platform as a personal learning environment, this narrative explores the pedagogical prospects of the read/write Web, and illustrates the way in which students use social networks for creative produsage (Bruns, 2008). Students were positive about the pedagogical approach, and the opportunities to gain valuable hands-on experience in their chosen field of study.

INTRODUCTION

The web is coming of age. Predicted almost 20 years ago, users with relatively unsophisticated information technology skills are now able to use the internet as a medium to communicate and publish in what we have chosen to describe as the read/write web. (Also known as Web 2.0 technology, the "read/write web" seems to us a more descriptive appellation.) The increasingly ubiquitous nature of the web, and its unquestioned affordances, now challenge the academy to embrace technology in appropri-

ate curricula and, in the process, to investigate the move from an industrial production model to the pragmatics of the web-led produsage, or user-led production, approach. Bruns (2008) focuses on the fluidity of the produsage process as a main characteristic – it is in the evaluation, the flexible leadership, its iterative nature and the attribution of social capital, rather than an end product, that the concept is defined.

Produsage in the higher education setting is the underlying theme of the chapter which maps this particular instance of produsage onto Bruns' model. In the process, it describes the pedagogical underpinnings of the inquiry through the account of

DOI: 10.4018/978-1-60566-826-0.ch013

the use of the read/write web as an environment to teach students of digital photography; discusses the design of learning tasks and the engagement of students in the design of an assessment and feedback rubric; and explores the findings from the students' evaluation of the research intervention. Lastly, the implications of the research for future iterations of the digital photography units are set out.

BACKGROUND

The roots of the read/write web were described by Berners-Lee and Cailliau (1990); they explained hypertext and foresaw two phases in its development: firstly the use of existing browsers to access information (the read web) and also ease of publication on the web (the write web) with "the creation of new links and new material by readers. At this stage, authorship becomes universal." The authors predicted that "this phase [would] allow collaborative authorship" facilitated by the annotation of existing data, linking and adding documents.

Almost two decades later, their vision has become a reality. Online participatory culture is ubiquitous, and evidenced by the popularity of social network and media-sharing sites, multiplayer games and other applications generally know as social software.

The academy is slowly entering this stage of "collaborative authorship". The term "classroom of the read/write web," coined by Richardson (2006), uses a familiar metaphor to translate this into a teaching and learning construct. Educators can assemble their own toolbox of freely available applications using the self-publishing technologies now abundant on the Internet; these may include weblogs, wikis, aggregators, social bookmarking, photo-sharing, rubric-making tools and many others. In his model, Richardson provides a pedagogical framework for the integration of these technologies in teaching and learning, in the context of the publishing affordances of the read/write web, and emphasizes the four core literacies – reading, publishing, collaborating and information management – that can be developed in the online environment.

In practice, the read/write web classroom demands major shifts in the ways we think about content and curriculum. Richardson (2006) identifies these as follows: the web is viewed as an open classroom; learning takes place 24/7 in interaction between online peers and experts; collaboration leads to the social construction of meaningful knowledge; teaching is democratized, a conversation rather than a lecture; knowing where to find information takes precedence over the acquisition (and regurgitation) of facts; students aspire to edit information critically, to develop active reading and writing skills; web applications are used as digital notebooks to store and share information found online; writing is lent richness by augmentation with photography, audio and video; mastery of skills is demonstrated and assessed in the product (e.g. digital content creation) and marked tests are dispensed with; and, finally, course materials and coursework are a contribution to a larger body of knowledge (the web), can be reused by others, and are not completed and discarded at the end of the semester.

This model of the open classroom is a major challenge for the academy. Many artists and designers already use the read/write web in their everyday life, but universities seem reluctant to make the transition from an industrial age concept of knowledge (production) to one more in tune with the information age model of user-led education (produsage). Bruns (2008) coined the word produsage to describe the process of user-led production in the setting of networked practices.

Engagement in the read/write web or, more specifically in this instance, in the contemporary online self-publishing environment, allows academe to explore novel opportunities for teaching and learning. These are underpinned by the four key principles of produsage: the implicit evalua-

tion by the community of users of artifacts pro-
dused by individuals; the flexible leadership of
projects which is grounded in personal strengths;
the recognition of the iterative and inherently
"unfinished" nature of the produsage process
which is constantly revised by interested parts of
the community; and the recognition of excellent
individual contributions to the community by
attributing social capital.

The model of the creative as an online produser
(Bruns, 2008) is useful as it expresses the authentic
practice of artist-teachers and artist-students. The
term encapsulates the reality of artistic creative
environments such as photograph- and video-
sharing blogs, and social network sites like Flickr,
YouTube, MySpace and Facebook and 3-D multi-
user spaces like Second Life.

The focus is often on the personal content that
circulates in these sites. While life caching (uploading of personal content for friends and family)
may be one application of these platforms, specific
groups of users have emerged which engage in
the proper produsage of creative content:

*... within such produser groups, content is ex-
changed not merely for its inherent personal or
communicative value, but overtly as creative work
to be showcased to and exchanged with other
members of the community. Participants both
comment on and critique one another's works;
they collaborate on creative projects both by
pooling together their individual collaborations
to form a composite whole, and by directly editing,
rearranging and remixing the material already
provided by others; and in the process they in
effect collaboratively curate an ever-expanding,
constantly changing exhibition of the community's
creative works. From such practices also emerge
heterarchical structures of recognition and merit
within the community. (Bruns, 2008, p229)*

Specific studies on the impact of Flickr in
photographic creative practices have revealed
the personal and learning implications of the

photo-sharing site. From her study, Van House
(2007) reveals four social uses of personal photography: firstly, it is a memory device to build
narratives of the self; it also serves as a form of
self-representation or self-portrait; it may be a way
of creating a relational sense of togetherness, an
expression of sociability; and it can also have the
purpose of displaying one's artistic and creative
work, a kind of sociable exhibition. In the academic
context, the use of Flickr in blended teaching for
a first year photography unit articulates with the
students' daily use of social networking sites for
their photo practices (Robbie & Zeeng, 2008).
Flickr's tools for commenting on and notating
each other's images facilitates analytical critical
reflection and feedback between students. It also
situates their work in the nexus between students'
studies and their professional practice; allows
conversations to develop beyond the classroom,
which addresses the balance between work and
study; and is an affordable way of exhibiting images publically.

Studies of print-on-demand, and its relationship with photography and design communities,
are also available. Lulu.com, in particular, is
referenced in studies of the relationship between
self-publishing and emerging online economies.
Anderson (2006) explores Lulu as a prime example
of the existence of long-tail markets, which are
possible because of the unlimited shelf space provided by online digital databases. The reputation
economy is a description of the self-promotion
value attached to publishing; it explains the added
attraction of publishing online, a motivational
factor that outweighs the small sales volumes that
characterise these niche markets. Specifically,
the adoption of print-on-demand to self-publish
photobooks allows emerging photographers to
bypass the lengthy process involved in traditional
publishing, with total financial independence –
there is no need to fundraise – and full editorial
control (Forrester, 2007).

Against this background, the possibility of
teaching units on photobook publishing in an

authentic produsage environment was a motivating factor in engaging in this qualitative pedagogical project. Other higher education projects using Lulu.com for graphic design are available (Philippin, 2008; Hochschule Darmstadt, 2008) but none comments on the pedagogical process involved in using the platform, choosing instead to present the students' work as an enquiry into the digital printing output achievable at Lulu. Our study explores the features of lulu.com that can be used as part of a "classroom of the read/write web" and discusses the results with reference to the self-publishing capacities involved in reaching the learning outcomes.

CASE STUDY: PHOTOBOOK PROJECT FOR PHOTOGRAPHY STUDENTS

There is an expanding field of inquiry into what constitutes artists' publications. Critical features of this interest are the combination of artistic approaches with networked practices, and the investigation of the latest technologies that many artists and publishing groups have started to explore as an alternative to traditional press. An artist's book, in this genre, is not an illustrated book characterized by high production values and a conventional separation text-image; nor is it a photo album containing the family's best moment's snapshots. Instead, it means working within a "zone of activity" (Drucker, 2004) at the intersect of conceptual art and photography, independent publishing, activism, fine art practice, sculpture, installation, book arts, performance, self-publishing fairs, and online produsage environments and social networks. The terms of reference for artists' publications may still be vague, but there is general agreement amongst practitioners and scholars that the final criteria rest upon the engagement of the work with the specific features of a book; this is the expression of the work's 'bookness'.

The emphasis of the photo publishing unit of this study is the genre of the photobook, "a book – with or without text – where the work's primary message is carried by photographs … an event in itself … a concise world where the collective meaning is more important than images" (Parr & Badger, 2006). This implies that the students come to think of the photograph in relational terms, develop skills as curators or editors, and learn to use current available digital technologies to publish and distribute independently. The genre has been developing since the conception of photography, but as printing technologies have gravitated towards a networked model, photographers have adapted their practices to take advantage offered by print-on-demand (POD) publishing models.

Teaching photographers to develop photobooks also means going beyond focusing on the 'best photo' to consider photographs as groups or collections. Free from the conventional photo-to-print relationship, the learner starts thinking in terms of the book's visual structure (Smith, 2005). The unit of meaning – the graphic layout as double page spread or as subchapter – conceptualises the narrative or meta-narrative aspects implied in grouping, serializing and sequencing the photos. Experimenting with the conventions of the book page becomes a key pedagogic strategy. The process allows deliberate disruption of conventional book flow – the distribution of text and image to create movement from page to page – to raise awareness of the relationship between page and image.

The book-making process starts with the creation of book dummies, 3-D mock-ups of the book that provide an excellent tool to play with the images and develop understanding of visual structures. Teaching the fundamentals of photobook publishing also implicitly equips students with in-depth knowledge of prepress, the steps necessary to prepare the work for a commercial printer. In the adoption of the desktop environment for publication design, creating a book means assuming responsibility for a series of processes: layout, typography and text formatting, preparation of images in Photoshop (color space and resolution), preflight and the creation of a robust .pdf file that the commercial printer will translate into a professional-looking photobook. Understanding and anticipating the printer's output environment is thus an important part of the learning program.

Why Teach Book Arts in a Produsage Environment?

While opportunities for self-publishing of photography online abound, few students take full advantage of the possibilities offered by the online photobook companies, like Lulu or Blurb. While students already use Flickr, deviantART and other photo-sharing sites for their photos, research shows that many photographers are exploring the professional photobook companies' sites for publishing their book works (Forrester, 2007). For our students, engaging in the professional environment represents the next step in their development; having completed a photographic brief, their focus changes to considering the editing of their work with a view to publication. Whilst other university assignments are produced for the teacher and the classroom, studying this unit unlocks the many possibilities of the classroom of the web.

With the availability of these technologies and the widespread opportunities for online publication, creating a photobook implies thinking beyond the screen and positioning the photographic work in the wider publishing context. Taking into account the current interest in e-books and readers, it is still a challenge in this unit to combine the best of digital technologies and paper-based media. Facilitating a semester unit on book-making for digital photographers means considering the book in the age of the digital press; the enterprise of the online print-on-demand photobook companies offering the latest developments in "digital/paper

hybrid product" (Sarvas, Mäntylä & Turpeinen, 2007); and the paper-digital technologies that allow for both printed and online book publishing outputs.

An additional opportunity in such produsage environments is the uploading and sharing of images, mainly an individual activity, or the creation of personal sets of photos. The art of produsage, however, also offers other possibilities, such as the sourcing of images from pools, or creating groups on particular themes; this activity exemplifies a shift from the photographer-author to the photographer-editor, involved in the curation of collections. Such collective (or networked) projects are exemplified by photographers editing found photography (Brittain, 2006) or the management of photos uploaded by participants into paper-based publications, as in JPG magazine (Bruns, 2008). Thus, the opportunity of teaching students to work as editors of someone else's material is indispensable to publishing practice and in this instance the involvement in social networks is an essential way of sourcing images.

The unit aims were to:

- identify and analyze the context of self-publishing practices, as evidenced by participation in rubric-led assessment and feedback, and the participation on e-tivities at Lulu.com;
- demonstrate a critical understanding of the genre of photo publishing, as evidenced by the output of two photo publications (a photobook and a photo magazine);
- develop skills in visual communication, as evidenced by their work with the structure of the visual book including creating a book dummy, using InDesign to layout photo and text; and
- use the print-on-demand publishing model, as evidenced by the use of Lulu publishing and networking platform.

Research Methodology

This study is shaped by an action research methodology. A qualitative research paradigm, the aim of an action research cycle in an educational setting is to identify an area of practice that might benefit from improvement, to design an intervention and implement it and then to observe the effect on the learning experience (Arhar, Holly, Kasten, 2001). This case study describes a single iteration of this "reflect, act and observe" cycle with relation to the two cohorts of students that participated in the research; it builds, however, on an earlier intervention described below and anticipates a further cycle in the final reflection.

The Choice of a Produsage Environment

The project built on an earlier photo publishing unit, from the first semester of the 2006/07 academic year. In this earlier (level 3) unit, the digital photography students used WordPress blogging platform, to publish their coursework and Lulu.com to publish the finished photobook. As they were entering the final year of their studies, it was important to address the acquisition and consolidation of a series of digital literacies and capacities that allowed them to engage critically with these online environments, whilst simultaneously creating quality professional work in them. This included the publication of their critical writing as well as their photographic portfolios and, in particular, introduced the use of the digital press for the publication of paper-based photo books.

We noticed, however, that not all students participated at the same level of engagement. Whilst some engaged with the produsage environments, finding and analyzing pertinent information and contributing to the conversation via posts and comments, others needed extra support to actively engage with the produsage tools. We also

Figure 1. The produser. (© 2008, Axel Bruns. Used with permission.)

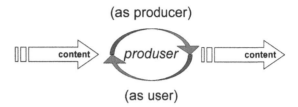

found evidence of what Bruns describes as a new form of digital divide, "between those already tuned in to the produsage process and those not yet motivated to participate, as well as between those who already have the skills and capacities to contribute ...and those for whom participation in such environments remains an apparently insurmountable challenge." (2008, p.338)

The development of a blended learning pedagogical approach with the selection of Lulu.com as the main produsage environment – both as a digital notebook and publishing platform – and the inclusion of e-tivities and rubrics to encourage peer feedback aims at improving on the earlier pedagogical framework.

According to a recent study (Forrester, 2007), there are more than 55 online photobook companies all offering similar print-on-demand services. In each, the user downloads the company's software (or the software is browser-based), inserts the photos and text in pre-designed templates, chooses a binding and cover format, and places an order which is printed and delivered, typically, in 10 days.

Lulu, however, has special produsage features that make it a preferred choice for teaching: it may be viewed as a two-sided produce-sell (or dashboard-storefront) platform. The dashboard is a private node (accessible only when the user is logged in), which accesses 'my projects' (a catalog of all the user's books), as well as the user's storefront, blog, groups, message box and friends. Additional account management features

Figure 2. An example of a student's book page from Lulu.com

such as account preferences and access to the files associated with the user's publishing activity are also available from the dashboard.

On finding a (prod)user's name in Lulu (often through a search box), one is directed to their storefront – a public-facing interface which can be fully customized by the seller, and which provides a variety of information about their associated activities: a profile, list of lulu friends, group memberships, lulu interests, published books, blogs and other feeds (del.icio.us bookmarks, for example).

An important storefront feature is the book page, which offers information about the book: a preview, publisher and licensing information, a description of the book content, and the book specifications (number of pages, use of color or black-and-white, format and binding). The page also states the prices for printing and downloading (which may be dif-

ferent), the book's tags, categories, reviews, and sales information such as the lulu sales ranking and other books bought by the customers who bought the book. A link to the shopping basket allows the viewer to place an order, pay and enter a (virtual or actual) shipping address. If the book download is free, clicking on the 'download now' button initiates its download. Opening the tags or categories reveals a catalog of other publications with similar tags and categories, and the licensing link accesses the licensing deed: either copyright or a chosen variation of creative commons.

The Lulu community supports forums, groups, a newsletter and the Lulu blog. The forums, in a variety of subjects related to self-publishing such as cover art, or storefront, are maintained by Lulu experts and archived in a variety of self-publishing related threads, easily accessible via search menus. International forums provide support in a wide number of languages, and users can also start their own group for more focused interests such as book promotion or teen literature.

Of all the online photobook companies, Lulu is the one that offers the platform with the most interesting blend of features with which to teach digital photobook publishing. In the first place, the dashboard is the most project-oriented of all the photobook companies; it allows students to design their books using InDesign, the desktop publishing software used in class, and to upload the resulting PDF file, while other companies require the use of their own software. Further, unlike other companies that keep the design document in-house for printing-on-demand purposes only, Lulu allows the design document to be accessed and shared digitally.

The online store also offers two methods of making the content available: the print version delivers a paperback that can be purchased using the online ordering process (shopping basket; online payment and delivery to the shipping address); and the download version, either as a paid or free PDF download. Whilst other companies may offer an online store, they do not offer access to the digital files. The dual options of the Lulu online store integrate well with the principle of common gains/individual rewards of the produsage environments.

Blogs, another of Lulu's tools, create opportunities to publish works-in-progress and to receive feedback from peers; the comments feature encourages analytical reflection and an extension of the online conversation beyond the classroom. The groups and friends' lists (social networking features) promote working as a group and extending classroom support into the online space.

Lastly, the forums in which users and experts exchange information on topics related to many aspects of digital online publishing offer a pool of extra teachers, available 24/7, that are supplemented by live help from Lulu, a feature that makes possible to obtain support from a company representative via a chat board.

The Design of Learning Tasks

The embedding of the teaching in this produsage environment was achieved by using a blended pedagogical framework, which consisted of twelve weekly face-to-face meetings in the media lab interspersed with eleven weekly e-tivities.

A particular intention in the design was a balance between individual expression and group work. The first project, an individual photobook, called for the selection of photos from students' own archives, the development of a visual structure for the book, the preparation of a book dummy, and the final production of the photobook. This project carried 25% of the marks for the unit. The second assignment was a collaborative one: working as editorial team, each group created a collective photo magazine using photos selected from a social network situation. They were required to prepare and submit a magazine dummy showing the visual structure, and to publish the photo magazine in Lulu.com. This, too, accounted for 25% of the marks for the unit.

The balance of the assessment was by way of weekly structured e-tivities (Salmon, 2004), posted to Lulu.com. The e-tivities supported the process in which students were required to analyze the production process and to reflect on online research and peer feedback. Each week's e-tivity was designed to further embed the online publishing environment in the students' experience, and dovetailed with the face-to-face activity for the week. In week one, for instance, the e-tivity was designed to help students become familiar with Lulu's tools. Subsequent e-tivities explored the definition of photobook, the structure of a visual book, how to create book and photo magazine proposals and dummies, participation in group forums, customizing the storefront for a book, bookmarking using del.icio.us, and book reviews. The last e-tivity required the students to reflect on their Lulu experience.

In addition to those available in Lulu.com, students used a variety of other digital tools for this project, including proprietary software and a free online platform. Adobe CS3 software was used for photo publishing. This package has been developed for desktop publishing and includes InDesign (for publication design), Photoshop (for color space management and photo optimization) and Bridge (for photo management). All the pre-press was handled in InDesign.

To operate in the Lulu.com environment, students created personal profiles and learned to use the various features related to managing publishing projects; they customized their blogs and storefronts, and developed a social network with their peers and the lulu community. In order to participate in the weekly e-tivities, they learnt how to blog (using the Lulu.com blogging tool), how to create links and post images, and how to reply to each other's messages. To collaborate during the design phase, they subscribed to the group's forum and participated by posting their questions and replies. To share their research on photo publishing with each other, they learned how to create a del.icio.us account and to use the features of social bookmarking.

Creating a Framework for Feeding Back and Assessing the Process and the Product

A fundamental philosophy underlying the development of this unit was Biggs' constructive alignment (2002). In this approach, it is the articulation between the stated learning outcomes, the teaching (and learning) activity and assessment that results in a meaningful learning experience. The approach to assessment that was used in this unit is commonly referred to as "criterion-referenced". Biggs (1999) states that there is "no *educational* justification for grading on a curve" (emphasis in original), a reference to the relatively common practice of measuring students' performance against that of the rest of the group. We believe that assessing against criteria measures more objectively the

extent to which students have achieved learning outcomes, and that, for this reason, it is a more student-centred approach.

It is apparent from the statement of the learning outcomes and the description of the learning activities that there is a causal connection between the two. This is no quirk of fate; the relationship was built into the design of the unit by adopting a constructive alignment approach. Similarly, attention was paid to the crafting of the assessment criteria. They were developed by the students in a joint activity with the teacher; in the process, the students not only gained insight into the purpose of assessment but were also empowered by the process of identifying the most important criteria against which to evaluate their work.

Using the learning outcomes as a point of reference, the learners were required to develop assessment criteria that would be used in rubric form to mark their projects. They were provided with a list of questions to guide their discussion, and were asked to engage with the following tasks: firstly, they had to develop six assessment criteria that articulated with the learning outcomes; then they were asked to rank these criteria, from most to least important; and finally, each group presented their two top criteria to the whole class.

During this report back process, all the groups' top criteria were written up on the board, and the whole class agreed on the four criteria that articulated most closely with the learning outcomes for the unit; these criteria then formed the basis of the assessment. This engagement in formulating the criteria against which their work would be measured empowers students with a sense of ownership, and a real interest in their own learning process (Stix, 1997). Andrade and Du (2005) point out the added value of using rubrics "to clarify the standards for quality performance, and to guide ongoing feedback about progress toward those standards." The incorporation of rubrics into learning design helps the students to visualize what it means to successfully address the learning outcome and to adjudge the quality of their own and others' work; in this sense, rubrics can also be said to be an instructional tool.

Once the assessment criteria were agreed upon, the class created an "irubric"which was developed using RubricStudio software from FacultyCentral. com. We define an irubric as a carefully crafted matrix that lists the assessment criteria and qualitatively describes different levels of excellence in achieving each criterion. This matrix constitutes the marking grid used by the teacher and students. The assessment criteria were listed down the left side of the rubric and the excellence descriptors for each criterion were entered in columns headed 0-5 (the potential marks for each criterion). The irubrics were used in two distinct ways: firstly, they provided a frame of reference within which to generate peer and tutor feedback. They were also used by the students and the tutor, as well as the second marker, as the statements against which the students were graded.

Different Approaches to Feedback

Rubrics are often used for assessment, but our review of literature on rubric-referenced assessment revealed that they can be a good tool for both assessment and feedback. Mertler (2001) points out that the analytic nature of the rubrics offers added advantage: the degree of feedback offered to students – and to teachers – is significant, and students receive specific feedback on their performance with respect to each of the individual scoring criteria – something that is unlikely to occur when using other forms of feedback.

In addition to this use of what we term "rubric-referenced feedback", students were required to provide feedback on the development of their peers' projects in the e-tivities. In that this second kind of feedback takes place in the distributed learning environment of the students, we have chosen to call it "distributed feedback".

It is clear that working online guarantees nei-

Figure 3. E-tivity 11: My Lulu experience (after Salmon's e-tivity model, 2004)

E-tivity 11: My Lulu experience
Purpose: Now that you are an expert in photo publishing, Lulu and print-on-demand, it's time to review all that happened, and share what you've learnt. This can help you put your experience in perspective and also help other people who are still on the look out for a way to publish their photobook. The best thing you can do to help others is to share your experience with them!
Task: Write about your experience in photo publishing with Lulu. Your reflection should include at least one of the following issues:
- Digital pedagogy: what are the differences between learning digital media in online and in offline environments?
- Communities of practice: what does it means to learn in a community that extends the classroom into the publishing market?.
- Vernacular versus academic culture: what are the implications of circulating the work in the field of popular culture side by side with non academic, 'amateur", production?
- A challenge to the hierarchical nature of the institution; what is the personal and social impact of starting publishing while you are still a student?
- The meaning of self-publishing: what does it mean to publish independently of a selection by committee (editors/ curators)?
- The value of publishing as a group, relying on the support of your peers' network.
- The advantages/constraints imposed by the POD templates on the format of the photobook.
- The lulu environment compared to other (publishing) social network sites.

ther student participation nor feedback. E-tivities (Salmon, 2004) are, however, a useful approach to increase online peer-feedback and their potential was explored throughout the 12 week teaching semester. In addition to the articulation between learning tasks and the e-tivities, outlined above, the e-tivities were used to enhance the feedback activity in various ways. Firstly, students were required to give feedback each week on each others' posts (the e-tivity defined the task to be completed and the requirement to respond to peers' work). Then Salmon's weaving technique was used to integrate the themes of the students' posts and to create a weekly summary that was posted to the blog. In two e-tivities, learners were asked to contribute to group discussions on photo publishing, and in another, they were asked to swap reviews of each others' books and post them to each others' storefronts. The last e-tivity required that learners reflect on the Lulu.com experience: their work, their peer's feedback about the course and the technology used. Figure 3, below, sets out the last e-tivity:

THE FINDINGS: STUDENTS' PERCEPTIONS OF THEIR ENGAGEMENT IN THE READ/ WRITE WEB ENVIRONMENT

We have described, this far, the rationale for (and the design and implementation of) the interventions that engaged the digital photography students in the produsage environment of the read/write web. In this section, we will report the students' own perceptions of the experience.

While students were free to write about any of the issues suggested in e-tivity 11, four emerged as particularly important to them: digital pedagogy; communities of practice; the value of publishing as a group; and the comparison of the Lulu.com environment with other social networking sites.

Digital Pedagogy

The Lulu.com environment forced a steep learning curve for both teacher and students. While really good for publishing, Lulu is not particularly appropriate for communication and group work; searches for information are painful, the menus badly organized, and the navigation system awful! Nonetheless, students identified positive benefits from the experience. The novelty of the method was deemed appropriate by students: *"Learning mostly online through practical demonstrations and experimentation on various related websites with self-publishing and online collaborative rubrics to assess our projects provided a new experience, for me at least"*, and *"Personally I believe anything that challenges the norm and gets you thinking in different ways is a good thing. This module is not presented to us in a traditional, stuffy, listen and take notes old school university style. We are studying a new art form and our lecture methods should reflect the move away from tradition."*

Another student remarked on the benefit of the hands-on approach: *"It is easier in my opinion to learn digital media practices on the Internet as opposed to the classroom or lecture hall – personally I am a more practical individual and feel the need to actively do something to learn effectively"*, which underscores the need to recognize different students' different learning styles. There was also a link made between the day-to-day online activities of students and the shift towards the Internet as a teaching medium: *"I welcome online learning as an idea very warmly. As most of my generation is connected to the Internet one way or another anyway, it's only a matter of when digital pedagogy becomes a standard."*

A caveat against seeing online learning as a silver bullet came from two students who showed their appreciation of more traditional approaches. *"Learning about digital media in an online environment as opposed to a more traditional format (i.e. a classroom) has been slightly chaotic at times.*

It's an unfortunate fact that sometimes you simply need a person on hand to help with problems, and online learning cannot always provide this." and *"The printed handouts on prepress fundamentals for InDesign were very useful too, as most of the class had not used this software previously."*

Communities of Practice

Students explored the concept of community of practice in a very practical way in these units. This student seems to doubt the personal value, but clearly recognizes the benefits to classmates: *"Learning by way of a community has been great for this unit, though I have not myself benefited from being part of a community it has clearly been a help to some members of the class who find websites and concepts such as those we have been studying more difficult than the theoretical issues in photography."* Another student came face to face with the diversity to be found in such a group: *"Become* [sic] *an online community was an interesting look at the class and how each person expressed themselves. There was such an array of difference in style of each person's e-tivities and how they coped with doing them."*

A particularly interesting comment was from a student who clearly found the online community too large for their liking but who had come to recognize that there were certain benefits. *"Like many others in our class, I found publishing our work online and making it available for anyone in the world to buy a very exciting aspect of the unit, and probably one which we would be keen to explore in the future. Publishing on Lulu however does put our work in with thousands of similar pieces, some interesting pieces and some rather less well put together. It would be good to find a more specialist online publishing site for our photobooks & photomags, however this would mean losing the huge numbers of visitors to Lulu. It's a trade-off I guess."*

The Value of Publishing as a Group

The principle value related to working as a group that was identified by the students was that help was immediately available: *"The support of the group was very helpful, especially the ability to post questions to the online forums and answer other's queries very quickly."*

Another student valued the collaboration in the community, too: *"There was a lot of help being given through blogs, forums and in person between all classmates during this period. Considering so many seemed unfamiliar with Indesign only a few weeks ago we all managed to create and upload an interesting mix of books into the Lulu store."*

It is interesting that none of the students identified any of Johnson and Johnson's five pillars of group work (n.d.): positive interdependence; group interaction; individual and group accountability; interpersonal skills; and group processing as valuable in the course of this unit. Their focus appears to be at a micro- rather than a macro-level.

A Comparison of Lulu with Other (Publishing) Social Networking Sites

There were varying opinions about the usability of Lulu.com relative to other social networking sites. One student commented that, *"Other social networking sites feature the same kind of real time features that Lulu does but many offer better usability and are far more effective."* Another clearly felt that the social side of the site was a positive: *"Lulu.com has much more of a social side to it than most other self-publishing websites"* but agreed with the critique on its usability: *"Whilst the design of the site is at the very least questionable, it does for the most part work well if you have the time and patience to figure it out!"*

This student pointed out that the cost effectiveness of Lulu was possibly outweighed by its design. *"To be able to publish your work cheaply and easily is a great asset afforded to us as a group, but Lulu seems to be experiencing prob-*

lems with the way it functions. It is tricky to use and everything seems to take a long time to do. Unlike other sites that involve social-networking, Lulu suffers from a lack of user friendly features." In addition, she offered some useful comments on the overall impact of using a better managed site: *"Overall, I see Lulu's merits and potential and also value certain aspects of the site but I think that with a better technical support and development the site should be more accessible and thus would have more of an impact and not come across as amateurish as it does now. Would the site be more interactive like Facebook with constant technical updates which facilitate the use it would be more popular and more people would use it, thus creating a bigger market for self-publishing."*

Possibly the view of the majority is summed up in this student's comment: *"Unfortunately, Lulu.com is not exactly a user-friendly environment and it isn't welcoming enough for constant digital activities like blogging, commenting and change of information. There are other, far more sophisticated environments for that (e.g. Facebook), which make users want to spend as much time as possible online."*

It is apparent from some of these remarks that the students lost sight of the requirement to compare Lulu.com with other publishing social networks. Nonetheless, their comments clearly indicate that they were at times frustrated by the Lulu experience.

Other Themes that Emerged from the Students' Writings

Some additional themes surface in the reading of the students' reflections. Firstly there is a concern about the ownership of their work: *"Another issue that was voiced by a large amount of our group was the fact that, while publishing as students, we do not control the simple intellectual copyright to our work. This is instead handed to the University who could, in theory (I hope not practice),*

profit from our work and charge us royalties for what is essentially our own personal art." They also expressed a lack of experience and a lack of confidence with the medium: *"Having set tasks within Lulu really made me play around and explore the system, something I have previously not done before. I do tend still to be scared of computers and really have no idea what they are capable of doing for me. Throughout this term I have had to face this fear and play around, do a lot of problem solving on my own and learn that these systems actually have everything explained for you if you use their 'help' and 'search' options."* Another student said: *"This has been a great struggle for me as I rarely use the Internet for social networking, I barely knew what a blog was. This unit was not something I enjoyed but I feel it helped me to get an understanding of how modern photographic practice operates on the Internet. I have learned how to produce my own book, which will be useful in the future I'm sure"*, which is a confident note upon which to wind up this discussion!

OVERVIEW OF OTHER FINDINGS FROM THE STUDY

From this study about the use of social networks for self-publishing, and engaging the students in the design of assessment criteria and the provision of feedback, we can confidently say that in a self-regulated learning environment, students can become a valuable source of feedback for their peers. It is also apparent that, with the right technology, feedback can be a tool for students to monitor their learning and guide them to achieve their learning outcomes.

In the Lulu.com domain, students viewed feedback through their familiarity with other social networking sites (SNSs). Throughout the semester, there was incidental collection of data which, when viewed holistically, points to cohorts of students who were generally comfortable in the online environment; who wanted a critique of their work in the form of feedback from the tutor, peers and the wider digital publishing community; and who would like to retain the benefits of face-to-face interaction in the classroom.

From a survey on their experience of SNSs, it was plain that the majority of the students (more than 90%) were competent in their use; almost 60% actively participated in more than one such site. While some of the students use SNSs to post pictures and stay in touch with friends – with some showing a preference for one SNS over another – their primary interest was to get feedback on their creative practice. One student explained, *"I use Flickr as a means of receiving feedback on my photographs and as an online portfolio - I prefer its emphasis on the work I produce and not on social aspects prevalent in many other sites with similar intentions"*, while another said, *"I use deviantART - a large artistic network which supports other artists and generally gives lots of feedback."* A third said, *"I use deviantart. com - to showcase my photography and receive detailed critiques based upon them. Also used to socialise with people who have similar interests. Research tool."*

This desire for feedback carried over into the Lulu environment. While Facebook, MySpace, Flickr and deviantART are used to post images and communicate with friends, they are also perceived as a way to get feedback about their creative practice from a like-minded community of artists. In the same way, students expected similar opportunities for feedback in a pedagogical project that is situated on a SNS; some saw this as a major advantage of delivering the course on Lulu as opposed to the classroom: *"The support of the group was very helpful, especially the ability to post questions to the online forums and answer other's queries very quickly."*

But others expected more! *"I do not see any advantages from publishing my book in a group (apart from getting one review) as only a few people downloaded it (which I cannot change*

and it's okay) and even less left comments in my development blog, which was incredibly disappointing as I put a lot of work into it and hoped to get some good feedback and constructive criticism. However, this is not lulu's fault but more the group motivation so I think next time there is a unit with such a heavy reliance on online media there should be more emphasis on the importance of this online activity and networking."

DISCUSSION

This study explored the features of read/write web to teach digital photobook publishing in a higher education context. The choice of Lulu.com as a software environment was partly a response to the hybrid digital-paper nature of the print-on-demand photobook project. The variety of tools available on the Lulu.com platform allowed us to view in context the core capacities of the digital art worker, the 5Cs of creative, collaborative, critical, combinatory and communicative work that characterize the art of produsage (Bruns, 2008). Figure 4 depicts the Bruns' produsage model in the context of this study:

Using the software to explore the meaning of **co-creativity**, and developing new work in dialogue with other creators was successful; meaningful learning was achieved in the group process, from establishing the cohort's online community to engaging in authentic group work by publishing the collective magazines. As has been noted, however, the technologies that support this interdependency are still in their infancy and in need of further development. Lulu.com is no exception. Studies have shown that people use social networking sites and media-sharing platforms to find people they already know with whom to work. If the interfaces make it difficult to find such friends and classmates, this can be a major barrier (Boyd & Ellison, 2007). The social browsing, for example, that is such a great feature of Flickr and Facebook, is still very limited

Figure 4. The produser in the Lulu.com environment. Adapted from The produser (Figure 1 above.)

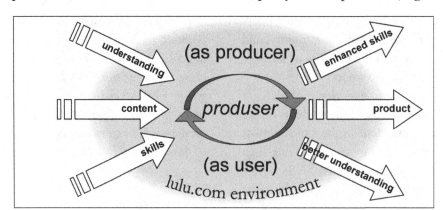

in Lulu; enhancing this tool to the level of other SNSs would be a great asset. There is, in general, a need for better interfaces to facilitate produsage (Lerman & Jones, 2006):

As social networks grow, it will be impossible for users to keep track of their contacts through the kinds of simple interfaces now offered. Better interfaces, for instance ones that create personal Explore pages by finding 'interesting' images from among those produced by the user's contacts, are a feasible solution to information overload. (p8)

The **collaborative** aspects associated with sharing one's work on the Internet require an understanding of appropriate legal frameworks, and this is greatly encouraged by Lulu's support of varied licensing deeds. The software's embedded licensing menus – with scope for creative commons licensing – provide a good opportunity to discuss the licensing of creative work, whether this is available as a free download, or as a profitable POD. The legal framework for this project – the Creative Commons Attribution Non Commercial Share Alike 2.0 negotiated with the University's copyright lawyer – offers a context within which to discuss issues of intellectual property in the academic environment. For the students, the principle of sharing their photographic work as a free downloadable PDF can be a watershed; this may be the first occasion in their time at university that

their work is placed online, and made available for others to use.

The **critical** tools embedded in the software – the use of blogs for commentary and feedback, and the potential for peer review in the book pages – generated possibilities for giving and receiving constructive feedback as part of the ongoing collaborative process. The traditional domain of the "crit" session in art and design studio practice was partially moved into an online environment: this is a way of addressing the changing patterns of student learning and the students' push for independent learning (Percy, 2004).

In the read/write environment, students can explore each other's work in their own domain and engage at their own pace; the opportunity appears greatly appreciated as time pressures arise as a result of the new work/study balance (Robbie & Zeeng, 2008). There are also issues raised that relate to an understanding of the students' needs and expectations in relation to online critical engagement. When used in the context of book reviews, the peer review in Lulu.com can be as effective as that on fanficton sites where beta-readers working in the same genre can help emerging authors develop genre-specific skills (Black, 2005). On the other hand, using the software to facilitate feedback can be disappointing, for instance when students invest a lot of effort in customizing their blogs and there is a lack of comments or, specifically, substantive ones (Stern, 2008).

The process of breaking down the complex assignments of photo publishing into a granular sequence of simpler tasks (from photo editing to online publishing) engaged the students in a series of mix and remix **combinatory** processes, and encouraged them to harness individual chunks of information. This is associated with engagement with multiple literacies; additional online tasks such as customizing profiles and storefronts, creating links, and uploading images side by side with text all encourage the development of all-round skills, and create a measure of granularity that is reinforced by drawing on the software's ability to aggregate feeds. This multimodality hallmarks young people's creative online practices (Thomas, 2007) and is connected with the aesthetic of remixing. It is a sign of new networked material, intelligences and tools (Perkel, 2008) that characterizes the photobook and photo magazine assignments through the remixing of one's own work and the work of others for the photo magazine.

The **communicative** aspects of the software, used by the students to publish their book analysis, pitch for their proposals, post questions and get technical help, were central to eliciting mutual constructive criticism between the participants; overall, the publishing of the work process as a digital sketchbook serves as "tangible evidence of participation" (Soules, 2001). This archive of works in progress and the development of ideas is still available online at http://stores.lulu.com/photocultures, and can be accessed by others.

Lastly, the platform provided an opportunity for the students to publish a photobook and a photo magazine in 12 weeks, a work flow that is only possible using an online photobook company. They did this with no financial burden and with total editorial control, a real achievement considering the limited opportunities available and the restrictive editorial policies of most established publishing houses. Whilst the field of artists' publications has always been strategically

associated with independent publishing initiatives, self-publishing is still considered a stigma for some (Forrester, 2007). With the increasing availability of print-on-demand it may be the best opportunity for emerging and established photographers alike to embrace it.

FUTURE IMPROVEMENTS AND RECOMMENDATIONS FOR PRACTICE

Feedback received from students and colleagues has been used to develop the latest version of the course, which is currently running with 34 level 2 digital photography students. For example, we removed the magazine brief and concentrated instead in the photobook, so that students can focus on developing critical thinking in the process of creating a single photo publication.

This is complemented by a move to reduce the number of e-tivities. Developed by Professor Gilly Salmon of Beyond Distance Research Alliance at the University of Leicester, *Carpe Diem* is quick prototyping methology to repurpose existing material for online delivery. Feedback from a *Carpe Diem* workshop that focused on this unit helped us to identify and retain the most successful e-tivities and discard the rest. The four e-tivities that remain address two particular areas: two encourage students to write about their own photobook and publishing practice, and the other two involve writing about their peers' photobooks and publishing practices. This allows for both self-reflection and collaboration, and students are supported by particular readings that coincide with the start of the e-tivities and help them to develop reflexive and critical skills in the analysis of photobooks, a zone of critical activity.

Finally, in response to the critique of the social aspects of Lulu as a networking environment, we decided to diversify. In addition to Lulu.com as the publishing site, in the latest action research cycle we use Facebook as the main social networking site for group communication and Blackboard, the University's virtual learning environment, as the repository/archive for all course documents.

REFERENCES

Anderson, C. (2007). *The long tail: How endless choice is creating unlimited demand.* London: Random House.

Andrade, H., & Du, Y. (2005). Student perspectives on rubric-referenced assessment. *Practical Assessment, Research, and Evaluation, 10*(3). Retrieved on October 9, 2008, from http://pare-online.net/pdf/v10n3.pdf

Arhar, J. M., Holly, M. L., & Kasten, W. C. (2001). *Action research for teachers: Travelling the yellow brick road.* Upper Saddle River, NJ: Merrill Prentice Hall.

Berners-Lee, T., & Cailliau, R. (1990). *WorldWide-Web: Proposal for a hypertext project.* Retrieved on November 12, 2008, from http://www.w3.org/Proposal.html

Biggs, J. (1999). What the student does: Teaching for enhanced learning. *Higher Education Research & Development, 18*(1), 57–75. doi:10.1080/0729436990180105

Biggs, J. (2002, November 4). *Aligning the curriculum to promote good learning.* Paper presented at Constructive Alignment in Action: Imaginative Curriculum Symposium. Retrieved on November 15, 2008, from http://www.palatine.ac.uk/files/1023.pdf

Black, R. B. (2005). *Online fanfiction: What technology and popular culture can teach us about writing and literacy instruction.* Retrieved on October 10, 2008, from http://newhorizons.org/strategies/literacy/black.htm

Boyd, D. M., & Ellison, N. B. (2007). Social network sites: Definition, history, and scholarship. *Journal of Computer-Mediated Communication, 13*(1), article 11. Retrieved on October 21, 2008, from http://jcmc.indiana.edu/vol13/issue1/boyd.ellison.html

Brittain, D. (2006). *Found, shared: The magazine photowork.* Brighton: Brighton Press.

Bruns, A. (2008). *Blogs, Wikipedia, Second Life, and beyond: From production to produsage.* New York: Peter Lang.

Drucker, J. (2004). *The century of artists' books.* New York: Granary Books.

Forrester, L. (2007). *Self-publishing photobooks.* London: Louise Forrester. Retrieved on November 22, 2008, from http://www.lulu.com/content/4052229

Hochschule Darmstadt. (2008). *Dear Lulu.* London: Hochschule Darmstadt/Practise. Retrieved on November 22, 2008, from http://www.lulu.com/content/2709735

Johnson, R. T., & Johnson, D. W. (n.d.). *Cooperative learning.* Retrieved on July 22, 2008, from http://www.co-operation.org/pages/cl.html

Lerman, K., & Jones, L. (2006). *Social browsing on flickr.* Retrieved on October 21, 2008, from http://arxiv.org/abs/cs/0612047

Mertler, C. (2001). Designing scoring rubrics for your classroom. *Practical Assessment, Research, & Evaluation, 7*(25). Retrieved on October 10, 2008, from http://pareonline.net/getvn.asp?v=7&n=25

Parr, M., & Badger, G. (2004). *The photobook: A history* (Volumes I and II). London: Phaidon.

Percy, C. (2004). Critical absence versus critical engagement: Problematics of the crit in design learning and teaching. *Art, Design, & [ADCHE]. Communication in Higher Education Journal, 2*(3), 143–154.

Perkel, D. (2008). Copy and paste literacy: Literacy practices in the production of a MySpace profile. In K. Drotner, H. S. Jensen & K. C. Schroeder (Eds.), *Informal learning and digital media: Constructions, contexts, consequences* (pp. 203-224). Newcastle, UK: Cambridge Scholars Press. Retrieved on October 10, 2008, from http://sims.berkeley.edu/~dperkel/media/dperkel_literacymyspace.pdf

Philippin, F. (2008). *Reaktionen*. Retrieved on October 10, 2008, from http://www.lulu.com/content/3978261

Richardson, W. (2006). *Blogs, wikis, podcasts, and other powerful Web tools for classrooms.* Thousand Oaks, CA: Corwin.

Robbie, D., & Zeeng, L. (2008). Engaging student social networks to motivate learning: Capturing, analysing, and critiquing the visual image. *The International Journal of Learning, 15*(3).

Salmon, G. (2004). *E-tivities: The key to active online learning.* Abingdon, Oxon: Routledge-Falmer.

Sarvas, R., Mäntylä, M., & Turpeinen, M. (2007). *Human-centric design of future print media.* Helsinki: PulPaper. Retrieved on October 10, 2008, from http://pong.hiit.fi/dcc/papers/FuturePrintMedia_PulPaper07.pdf

Smith, K. A. (2005). *Structure of the visual book.* Rochester, NY: Keith Smith.

Soules, M. (2001). *Collaboration and publication in hybrid online courses.* Retrieved on October 7, 2008, from http://records.viu.ca/~soules/hybrid2.htm

Stern, S. (2008). Producing sites, exploring identities: Youth online authorship. In D. Buckingham (Ed.), *Youth, identity, and digital media* (pp. 95–118). Cambridge, MA: MIT Press. Retrieved on October 10, 2008, from http://www.mitpressjournals.org/doi/abs/10.1162/dmal.9780262524834.095

Stix, A. (1997). *Creating rubrics through negotiable contracting and assessment.* Retrieved on October 10, 2008, from http://interactiveclassroom.com/article_07.html

Thomas, A. (2007). *Youth online: Identity and literacy in the digital age.* New York: Peter Lang.

Van House, N. A. (2007, April 28-May 3). Flickr and public image-sharing: Distant closeness and photo exhibition. In M. B. Rosson & D. J. Gilmore (Eds.), *Extended Abstracts Proceedings of the 2007 Conference on Human Factors in Computing Systems, CHI 2007* (pp. 2717-2722) San Jose, CA.

ADDITIONAL READING

Berners-Lee, T. (2001). *Weaving the Web.* London: Texere.

Burgos, D. (2006). *The structure and behavior of virtual communities engaged in informal learning about e-learning standards* (Estudio de la estructura y del comportamiento de las comunidades virtuales de aprendizaje no formal sobre estandarización del e-learning). Unpublished doctoral dissertation, European University of Madrid, Villaviciosa de Odón, Madrid, Spain.

Burgos, D., Hummel, H. G. K., Tattersall, C., Brouns, F., & Koper, R. (2008). Design guidelines for collaboration and participation with examples from the LN4LD (Learning Network for Learning Design). In *LN: Publications and preprints.* Heerlen, NL: Open Universiteit Nederland.

Figallo, C. (1998). *Hosting Web communities.* New York: John Wiley.

Hagel, J., III, & Armstrong, A. (1997). *Net.gain: Expanding markets through virtual communities.* Boston, MA: Harvard Business School Press.

Lave, J., & Wenger, E. (1991). *Situated learning: Legitimate peripheral participation.* Cambridge, UK: Cambridge University Press.

Lockyer, L., Bennet, S., Agostinho, S., & Harper, B. (Eds.). (2008). *Handbook of research on learning design and learning objects: Issues, applications, and technologies.* Hershey, PA: IGI Global.

Mitchell, C., & Weber, S. (1999). *Reinventing ourselves as teachers: Beyond nostalgia.* London: Falmer.

Redecker, C. (2008). *Fostering innovation with Web 2.0.* Retrieved from http://www.checkpoint-elearning.com/article/6115.html

Rheingold, H. (1993). *The virtual community.* London: Secker & Warburg.

Weber, S., Mitchell, C., & Dziewirz, S. (2008). *The image and identity research collective (IIRC).* Retrieved from http://iirc.mcgill.ca/

Wells, G. (2001). *Indagación dialógica. Hacia una teoría y una práctica socioculturales de la educación.* Barcelona: Paidós.

Williams, K. (2000, February 2-4). Self directed learning in the visual arts. In A. Herrmann & M. M. Kulski (Eds), *Flexible futures in tertiary teaching. Proceedings of the 9th Annual Teaching Learning Forum.* Perth: Curtin University of Technology. Retrieved from http://lsn.curtin.edu.au/tlf/tlf2000/williams.html

Chapter 14
Revising the Framework of Knowledge Ecologies:
How Activity Patterns Define Learning Spaces

Kai Pata
Tallinn University, Estonia

ABSTRACT

This chapter describes the Web of social software tools with its inhabitants as an evolving and ecological environment, discussing and elaborating the connectivist framework coined by George Siemens in his book Knowing Knowledge. This new perspective to ecological learning in social software environments resides on the ideas of Gibson's and his followers approach to ecological psychology, the rising theory of embodied simulation and Lotman's theory of cultural semiosis. In the empirical part of the chapter, we focus on the methods of investigating how social software systems become accommodated with their users forming learning spaces. Analysis discusses such ecologically defined spaces for individual and collaborative learning.

INTRODUCTION

Recently, the widespread public use of social software in Web has triggered for the need to theoretically ground the learning phenomena in this new environment using the ecological view. Favouring the biological human-centred understanding of information systems, Davenport and Prusack (1997, p. 11) primarily used the information ecology as a metaphorical term to capture holistic and human-centred management of information. Next,

the knowledge ecology and knowledge ecosystem terms were coined, which started to mark the rapidly developing area that binds knowledge creation and utilization with the social and management aspects in human networks (Pór & Malloy, 2000; Pór & Spivak, 2000). The Web visionaries like John Seeley Brown (1999; 2002), and George Siemens (2005; 2006) related knowledge ecology and knowledge ecosystem terms with weaving information and artefacts, meanings and knowledge, networks and connections. G. Siemens published a book "Knowing Knowledge" (2006), which received wide public recognition in social Web communi-

DOI: 10.4018/978-1-60566-826-0.ch011

ties. He suggested Connectivism as the learning theory for new Digital Age. While the book captures a new knowledge ecology vision, it has yet several limitations, which will be discussed in this chapter.

G. Siemens formulated that Connectivism is the assertion that learning is primarily a network-forming process (Siemens, 2006, p. 15). He relies on the ideas of Downes (2005) who wrote that: *A property of one entity must lead to or become a property of another entity in order for them to be considered connected; the knowledge that results from such connections is connective knowledge. The act of learning is one of creating an external network of nodes – where we connect and form information and knowledge sources* (Siemens, 2006, p. 29). Connectivism focuses on the knowledge, situated externally from people in the web. Several authors address this knowledge using different terms e.g. cultural knowledge (Heft, 2001); semiotic niche (Hoffmeyer, 1995) or cognitive niche (Magnani, 2008; Magnani & Bardone, 2008). These terms will be elaborated in the further parts of the paper.

G. Siemens (2005; 2006) assumes that creating meanings and relations publicly in social software environments would aid through connective processes the formation of new knowledge ecologies and learning cultures. In the Connectivism framework Siemens takes an approach that is strongly tilted towards knowledge, meanings, communities and networks and their spaces – knowledge ecosystems. However, the Connectivism framework is inconsistent in elaborating the ecological role of tools, activities, and communities in the formation and evolvement of knowledge ecologies. Siemens writes: *The pipe is more important than the content in the pipe. 'Know where' and 'know who' are more important today that 'knowing what' and 'how'* (Siemens, 2006, p. 32). In this chapter we attempt to argue against this metaphoric claim. We suggest that the use of static 'pipe' metaphor, and diminishing the role of activities, the 'knowing how' part, may theoretically lead to

losing the ecological nature of knowledge ecologies framework.

Studies of communities and networks assume that these are formations of people (Lin, Sundaram, Li, Tatemura & Cheng, 2006; Kumar, Novak & Tompkins, 2006) or their artifacts in the Web (Klamma, Spaniol, Cao & Jarke, 2006). What yet is missing is seeing Web 2.0 as a united ecological system with its inhabitants. The interrelations between communities, the environment and the culture left there by people - the traces of meanings (Llor`a, Imafuji, Welge, & Goldberg, 2006; Magnani, 2008) and the traces of activities - are important in the ecological framework. Similar tiltedness towards artifacts and meanings appears in the development of most of the social software tools. In social software systems we can find several possibilities of organising and filtering content by socially defined meanings, however, to see what activities take place in the communities that use these systems is often possible only if participating in the communities. We assume in this chapter that the ecological formation of common places, where communities and networks exist and take action, needs to be integrated into the theoretical explanations about connectivist learning in these systems.

The remaining chapter is organized in the following order. We introduce the enlarged ecological framework of learning in social software systems. The ecological learning framework is illustrated in the case study from formal higher education. This study is discussing the methodologies of detecting ecological learning spaces of the communities that use social software. The analytical part demonstrates learning spaces of individual and collaborative learners who use social software at the course. The analysis focuses on the importance of activity-related aspects in the ecological model. We provide answers to the two research questions:

What characterizes the learning spaces of individual and collaborative learners who use social software at the formal higher education course?

Which differences in the learning culture with social software do the learning spaces of individual and collaborative learners reveal?

KNOWLEDGE ECOSYSTEMS IN THE CONNECTIVISM FRAMEWORK: FLOWING KNOWLEDGE IN THE CONNECTED PIPES

Siemens (2006) wrote in his book *Knowing Knowledge* that Connectivism is a staged view of how individuals encounter and explore knowledge in a networked/ecological manner. The central concepts Siemens discusses are: knowledge, learning, spaces, networks and knowledge ecosystems. He illustrated his framework with the following metaphor: *The pipe is more important than the content in the pipe. 'Know where' and 'know who' are more important today that 'knowing what' and 'how'* (p. 32). Subsequently we introduce his position in concerns of these terms, asking also some questions, which reveal the areas where Connectivism framework must be elaborated. The answers to these questions will be further discussed in the next chapters.

Knowledge: *Knowledge rests in networks. Knowledge may reside in non-human appliances, and learning is enabled/facilitated by technology (p. 31). The act of knowing is offloaded onto the network itself – to a connected network of specialists. The network (or web) of connections is the structure, which holds the knowledge of individuals in a holistic manner (p. 33). Content is imbued with new meaning when situated in network (or is more accurate to say that the network acquires new meaning when new content is added?) (p. 43).*

Learning: *Learning is a network formation process of connecting specialized nodes or information sources (p. 31). The elements that create understanding are scattered across many structures and spaces. We 'know' when we seek and pull elements together – when we create a meaning-laden view of an entity (p. 45).*

Q: How technology enables/facilitates ecologies?

Q: How network holds knowledge and acquires new meanings?

Spaces: *We create spaces where we can dialogue about and enact knowledge (p. 4). Ecologies and networks provide the solution to needed structures and spaces to house and facilitate knowledge flow (p. 86). Understanding knowledge in a particular era is important in ensuring that we have aligned our spaces and structures with the nature of knowledge (p. 10). Spaces are themselves agents for change. Changed spaces will change practice (p. 87).*

Q: How spaces enable enacting knowledge?

Q: Can we separate the knowledge flow from the structures and spaces – networks and ecologies – where knowledge flows?

Networks: *Our mind is a network... and ecology. It adapts to the environment (p. 27). The network is a structure that individuals create on their own (p. 132). Content is imbued with new meaning when situated in network (or is more accurate to say that the network acquires new meaning when new content is added?) (p. 43). Better quality of networks and connections result in better quality knowledge sharing (p. 20). Networks occur within ecologies. Ecology is a living organism. It influences the formation of the network itself. The health of each personal learning network is influenced by the suitability of the ecology in which the learner exists (p. 92).*

Q: What are networks: Personal learning environments (PLEs)? Connections between artifacts a person creates? Connections between people a person interacts with?

Ecology:*Ecologies and networks provide the solution to needed structures and spaces to house and facilitate knowledge flow (p. 86). Ecology is a knowledge-sharing environment (p. 87). The ecology fosters connections to original and knowledge sources, allowing for currency. The ecology fosters rich interaction between disparate fields of knowledge, allowing growth and adaptation of ideas and concepts. Each participant in the ecology pursues his/her own objectives, but within the organized domain of knowledge of a particular field (p. 117). Ecologies permit diverse, multi-faceted concepts... and meanings to emerge based on how items are organized or self-organize (p. 87). The creation of the ecology permits a broad-scale implementation of differing knowledge and learning experiences, permitting employees to achieve knowledge-based needs in a multi-faceted manner, multiple ways, and through multiple devices (p. 132). Ecologies are nurtured and fostered...instead of constructed, organized and mandated (p. 90). Ecologies are capable of rapid growth, adapting to new competition, differing perspectives, and enabling innovative concepts and ideas to gain traction (p. 87). Ecology is a living organism (p. 92). Ecologies are: loose, free, dynamic, adaptable, messy, and chaotic (p. 90). The ecology influences the formation of the network itself. The health of each personal learning network is influenced by the suitability of the ecology in which the learner exists (p. 92).*

Q: How does the ecology influence personal networks?

Siemens (2006, p. 87) also discusses the characteristics of ecologies that promote knowledge sharing. He emphasizes the freedom of choice to use different systems and tools that meet the needs of each person, and which they perceive easy to use. This suggests owning a personal learning environment (PLE), the autonomously combined various tools, material- and human resources for facilitating person's cognitive learning activities, which are accommodated to certain person's needs and may be interconnected with other persons' PLEs (Attwell, 2007; Underwood & Banyard, 2008). Secondly, the variety of systems and tools that individuals use is considered important. This may increase the possibility of making connections between people and between artifacts across the various borders. The personal choice in making connections is of importance to hold motivation and inquiry spirit. Because knowledge is supposed to be situated in networks and connections, the deep and trusting connections between individuals, who uptake knowledge from the ecologies, and tolerance among these individuals must be achieved. Thirdly, the consistency of participating in certain practices with knowledge is suggested, which may increase the probability that patterns will emerge within ecologies, and that persons will notice them.

Siemens (2006, p. 45) explains the functioning of knowledge networks as follows: *Individuals are active in the learning ecology/space in terms of* **consuming or acquiring new resources and tools**. *The learner begins to actively contribute to the network/ecology essentially, becoming a visible node. Time in the network has resulted in the learner developing an* **increased sense of what is happening** *in the network/ecology as a whole. She/he will become more adept at* **recognizing new patterns or changing winds of information of knowledge**. *Individuals are capable of understanding* **what do the emerging patterns mean**. *The learner is also* **focused on active reflection of the shape of the ecology itself**. *The learner may engage in* **attempts to transform the ecology beyond his/her own network**.

In the practical implementation of Connectivism ideas into learning Siemens (2006, p. 140) suggests three key aspects of ecologies – they must be *holistic, adaptive* and *result-focused*. These concepts may also serve as the starting-points into taking the fresh look at the knowledge ecologies.

Siemens suggests that holistic ecologies represent the situation diversely, allowing multiple perspectives and views. We can further argue that holistic view means that we may find several subspaces in the ecologies, which differ from each other by perspectives. Ecologies are formed of many individuals who try to realize their personal objectives, often individually and without being consciously involved into group actions. The view at the ecology level permits to see these individuals forming various communities who share similar views or act in a certain way without even knowing each other or forming networks. However, the *communities inhabit sub-spaces in the ecology*, which are evolving, and dynamically changing. Across the vaguely defined borders of community subspaces, knowledge can be interpreted and translated, creating new knowledge. The abstract sub-space concept, which we formulize as a *learning niche for certain community*, is central in the revisions of Connectivism framework. A learning niche is a community-specific activity- and meaning subspace for learning in the larger learning space of the knowledge ecology or knowledge ecosystem.

Secondly, Siemens suggests that ecologies must be adaptive and able to adjust and change as the environment changes. These characteristics are elaborated further in the next subchapter, introducing the ecological idea of *affordances that define niches*. Affordances denote the relations between particular aspects of the situations and people planning or taking action. If the persons are linked to their existing habits, activities, processes and tools, like Siemens suggests, any change in their objectives and preferences would cause the changes in the whole environment, in these communities. People, activities, and tools what they find to fulfill their objectives are ecologically interrelated. People rely on the cultural behaviors that take place in certain social environments – e.g. 'tagging of personal meanings' or 'reflecting in public spaces' etc. Thus, community activities influence, which perspectives of meanings, actions and tool functionalities and objectives

would be actual for the learners. Everything what people do in Web remains as the *feedback into the systems.* It is interpreted as an *ecological knowledge,* influencing not only this community, but also potentially other communities. Ecological knowledge is everything what people do in Web, e.g. the content and meanings, the process traces from actions taken with certain tools with certain artifacts with certain people that remains to the Web and can be used as a feedback for communities or as a cultural knowledge embedded to Web systems.

Thirdly, Siemens emphasizes the intended targets and desired outcomes that the ecologies might have. This view would obtain a new meaning if we stop seeing the formation of ecologies as the systems purposefully designed by groups, but as *emergent and evolving activity systems.* The mutual interrelations between individuals, their objectives, and what they see and use in the surrounding system, when constructing knowledge, are triggered ecologically. The ecological knowledge is always being formed and always influencing what is being formed, and how it is being formed. This *ecological knowledge is not only content* and meanings left into the Web systems, but also the *process traces from actions* taken with certain tools with certain artifacts, with certain people. Thus, the communities always shape their spaces and these spaces shape the communities.

ENACTMENT WHEN LEARNING IN KNOWLEDGE ECOSYSTEMS: COMMUNITIES CONSTRUCT NICHES

In the previous discussion several questions where addressed when analyzing the Connectivism framework. These questions revealed that there are unclear aspects, suggesting the necessity to take a more in-depth look into the knowledge ecologies. We have reorganised the order of these questions to frame our argumentation about the nature of

Figure 1. Components in the learning ecology framework

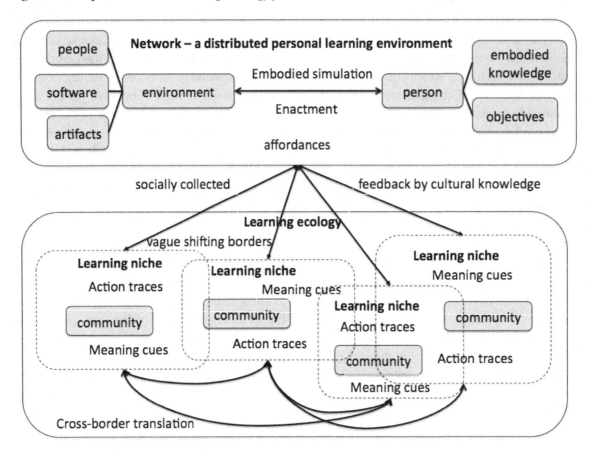

knowledge, networks, knowledge ecologies and their interrelations.

Q: What are networks: Personal learning environments (PLEs)? Connections between artifacts a person creates? Connections between people a person interacts with?

Q: How network holds knowledge and acquires new meanings?

Q: Can we separate the knowledge flow from the structures and spaces (networks and ecologies) where knowledge flows?

Q: How technology enables/facilitates knowledge ecologies?

Q: How spaces enable enacting knowledge?

Q: How does the ecology influence personal networks?

To answer these questions we introduce some more concepts to the ecological learning framework: *niches* as abstract community spaces, *affordances* that define niches, ecological knowledge as the *feedback* that communities create, *enactment* and *embodied simulation* as the possible processes that cause ecology formation. Siemens (2005, 2006) has built his Connectivist framework on the ecological understanding. However, deepening of the ecological approach enables to see activities in the more central position in the knowledge ecologies. We aim to elaborate the knowledge ecosystem idea, strengthening the role of activities and introducing the theoretical framework how activities are related to the knowledge ecosystems. Figure 1 illustrates the components of our knowledge ecologies framework.

Network-Knowledge Interrelations

Q1: What are networks: Personal learning environments (PLEs)? Connections between artifacts a person creates? Connections between people a person interacts with?

We do not want to criticise the main idea expressed by Siemens (2006) in Knowing Knowledge, declaring that knowledge rests and changes in the networks that connect people and their artifacts. Asking, what these networks are, we want to emphasise *the role of tools and activities as an ecologically entwined parts of the network*. We emphasise that knowledge, is more than information and meanings – *knowledge has an activity- and tool-related dimension*. Personal learning environments (PLEs) that people construct and use in their daily activities are not merely the mediators, 'the inactive pipes' that enable knowledge flow. PLEs are dynamically evolving activity systems in which the personal objectives and human and material resources are integrated in the course of action.

We want to emphasize the *distributed nature of what we define as PLEs*. Here, we do not mean only that each PLE may be constructed of many separate tools forming a distributed system. PLE is also distributed ecologically, integrating our minds with the elements of the environment. Zhang and Patel (2006) suggested that people perform the distributed cognition evoking simultaneously affordances, the allowable actions specified by the environment coupled with the properties of the organisms, in the form of distributed representations extended across external (the environment) and internal (the organism) representations.

Hommel (2003), has written that action control to all behavioral acts is ecologically delegated to the environment - when planning actions in terms of anticipated goals, the sensory-motor assemblies needed to reach the goal are simultaneously selectively activated in the environment, and bind together into a coherent whole that serves as an action-plan, facilitating the execution of the goal-directed actions through the interaction between the environment and its embodied sensory-motor activations. In the frames of ecologically defined learning systems, we can assume that our embodied sensory-motor knowledge of previous meaningful actions and its environmental correlates that we find around us form one emergent distributed system. In the course of learning our PLE is always in change. We actualize certain dimensions from the environment around us integrating it to the action-plans, and simultaneously the environment extends certain dimensions to us changing and shaping our intentions. Deliberately, we do not talk of the environment as merely of tools and systems. Environment involves all kind of resources in PLEs – people, artifacts, software systems and services. Thus, *the network in the ecological framework may be interpreted as a cognitively distributed system continuously constructed of our minds and the environment components*.

Q2: How network holds knowledge and acquires new meanings?

Applying the previous interpretation of networks in ecological framework we can assume that knowledge that the networks hold is pattern-like, cognitively distributed between the environment and person(s), and dynamically emergent in activities. Two perspectives are important about the nature of knowledge – knowledge is always developed within the distributed systems personally and culturally. These personal and cultural ways to create knowledge are interrelated.

Varela, Thompson & Rosch (1991, p. 149) wrote that knowledge is the result of ongoing interpretation that emerges from our capacities of understanding. These capacities are rooted in the structures of our biological embodiment but are lived and experienced within a domain of consensual action and cultural history. They coined the term *embodied action* to transmit the idea that cognition depends upon the kinds of experience that come from having a body with various sensory-motor capacities, and second that these individual sensory-motor capacities are themselves embedded in a more encompassing biological, psychological, and cultural context. The authors assumed that sensory and motor processes, perception and action are fundamentally inseparable in lived cognition (p. 172-173). Using the term *enaction* they focused on two points: 1) perception consists of perceptually guided action, and 2) cognitive structures emerge from recurrent sensory-motor patterns that enable action to be perceptually guided (Varela et al., 1991, p. 173).

Bereiter (2002, p. 57) framed and answered the question about the nature of knowledge as follows: *Where is knowledge if it isn't contained in individual minds? The kind of answer coming from activity and situated cognition theorists runs along the following lines: Knowledge is not lodged in any physical or metaphysical organ. Rather knowledge inheres in social practices and in the tools and artifacts used in those practices. Knowledge is regarded as distributed. This does not mean merely that it is spread around, a bit here and a bit there... knowledge does not consist of little bits...all the knowledge is in the relationships – relationships among the people engaged in an activity, the tools they use, and the material conditions of the environment in which action takes place.* Yet, Varela et al. (1991) and Bereiter (2002) do not offer explanations of how network holds knowledge and how this knowledge can change.

Recently researchers have come up to the idea how this distributed knowledge emerges as a result of *embodied simulation*. Discoveries in cognitive and neuroscience about the functioning of mirror-neuron systems (Gallese et al., 1996), claim, that cognition is embodied through grounding knowledge directly in sensory-motor experiences without the mediation of symbolic representations (Pecher & Zwaan, 2005). Research indicates that from observation of others and the environment (Rizzolatti et al., 2001), from listening narratives (Rizzolatti & Arbib, 1998; Iaccoboni, 2005) or from reading narratives (Scorolli & Borghi, 2007) and looking everyday images of objects or works of art (Gallese & Freedberg, 2007) we perceptually activate certain multi-modal action-potentialites of embodied symbols that directly mediate our purposeful and goal-directed actions (see Gallese & Lakoff, 2005). These findings suggest an additional way of how distributed cognition works without representational processes suggested by Zhang and Patel (2006). When acting in social learning environments not only the meanings are newly created from found information, but also the action-related cues are picked up from different narratives and from the whole systems, and they are integrated into our action plans. These findings indicate, that besides possibilities of organizing meanings with various ways in social learning environments, much more attention needs to be put on these *action-related cues individuals and communities interact within the environment.* Knowledge is always in change because of personal nature of embodied simulation processes and the influence or *feedback* that people make with their actions, action- and meaning traces, and their specific way of activation of PLEs from the environment.

Q3: Can we separate the knowledge flow from the structures and spaces (networks and ecologies) where knowledge flows?

In the revised ecological framework knowledge and networks are integrated. Our ecological learning framework binds together three assumptions: i) network may be interpreted as a cognitively distributed system continuously constructed of our minds and the environment components in the course of action; ii) knowledge is pattern-like, distributed between the environment and people, and is dynamically emergent in activities,

iii) knowledge emerges as a result of embodied simulation, when people perceptually activate certain multi-modal action-potentialites from the environment that mediate their purposeful and goal-directed actions, and leave action- and meaning traces as a feedback to the environment.

Network-Ecosystem Interrelations

Q: How technology enables/facilitates knowledge ecologies?

The concept of ecology plays an important part in the Connectivism framework of learning. However, Siemens (2006) is not very precise in explaining how ecologies and networks influence each other. In our main amendments to Connectivism we try to elaborate the emergent nature of ecologies with bottom-up social definition of learning niches, discuss what is the role of using software systems in these ecologies, and describe how feedback through ecological knowledge connects ecologies and networks.

Ecologies are formed as a result of many individuals taking actions. Thus, people with various perspectives are simultaneously at present in these ecologies and influencing them. Many abstract sub-spaces can be formed within ecologies. Such sub-spaces emerge when parts of the environment are embodied and used similar way by many people. They are more general than networks of one individual – they come to existence and can be identified only if many individuals actualize similar personal learning environments (PLEs) for the same purposes with certain frequency at the certain period of time. These groups of individuals have something in common in their identity. Hoffmeyer (1995) coined the *semiotic niche* term to signify the semiotic spaces that are actualized by certain organisms in species' specific semiotic processes when interacting with their environment. Magnani (2008), and Magnani and Bardone (2008) use the term *cognitive niche* to mark the distributed

space that people create by interrelating individual cognition and the environment through the continuous interplay through abductive processes in which they alter and modify the environment. In the knowledge ecologies we can use the learning niche term that marks the cognitive niches that are related to learning-related activities. Learning communities inhabit *learning niches – the abstract sub-spaces for learning in the space of knowledge ecosystem.*

Hutchinson (1957) defined niche as a region (n-dimensional hypervolume) in a multi-dimensional space of environmental factors that affect the welfare of a species. Niches have been conceptualized as the collections of environmental gradients with certain ecological amplitude, where the ecological optimum marks the gradient peaks where the organisms are most abundant. The welfare of species can be determined by meaning-creation and action-taking possibilities in the environment. For example Hoffmeyer (1998) coined the term semiotic fitness to describe the relation how organisms contribute to the emergence of semiotic niches. Semiotic fitness measures the semiotic competence or success of natural systems in managing the genotype-environtype translation processes. The optimization of semiotic fitness results in the continuing growth in the depth of interpretative patterns accessible to life. In the gradient concept structural ecosystem properties are comprehended as concentration gradients in space and time (Müller, 1998). Any niche gradient is a peak of the fitness landscape of one environmental characteristic (Wright, 1931), which can be visualized in two-dimensional space as a graph with certain skew and width, determining the ecological amplitude. The shape of the fitness graph for certain characteristic can be plotted through the abundance of certain specimen benefitting of this characteristic. All niche gradients are situated and establish a multi-dimensional hyper-room, which axes are different environmental parameters.

The formation of learning niches for specific learning-related activities happens through the social definition of several factors that influence learning. It is assumed that any learning niche in social systems is determined as a set of characteristics that people perceive and actualize as useful for their activities and wellbeing individually or in groups. The meaning- and action-relevant information should be considered important in niche formation. Each niche gradient defines one dimension of the learning space. Hutchinson (1957) made difference of fundamental and realized niche – the former exist as the complex of all necessary environmental characteristics for certain species, the latter is formed under the pressure of all the currently available environmental characteristics in the competitive conditions with other species. On our learning ecology framework, the fundamental cognitive learning niche term applies for all the possibly usable software tools and services, artifacts and people, while the realized niches form under the constrained conditions of resource availability.

What is the mechanism how niches appear? Previously we have described the distributed cognition (see Zhang & Patel, 2006; Magnani, 2008; Magnani & Bardone, 2008) and embodied simulation (see Gallese et al., 1996; Pecher & Zwaan, 2005; Gallese & Lakoff, 2005) as the candidates of ecological emergence of knowledge in systems from individual activities in interrelation to the ecosystem knowledge. Both approaches may be related with the *affordance* concept from ecological psychology. This concept we use in our elaborated framework to describe the different dimensions people actualize in the course of action with the environment.

Gibson (1979) originally defined affordances as opportunities for action for an observer, provided by an environment. The mainstream view on affordances in educational technology settings considers them as objective properties of the tools, which are perceptible in the context of certain activities. Thus, it is commonly suggested that tools have concrete technological affordances for certain performances that can be brought into

a learner's perception with specific instructions (Norman, 1988; Gaver, 1996). This use of the concept tends to ignore its relativistic nature and observer-dependence, and seems to imply that affordances should be located in the environment or specific artifacts or tools.

The interactional affordance concept that supports the embodied simulation mechanisms appears in a number of studies. Chemero (2003), a researcher from the school of Gibsonian ecological psychology, has suggested that affordances are rather the relations between particular aspects of the animal and the situations. Chemero wrote that affordances are features of whole situations (meaning the actors are part of this situation). Gaver (1996) emphasized that affordances emerge in human action and interaction and, thus, go beyond mere perception. Michaels (2003) claimed that perceiving affordances is more than perceiving relations, but it brings attention to the action-guiding information and sets up action systems to act. Magnani and Bardone (2008) also stress that human and non-human animals can "modify" or "create" affordances by manipulating their cognitive niches.

Barab and Roth (2006) have noted that connecting learners to ecological networks, where they can learn through engaged participation, activates the affordance networks. Affordance networks, in contrast to the perceptual affordances described by Gibson, are extended in both time and space and can include sets of perceptual and cognitive affordances that collectively come to form the network for particular goal sets. According to Barab and Roth (2006) affordance networks are not entirely delimited by their material, social, or cultural structure, although one may have elements of all of these; instead, they are functionally bound in terms of the facts, concepts, tools, methods, practices, commitments, and even people that can be enlisted toward the satisfaction of a particular goal. In this way, affordance networks are dynamic socio-cultural configurations that take on particular shape as a result of material, social, political, economic, cultural, historical, and even personal factors but always in relation to particular functions. Barab and Roth (2006) assumed that affordance networks are not read onto the world, but instead continually "transact" (are coupled) with the world as part of a perception-action cycle in which each new action potentially expands or contracts one's affordance network.

Affordances emerge and potentially become observable in actions what people undertake to realize their goals. Actions of other people in the environment or traces of their action serve as the triggers of new action plans. Vyas and Dix (2007) distinguished 3 levels of affordances: personal, organization/community, and culture level, which differ also on the level of how rapidly they can change. They claim that affordances of different levels influence each other. For example affordances one person can perceive may depend on the affordances the community perceives or culture uses as norms. Heft (2001) wrote that: "*we engage a meaningful environment of affordances and refashion some aspects of them... These latter constructed embodiments of what is known – which include tools, artifacts, representations, social patterns of actions, and institutions – can be called ecological knowledge. Ecological knowledge through its various structural, material culture, human setting manifestations becomes an integral social and cultural part of 'the environment', with these social and cultural affordances constituting effective, largely material, forms of knowledge with their own functional significance, cultural transmission, and adaptation implications.*" Heft's interpretation enables to view both the information from the artifacts but also the traces of action in social software systems as important components that define knowledge ecologies.

We can conclude that in our elaborated framework of ecological learning *we support the idea that affordances are the perceived possibilities for both thinking and doing, what learners evoke and signify during their actual interaction with an artifact or tool and with each other.* People

determine the personal learning affordances within their PLEs. Hence, the learning affordance descriptions involve the learning action verbs, people who are involved in action, and mediators of actions (various tools, services and artifacts). Any individual conceptualizes learning affordances personally, but the range of similar learning affordance conceptualizations may be clustered into more general affordance groups e.g. 'pulling social awareness information' or 'searching artifacts by social filtering' etc. These *affordance clusters may be interpreted and used as the abstract learning niche gradients.* The affordances as niche gradients are socially developed.

Using the affordance conception for defining learning space dimensions for the communities, we can bring the emergent ecological properties from the individual network level to the new structural level that is niches in the ecologies. *Ecologies integrate many niches of different communities.* The awareness of different niches is obtained by tracing the meaning-spaces and activity patterns of other people twined between the distributed real and virtual places they inhabit. If the dimensions of learning niches become unfolded, they become usable for our own self-directed learning. Two aspects here are important. The meaning centred aspect suggests to use distributed PLEs to be aware of more communities and their *meaning niches*, and to create conditions for transferring information from one conceptual dimension to another. This precondition for cross-border meaning-building activities has been focused both in cultural semiotics (Lotman, 1990; Hoffmayer, 1995) as well as in the theory of Connectivism. Second aspect is finding people to learn together with. To be involved in the similar activities, similar *action niches* need to be used for interaction. *Learning affordances enable to characterize these action niches.*

Q: How spaces enable enacting knowledge?
Q: How does the ecology influence personal networks?

Previously we have defined the various subspaces in the Connectivism framework as learning niches. Here we assume that *niches enable to enact knowledge and influence personal networks because of ecological inheritance left as feedback to the social software systems.* We suggest that this *ecological inheritance is the particular set of affordances and meanings left into the systems by various communities in the form of meaning- and action-relevant cues.*

Hoffmeyer (1995) assumes that in the semiotic communication through their semiotic places the organisms' have capacity for anticipation, and the possibility of foreseeing actual events and protecting oneself against them or otherwise deriving advantage from them. A recent literature in evolutionary theory provides the idea of niche construction (Odling-Smee et al., 2003) as an ecological factor that enables organisms to contribute for and benefit from environmental information. It is argued, the organism has a profound effect on the very environment as a feedback loop. Organisms have influence on their environment, and the affected environment can have a reciprocal effect on other organisms of this species or on other species, creating an environment different from what it would have been before it was modified. This niche construction challenges the convention of a distinct separation between organism and its environment. The niche-construction perspective stresses two legacies that organisms inherit from their ancestors, genes and a modified environment with its associated selection pressures. The authors assume that the feedback must persist for long enough, and with enough local consistency, to be able to have an evolutionary effect. They introduce the term *ecological inheritance.* Ecological inheritance is a modified environment influenced by organisms, their ancestors or other organism communities what has evolutionary effect and selection pressure to organisms. Genetic inheritance depends on the capacity of reproducing parent organisms to pass on replicas of their genes to their offspring. Ecological inheritance,

however, does not depend on the presence of any environmental replicators, but merely on the persistence, between generations, of whatever physical changes are caused by ancestral organisms in the local selective environments of their descendants. If organisms evolve in response to selection pressures modified by themselves and their ancestors, there is feedback in the system.

Magnani (2008), and Magnani and Bardone (2008) note that human and non-human animals "modify" or "create" affordances by manipulating their cognitive niches. This manipulation in social software systems takes place in the form of creating PLEs as cognitive personal learning environments constructed of various personally activated tools and system functions, networks of people and artifacts and interaction patterns, and interacting with PLEs in various knowledge building communities. In accordance with the ecological inheritance ideas, social software systems demonstrate similar interdependency between user-generated environmental influence and the development of user culture. The activities in social systems make them into the arenas of 'produsage' where learners' production and consumption cannot be separated from the surrounding environment (Bruns, 2008). The concept of 'produsage' as a term highlights the idea of embodied action, suggesting that within the communities, which engage in the collaborative creation and extension of information and knowledge, the role of consumer and even that of end user have long disappeared, and the distinctions between producers and users of content have faded into comparative insignificance. People actively participating in social web culture and technological systems form an ecological system.

It is generally accepted that learning, and tools used by certain culture from one side, and individuals of this culture and their learning and tool-using habits from another side, are influencing and shaping each other mutually (see Vygotsky, 1978). By definition, the more social software tools are used, the better they become adjusted to the cultural habits of their users. The more user-defined interrelations between the meanings exist and can be activated by social-software, the better the systems get for social retrieval of information. The more users' activities in social environments are externally marked by the users, for example with machine-readable formats describing people, the links between them, and the things they create and do, the better the access to the activity-related information and people becomes. The positive side effect of it is also, that the systems obtain new qualities for monitoring and getting awareness, that would open the gateway to the otherwise non-traceble communities in which the members are not personally related into social networks through shared activities. They may or may not have an awareness of each other, but they share similar meanings or perform same type of activities.

Access to such people in new environments is potentially opening a multi-dimensional place where individuals can learn from each other or where shared group activities can be initiated for learning purposes. The more people get involved into the similar activities, while evoking for themselves certain functions the social tools offer, the stronger the pressure gets of developing the systems towards facilitating this activity, and the more this activity becomes part of the learning culture in this environment. This presumes the ecological relationships between people and their objectives for action in certain learning environments, and the personally differentiated perception of meanings and tools in their surrounding environments. Such relations would alltogether dynamically shape the social software environments as places for learning.

An interesting aspect about ecological knowledge is its influence to the subsequent members of the community or other communities. Niches and their communities have interdependence and they cannot exist without each other. Besides this, some communities benefit from the niches of other communities, but these may not be existential for their wellbeing. Vandermeer (2008) explains that

if organisms construct their environments, there must be ecological consequences in addition to the evolutionary ones. He distinguishes between obligate and facultative organisms and niches, formulating assumptions how these organisms are influenced by niche construction: a) In an obligate constructive niche the organism dies in the absence of niche construction; b) In a facultative constructive niche the organism survives even in the absence of niche construction, nevertheless will benefit further from the construction, c) A facultative organism survives even in a non-constructive niche, but benefits further from the construction, and d) An obligate organism does not survive unless a constructed niche becomes available.

These assumptions can be transferred to the social web environments. For example: a) Wikis and microblogging environments can be considered obligate constructive niches, where single person without the community has very little benefit of the system; while b) Blogs or social bookmarking systems may be seen as facultative constructive niches, in which keeping individual diary or collecting bookmarks gives some additional value even without the community; c) A facultative user of web systems will not rely on its' activities on the niche construction of the other users; but d) An obligate web user has constructed its personal learning environment of community tools and services e.g. of 'pulling feeds', and cannot function effectively without this niche construction.

HOW ECOLOGIES ENABLE LEARNING AND KNOWLEDGE?

In this subchapter we try to elaborate some ideas how learning happens within ecologies. We can view niches as semiotic formations. Deeley (1990) defines semiosis as a process of applying signs to understand some phenomena, reasoning from sign to sign, and intervention of new signs to make sense of some new experiences. Processes of operating within the same or between different sign systems are characteristic to learning new things. The simplified way of interpreting semiotic processes is by claiming that there is a complete mutual translability between signs from different systems and all the information can be transformed from one system to another without any loss until new understanding of the phenomenon under investigation has reached learners' minds. As an improvement, Eco (2000) suggested that semiotic processes are more complex. He interpreted signs as not fixed semiotic entities but rather the meeting ground for independent elements coming from different planes and meeting on the basis of coding correlation.

Using semiotic model in knowldge ecology framework we rely heavily on the model created by Lotman (1990) of the semiosphere to explain cultural semiosis. His model depicts semiosis as a knowledge creation between cultural spaces on the basis of meanings. Similarly, Hoffmayer (1995, 1998) has proposed that semiotically determined niches are places where semiotic processes take place, and survival through semiosis implies a dynamic creativity. Lotman (1990) defined the conception of the semiosphere as a living space of dialogical events, in which the production of consciousness and meaning can only take place through contact with an 'Other'. He explained that during semiotic processes people always focus on those aspects of the sign systems, which are important to them. They systematize their perceptions into structured descriptions of the system, by this distinguishing also the elements that are perceived as belonging to out-of-system area or to other systems for them. Thus, a dynamic binary structure is formed in their minds that Lotman described as the semiosphere. Binary parts of semiotic spaces – common and align contexts – are connected by translation. Lotman (1990) assumed that separate sign systems do not have mutual semantic correspondence. He wrote that any cultural semiosphere and its text-generating mechanisms depend on otherness and its semiotic

input in order to forge appropriate conditions for semiotic enrichment and change. He assumed that the dynamic reconstruction of context, the alteration of meanings, and the construction of new information happen only in the communication between differences when the lack of fit between cultural 'languages' creates the conditions for translation. According to his theory, fixed elementary semiotic systems are abstractions. Instead, *semiosphere should be regarded as an initial unit where semiotic processes take place between inconsistent semiotic spaces that people create in their minds.*

Stecconi (2004) suggested that during semiosis the translator relies on his notion of similarity to find and generate intuitively equivalent relations between sign systems, using abduction to make certain elements of these systems that may not have similar meanings equivalent. By this, the dynamics of semiotic structures emerge from the involvement of the out-of-system elements to the system and the upstage of the system elements to the regions with less systematic nature.

Learning ecologies are similar to the semiosphere model. Niches support the formation of binary structures, the places where learners must apply different rule-systems and languages, and can yield knowledge or find new ways how to yield knowledge. Niches enable to translate between common and align contexts not only meaning-based, but also the affordances of different niches may be integrated temporarily into ones personal learning environment for performing certain actions. Magnani (2008) and Magnani and Bardone (2008) assume that affordances are the important determinants of cognitive niches created by humans. Thus we can consider that similarly to meaning-creation and semiosis also the action-related information is re-interpreted and translated in niches, creating new possibilities for enactment. Magnani and Bardone (2008) write that finding and constructing affordances refers to a (semiotic) inferential activity: we come up with affordance insofar as an object exhibits those signs from which we infer a possible way to interact with it and to perform suitable actions. This inferential process relies on various cognitive endowments, both instinctual and learnt, and occurs in the eco-cognitive interaction between environment and organisms.

The formation of the dynamic ecology for the learners depends on whether their personal learning environment evokes certain affordances from different niches enabling their interrelations with various communities, and if learners perceive and start using the interrelated binary structures manifested by these emerging affordances. For example Pata & Fiedler (2009) describe that learners perceive different affordances of the group environment while composing a shared learning environment from PLEs, and grounding of affordances as a necessary procedure. Secondly, integrating one new tool may restructure the whole set of affordances people perceive in concerns of other software in their PLE. The software use at different, non-familiar communities may in some cases attribute totally new affordances to the software that differ from the previous cultural use of this software. One example of how this translation of affordances has appeared may be taken from microblogging environments (Mackie, 2007).

THE CASE STUDY FROM FORMAL HIGHER EDUCATION

We illustrate the enlarged ecological framework of learning in social software systems with the case study from formal higher education conducted in Tallinn University.

In this study we demonstrate the methods of detecting ecological learning spaces of the communities that use social software. The results part demonstrates learning spaces of individual and collaborative learners who use social software, answering two research questions: What characterizes the learning spaces of individual and collaborative learners who use social software at

the formal higher education course? Which differences in the learning culture with social software do the learning spaces of individual and collaborative learners reveal? We discuss the results in the frames of using ecological framework.

Methods

Sample

The participants of the study were master students of Tallinn University, mainly from Institute of Informatics who participated in the course „Learning with social media". The two groups of students were involved in the development of the course design in two separate studies. In the first study, held in spring 2007, 25 second-year master students participated at the course. In the fall 2007, 28 first year master students participated at the course. The master students of the Tallinn University, Institute of Informatics originated from heterogeneous backgrounds – there were practicing schoolteachers of different subjects or informatics, educational technologists of different governmental and military institutions or private enterprisers. Thus, they all had needs for different competences and their contact with social media had been quite minimal so far. Due to the authentic settings of the study, convenient sampling was used. Thus the conclusions from this research must be regarded in the particular contextual setting. Two facilitators of the course were involved in research.

Course Settings

The first year the course was run aiming to develop primarily the learners' competencies of using Web 2.0 environments for planning learning landscapes and activity patterns, both for personal and collaborative use (see Väljataga, Pata, Tammets, in press). At the second year the structure of the course was changed, the new focus was on developing self-directed learning competences

Figure 2. Personal learning environment scheme of one student

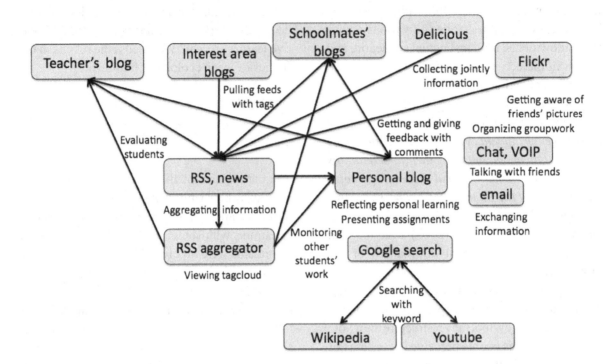

through individual and collaborative activities with Web 2.0 software (see Tammets, Väljataga & Pata, 2008). This meant mainly that the task of self-reflection on personal learning contracts in weblog was part of the learning tasks in addition to the previous tasks that were used at the first year of the course.

The general planning of the course was the following. Together with facilitators, the distributed learning environment of the course was created, which was used and developed during the course. Every student individually developed his or her personal distributed learning environment (see Figure 2) and described and tested it in action. In order to perform collaborative learning tasks, learners had to combine their personal learning environments, to conduct collaborative activities.

Course had three face-to-face contact days, meantime learners were asked to do independent work, either individually or in groups. At contact days, facilitators gave theoretical lectures and

modeled practical competences of using different social media tools and services for educational purposes. At the same time learners were expected to get practical experiences with different social media tools in order to plan their individual and collaborative learning environments and activities with those tools.

The distributed web-based learning environment of the course was conducted dynamically under learners' eyes with their active participation. Creating such joint learning environment together with learners, improved the learners' competencies of conceptualizing the affordances of the learning space similarly as the facilitator, and enabled the facilitator to make corrections in the learning environment in accordance with the learners' perception of affordances. Students could see, that their role was equal to the facilitator, and monitor how each member was contributing to the development of the distributed learning environment of the course.

The central feedback and learning material service of the course was a blog at Wordpress.com provider, which was maintained by two facilitators. The primary function of the blog was organizing learning materials and assignments, it also served as the feedback channel between learners and facilitators. The second part of web-based distributed learning course environment was the social bookmarking service Delicious (http://delicious.com/mii7008), where facilitators collected bookmarks of the materials related to the course. The Slideshare.net tool and Splashcast were used to present slideshows, which were also embedded to learning materials at the course blog. The third central tool of the course was a shared aggregator in Pageflakes.com provider (http://www.pageflakes.com/kpata/12983138). This aggregator enabled to integrate different distributed course tools, using feed and mashup technologies. The course aggregator collected into the shared place the feeds from course weblog and learners' weblogs enabling the monitoring between learners themselves and between facilitators and learners (Väljataga, Pata & Tammets, 2008). The tagcloud feed from the course bookmarks and the mashed feed from social bookmarks accounts were pulled to the aggregator.

The students' distributed learning environments consisted of weblog, social bookmarking service and Slideshare accounts, web-based office software, wiki, instant messaging services, and aggregators. Individual weblog was a compulsory tool for each student. Using Delicious for bookmarking was required. The rest of the tools were not optional. Some students used very actively wiki, some web-based office service, Flickr and Youtube social repositories. That kind of usage of tools and services supported personalized mediation of self-directed learning. Every learner made the choice of most suitable tools for her/him. Learners had chance to decide what is useful for them and they used only those tools, but not the services, that teacher has thought might be the most suitable. The shared learning environments of the groups were developed as part of the course

assignments. In general individual weblogs, collaborative writing/drawing environments like wiki, google.docs, Vyew.com or bubble.us, and instant messaging services like Gabbly.com, MSN and Skype.com were used, but the landscapes differed from each other. The case, where learners teamed up themselves, then selected tools what they need in order to complete assignments gave them competence, how to plan the group work, select the tools, which are suitable to everyone, how to organize the communication between team members and how to divide the responsibility. In other words, the assignment developed their competencies, which are required in their professional life.

Data Collection and Analysis

Learners were expected to draw visual schemas of individual and collaborative learning environments and activity diagrams, write an essay, and fill in a questionnaire as assignments. Schemas of personal and shared distributed learning environments and activity diagrams were collected from learners' blogs. Essays and schemes from learners' blogs were used as research instruments in the design-based research process. In that kind of authentic settings it was important to use those data gathering instruments in order to get the ideas of learners' ideas and perceptions of learning affordances without intervention. Thus, the same data-collection instruments served as a natural part of learners' assignments supporting their competence development.

For the data analysis the visual and narrative data collected from the course was used. The students composed personal learning environments from Web 2.0 tools and described these composing learning landscape schemes. They also draw activity patterns to describe activities at their personal learning landscapes. Several of the landscape and activity pattern descriptions were composed for collaborative groups. Each figure was accompanied by narrative descriptions mentioning several learning affordances in relation with the tools the student(s) used for activities and for constructing distributed learning landscapes.

For the study two researchers analyzed from schemata and narratives, what kind of tools consisted learners' distributed learning environments, and what kind of tools they used for planning individual activities. It was investigated, what kind of tools were perceived useful for individual and collaborative learning. It was studied, which learning affordances the students perceived in relation to every tool in their learning environment in individual and collaborative cases. Each affordance was listed only once in relation to mentioning it with the certain tool. The differences between two researchers' categorization were resolved after comparison and discussions.

The analysis of 63 activity- and learning landscape descriptions was conducted. From the figures and from the narratives the learning affordances were collected and categorized. The categorization scheme separated each affordance according to its belonging to individual or collaborative learning activity. The relationship of the learning affordance with the tool(s) was categorized using binary system. The main tool categories were: blog, wiki, chat tools (MSN, Skype, Gabbly), email, search engines, RSS aggregator, social bookmarking tools, forums, co-writing tools (e.g. Zoho or Google Documents), co-drawing tools (e.g. Vyew, Gliffy), and social repositories of Flickr and Youtube. These were selected because these tools were mostly in use by the students during the course and they also appeared at their schemes frequently. These data reflect specifically the learning affordance perception of the students of the course (beginner users of Web 2.0 tools), and cannot be broadened to the perception of learning affordances of the active Web 2.0 users in various settings.

Analytically, conducting ANOVA, Cross tabulation, and Chi square analysis with SPSS 16.0 were used as methods to show if there was a difference in the distribution of learning affordances at individual and collaborative cases. The learning affordances were categorized into specific types representing similar affordances: assembling, managing, creating, reading, presenting, changing and adding, collaborating and communicating, sharing, exchanging, searching, filtering and mashing, collecting, storing, tagging, reflecting and argumenting, monitoring, giving tasks and supporting, asking and giving-getting feedback, and evaluating. These types were deduced from the main verbs the students tended to use in their learning affordance descriptions. Cross tabulation was performed to demonstrate learning niches. The frequency of learning affordance categories was found for each tool both in case of individual and collaborative activities. Each learning affordance e.g. searching was considered as a variable defining the niche. Niches have been defined as the collections of environmental gradients with certain ecological amplitude, where the ecological optimum marks the gradient peaks where the organisms are most abundant. In all activity/landscape descriptions the optimum for certain learning affordance category was calculated dividing the frequency of this affordance per certain tool to the total frequency of certain learning affordance category for all tools. The results were plotted on the maps with MS Excel.

Results

What characterizes the learning spaces of individual and collaborative learners who use social software at the formal higher education course?

Table 1 presents the results of ANOVA analysis demonstrating that there were no significant differences between the frequency of tool use in case of how students planned their individual and collaborative diagrams of activities and learning landscapes (see Table 1). The number of affordances, mentioned in case of the tools in individual and collaborative settings did not differ. Thus, viewing only the tool use is not distinguishing two types of activities.

Table 1. ANOVA analysis of the distribution of learning affordances between tools at individual and collaborative learning situation descriptions

Tools	Activity	N	df	Mean square	F	Sig
blog	I	151	1	0.001	0.001	0.99
	C	143		0.247		
wiki	I	18	1	0.076	1.29	0.25
	C	24		0.059		
chat	I	27	1	0.285	3.20	0.07
	C	39		0.089		
bookmarks	I	49	1	0.001	0.002	0.96
	C	46		0.123		
aggregator	I	61	1	0.165	1.05	0.30
	C	68		0.156		
email	I	21	1	0.015	0.24	0.61
	C	23		0.062		
search engine	I	33	1	0.084	1.06	0.30
	C	24		0.078		
co-writing	I	30	1	0.047	0.63	0.42
	C	23		0.073		
forum	I	10	1	0.003	0.13	0.71
	C	8		0.026		
co-drawing	I	11	1	0.033	0.88	0.34
	C	15		0.038		
flickr	I	14	1	0.008	0.22	0.63
	C	11		0.036		
youtube	I	24	1	0.099	1.70	0.19
	C	17		0.058		

**p<0.001 *p<0.01 I – Individual activity C – Collaborative activity

Next, it was investigated, if learners perceive the learning affordances of individual and collaborative activities differently. ANOVA (see Table 2) and Chi Square analysis indicated that differencies between individual and collaborative descriptions were significant for collaborating and communicating (χ^2=2.062, df=2, p<0.001), sharing (χ^2=7.028, df=2, p=0.030) and tagging (χ^2=9.008, df=2, p=0.01) affordances. Collaborative activity niche involved significantly more affordances of 'collaborating and communicating', and 'sharing', while 'tagging' was the only specific affordance type descriptor, distinguishing the individual activity niches. Affordances of 'giving tasks and supporting' were more frequent in case of collaborative activity niches.

Comparison of the differencies of individual and collaborative activities in Table 1 and 2 enabled to assume that two distinct learning niches were found comparing the means of affordance use, but not on the basis of tool usage differences.

Which differences in the learning culture with social software do the learning spaces of individual and collaborative learners reveal?

Table 2. ANOVA analysis of the distribution of learning affordance types in individual and collaborative descriptions

Affordance types	Description	N	df	Means square	F	Sig
assembling	I	41	2	0.203	1.629	0.19
	C	55		0.124		
managing	I	10	2	0.013	0.440	0.64
	C	9		0.029		
creating	I	41	2	0.152	1.613	0.20
	C	27		0.094		
reading	I	14	2	0.027	0.797	0.45
	C	9		0.033		
presenting	I	34	2	0.048	0.468	0.62
	C	41		0.103		
changing and adding	I	20	2	0.051	0.909	0.40
	C	18		0.057		
collaborating and commu-nicating	I	34	2	1.391	10.594	0.001**
	C	73		0.131		
sharing	I	10	2	0.180	3.536	0.03
	C	25		0.051		
exchanging	I	5	2	0.010	0.521	0.59
	C	8		0.019		
searching	I	29	2	0.054	0.714	0.49
	C	26		0.076		
filtering and mashing	I	42	2	0.186	1.932	0.14
	C	30		0.096		
collecting	I	14	2	0.021	0.593	0.55
	C	10		0.035		
storing	I	21	2	0.055	1.104	0.33
	C	14		0.050		
tagging	I	19	2	0.156	4.545	0.01*
	C	5		0.034		
argumenting and reflecting	I	30	2	0.132	1.666	0.19
	C	25		0.079		
monitoring	I	11	2	0.069	1.502	0.22
	C	20		0.046		
give tasks supporting	I	24	2	0.266	2.951	0.053
	C	42		0.090		
asking giving and getting feedback	I	36	2	0.186	2.305	0.10
	C	21		0.081		
evaluating	I	12	2	0.082	1.903	0.15
	C	16		0.043		

**p<0.001 *p<0.01 I – Individual description C – Collaborative description

Figure 3 demonstrates the learning niches of individual and collaborative activities, calculated on the basis of Cross-tabulation of affordances with tools. The figure shows the map of isoclines indicating the gradient of each affordance type in case of using particular set of tools. This map-like niche landscape shows the areas where certain affordances were perceived in relation with using specific social software tools. It was found that collaborative activity niche was different from the individual activity niche by the following characteristics:

Blog (e.g. Wordpress, Blogger) had similar affordances in individual and collaborative learning activities e.g. assembling, managing, presenting, reading, changing and adding, collaborating and communicating, storing, reflecting and argumenting, monitoring, asking and getting feedback and giving tasks, and supporting and evaluating. The exception in this pattern was the fact that in the

collaborative activity niche blog was seen useful for the tagging, filtering and mashing, and collecting information.

Wiki (e.g. PBWiki, Wikispaces) was used seldom at the course, thus, wiki-related affordances do not show up on individual and collaborative niches. These students had no experience with using a wiki tool.

Chat tools (e.g. MSN, Gabbly, Skype) were perceived useful for managing and exchanging in collaborative activity niche, while in individual activity niche chat was attributed the affordance of collaborating and communicating. This indicates that in the collaborative setting the need for managing the learning-related issues is a necessary part of learning culture and this socially defined need would activate the perception of this type of affordances in relation to chat tool.

Social bookmarking tool (e.g. Delicious) was perceived obtaining the filtering and collect-

Figure 3. Niche maps for individual and collaborative activities (the importance of certain tool type among other tools in evoking some specific affordance is presented as isoclines using the scale between 0-100%).

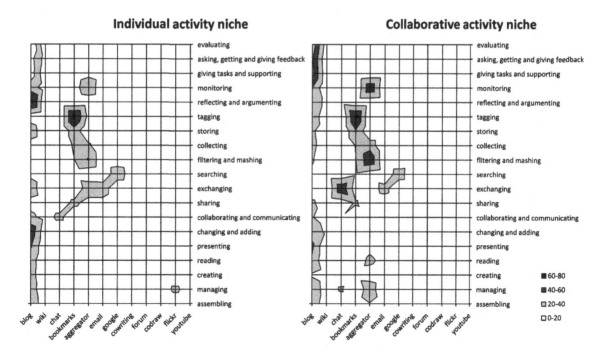

ing, sharing and searching affordances in both individual and collaborative activity niches. It was supposed that students of the course did not learn to use the whole range of social bookmarking functionalities, thus affordances that indicate group use activities like collaborating, changing and adding, and exchanging were not part of collaborative activity patterns and landscapes.

The affordances of filtering and collecting and monitoring with the aggregator (e.g. Netvibes) were common to both niches. Aggregator was seen useful for managing, assembling and reading in the collaborative activity niche, while in the individual activity niche it obtained also the role of sharing and exchanging. These results were unexpected and indicate that there is a certain other-directed aim in individual activities with social media. Learning from the others seems to be already part of the individual learning culture. The attribution of managing affordances to the aggregator in collaborative settings indicates that groups perceive the need to organize their learning with PLEs, assembling them with the aggregators.

Email was perceived useful of sharing and exchanging in the individual activity niche, while in the collaborative niche only the exchanging affordance remained important. Thus it is possible to assume, that students perceived some difference between these seemingly close types of affordances.

The search engines (e.g. Google) had the same role of searching in both individual and collaborative activity niches. Other tools for co-drawing (whiteboard tools), co-writing (e.g. Google.docs), and social repositories (e.g. Flickr, Youtube) were mentioned with lower frequency, and therefore they did not appear at the maps of the individual and collaborative learning niches.

Presenting the differences of individual and collaborative activities according to the tool-use, affordance selection and niche theory we could demonstrate that the last method was most effective in revealing considerable differences between two types of activities from the learners' perspective.

DISCUSSION

In this paper we have proposed a framework explaining the bottom-up social determination of learning niches within the knowledge ecologies using the affordances as niche gradients. In the limited space of this chapter we do not provide evidence to all elements of this framework. The empirical case demonstrates the formation of two partially overlapping niches for individual and collaborative activities using the dataset collected from the course of self-directed learning with social media.

We have analysed the students' understanding of their activity-patterns within social software environments using three different methods: comparing the frequence of mentioning certain tools, comparing the frequence of mentioning certain affordance dimensions, and plotting the affordances as niche gradients on tool landscape. Three general findings were: i) The frequency of use of social software was not different in individual and collaborative activities. ii) The frequency of use of some affordance dimensions was different in individual and collaborative activities, but many affordances appeared with similar frequency in both activities. iii) The comparison of individual and collaborative niche landscapes demonstrated that these niches differed on the basis of niche gradients – some tools appeared to be more frequently selected compared with other tools in relation to certain affordances.

The following assumptions could be made:

i)   When learning with social software people use same tools for individual and collaborative activities. The tools in personal learning environments are switched to the distributed learning environments for collaboration and vice versa, collaborative tools are used for organising individual learning. Thus, merely the tool use frequency would not distinguish the learning cultures related to individual or collaborative assignments.

ii) However, students evoked different learning affordances in relation to these tools in the individual and collaborative settings. This suggests that different objectives of individual and collaborative assignments might actualize different sets of affordances within learning ecologies. There seems to be an overlap of what types of affordances would be actualized in indvidual and collaborative learning activities with social software. We can assume that same types of affordances are in general useful nevertheless if learning at individual or collaborative settings with social software. This indicates also, that the paradigm of learning with social media is other-directed and entails various aspects of benefitting from the ideas of others', and sharing knowledge with other people both in individual and collaborative learning modes.

iii) The activity setting (individual or collaborative) has influence on how learners would activate certain sets of affordances in relation to certain social software. It suggests that different objectives might enable learners to actualize and integrate into their action plans different action perspectives rising from the use of the learning environment. This supports the idea that affordances are by nature emergent aspects in the learning situations.

Currently, there are few sufficient automatic ways of collecting learners' action relevant information when people use social software. The user modelling approaches are only appearing at the frontlines of scientific conferences and yet the meaning-based user-modelling techniques prevail (e.g. using personal information and tags) (see Carmagnola, Cena & Gena, 2008). However,

if action-relevant information was available for individuals and communities, it would enable to predict and control the learning niches dynamically in the course of action. Secondly, the niche visualization and exploration aspects are important if people want to use niches more effectively in the learning design. In this paper we have used a simple method of plotting the niche gradients in two-dimensional space. The affordance data were collected in the active design sessions where learners had to visualize their learning landscapes and activity patterns. For learners this activity proved to be a useful method for gaining control of their learning, yet, a lot of manual work was needed to demonstrate the niches. Thus, better tools are needed that enable to collect this learning landscape and activity pattern information from learners' personal learning environments or from group environments. One tool prototype for determining the learning affordances in respect to social software tools has been developed to plan the affordances and explore the niches (Väljataga, Pata, Laanpere & Kaipainen, 2007). Another interesting approach has been taken in a new type of mashup tool Mupple prototype for constructing PLEs, which enables users to collect their activity-related data in the phase of planning (Mödritscher, Wild & Sigurdarson, 2008). It is predicted that in the forthcoming years the tracing of activity-patterns in social software environments will undergo a rapid development and it would gain an equal position in the theoretical and practical solutions that support learning in social communities.

CONCLUSION

In this paper we have demonstrated that niche conception might add the missing link between knowledge network and knowledge ecology levels in the Connectivist framework. Data from the empirical case study indicated that exploration of learning niches might give useful information for evaluating learners' perspectives to certain learning approaches. Accordingly, the niche monitoring and evaluation can be used in planning and facilitating learning and the community identity formation according to the ecological principles.

ACKNOWLEDGMENT

This study was funded by Estonian SF grant 7663 and MER targeted research 0130159s08. Anatole Pierre Fuksas from Università degli Studi di Cassino, Kairit Tammets and Terje Väljataga from Tallinn University are acknowledged for triggering the fruitful discussions around the ideas of this paper, and participating in the study.

REFERENCES

Attwell, G. (2007). Personal learning environments-the future of e-learning? *E-Learning Papers, 2*. Retrieved from http://www.elearningpapers.eu/index.php?page=doc&doc_id=8553&doclng=6

Barab, S. A., & Roth, W.-M. (2006). Intentionally-bound systems and curricular-based ecosystems: An ecological perspective on knowing. *Educational Researcher, 35*(5), 3–13. doi:10.3102/0013189X035005003

Bereiter, C. (2002). *Education and mind in the knowledge age*. Mahwah, NJ: Lawrence Erlbaum Associates.

Brown, J. S. (1999, 2002). *Learning, working, and playing in the digital age*. Retrieved from http://serendip.brynmawr.edu/sci_edu/seelybrown/seelybrown.html

Bruns, A. (2008). *Blogs, Wikipedia, Second Life, and Beyond: From production to produsage*. New York: Peter Lang.

Carmagnola, F., Cena, F., & Gena, C. (2008). User modeling in the social Web. In *Knowledge-based intelligent information and engineering systems* (pp. 745-752). 11th International Conference, KES 2007, XVII Italian Workshop on Neural Networks, Vietri sul Mare, Italy, September 12-14, 2007, Proceedings, Part III. (LNCS 4694). Springer Berlin/Heidelberg.

Chemero, A. (2003). An outline of a theory of affordances. *Ecological Psychology, 15*(2), 181–195. doi:10.1207/S15326969ECO1502_5

Davenport, T. H., & Prusak, L. (1997). *Information ecology: Mastering the information and knowledge environment*. New York: Oxford University Press.

Deeley, J. (1990). *Basics of semiotics*. Bloomington: Indiana University Press.

Downes, S. (2005). *An introduction to connective knowledge*. Retrieved from http://www.downes.ca/cgi-bin/page.cgi?post=33034

Eco, U. (2000). *Experiences in translation*. Toronto: Toronto U.P.

Fiedler, S., & Pata, K. (2009). Distributed learning environments and social software: In search for a framework of design. In S. Hatzipanagos & S. Warburton (Eds.), *Handbook of research on social software and developing community ontologies* (pp. 151-164). Hershey, PA: IGI Global.

Gallese, V., Fadiga, L., Fogassi, L., & Rizzolatti, G. (1996). Action recognition in the premotor cortex. *Brain, 119*, 593–609. doi:10.1093/brain/119.2.593

Gallese, V., & Freedberg, D. (2007). Mirror and canonical neurons are crucial elements in esthetic response. *Trends in Cognitive Sciences, 11*, 411. doi:10.1016/j.tics.2007.07.006

Gallese, V., & Lakoff, G. (2005). The brain's concepts: The role of the sensory-motor system in reason and language. *Cognitive Neuropsychology, 22*, 455–479. doi:10.1080/02643290442000310

Gaver, W. W. (1996). Affordances for interaction: The social is material for design. *Ecological Psychology, 8*(2), 111–129. Retrieved from http://www.cs.ubc.ca/labs/spin/publications/related/gaver96.pdf

Gibson, J. J. (1979). *The ecological approach to visual perception*. Boston: Houghton Mifflin.

Heft, H. (2001). *Ecological psychology in context. James Gibson, Roger Baker, and the legacy of William James's radical empiricism*. Lawrence Erlbaum Associates, Publishers.

Hoffmeyer, J. (1995, June). *The global semiosphere*. Paper presented at the 5ᵗʰ IASS Congress in Berkeley. In I. Rauch & G. F. Carr (Eds.), *Semiotics around the world. Proceedings of the Fifth Congress of the International Association for Semiotic Studies* (pp. 933-936), Berkeley 1994. Berlin/New York: Mouton de Gruyter 1997.

Hoffmeyer, J. (1998). The unfolding semiosphere. In G. Van de Vijver, S. Salthe & M. Delpos (Eds.), *Evolutionary systems. Biological and epistemological perspectives on selection and self-organization* (pp. 281-293). Dordrecht: Kluwer.

Hommel, B. (2003). Planning and representing intentional action. *TheScientificWorldJournal, 3*, 593–608. doi:10.1100/tsw.2003.46

Hutchinson, G. E. (1957). Concluding remarks. *Cold Spring Harbor Symposia on Quantitative Biology, 22*, 145–159.

Iaccoboni, M. (2005). Understanding others: Imitation, language, empathy. In S. Hurley & N. Chater, (Eds.), *Perspectives on imitation: From mirror neurons to memes, volume 1. Mechanisms of imitation and imitation in animals*. MIT Press.

Klamma, R., Spaniol, M., Cao, Y., & Jarke, M. (2006). Pattern-based cross media social network analysis for technology enhanced learning in Europe. In W. Nejdl & K. Tochtermann (Eds.), *Innovative approaches to learning and knowledge sharing, Proceedings of the 1ˢᵗ European Conference on Technology Enhanced Learning (EC-TEL 2006)*, Hersonissou, Greece, October 1-3. (LNCS 4227, pp. 242–256). Springer-Verlag.

Kumar, R., Novak, J., & Tomkins, A. (2006). Structure and evolution of online social networks. In *Proceedings of the 12ᵗʰ ACM SIGKDD International Conference on Knowledge Discovery and Data Mining Table of Contents* (pp. 611–617). Philadelphia, PA.

Lin, Y.-R., Sundaram, H., Chi, Y., Tatemura, J., & Tseng, B. (2006). Discovery of blog communities based on mutual awareness. In *Proceedings of the 3ʳᵈ Annual Workshop on the Webblogging Ecosystem: Aggregation, Analysis and Dynamics*. Retrieved from http://www.blogpulse.com/www2006-workshop/papers/wwe2006-discovery-lin-final.pdf

Llor`a. X., Imafuji, N., Welge, Y. M., & Goldberg, D. E. (2006). *Human-centered analysis and visualization tools for the blogosphere*. (Illinois Tech. Rep. No. 2006023). Retrieved from http://www-discus.ge.uiuc.edu/discussite/2006/11/29/human-centered-analysis-and-visualization-tools-for-the-blogosphere/

Lotman, Y. (1990). *Universe of the mind: A semiotic theory of culture*. (ed. & trans. by A. Shukman). Bloomington, IN: Indiana University Press.

Mackie, K. (2007). *A brief history of microblogging*. Retrieved from http://www.blogschmog.net/2007/11/17/a-brief-history-of-microblogging/

Magnani, L. (2008). Chances, affordances, niche construction. In *Proceedings of the 12th International Conference on Knowledge-based Intelligent Information and Engineering Systems* (LNAI 5178, pp. 719-726).

Magnani, L., & Bardone, E. (2008). Sharing representations and creating chances through cognitive niche construction. The role of affordances and abduction. In S. Iwata, Y. Ohsawa, S. Tsumoto, N. Zhong, Y. Shi & L. Magnani (Eds.), *Communications and discoveries from multidisciplinary data* (pp.3-40). New York/Berlin: Springer.

Michaels, C. F. (2003). Affordances: Four points of debate. *Ecological Psychology, 15*(2), 135–148. doi:10.1207/S15326969ECO1502_3

Mödritscher, F., Wild, F., & Sigurdarson, S. (2008). *Language design for a personal learning environment design language. E-learning.* Retrieved on July 9, 2008, from http://www.elearningeuropa. info/files/media/media15972.pdf

Müller, F. (1998). Gradients in ecological systems. *Ecological Modelling, 108*(1–3), 3–21. doi:10.1016/S0304-3800(98)00015-5

Norman, D. A. (1988). *The design of everyday things*. New York: Basic Books.

Odling-Smee, F. J., Laland, K. N., & Feldman, M. W. (2003). Niche construction: The neglected process in evolution. *Monographs in Population Biology, 37*. Princeton University Press.

Pecher, D., & Zwaan, R. A. (2005). *Grounding cognition: The role of perception and action in memory, language, and thinking.* Cambridge University Press.

Pór, G., & Molloy, J. (2000). Nurturing systemic wisdom through knowledge ecology. *The Systems Thinker, 11*(8). Retrieved from http://www.co-i-l. com/coil/knowledge-garden/kd/KE.pdf

Pór, G., & Spivak, J. (2000, May 23-24). *The ecology of knowledge: A field theory and practice, key to research, & technology development.* Paper presented at the Consultation Meeting on the Future of Organisations and Knowledge Management of the European Commission's Directorate-General Information Society Technologies, Brussels. Retrieved from http://www.co-i-l.com/coil/knowledge-garden/kd/eoknowledge.shtml

Rizzolatti, G., & Arbib, M. A. (1998). Language within our grasp. *Trends in Neurosciences, 21*(5), 188–194. doi:10.1016/S0166-2236(98)01260-0

Rizzolatti, G., Fogassi, L., & Gallese, V. (2001). Neurophysiological mechanisms underlying the understanding and imitation of action. *Nature Reviews. Neuroscience, 2*, 661–670. doi:10.1038/35090060

Scorolli, C., & Borghi, A. (2007). Sentence comprehension and action: Effect or specific modulation of the motor system. *Brain Research, 1130*, 119–124. doi:10.1016/j.brainres.2006.10.033

Siemens, G. (2005). *Connectivism: A learning theory for digital age.* Retrieved from http://www.elearnspace.org/Articles/connectivism.htm

Siemens, G. (2006). *Knowing knowledge.* Retrieved from http://www.knowingknowledge.com/2006/10/knowing_knowledge_pdf_files.php

Stecconi, U. (2004). Interpretive semiotics and translation theory: The semiotic conditions to translation. *Semiotica, 150*(1/4), 471–489. doi:10.1515/semi.2004.056

Tammets, K., Väljataga, T., & Pata, K. (2008, June 30-July 4). Self-directing at social spaces: Conceptual framework for course design. In *Proceedings of ED-MEDIA 2008-World Conference on Educational Multimedia, Hypermedia, & Telecommunications* (pp. 6337–6342), Vienna, Austria. Vienna: Association for the Advancement of Computing in Education (AACE).

Underwood, J., & Banyard, P. E. (2008). Understanding the learning space. *eLearning papers, 9*. Retrieved from http://www.elearningpapers.eu/index.php?page=doc&doc_id=11937&doclng=6

Väljataga, T., Pata, K., Laanpere, M., & Kaipainen, M. (2007). Theoretical framework of the iCamp-Folio-new approach to evaluation and comparison of systems and tools for learning purposes. In E. Duval, R. Klamma, & M. Wolpers (Eds.), *Creating new learning experiences on a global scale* (pp. 349-363). Berlin/Heidelberg.

Väljataga, T., Pata, K., & Tammets, K. (forthcoming). Considering learners' perspectives to personal learning environments in course design. In M. J. W. Lee & C. McLoughlin (Eds.), *Web 2.0-based e-learning: Applying social informatics for tertiary teaching*. Hershey, PA: IGI Global.

Vandermeer, J. (2008). The niche construction paradigm in ecological time. *Ecological Modelling, 214*, 385–390. doi:10.1016/j.ecolmodel.2008.03.009

Varela, F. J., Thompson, E., & Rosch, E. (1991). *The embodied mind*. Cambridge, MA: MIT Press.

Vyas, D., & Dix, A. (2007, September 16). Artefact ecologies: Supporting embodied meeting practices with distance access. In *Proceedings of UbiComp (Ubiquitous Computing) 2007 Workshops, Innsbruck, Austria* (pp. 117–122). University of Innsbruck.

Vygotsky, L. S. (1978). *Mind in society*. Cambridge: Harvard University Press.

Wright, S. (1931). The roles of mutation, inbreeding, cross-breeding, and selection in evolution. In *Proceedings of the Sixth International Congress of Genetics, 1*, 356–366.

Zhang, J., & Patel, V. L. (2006). Distributed cognition, representation, and affordance. *Cognition &Pragmatics, 14*(2), 333–341. doi:10.1075/pc.14.2.12zha

268

Compilation of References

37signals. (n. d.). *Collaborative writing software online with writeboard, write, share, revise, compare.* Retrieved on December 4, 2008, from http://www.writeboard.com/

Abbeduto, L., Short-Meyerson, K., Benson, G., & Dolish, J. (2004). Relationship between theory of mind and language ability in children and adolescents with intellectual disability. *Journal of Intellectual Disability Research, 48*(2), 150–159. doi:10.1111/j.1365-2788.2004.00524.x

Abram, S. (2005). Web 2.0—huh? Library 2.0, librarian 2.0. *Information Outlook, 9*(12), 44–46.

Abrami, P. C., & Barrett, H. (Eds.). (2005). Electronic portfolios [special issue]. *Canadian Journal of Learning Technology, 31*(3).

Adams, R. B., & Kleck, R. E. (2005). Effects of direct and averted gaze on the perception of facially communicated emotion. *Emotions, 5*(1), 3–11. doi:10.1037/1528-3542.5.1.3

Adams, R., B., & Kleck, R. E. (2003). Perceived gaze direction and the processing of facial displays of emotion. *Psychological Science, 14*(6), 644–647. doi:10.1046/j.0956-7976.2003.psci_1479.x

Adell, J. (2003). *Internet en el aula: A la caza del tesoro* [online]. *Edutec, Revista Electrónica de Tecnología Educativa, 16.* Retrieved from http://edutec.rediris.es/Revelec2/revelec16/adell.htm

Adell, J., & Sales, A. (1999). *El profesor online: Elementos para la definición de un nuevo rol docente* [en línia]. Retrieved on November 16, 2005, from http://tecnologiaedu.us.es/edutec/paginas/105.html

Advanced Video Communications, Inc. (2008). *Stickam—the live community, live streaming video.* Retrieved on December 3, 2008, from http://www.stickam.com/

Affordance. (2008). In *Wikipedia, the free encyclopedia.* Retrieved on December 4, 2008, from http://en.wikipedia.org/wiki/Affordance

Aggarwal, A. (2003). *Web-based education: Learning from experience.* Hershey, PA: IGI Global.

Ahern, S., Eckles, D., Good, N. S., King, S., Naaman, M., & Nair, R. (2007). Over-exposed? Privacy patterns and considerations in online and mobile photo sharing. *Proceedings of the SIGCHI Conference on Human Factors in Computing Systems.* San Jose, CA: ACM.

Ajjan, H., & Hartshorne, R. (2008). Investigating faculty decisions to adopt Web 2.0 technologies: Theory and empirical tests. *The Internet and Higher Education, 11*(2), 71–80. doi:10.1016/j.iheduc.2008.05.002

Alexander, B. (2006). Web 2.0: A new wave of innovation for teaching and learning? *EDUCAUSE Review, 41*(2), 32–44.

Alexander, B. (2006). Web 2.0: A new wave of innovation for teaching and learning? *Educause Review.*

Allee, V. (2000). Knowledge networks and communities of practice. *OD Practitioner . Journal of the Organizational Development Network, 32*(4).

Allen, C. (2004). *Tracing the evolution of social software.* Retrieved on June 4, 2007, from http://www.lifewithalacrity.com/2004/10/tracing_the_evo.html

Allen, S., Ure, D., & Evans, S. (2003). *Virtual communities of practice as learning networks*. Provo, UT: Brigham Young University Instructional Psychology and Technology.

Álvarez, I., Ayuste, A., Gros, B., Guerra, V., & Romañá, T. (2005). Construir conocimiento con soporte tecnológico para un aprendizaje colaborativo [en línia]. *Revista Iberoamericana de Educación* (ISSN: 1681-5653). Retrieved on April 2, 2006, from http://www.rieoei.org/deloslectores/1058alvarez.pdf

Anderson, C. (2007). *The long tail: How endless choice is creating unlimited demand*. London: Random House.

Anderson, J. (1995). Cybarites, knowledge workers and the new Creoles on the superhighway. *Anthropology Today, 11*(4), 13–15.

Anderson, P. (2007). What is Web 2.0? Ideas, technologies, and implications for education. *JISC, Technology & Standards Watch*. Retrieved on August 14, 2008, from http://www.jisc.ac.uk/media/documents/techwatch/tsw0701b.pdf

Anderson, T. (2007, June). Book review–control and constraint in e-learning: Choosing when to choose. *International Review of Research in Open and Distance Learning, 8*(2), 1–3.

Anderson, T., & Elloumi, F. (Eds.). (2004). *Theory and practice of online learning*. Canada: Athabasca University.

Andrade, H., & Du, Y. (2005). Student perspectives on rubric-referenced assessment. *Practical Assessment, Research, and Evaluation, 10*(3). Retrieved on October 9, 2008, from http://pareonline.net/pdf/v10n3.pdf

Ardichvili, A., Page, V., & Wentling, T. (2003). Motivation and barriers to participation in virtual knowledge sharing teams. *Journal of Knowledge Management, 7*(1), 64–77. doi:10.1108/13673270310463626

Arhar, J. M., Holly, M. L., & Kasten, W. C. (2001). *Action research for teachers: Travelling the yellow brick road*. Upper Saddle River, NJ: Merrill Prentice Hall.

Artigue, M. (2002). Learning mathematics in a CAS environment: The genesis of a reflection about instrumentation and the dialectics between technical and conceptual work. *International Journal of Computers for Mathematical Learning, 7*(3), 245–274. doi:10.1023/A:1022103903080

Artigue, M. (2004). Problemas y desafíos en educación matemática:¿qué nos ofrece hoy la didáctica de la matemática para afrontarlos? *Educación Matemática, 16*(3), 5–28.

Assor, A., Kaplan, H., & Roth, G. (2002). Choice is good, but relevance is excellent: Autonomy-enhancing and suppressing teacher behaviors predicting students' engagement in schoolwork. *The British Journal of Educational Psychology, 72*(2), 261–278. doi:10.1348/000709902158883

Atherton, J. S. (2002). *Learning and teaching: Learning from experience* [online]. Retrieved on September 26, 2004, from the http://www.dmu.ac.uk/~jamesa/learning/experien.htm

Attwell, G. (2007). Personal learning environments-the future of e-learning? *E-Learning Papers, 2*. Retrieved from http://www.elearningpapers.eu/index.php?page=doc&doc_id=8553&doclng=6

Atwell, G. (2007). E-portfolio: The DNA of the personal learning environment? *Journal of E-Learning and Knowledge Society*.

Azcárate, C., et al. (1996). *Cálculo diferencial e integral*. Madrid, España: Editorial Síntesis, S.A.

Azevedo, R. (2005). Computers environments as metacognitive tools for enhancing learning. [Special Issue on Computers as Metacognitive Tools for Enhancing Student Learning]. *Educational Psychologist, 40*(4), 193–197. doi:10.1207/s15326985ep4004_1

Baggetun, R. (2006). Emergent Web practices and new educational opportunities [online]. *TELOS, Cuadernos de Comunicación e Innovación, 67*. Retrieved from http://www.campusred.net/telos/articulocuaderno.asp?idarticulo=9&rev=67

Bandura, A. (1997). *Self-efficacy: The exercise of control*. New York: W.H. Freeman.

Bandura, A. (1997). *Social learning theory.* Englewood Cliffs, NJ: Prentice Hall.

Bandura, A. (2001). Social cognitive theory: An agentic perspective. *Annual Review of Psychology, 52*(1), 1–26. doi:10.1146/annurev.psych.52.1.1

Barab, S. A., & Roth, W.-M. (2006). Intentionally-bound systems and curricular-based ecosystems: An ecological perspective on knowing. *Educational Researcher, 35*(5), 3–13. doi:10.3102/0013189X035005003

Barberà, E. (2006). Aportaciones de la tecnología a la e-evaluación. *RED Revista de Educación a Distancia, monographic number VI.* Retrieved on January 15, 2009, from http://www.um.es/ead/red/M6

Barker, P. (2002). On being an online tutor. *Innovations in Education and Teaching International, 39*(1), 3–13. doi:10.1080/13558000110097082

Bauman, Z. (2000). *Liquid modernity.* Cambridge, MA: Polity Press.

Beldarrain, Y. (2006). Distance education trends: Integrating new technologies to foster student interaction and collaboration. *Distance Education, 27*(2), 139–153. doi:10.1080/01587910600789498

Bennet, A. (2004). Supporting collaborative project teams using computer-based technologies. In T. Roberts (Ed.), *Online collaborative learning: Theory and practice.* London: Information Science Publishing.

Bereiter, C. (2002). *Education and mind in the knowledge age.* Mahwah, NJ: Lawrence Erlbaum Associates.

Berg, J., Berquam, L., & Christoph, K. (2007, March/April). Social networking technologies: A "poke" for campus services. *EDUCAUSE Review, 42*(2), 32–44.

Berge, Z. L., & Collins, M. P. (Eds.). (1995). Computer mediated communication and the online classroom (Vols. 1-3). Cresskill, NJ: Hampton Press.

Berners-Lee, T., & Cailliau, R. (1990). *WorldWideWeb: Proposal for a hypertext project.* Retrieved on November 12, 2008, from http://www.w3.org/Proposal.html

Beshears, F. M. (2005, October 4). Viewpoint: The economic case for creative commons textbooks. *Campus Technology.* Retrieved on May 10, 2007, from http://campustechnology.com/articles/40535/

Bhattacharya, M., & Dron, J. (2007). Cultivating the Web 2.0 jungle. *Seventh IEEE International Conference on Advanced Learning Technologies, ICALT 2007.*

Biggs, J. (1999). What the student does: Teaching for enhanced learning. *Higher Education Research & Development, 18*(1), 57–75. doi:10.1080/0729436990180105

Biggs, J. (2002, November 4). *Aligning the curriculum to promote good learning.* Paper presented at Constructive Alignment in Action: Imaginative Curriculum Symposium. Retrieved on November 15, 2008, from http://www.palatine.ac.uk/files/1023.pdf

Bijker, W., Hughes, T., & Pinch, T. (Eds.). (1987). *Social construction of technological systems: New directions in the sociology and history of technology.* Cambridge, MA: MIT Press.

Biolghini, D. (Ed.). (2001). *Comunità in rete e Net learning. Innovazione dei sistemi organizzativi e processi di apprendimento nelle comunità virtuali.* Milano: Etas.

Bishop, J. (2003). The Internet for educating individuals with social impairments. *Journal of Computer Assisted Learning, 19*(4), 546–556. doi:10.1046/j.0266-4909.2003.00057.x

Black, R. B. (2005). *Online fanfiction: What technology and popular culture can teach us about writing and literacy instruction.* Retrieved on October 10, 2008, from http://newhorizons.org/strategies/literacy/black.htm

Blokland, T. (2002). Neighbourhood social capital: Does an urban gentry help? Some stories of defining shared interests, collective action, and mutual support. *Sociological Research Online, 7*(3).

Bloom, B. (1974). *Taxonomy of educational objectives: The classification of educational goals.* New York: D. McKay.

Boettcher, J. V. (2006, February 28). The rise of student performance content. *Campus Technology.* Retrieved on

February 11, 2007, from http://www.campustechnology/article.aspx?aid=40747

Bolter, J., & Grusin, R. (1999). *Remediation. Understanding new media*. Cambridge, MA: The MIT Press.

Bonaiuti, G. (Ed.). (2006). *E-learning 2.0. Il futuro dell'apprendimento in rete tra formale e informale*. Trento: Erickson.

Boone, R. T., & Buck, R. (2003). Emotional expressivity and trustworthiness: The role of nonverbal behavior in the evolution of cooperation. *Journal of Nonverbal Behavior, 27*(3), 163–182. doi:10.1023/A:1025341931128

Borowicz, S. (2004). The effect of synchronous chat on student performance in an undergraduate introductory accounting course. In G. Richards (Ed.), *Proceedings of World Conference on E-Learning in Corporate, Government, Healthcare, and Higher Education 2004* (pp. 1790-1793). Chesapeake, VA: AACE.

Bosley, M. E. (1998). An analysis of language maturity, verbal aggression, argumentativeness, and propensity toward violence in middle school adolescents. *Dissertation Abstracts International Section A: Humanities and Social Sciences, 58*(10A), 3773.

Botting, N., & Conti-Ramsden, G. (2008). The role of language, social cognition, and social skill in the functional social outcomes of young adolescents with and without a history of SLI. *The British Journal of Developmental Psychology, 26*(2), 281–300. doi:10.1348/026151007X235891

Botting, N., Faragher, B., Simkin, Z., Knox, E., & Conti-Ramsden, G. (2001). Predicting pathways of specific language impairment: What differentiates good and poor outcome? *Journal of Child Psychology and Psychiatry, and Allied Disciplines, 42*(8), 1013–1020. doi:10.1111/1469-7610.00799

Bourdieu, P. (1983). The forms of capital [originally published as Ökonomisches Kapital, kulturelles Kapital, soziales Kapital]. In R. Kreckel (Ed.), *Soziale Ungleichheiten (Soziale Welt, Sonderheft 2)* (pp. 183-198). Goettingen: Otto Schartz & Co.

Bourke, M. L. (2001). Social problem-solving skills training for incarcerated offenders: A treatment manual. *Behavior Modification, 25*(2), 163–188. doi:10.1177/0145445501252001

Bowker, N. I. (2001). Understanding online communities through multiple methodologies combined under a postmodern research endeavour. *Forum Qualitative Sozialforschung/Forum: Qualitative Social Research.*

Boyd, D. (2007). The significance of social software. In T. N. Burg & J. Schmidt (Eds.), *BlogTalks reloaded: Social software research & cases* (pp. 15–30). Norderstedt, Germany: Books on Demand.

Boyd, D. M., & Ellison, N. B. (2007). Social network sites: Definition, history, and scholarship. *Journal of Computer-Mediated Communication, 13*(1), article 11. Retrieved on October 21, 2008, from http://jcmc.indiana.edu/vol13/issue1/boyd.ellison.html

Brandsma, J. (1998). Financement de l'éducation et de la formation tout au long de la vie: Problèmes clés. In *Peut-on mesurer les bénéfices de l'investissement dans les ressources humaines. Formation professionnelle . Revue Européenne, 14*, 1–6.

Breu, K., & Hemingway, C. (2002). Collaborative processes and knowledge creation in communities of practice. *Creativity and Innovation Management, 11*(3), 147–153. doi:10.1111/1467-8691.00247

Brewer, W. F., & Treyens, J. C. (1981). Role of schemata in memory for places. *Cognitive Psychology, 13*, 207–230. doi:10.1016/0010-0285(81)90008-6

Brittain, D. (2006). *Found, shared: The magazine photowork*. Brighton: Brighton Press.

Brown, A. L. (1987). Metacognition, executive control, self-regulation, and other more mysterious mechanisms. In F. E. Weinert & R. H. Kluwe (Eds.), *Metacognition, motivation, and understanding* (pp. 65-116). Hillsdale, NJ: Lawrence Erlbaum Associates.

Brown, J. S. (1999, 2002). *Learning, working, and playing in the digital age*. Retrieved from http://serendip.brynmawr.edu/sci_edu/seelybrown/seelybrown.html

Brown, J. S., & Duguid, P. (2000). *The social life of information.* Boston: Harvard Business School Press.

Brown, J. S., & Duguid, P. (2001). Knowledge and organization: A social-practice perspective. *Organization Science, 12*(2), 198–213. doi:10.1287/orsc.12.2.198.10116

Brown, J. S., Collins, A., & Duguid, P. (1989). Situated cognition and the culture of learning. *Educational Researcher, 18*(1), 32–42.

Brualdi, A. C. (1996). Multiple intelligences: Gardner's theory. *ERIC Digest.* Retrieved on June 15, 2008, from http://www.ericdigests.org/1998-1/multiple.htm

Bruns, A. (2008). *Blogs, Wikipedia, Second Life, and beyond: From production to produsage.* New York: Peter Lang.

Brush, T., & Saye, J. (2001). The use of embedded scaffolds with hypermedia-supported student-centered learning. *Journal of Educational Multimedia and Hypermedia, 10*(4), 333–356.

Bryant, T. (2006). Social software in academia. *EDUCAUSE Quarterly, 29*(2), 61–64.

Burgos, D., Hummel, H. G. K., Tattersall, C., Brouns, F., & Koper, R. (2008). Design guidelines for collaboration and participation with examples from the LN4LD. In L. Lockyer, S. Bennett, S. Agostinho & B. Harper (Eds.), *Handbook of research on learning design and learning objects: Issues, applications, and technologies* (Vol. 1, pp. 373–389). Hershey, PA: IGI Global.

Butcher, H. K., & Taylor, J. Y. (2008). Using a wiki to enhance knowing participation in change in the teaching-learning process. *Visions, 15*(1), 30–44.

Caire, J. B., & Cosgrove, S. M. (1995). An expert-novice approach to self. *Behavior Therapist, 18*, 137–140.

Caire, J., Pliner, P., & Stoker, S. C. (1998). An expert-novice approach to assessing implicit models of the self. In A. Colby, J. James & D. Hart (Eds.), *Competence and character through life.* Chicago: The University of Chicago Press.

Callicott, K. J. (2003). Effects of self-talk on academic engagement and academic responding. *Behavioral Disorders, 29*(1), 48–64.

Calvani, A., & Rotta, M. (2000). *Fare formazione in Internet.* Trento: Erickson.

Calvani, A., Bonaiuti, G., & Fini, A. (2008). Lifelong learning: What role for e-learning 2.0. *Journal of e-Learning and Knowledge Society, 4*(1), 2008. Retrieved from http://www.je-lks.it/en/08_01/06Metcalv_enl.pdf

Cambra, T. (2008). El Web 2.0 com a distòpia en la recent Internet [online]. *Digithum, 10.* UOC. Retrieved from http://www.uoc.edu/digithum/10/dt/cat/cambra.pdf

Cameron, D., & Anderson, T. (2006). Comparing weblogs to threaded discussion tools in online educational contexts. *International Journal of Instructional Technology and Distance Learning, 3*(11), 3–15.

Canzi, A., Folcio, A., Dilani, M., Radice, S., Santangelo, E., & Zanoni, E. (2004, May 10-12). *Da tutor-facilitatore a tutor-instructional designer: Evoluzione del ruolo in contesti di blended learning, in AICA (Ed.), Didamatica 2004.* Ferrara.

Carbonaro, M., Cutumisu, M., Duff, H., Gillis, S., Onuczko, C., & Siegel, J. (2008). Interactive story authoring: A viable form of creative expression for the classroom. *Computers & Education, 51*(2), 687–707. doi:10.1016/j.compedu.2007.07.007

Carmagnola, F., Cena, F., & Gena, C. (2008). User modeling in the social Web. In *Knowledge-based intelligent information and engineering systems* (pp. 745-752). 11th International Conference, KES 2007, XVII Italian Workshop on Neural Networks, Vietri sul Mare, Italy, September 12-14, 2007, Proceedings, Part III. (LNCS 4694). Springer Berlin/Heidelberg.

Carnevale, A. P., Gainer, L. J., & Villet, J. (1990). Training in America. San Francisco: Jossey-Bass.

Carr, E. G., & Durand, V. M. (1985). Reducing behavior problems through functional communication training. *Journal of Applied Behavior Analysis, 18*(2), 111–126. doi:10.1901/jaba.1985.18-111

Castells, M. (1996). *The rise of the network society* (Vol. 1). Oxford: Blackwell Publishers.

Cattuto, C., Loreto, V., & Pietronero, L. (2007). Semiotic dynamics and collaborative tagging. *Proceedings of the National Academy of Sciences of the United States of America, 104*, 1461–1464. doi:10.1073/pnas.0610487104

Chemero, A. (2003). An outline of a theory of affordances. *Ecological Psychology, 15*(2), 181–195. doi:10.1207/S15326969ECO1502_5

Chen, G., & Chiu, M. M. (2008). Online discussion processes: Effects of earlier messages' evaluations, knowledge content, social cues, and personal information on later messages. *Computers & Education, 50*, 678–692. doi:10.1016/j.compedu.2006.07.007

Chin, J., Fu, W.-T., & Kannampalil, T. G. (2009). Adaptive information search: Age-dependent interactions between cognitive profiles and strategies. In *Proceedings of the ACM Conference on Computer-Human Interaction (CHI)*, Boston, MA.

Clark, D. (2003). *The napsterisation of learning (P2P)*. Brighton, England: Epic Group.

Clark, D. (2006). *E-tutoring*. EPIC, White Papers. Retrieved on August 14, 2008, from http://www.epic.co.uk/content/resources/white_papers/pdf_versions/Delivery/Epic_White_Paper_E_tutoring.pdf

Clark, R. E. (1982). Antagonism between achievement and enjoyment in ATI studies. *Educational Psychologist, 17*, 92–101.

Clark, R. E. (1989). When teaching kills learning: Research on mathematics. In H. N. Mandl, N. Bennett, E. de Corte, & H. F. Freidrich (Eds.), *Learning and instruction: European research in an international context* (Vol. 2, pp. 1–22). London: Pergamon.

Clarke, E., & Emerson, A. (1981). Design and synthesis of synchronization skeletons using branching-time temporal logic. *Logic of Programs, 1981*, 52–71.

Clements, D. H., & Nastasi, B. K. (1999). Metacognition, learning, and educational computer environments. *Information Technology in Childhood Education Annual, 1*, 5–38.

Cochrane, T. (2008). Mobile Web 2.0: The new frontier. In *Hello! Where are you in the landscape of educational technology?* [Melbourne, Australia: Deakin University.]. *Proceedings Ascilite Melbourne, 2008*, 177–186.

Cohen, N. J. (2001). *Language impairment and psychopathology in infants, children, and adolescents*. Thousand Oaks, CA: Sage Publications, Inc.

Cohen, N. J., Barwick, M. A., Horodezky, N. B., Vallance, D. D., & Im, N. (1998). Language, achievement, and cognitive processing in psychiatrically disturbed children with previously identified and unsuspected language impairments. *Journal of Child Psychology and Psychiatry, and Allied Disciplines, 39*(6), 865–877. doi:10.1111/1469-7610.00387

Cohen, N. J., Davine, M., & Meloche-Kelly, M. (1989). Prevalence of unsuspected language disorders in a child psychiatric population. *Journal of the American Academy of Child and Adolescent Psychiatry, 28*(1), 107(5)-112.

Cohen, N. J., Menna, R., Vallance, D. D., Barwick, M. A., Im, N., & Horodezky, N. B. (1998). Language, social cognitive processing, and behavioral characteristics of psychiatrically disturbed children with previously identified and unsuspected language impairments. *Journal of Child Psychology and Psychiatry, and Allied Disciplines, 39*(6), 853–864. doi:10.1017/S0021963098002789

Cohen, N., Vallance, D. D., Barwick, M., Im, N., Menna, R., & Horodezky, N. B. (2000). The interface between ADHD and language impairment: An examination of language, achievement, and cognitive processing. *Journal of Child Psychology and Psychiatry, and Allied Disciplines, 41*(3), 353–362. doi:10.1111/1469-7610.00619

Coleman, J. (1988). Social capital in the creation of human capital. *American Journal of Sociology, 94*, S95–S120. doi:10.1086/228943

Coleman, J., Catan, L., & Dennison, C. (1997). You're the last person I'd talk to. In S. Tucker & J. Roche (Eds.), *Youth in society: Contemporary theory, policy, and practice* (pp. 227-234). Thousand Oaks, CA: Sage Publications, Inc.

Collins, A., Brown, J. S., & Newman, S. E. (1987). *Cognitive apprenticeship: Teaching the art of reading, writing, and mathematics.* (Tech. Rep. 403). Washington, D.C.: National Institute of Education. (ERIC Document Reproduction Service No. ED 284 181).

Collis, B., & Moonen, J. (2008). Web 2.0 tools and processes in higher education: Quality perspectives. *Educational Media International, 45*(2), 93–106. doi:10.1080/09523980802107179

Collison, G., Elbaum, B., Haavind, S., & Tinker, R. (2000). *Facilitating online learning. Effective strategies for moderators.* Madison, WI: Atwood Publishing.

Conger, R. D., Neppl, T., & Kim, K. J. (2003). Angry and aggressive behavior across three generations: A prospective, longitudinal study of parents and children. *Journal of Abnormal Child Psychology, 31*(2), 143–160. doi:10.1023/A:1022570107457

Conti-Ramsden, G., & Botting, N. (2004). Social difficulties and victimization in children with SLI at 11 years of age. *Journal of Speech, Language, and Hearing Research: JSLHR, 47*(1), 147–162. doi:10.1044/1092-4388(2004/013)

Cook-Sather, A. (2007). Direct links: Using e-mail to connect preservice teachers, experienced teachers, and high school students within an undergraduate teacher preparation program. *Journal of Technology and Teacher Education, 15*(1), 11–37.

Corcos, E. (2003). *Teaching children and adolescents with behavioral difficulties: An educational approach.* Toronto, Canada: Tigress Publications.

Corlett, D., Chan, T., Ting, J., & Sharples, M. (2005). Interactive logbook: A mobile portfolio and personal development planning tool. In *M-Learn 2005 Proceedings.* Cape Town, M-Learn. Retrieved from http://www.mlearn.org.za/CD/papers/Corlett.pdf

Cornelius, S., & Higgison, C. (2000). *Online tutoring e-book.* OTIS Research Group, Online Tutoring Skills Project. Retrieved on August 14, 2008, from http://otis.scotcit.ac.uk/onlinebook/

Covington, M. V. (2000). Goal theory, motivation, and school achievement: An integrative review. *Annual Review of Psychology, 51*(1Journal Article), 171-200.

Creative Commons. (2008). Retrieved on December 30, 2008, from http://creativecommons.org/

Crook, C. (1998). *Ordenadores y aprendizaje colaborativo.* Madrid: Morata.

Crook, C., Cummings, J., Fisher, T., Graber, R., Harrison, C., Lewin, C., et al. (2008). *Web 2.0 technologies for learning: The current landscape—opportunities, challenges, and tensions.* Coventry, England: Becta. Retrieved on December 29, 2008, from http://partners.becta.org.uk/upload-dir/downloads/page_documents/research/web2_technologies_learning.pdf

Cross, J. (2007). Informal learning: Rediscovering the natural pathways that inspire innovation and performance. San Francisco: John Wiley & Sons, Inc.

Cych, L. (2006). *Social networks. Emerging technologies for learning.* British Educational Communications and Technology Agency (Becta) ICT Research.

Dabbagh, N. (2003). Scaffolding: An important teacher competency in online learning. *TechTrends, 47*(2), 39–44. doi:10.1007/BF02763424

Dalsgaard, C. (2006). Social software: E-learning beyond learning management systems. *European Journal of Open, Distance, and E-learning.* Retrieved on January 3, 2009 from [REMOVED HYPERLINK FIELD]http://www.eurodl.org/materials/contrib/2006/Christian_Dalsgaard.htm

Daniel, B., Schwier, R. A., & McCalla, G. (2003). Social capital in virtual learning communities and distributed communities of practice. *Canadian Journal of Learning and Technology, 29*(3), 2003.

Davenport, T. H., & Prusak, L. (1997). *Information ecology: Mastering the information and knowledge environment.* New York: Oxford University Press.

Davis, A. D., Sanger, D. D., & Morris-Friehe, M. (1991). Language skills of delinquent and nondelinquent adolescent males. *Journal of Communication Disorders*, *24*(4), 251–266. doi:10.1016/0021-9924(91)90001-Y

de Castell, S., & Jenson, J. (2004). Paying attention to attention: New economies for learning. *Educational Theory*, *54*(4), 381–397. doi:10.1111/j.0013-2004.2004.00026.x

de Castell, S., Bryson, M., & Jenson, J. (2002). Object lessons: Towards an educational theory of technology. *First Monday*, *7*(1), 1–18.

de Montes, L. G., Semin, G. R., & Valencia, J. F. (2003). Communication patterns in interdependent relationships. *Journal of Language and Social Psychology*, *22*(3), 259–281. doi:10.1177/0261927X03255381

De Vita, A. (2007). *L'e-learning nella formazione professionale. Strategie, modelli e metodi*. Trento: Erickson.

Deeley, J. (1990). *Basics of semiotics*. Bloomington: Indiana University Press.

DeKerckhove, D. (Ed.). (2003). *La conquista del tempo. Società e democrazia nell'era della rete*. Roma: Editori Riuniti.

Delicious. (2008). Retrieved on December 30, 2008, from http://www.delicious.com/

Denis, B. (2003). Quels rôles et quelle formation pour les tuteurs intervenant dans des dispositifs de formation à distance? *Distances et savoirs, 1*(1), 2003.

Denis, B., Watland, P., Pirotte, S., & Verday, N. (2004). Roles and competencies of the e-tutor. In *NCL2004*. Retrieved from http://www.shef.ac.uk/ncl2004/Proceedings/Symposium

Desharnais, R. A., & Limson, M. (2007). Designing and implementing virtual courseware to promote inquiry-based learning. *Journal of Online Learning and Teaching*, *3*(1), 30–39.

Diener, E., Oishi, S., & Lucas, R. E. (2003). Personality, culture, and subjective well-being: Emotional and cognitive evaluations of life. *Annual Review of Psychology*, *54*(1), 403–425. doi:10.1146/annurev.psych.54.101601.145056

DiGiammarino, F., & Trudeau, L. (2008). Virtual networks: An opportunity for government. *Public Management*, *37*(1), 5–11.

Dillenbourg, P. (2006). The solo/duo gap. *Computers in Human Behavior*, *22*(1), 155–159. doi:10.1016/j.chb.2005.05.001

Dodge, B. (1995). *Some thoughts about Webquests*. [online]. Retrieved from http://webquest.sdsu.edu/about_webquests.html

Doheny-Farina, S. (1996). *The wired neighborhood*. New Haven: Yale University Press.

Downes, S. (2004). Educational blogging. *EDUCAUSE Review*, *39*(5), 14–26.

Downes, S. (2005). *An introduction to connective knowledge*. Retrieved from http://www.downes.ca/cgi-bin/page.cgi?post=33034

Downes, S. (2005, October). *E-learning 2.0. ELearn*. Retrieved on June 3, 2007, from http://www.elearnmag.org/subpage.cfm?section=articles&article=29-1

Downes, S. (2006a). Learning networks and connective knowledge. Retrieved on August 14, 2008, from http://it.coe.uga.edu/itforum/upcoming.html

Downes, S. (2006b). Web 2.0, e-learning 2.0, and personal learning environments. Retrieved on August 14, 2008, from http://www.downes.ca/files/nutn2006.ppt

Dron, J. (2006). Social software and the emergence of control. In *Proceedings of the Sixth International Conference on Advanced Learning Technologies* (pp. 904–908). New York: ACM.

Dron, J. (2006). The teacher, the learner, and the collective mind. *AI & Society*, *21*(1), 200–216. doi:10.1007/s00146-005-0031-4

Dron, J. (2007). *Control and constraint in e-learning: Choosing when to choose*. Hershey, PA: Information Science Publishing.

Dron, J. (2007). Designing the undesignable: Social software and control. *Educational Technology & Society*, *10*(3), 60–71.

Drucker, J. (2004). *The century of artists' books.* New York: Granary Books.

Dutil, P., & Reid, T. (2007). Time for a new networked public service. *Policy Options, 28*(1), 80–84.

Dybwad, B. (2005, September 29). Approaching a definition of Web 2.0. *The social software weblog* [weblog]. Retrieved on January 10, 2007, from http://socialsoftware.weblogsinc.com/2005/09/29/approaching-a-definition-of-web-2-0/

Eco, U. (2000). *Experiences in translation.* Toronto: Toronto U.P.

Edelson, D. C., Gordin, D. N., & Pea, R. D. (1999). Addressing the challenges of inquiry-based learning through technology and curriculum design. *Journal of the Learning Sciences, 8*(3/4), 391–450. doi:10.1207/s15327809jls0803&4_3

Eisenberg, N. (2000). Emotion, regulation, and moral development. *Annual Review of Psychology, 51*(1), 665–697. doi:10.1146/annurev.psych.51.1.665

Elias, M. J. (2004). The connection between social-emotional learning and learning disabilities: Implications for intervention. *Learning Disability Quarterly, 27*(1), 53–63. doi:10.2307/1593632

Ellemers, N., Spears, R., & Doosje, B. (2002). Self and social identity. *Annual Review of Psychology, 53*(1), 161–186. doi:10.1146/annurev.psych.53.100901.135228

Ellison, N. B., & Wu, Y. (2008). Blogging in the classroom: A preliminary exploration of student attitudes and impact on comprehension. *Journal of Educational Multimedia and Hypermedia, 17*(1), 99–122.

Encyclopædia Britannica Online. (2007). Retrieved on August 10, 2007, from http://www.britannica.com/

Engeström, Y. (1987). *Learning by expanding.* Helsinki, Finland: Orienta-Konsultit Oy.

Engeström, Y. (1999). Innovative learning in work teams: Analyzing cycles of knowledge creation in practice. In Y. Engeström, R. Miettinen & R.-L. Punamäki (Eds.), *Perspectives on activity theory* (pp. 377–404). Cambridge, England: Cambridge University Press.

Eraut, M. (2000). Non-formal learning, implicit learning, and tacit knowledge in professional work. *The British Journal of Educational Psychology, 70*(1), 113–136. doi:10.1348/000709900158001

Erickson, K., & Schulkinb, J. (2003). Facial expressions of emotion: A cognitive neuroscience perspective. *Brain and Cognition, 52*, 52–60. doi:10.1016/S0278-2626(03)00008-3

Ertscheid, O. (2005). Google a les moyens de devenir un guichet d'accès unique à l'information. *Le Monde.*

Esteban, M., & Zapata, M. (2008). Estrategias de aprendizaje y e-learning. Un apunte para la fundamentación del diseño educativo en los entornos virtuales de aprendizaje. Consideraciones para la reflexión y el debate. Introducción al estudio de las estrategias y estilos de aprendizaje [online]. *Revista de Educación a Distancia, 19.* Retrieved from http://www.um.es/ead/red/19

Eustace, K. (2003). Educational value of e-learning in conventional and complementary computing education. In S. Mann & A. Williamson (Eds.), *Proceedings of the 16th Annual Conference of the National Advisory Committee on Computing Qualifications* (pp. 53–62). Hamilton, New Zealand: NACCQ.

Facebook. (2008). Retrieved on December 4, 2008, from http://www.facebook.com/

Fahy, P. J. (2006). Online and face-to-face group interaction processes compared using Bales' interaction process analysis (IPA). *European Journal of Open Distance and E-learning EURODL.*

Farmer, J. (2004). Communication dynamics: Discussion boards, weblogs, and the development of communities of inquiry in online learning environments. In R. Atkinson, C. McBeath, D. Jonas-Dwyer & R. Phillips (Eds.), *Beyond the comfort zone: Proceedings of the 21st ASCILITE Conference* (pp. 274–283). Perth, Australia: University of Western Australia.

Fazey, D. M., & Fazey, J. A. (2001). The potential for autonomy in learning: Perceptions of competence, motivation, and locus of control in first-year undergraduate students. *Studies in Higher Education, 26*(3), 345–361. doi:10.1080/03075070120076309

Federici, G., & Ragone, G. (2008). University and life-long learning in Italy: Policies and higher education, and training systems integration. *Journal of e-Learning and Knowledge Society, 4*(1). Retrieved from http://www.je-lks.it/en/08_01/03Metfed_en1.pdf

Fenstermacher, K., Olympia, D., & Sheridan, S. M. (2006). Effectiveness of a computer-facilitated interactive social skills training program for boys with attention deficit hyperactivity disorder. *School Psychology Quarterly, 21*(2), 197–224. doi:10.1521/scpq.2006.21.2.197

Ferdig, R. (2007). Examining social software in teacher education. *Journal of Technology and Teacher Education, 15*(1), 5–10.

Fiedler, S., & Pata, K. (2009). Distributed learning environments and social software: In search for a framework of design. In S. Hatzipanagos & S. Warburton (Eds.), *Handbook of research on social software and developing community ontologies* (pp. 151-164). Hershey, PA: IGI Global.

Fink, L. (2005, September 16). Making textbooks worthwhile. *Chronicle of Higher Education.* Retrieved on March 10, 2007, from http://chronicle.com/weekly/v52/i04/04b01201.htm

Fischer, G., & Konomi, S. (2005). Innovative media in support of distributed intelligence and lifelong learning. In *Proceedings of the Third IEEE International Workshop on Wireless and Mobile Technologies in Education* (pp. 3–10). Los Alamitos, CA: IEEE Computer Society.

Flavell, J. H. (1976). Metacognition aspects of problem solving. In L. B. Resnick (Ed.), *The nature of intelligence.* Hilldale, NJ: Lawrence Erlbaum.

Flavell, J. H. (1979). Metacognition and cognitive monitoring: A new area of cognitive-developmental inquiry. *The American Psychologist, 34*(10), 906–911. doi:10.1037/0003-066X.34.10.906

Forman, E. (1996). Learning mathematics as participation in classroom practice: Implications of sociocultural theory for educational reform. In L. Steffe, P. Nesher, P. Cobb, G. Goldin & B. Greer (Eds.), *Theories of mathematical learning* (pp. 115–130). Mahwah, NJ: Lawrence Erlbaum Associates.

Forrester, L. (2007). *Self-publishing photobooks.* London: Louise Forrester. Retrieved on November 22, 2008, from http://www.lulu.com/content/4052229

Fox News. (2006). *YouTube popularity eclipses, and influences, fall TV season.* Retrieved on August 20, 2008, from http://www.foxnews.com/story/0,2933,209022,00.html

Fox, G. C., Pierce, M. E., Mustacoglu, A. F., & Topcu, A. E. (2007). Web 2.0 for e-science environments. *Third International Conference on Semantics, Knowledge, and Grid.*

Fraenkel, J. R., & Wallen, N. E. (1996). *How to design and evaluate research in education,* 3rd ed. New York: McGraw-Hill Inc.

Frand, J., & Hixon, C. (1999). Personal knowledge management: Who, what, why, when, where, how? Berkeley, UCLA. Retrieved on August 14, 2008, from http://www.anderson.ucla.edu/faculty/jason.frand/researcher/speeches/PKM.htm

Frankel, F., & Feinberg, D. (2002). Social problems associated with ADHD vs. ODD in children referred for friendship problems. *Child Psychiatry and Human Development, 33*(2), 125–146. doi:10.1023/A:1020730224907

Friendster. (2008). Retrieved on December 4, 2008, from http://www.friendster.com/

Fu, W.-T. (2008). The microstructures of social tagging: A rational model. In *Proceedings of the ACM 2008 Conference on Computer Supported Cooperative Work (CSCW)* (pp. 229-238), San Diego, CA.

Fu, W.-T., & irolli, P. (2007). SNIF-ACT: A cognitive model of user navigation on the World Wide Web. *Human-Computer Interaction, 22,* 355–412.

Fukuyama, F. (1999). *Social capital and civil society.* Paper presented at the IMF Conference on Second Generation Reforms. Retrieved on April 10, 2005, from http://www.imf.org/external/pubs/ft/seminar/1999/reforms/fukuyama.htm

Furlong, M. J., & Smith, D. C. (1998). Raging Rick to tranquil Tom: An empirically based multidimensional anger typology for adolescent males. *Psychology in the Schools, 35*(3), 229–245. doi:10.1002/(SICI)1520-6807(199807)35:3<229::AID-PITS4>3.0.CO;2-I

Gallese, V., & Freedberg, D. (2007). Mirror and canonical neurons are crucial elements in esthetic response. *Trends in Cognitive Sciences, 11*, 411. doi:10.1016/j.tics.2007.07.006

Gallese, V., & Lakoff, G. (2005). The brain's concepts: The role of the sensory-motor system in reason and language. *Cognitive Neuropsychology, 22*, 455–479. doi:10.1080/02643290442000310

Gallese, V., Fadiga, L., Fogassi, L., & Rizzolatti, G. (1996). Action recognition in the premotor cortex. *Brain, 119*, 593–609. doi:10.1093/brain/119.2.593

Gambles, A. (2001, March). The headline personal information environment. *D-LIB Magazine*. Retrieved from http://www.dlib.org/dlib/march01/gambles/03gambles.html

Gannon-Leary, P., & Fontainha, E. (2007). Communities of practice and virtual learning communities: Benefits, barriers, and success factors. *E-learning Papers, 5*(1), 1887–1542.

Gardner, H. (1993). *Frames of mind: The theory of multiple intelligences*. USA: Basic Books.

Gardner, H. (2000). Can technology exploit our many ways of knowing? In D. T. Gordon (Ed.), *The digital classroom: How technology is changing the way we teach and learn* (pp. 32–35). Cambridge, MA: Harvard Education Letter.

Gardner, H. (2000). The complete tutor. *Technos: Quarterly for Education and Technology, 9*, 3.

Gardner, H. (2006). *Changing minds. The art and science of changing our own and other people's minds*. Boston, MA.: Harvard Business School Press.

Gardner, H., & Hatch, T. (1989). Multiple intelligences go to school: Educational implications of the theory of multiple intelligences. *Educational Researcher, 18*(8), 4–9.

Garrison, D. R. (2006). Online collaboration principles. *Journal of Asynchronous Learning Networks, 10*(1), 25–34.

Garrison, D. R., & Anderson, T. (2003). *E-learning in the 21st century: A framework for research and practice*. London: Routledge Falmer.

Gaver, W. W. (1996). Affordances for interaction: The social is material for design. *Ecological Psychology, 8*(2), 111–129. Retrieved from http://www.cs.ubc.ca/labs/spin/publications/related/gaver96.pdf

Gee, J. P. (2003). *What video games have to teach us about learning and literacy*. New York: Palgrave MacMillan.

Gee, J. P. (2004). *Situated language and learning: A critique of traditional schooling*. New York: Palmgrave-McMillan.

Gewerc, A. (2005). El uso de weblogs en la docencia universitaria [online]. *Revista Latinoamericana de Tecnología Educativa, 4*(1). Retrieved from http://campusvirtual.unex.es/cala/editio/index.php

Giannini, L., Nati, B., Pettinari, E., & Rotta, M. (2005, May 12-14). FAD: Didattica dell'italiano. Riflessioni tra contenuto e relazione nel progetto di formazione in rete Giunti Scuola. In AICA (Ed.), *Didamatica 2005*. Potenza.

Gibson, J. J. (1979). *The ecological approach to visual perception*. Boston: Houghton Mifflin.

Glogoff, S. (2005). Instructional blogging: Promoting interactivity, student-centered learning, and peer input. *Journal of Online Education, 1*(5). Retrieved on August 9, 2008, from http://www.innovateonline.info/index.php?view=article&id=126

Glover, D., Miller, D., Averis, D., & Door, V. (2007). The evolution of an effective pedagogy for teachers using the interactive whiteboard in mathematics and moderns languages: An empirical analysis from the secondary sector. *Learning, Media and Technology, 32*(1), 5–20. doi:10.1080/17439880601141146

Gobbo, C., & Chi, M. (1986). How knowledge is structured and used by experts and novice children.

Cognitive Development, 1, 221–237. doi:10.1016/S0885-2014(86)80002-8

Gokhale, A. A. (1995). Collaborative learning enhances critical thinking. *Journal of Technology Education, 7*(1). Retrieved from http://scholar.lib.vt.edu/ejournals/JTE/jte-v7n1/gokhale.jte-v7n1.html

Golder, S. A., & Huberman, B. A. (2006). Usage patterns of collaborative tagging systems. *Journal of Information Science, 32*(2), 198–208. doi:10.1177/0165551506062337

Goldsworthy, R., Schwartz, N., Barab, S., & Landa, A. (2007). Evaluation of a collaborative multimedia conflict resolution curriculum. *Educational Technology Research and Development, 55*(6), 597–625. doi:10.1007/s11423-006-9006-5

Goodyer, I. (2000). Language difficulties and psychopathology. In D. Bishop & L. Leonard (Eds.), *Speech and language impairment in children* (pp. 227-244). Hove, UK: Psychology Press.

Goos, M., Galbraith, P., Renshaw, P., & Geiger, V. (2000, July 31-August 6). *Classroom voices: Technology enriched interactions in a community of mathematical practice.* Paper presented at the Working Group for Action 11 (The Use of Technology in Mathematics Education) at the 9th International Congress on Mathematical Education, Tokyo/Makuhari.

Gordon, M. (Ed.). (1998). *A dictionary of sociology.* New York: Oxford University Press.

Gordon. (1996). Tracks for learning: Metacognition and learning technologies. *Australian Journal of Educational Technology, 12*(1), 46-55.

Green, H., Facer, K., Rudd, T., Dillon, P., & Humphreys, P. (2005). *Personalisation and digital technologies.* Bristol, England: Futurelab. Retrieved on October 23, 2007, from http://www.futurelab.org.uk/resources/documents/opening_education/Personalisation_report.pdf

Greiffenhagen, C. (2002). *Out of the office into the school: Electonic for education.* Retrieved on August 20, 2008, from ftp://ftp.comlab.ox.ac.uk/pub/Documents/techreports/TR-16-00.pdf

Gualtieru, C. T., Koriath, U., Van Bourgondien, M., & Saleeby, N. (1983). Language disorders in children referred for psychiatric-services. *Journal of the American Academy of Child and Adolescent Psychiatry, 22*(2), 165–171.

Guiller, J., & Durndell, A. (2007). Students' linguistic behaviour in online discussion groups: Does gender matter? *Computers in Human Behavior, 23*, 2240–2255. doi:10.1016/j.chb.2006.03.004

Hall, I., & Higgins, S. (2005). Primary school students' perceptions of interactive whiteboards. *Journal of Computer Assisted Learning, 21*(2), 102–117. doi:10.1111/j.1365-2729.2005.00118.x

Halliday, M. A. K. (1975). *Learning how to mean: Explorations in the development of language.* London: Edward Arnold (Publishers) Ltd.

Hamman, R. (1998). *The online/offline dichotomy: Debunking some myths about AOL users and the effects of their being online upon offline friendships and offline community.* University of Liverpool, Liverpool.

Hammond, M. (2000). Communication within online forums: The opportunities, the constraints, and the value of a communicative approach. *Computers & Education, 35*, 251–262. doi:10.1016/S0360-1315(00)00037-3

Han, S. Y., & Hill, J. R. (2007). Collaborate to learn, learn to collaborate: Examining the roles of context, community, and cognition in asynchronous discussion. *Journal of Educational Computing Research, 36*(1), 89–123. doi:10.2190/A138-6K63-7432-HL10

Harasim, L., Roxanne, S., Turoff, M., & Teles, L. (2000). *Redes de aprendizaje. Guía para la enseñanza y el aprendizaje en red.* Barcelona: Gedisa Editorial.

Hartley, J. (2007). Teaching, learning, and new technology: A review for teachers. *British Journal of Educational Technology, 38*(1), 42–62. doi:10.1111/j.1467-8535.2006.00634.x

Hastie, R. (2001). Problems for judgment and decision making. *Annual Review of Psychology, 52*(1), 653–683. doi:10.1146/annurev.psych.52.1.653

Hay, J. A., & Schmuck, M. F. (1993). *Problem-based learning: Development and analysis of a tutor evaluation form for use in small-group problem-based learning.* Paper presented at the Annual Meeting of the American Educational Research Association.

He, K. K., & Yu, S. Q. (2005). The education innovating in information age. *Basic Education Reference, 5,* 1–6.

Heaton, L. (1998). Preserving communication context: Virtual workspace and interpersonal space in Japanese CSCW. In C. Ess & F. Sudweeks (Eds.), *Cultural attitudes towards communication and technology* (pp. 163-186). Australia: University of Sydney.

Heft, H. (2001). *Ecological psychology in context. James Gibson, Roger Baker, and the legacy of William James's radical empiricism.* Lawrence Erlbaum Associates, Publishers.

Henning, E. (2003). I click therefore I am (not): Is cognition 'distributed' or is it 'contained' in borderless e-learning programmes? *International Journal of Training and Development, 7*(4), 303–317. doi:10.1046/j.1360-3736.2003.00188.x

Hermans, B. (1998). Desperately seeking: Helping hands and human touch. *First Monday, Peer Reviewed Journal on the Internet, 3,* 11. Retrieved from http://www.firstmonday.dk/issues/issue3_11/hermans/index.html

Hilton, J. (2006). The future for higher education: Sunrise or perfect storm? *EDUCAUSE Review, 41*(2), 58–71.

Hochschule Darmstadt. (2008). *Dear Lulu.* London: Hochschule Darmstadt/Practise. Retrieved on November 22, 2008, from http://www.lulu.com/content/2709735

Hofer, B., Yu, S., & Pintrich, P. (1998). Teaching college students to be self-regulated learners. In D. Schunk & B. Zimmerman (Eds.), *Self-regulated learners: From teaching to self-reflective practice* (pp. 57-85). New York: Guilford.

Hoffmeyer, J. (1995, June). *The global semiosphere.* Paper presented at the 5th IASS Congress in Berkeley. In I. Rauch & G. F. Carr (Eds.), *Semiotics around the world. Proceedings of the Fifth Congress of the International*

Association for Semiotic Studies (pp. 933-936), Berkeley 1994. Berlin/New York: Mouton de Gruyter 1997.

Hoffmeyer, J. (1998). The unfolding semiosphere. In G. Van de Vijver, S. Salthe & M. Delpos (Eds.), *Evolutionary systems. Biological and epistemological perspectives on selection and self-organization* (pp. 281-293). Dordrecht: Kluwer.

Hofstede, G. (1980). *Culture's consequences.* Beverly Hills, CA: Sage.

Hollan, J., Hutchins, E., & Kirsh, D. (2000). Distributed cognition: Toward a new foundation for human-computer interaction research. *ACM Transactions on Computer-Human Interaction, 7*(2), 174–196. doi:10.1145/353485.353487

Hommel, B. (2003). Planning and representing intentional action. *TheScientificWorldJournal, 3,* 593–608. doi:10.1100/tsw.2003.46

Horn, R. E. (1998). *Visual language: Global communication for the 21st century.* Beainbridge Island, WA: Macro Vu.

Horton, W. (2000). *Designing Web-based training.* USA: John Wiley & Sons, Inc.

Houssman, J. (1991). Self monitoring and learning proficiency. In *Computer classroom.* Hofstra University, EDD.

Hsu, C.-J., & Lin, J.-C. (2008). Acceptance of blog usage: The roles of technology acceptance, social influence, and knowledge sharing motivation. *Information & Management, 45,* 65–74. doi:10.1016/j.im.2007.11.001

Hsu, J. (2007). Innovative technologies for education and learning: Education and knowledge-oriented applications of blogs, wikis, podcasts, and more. *International Journal of Information and Communication Technology Education, 3*(3), 70–89.

Hubal, R. C., Fishbein, D. H., Sheppard, M. S., Paschall, M. J., Eldreth, D. L., & Hyde, C. T. (2008). How do varied populations interact with embodied conversational agents? Findings from inner-city adolescents and prisoners. *Computers in Human Behavior*, *24*(3), 1104–1138. doi:10.1016/j.chb.2007.03.010

Hurme, T.-R., & Merenluoto, K. (2008, June 9-13). *Socially shared metacognition and feelings of difficulty in a group's computer supported mathematical problem solving*. Kesäseminaari pidetään Physicumissa, Helsingin yliopistossa. Retrieved on October 1, 2008, from http://per.physics.helsinki.fi/Tutkijakoulun_kesaseminaari_2008/Hurme.pdf

Hutchins, E. (1995). How a cockpit remembers its speeds. *Cognitive Science*, *19*, 265–288.

Hutchinson, G. E. (1957). Concluding remarks. *Cold Spring Harbor Symposia on Quantitative Biology*, *22*, 145–159.

Iaccoboni, M. (2005). Understanding others: Imitation, language, empathy. In S. Hurley & N. Chater, (Eds.), *Perspectives on imitation: From mirror neurons to memes, volume 1. Mechanisms of imitation and imitation in animals*. MIT Press.

Iiskala, T., Vauras, M., & Lehtinen, E. (2004). Socially-shared metacognition in peer learning? *Hellenic Journal of Psychology*, *1*, 147–178.

Ingram, A. L., Hathorn, L. G., & Evans, A. (2000). Beyond chat on the Internet. *Computers & Education*, *35*, 21–35. doi:10.1016/S0360-1315(00)00015-4

Jacquinot, G. (2002). Absence et présence dans la médiation pédagogique ou comment faire circuler les signes de la presence. In *Pratiquer les TICE, former les enseignants et les formateurs à de nouveaux usages* (pp. 103-113). Bruxelles, De Boeck.

Jakes, D. (2006). Wild about wikis: Tools for taking students and teacher collaboration to the next level. *Technology and Learning*, *27*(1), 6.

Jarvis, P. (2000). Globalisation, the learning society, and comparative education. *Comparative Education*, *36*(3), 343–355. doi:10.1080/713656613

Jenkins, H. (2007). *Confronting the challenges of participatory vulture: Media education for the 21st century*. Chicago, IL: MacArthur Foundation. Retrieved on

January 4, 2008, from http://www.digitallearning.macfound.org/atf/cf/%7B7E45C7E0-A3E0-4B89-AC9C-E807E1B0AE4E%7D/JENKINS_WHITE_PAPER.PDF

Joffe, R. D., Dobson, K. S., Fine, S., & Marriage, K. (1990). Social problem-solving in depressed, conduct-disordered, and normal adolescents. *Journal of Abnormal Child Psychology*, *18*(5), 565–575. doi:10.1007/BF00911108

Johnson, C. M. (2001). A survey of current research on online communities of practice. *The Internet and Higher Education*, *4*(1), 45–60. doi:10.1016/S1096-7516(01)00047-1

Johnson, K., & Magusin, E. (2005). *Exploring the digital library. A guide for online teaching and learning*. San Francisco, CA: Jossey Bass.

Johnson, R. T., & Johnson, D. W. (1991). *Joining together*. Boston: Ally et Bacon.

Johnson, R. T., & Johnson, D. W. (n.d.). *Cooperative learning*. Retrieved on July 22, 2008, from http://www.co-operation.org/pages/cl.html

Jonassen, D. H., & Harris, N. D. (1990). Analyzing and selecting instructional strategies and tactics. *Performance Improvement Quarterly*, *3*(2), 29–47.

Jones, S. (Ed.). (1998). *Cybersociety 2.0: Revisiting computer-mediated communication and community*. London: SAGE Publications.

Kadish, T. E., Glaser, B. A., Calhoun, G. B., & Ginter, E. J. (2001). Identifying the developmental strengths of juvenile offenders: Assessing four life-skills dimensions. *Journal of Addictions & Offender Counseling*, *21*(2), 85–95.

Kaldoudi, E., Bamidis, P., Papaioakeim, M., & Vargemezis, V. (2008). Problem-based learning via Web 2.0 technologies. *21st IEEE International Symposium on Computer-Based Medical Systems, CBMS '08*.

Kamel Boulos, M., & Wheeler, S. (2007, March). The emerging Web 2.0 social software: An enabling suite of sociable technologies in health and healthcare education.

Health Information and Libraries Journal, 24(1), 2–23. doi:10.1111/j.1471-1842.2007.00701.x

Kanuka, H., Jugdev, K., Heller, B., & West, D. (2006). *The rise of the telecommuter and the fall of community: False promise.* Edmonton, Canada: Athabasca University. Retrieved from http://auspace.athabascau.ca:8080/dspace/handle/2149/1074

Karagiorgi, Y., & Symeou, L. (2005). Translating constructivism into instructional design: Potential and limitations. *Educational Technology & Society, 8*(1), 17–27.

Katz, I. R., & Macklin, A. S. (2007). Information and communication technology (ICT) literacy: Integration and assessment in higher education. *Systemics, Cybernetics, and Informatics, 5*(4), 50–55.

Kaufman, J. M. (1999). How we prevent the prevention of emotional and behavior disorders. *Exceptional Children, 65*(4), 448–468.

Kehle, T. J., & Bray, M. A. (2004). Commentary: Current perspectives on school-based behavioral interventions: Science and reality of the classroom. *School Psychology Review, 33*(3), 417–420.

Kelly, S. D. (2001). Broadening the units of analysis in communication: Speech and nonverbal behaviors in pragmatic comprehension. *Journal of Child Language, 28,* 325–349.

Kemshal-Bell, G. (2001). *The online teacher. Final report prepared for the Project Steering Committee of the VET Teachers and Online Learning Project.* ITAM ESD TAFENSW International Centre for VET Teaching and Learning. Retrieved on August 14, 2008, from http://cyberteacher.onestop.net/final%20report.pdf

Kenney, B. (2007, January). You 2.0. *School Library Journal, 53*(1), 11.

Keysar, B. (2000). The illusory transparency of intention: Does June understand what Mark means because he means it? *Discourse Processes, 29*(2), 161–172. doi:10.1207/S15326950dp2902_4

Keysar, B., Barr, D. J., Balin, J. A., & Brauner, J. S. (2000). Taking perspective in conversation: The role of mutual

knowledge in comprehension. *Psychological Science, 11*(1), 32–38. doi:10.1111/1467-9280.00211

Kirschner, P. A. (2002). Can we support CSCL? Educational, social, and technological affordances for learning. In P.A. Kirschner (Ed.), *Three worlds of CSCL: Can we support CSCL?* (pp. 7–47). Heerlen, The Netherlands: Open University of the Netherlands.

Kirschner, P. A., Sweller, J., & Clark, R. E. (2006). Why minimal guidance during instruction does not work: An analysis of the failure of constructivist, discovery, problem-based, experiential, and inquiry-based teaching. *Educational Psychologist, 41*(2), 75–86. doi:10.1207/s15326985ep4102_1

Klamma, R., Spaniol, M., Cao, Y., & Jarke, M. (2006). Pattern-based cross media social network analysis for technology enhanced learning in Europe. In W. Nejdl & K. Tochtermann (Eds.), *Innovative approaches to learning and knowledge sharing, Proceedings of the 1ˢᵗ European Conference on Technology Enhanced Learning (EC-TEL 2006),* Hersonissou, Greece, October 1-3. (LNCS 4227, pp. 242–256). Springer-Verlag.

Knight, P., Pennant, J., & Piggott, J. (2005)... *The Power of the Interactive Whiteboard, 21*(2), 11–15.

Kolb, D. A. (1984). *Experiential learning.* Englewood Cliffs, NJ: Prentice Hall.

Kolb, D. A., & Fry, R. (1975). Toward an applied theory of experiential learning. In C. L. Cooper (Ed.), *Theories of group process* (pp. 33–58). London: John Wiley.

Kolodner, J., & Guzdial, M. (1996). Effects with and of CSCL: Tracking learning in a new paradigm. In T. Koschmann (Ed.), *CSCL: Theory and practice of an emerging paradigm.* New Jersey: Lawrence Erlbaum Associates.

Kreijns, K., Kirschner, P. A., Jochems, W., & Van Buuren, H. (2005). Measuring perceived sociability of computer-supported collaborative learning environments. *Computers & Education.*

Kumar, R., Novak, J., & Tomkins, A. (2006). Structure and evolution of online social networks. In *Proceedings of the 12ᵗʰ ACM SIGKDD International Conference on Knowledge Discovery and Data Mining Table of Contents* (pp. 611–617). Philadelphia, PA.

Lam, S. K., & Churchill, E. (2007). The social Web: Global village or private cliques? *Proceedings of the 2007 Conference on Designing for User eXperiences.* Chicago, IL: ACM.

Lapadat, J. C. (1991). Pragmatic language skills of students with language and/or learning disabilities: A quantitative synthesis. *Journal of Learning Disabilities, 24*(3), 147–158. doi:10.1177/002221949102400303

Laplante, D., & Ambady, N. (2003). On how things are said: Voice tone, voice intensity, verbal content, and perceptions of politeness. *Journal of Language and Social Psychology, 22*(4), 434–441. doi:10.1177/0261927X03258084

Lashinsky, A. (2005). Facebook stares down success. *Fortune, 152*, 40.

Laurillard, D. (2001). *Rethinking university teaching: A framework for the effective use of educational technology* (2nd ed.). London: Routledge.

Lave, J., & Wenger, E. (1991). *Situated learning: Legitimate peripheral participation.* Cambridge, England: Cambridge University Press.

Le, T., & Le, Q. (2002). The nature of learners' email communication. [). Auckland, New Zealand.]. *Proceedings of the International Conference on Computers in Education, 1*, 468–471. doi:10.1109/CIE.2002.1185979

Lee, M. J. W. (2005). New tools for online collaboration: Blogs, wikis, RSS, and podcasting. *Training and Development in Australia, 32*(5), 17–20.

Lentell, H. (2003). The importance of the tutor in open and distance learning. In A. Tait & R. Mills (Eds.), *Rethinking learner support in distance education* (pp. 64-76). London: Routledge.

Lerman, K., & Jones, L. (2006). *Social browsing on flickr.* Retrieved on October 21, 2008, from http://arxiv.org/abs/cs/0612047

Lerner, M. (1957). *America as a civilization: Life and thought in the United States today.* New York: Simon & Schuster.

Lesser, E. (Ed.). (2000). *Knowledge and social capital: Foundations and applications.* Boston: Butterworth-Heinemann.

Leung, A. C. K. (2003). Contextual issues in the construction of computer-based learning programs. *Journal of Computer Assisted Learning, 19*(4), 501–516. doi:10.1046/j.0266-4909.2003.00053.x

Levy, P. (2004). *L'Intelligence collective. Pour une anthropologie du cyberespace.* Paris: La Découverte.

Levy, S. (2007, August 20). Facebook grows up. *Newsweek, 8*, 40-46.

Lightfoot, J. M. (2006). A comparative analysis of e-mail and face-to-face communication in an educational environment. *The Internet and Higher Education, 9*, 217–227. doi:10.1016/j.iheduc.2006.06.002

Ligorio, M. B., Talamo, A., & Pontecorvo, C. (2008). Building intersubjectivity at a distance during the collaborative writing of fairy tales. *Computers & Education, 5*, 357–374.

Lin, Y.-R., Sundaram, H., Chi, Y., Tatemura, J., & Tseng, B. (2006). Discovery of blog communities based on mutual awareness. In *Proceedings of the 3ʳᵈ Annual Workshop on the Webblogging Ecosystem: Aggregation, Analysis and Dynamics.* Retrieved from http://www.blogpulse.com/www2006-workshop/papers/wwe2006-discovery-lin-final.pdf

Lin, Y.-T., Chi, Y.-C., Chang, L.-C., Cheng, S.-C., & Huang, Y.-M. (2007). A Web 2.0 synchronous learning environment using ajax. *Ninth IEEE International Symposium on Multimedia 2007.*

Lindner, M. (2006). Use these tools, your mind will follow. Learning in immersive micromedia and microknowledge environments. In D. Whitelock & S. Wheeler (Eds.), *The next generation: Research proceedings of the 13ᵗʰ ALT-C conference* (pp. 41–49). Oxford: ALT.

Lindsay, G., & Dockrell, J. (2000). The behavior and self esteem of children with specific speech and language difficulties. *The British Journal of Educational Psychology, 70*, 583–601. doi:10.1348/000709900158317

Llor`a. X., Imafuji, N., Welge, Y. M., & Goldberg, D. E. (2006). *Human-centered analysis and visualization tools for the blogosphere*. (Illinois Tech. Rep. No. 2006023). Retrieved from http://www-discus.ge.uiuc. edu/discussite/2006/11/29/human-centered-analysis-and-visualization-tools-for-the-blogosphere/

LookSmart, Ltd. (2008). *Furl*. Retrieved on December 30, 2008, from http://www.furl.net/

Lorenzo, G., & Dziuban, C. (2006). *Ensuring the net generation is net savvy*. Washington, D.C.: EDUCUASE.

Losel, F., & Beelmann, A. (2003). Effects of child skills training in preventing antisocial behavior: A systematic review of randomized evaluations. *The Annals of the American Academy of Political and Social Science, 587*(1), 84–109. doi:10.1177/0002716202250793

Lotman, Y. (1990). *Universe of the mind: A semiotic theory of culture*. (ed. & trans. by A. Shukman). Bloomington, IN: Indiana University Press.

Love, D., McKean, G., & Gathercoal, P. (2002). Portfolios to webfolios and beyond: Levels of maturation. *EDUCAUSE Quarterly, 25*(2), 29–37.

Luckin, R. (2006). Understanding learning contexts as ecologies of resources: From the zone of proximal development to learner generated contexts. In T. Reeves & S. Yamashita (Eds.), *Proceedings of World Conference on E-Learning in Corporate, Government, Healthcare, and Higher Education 2006* (pp. 2195–2202). Chesapeake, VA: AACE.

Luckin, R., du Boulay, B., Smith, H., Underwood, J., Fitzpatrick, G., Holmberg, J., et al. (2005). Using mobile technology to create flexible learning contexts. *Journal of Interactive Media in Education, 22*. Retrieved on December 4, 2008, from http://jime.open.ac.uk/2005/22/luckin-2005-22.pdf

Lynch, K. G. (2007). Fourteenth annual report to the Prime Minister on the Public Service of Canada. Retrieved on July 31, 2008, from http://www.pco- bcp.gc.ca/index.as p?lang=eng&page=information&sub=publications&do c=ar-ra/15- 2008/rpt_e.htm

Lynch, K. G. (2008). Fifteenth annual report to the Prime Minister on the Public Service of Canada. Retrieved on July 31, 2008, from http://www.pco- bcp.gc.ca/index.as p?lang=eng&page=information&sub=publications&do c=ar-ra/15- 2008/rpt_e.htm

Lyons, N., & Freidus, H. (2004). The reflective portfolio in self-study: Inquiring into and representing a knowledge of practice. In J. J. Loughran, M. L. Hamilton, V. K. LaBoskey & T. L. Russell (Ed.), *International handbook of self-study of teaching and teacher education practices* (pp. 1073–1107). Dordrecht, The Netherlands: Springer.

Mackie, K. (2007). *A brief history of microblogging*. Retrieved from http://www.blogschmog.net/2007/11/17/a-brief-history-of-microblogging/

Mader, S. (2006). Ways to use wiki in education [online]. *Using Wiki in Education.* Retrieved from http://www.wikiineducation.com/display/ikiw/Ways+to+use+wiki+in+education

Magnani, L. (2008). Chances, affordances, niche construction. In *Proceedings of the 12th International Conference on Knowledge-based Intelligent Information and Engineering Systems* (LNAI 5178, pp. 719-726).

Magnani, L., & Bardone, E. (2008). Sharing representations and creating chances through cognitive niche construction. The role of affordances and abduction. In S. Iwata, Y. Ohsawa, S. Tsumoto, N. Zhong, Y. Shi & L. Magnani (Eds.), *Communications and discoveries from multidisciplinary data* (pp.3-40). New York/ Berlin: Springer.

Mangione, G. R., Cigognini, M. E., & Pettenati, M. C. (2007, July 4-6). Favorire l'uso critico creativo ed etico della rete nella gestione personale della conoscenza. In Sie-L Società italiana di e-Learning (Ed.), *E-Learning fra formale e informale*. Macerata, Università di Macerata.

Manion, V., & Alexander, J. (1997). The benefits of peer collaboration on strategy use, metacognitive causal attribution, and recall. *Journal of Experimental Child Psychology, 67*, 268–289. doi:10.1006/jecp.1997.2409

Marchionini, G. (2006). Exploratory search: From finding to understanding. *Communications of the ACM, 49*(4), 41–46. doi:10.1145/1121949.1121979

Marshall, C., & Rossman, G. (1999). *Designing qualitative research*. London: Sage Publications.

Martin, P. T. (1996). Email and the Internet as a teaching tool: A critical perspective. *Proceedings of the 26th Annual Frontiers in Education Conference* (pp. 823–825). Salt Lake City, UT.

Marzano, R. J. (1988). *Metacognition: The first step in teaching thinking. Professional handbook for the language arts*. Morristown, NJ: Silver Burdett and Ginn.

Marzano, R. J. (1998). *A theory-based meta-analysis of research on instruction*. Mid-continent Aurora, CO: Regional Educational Laboratory.

Mason, R. D., & Kaye, A. R. (1992). *Collaborative learning through computer conferencing*. Berlin: Springler Verlag.

Mason, R. D., & Weller, M. (2000). Factors affecting students' satisfaction on a Web course. *Australian Journal of Educational Technology, 16*(2), 173–200.

Mason, R., & Rennie, F. (2007). Using Web 2.0 for learning in the community. *The Internet and Higher Education, 10*(3), 196–203. doi:10.1016/j.iheduc.2007.06.003

Massachusetts Institute of Technology. (2008). *MIT OpenCourseWare*. Retrieved on December 30, 2008, from http://ocw.mit.edu/

Mathur, S. R., & Rutherford, R. B. (1994). Teaching conversational social skills to delinquent youth. *Behavioral Disorders, 19*(4), 294–305.

Matthys, W., Cuperus, J. M., & Van-Engeland, H. (1999). Deficient social problem-solving in boys with ODD/CD, with ADHD, and with both disorders. *Journal of the American Academy of Child and Adolescent Psychiatry, 38*(3), 311–321. doi:10.1097/00004583-199903000-00019

Mayer, R. E. (2001). *Multimedia learning*. Cambridge, England: Cambridge University Press.

Mazer, J. P., Murphy, R. E., & Simonds, C. J. (2007). I'll see you on Facebook: The effects of computer-mediated teacher self-disclosure on student motivation, affective learning, and classroom climate. *Communication Education, 56*(1), 1–17. doi:10.1080/03634520601009710

Mazzolini, M., & Maddison, S. (2003). Sage, guide, or ghost? The effect of instructor intervention on student participation in online discussion forums. *Computers & Education, 40*, 237–253. doi:10.1016/S0360-1315(02)00129-X

McCabe, P. C., & Meller, P. J. (2004). The relationship between language and social competence: How language impairment affects social growth. *Psychology in the Schools, 41*(3), 313–321. doi:10.1002/pits.10161

McClure, E. B., & Nowicki, S. Jr. (2001). Associations between social anxiety and nonverbal processing skill in preadolescent boys and girls. *Journal of Nonverbal Behavior, 25*(1), 3–19. doi:10.1023/A:1006753006870

McCoog, I. J. (2007). Integrated instruction: Multiple intelligences and technology. *Clearing House (Menasha, Wis.), 81*(1), 25–28. doi:10.3200/TCHS.81.1.25-28

McCreary, F. A., & Ehrich, R. W. (2001). Chat rooms as "virtual hangouts" for rural elementary students. *Information Technology in Childhood Education Annual*.

McHugh, L., Barnes-Holmes, Y., & Barnes-Holmes, D. (2004). Perspective-taking as relational responding: A developmental profile. *The Psychological Record, 54*(1), 115–144.

McKay, S. (2003). Adolescent risk behaviors and communication research: Current directions. *Journal of Language and Social Psychology, 22*(1), 74–82. doi:10.1177/0261927X02250058

Mejias, U. (2005). A nomad's guide to learning and social software. *The Knowledge Tree: An E-Journal of Learning Innovation, 7*. Retrieved on December 10, 2006, from http://knowledgetree.flexiblelearning.net.au/edition07/download/la_mejias.pdf

Mejias, U. (2005). A nomad's guide to learning and social software. *The Knowledge Tree*. Retrieved on October 20, 2007, from http://knowledgetree.flexiblelearning.net.au/edition07/html/la_mejias.html

Mejias, U. (2007). Teaching social software with social software. *Innovate: Journal of Online Education, 2*(5). Retrieved on December 2, 2007, from http://www.innovateonline.ifo/index.php?view=article&id=260

MERLOT. (2008). Retrieved on February 19, 2008, from http://www.merlot.org/

Merrill, M. D. (2002). First principles of instruction [online]. *Educational Technology, Research, and Development, 50*(3), 43-59. Retrieved from http://id2.usu.edu/Papers/5FirstPrinciples.PDF

Mertler, C. (2001). Designing scoring rubrics for your classroom. *Practical Assessment, Research, & Evaluation, 7*(25). Retrieved on October 10, 2008, from http://pareonline.net/getvn.asp?v=7&n=25

Michaels, C. F. (2003). Affordances: Four points of debate. *Ecological Psychology, 15*(2), 135–148. doi:10.1207/S15326969ECO1502_3

Mignault, A., & Chaudhuri, A. (2003). The many faces of a neutral face: Head tilt and perception of dominance and emotion. *Journal of Nonverbal Behavior, 27*(2), 111–132. doi:10.1023/A:1023914509763

Millard, D. E., & Ross, M. (2006). Web 2.0: Hypertext by any other name? *Proceedings of the Seventeenth Conference on Hypertext and Hypermedia*. Odense, Denmark: ACM.

Miller, D. T. (2001). Disrespect and the experience of injustice. *Annual Review of Psychology, 52*(1Journal Article), 527-553.

Miller, G. A. (1956). The magical number seven, plus or minus two: Some limits on our capacity for processing information. *Psychological Review, 63*(2), 81–97. doi:10.1037/h0043158

Milne, C. S. (2005, January). E-learning: Personal computing. How can mentoring or coaching by email help learners get more out of e-learning? *IT Training*. Retrieved from http://www.train-net.co.uk/news/full_news.cfm?ID=4676

Minowa, N. (1997). Lack of words, lack of control: Relationship between language proficiency and frequency of aggressive behavior. *Dissertation Abstracts International: Section B: The Sciences & Engineering, 58*(5-B), 2691.

Mödritscher, F., Wild, F., & Sigurdarson, S. (2008). *Language design for a personal learning environment design language. E-learning*. Retrieved on July 9, 2008, from http://www.elearningeuropa.info/files/media/media15972.pdf

Mohan, B., & van Naerssen, M. (1997). Understanding cause-effect: Learning through language. *Forum, 35*(4), 22–40.

Moisan, A., & Carré, P. (2002). *L'autoformation, fait social? Aspects historiques et sociologiques*. Paris: L'Harmattan.

Monereo, C., & Duran, D. (2001). *Entramats. Mètodes d'aprenentatge cooperatiu i collaboratiu*. Barcelona: Edebé.

Moore, J. W. (2003). Are textbooks dispensable? *Journal of Chemical Education, 80*(4), 359.

Müller, F. (1998). Gradients in ecological systems. *Ecological Modelling, 108*(1–3), 3–21. doi:10.1016/S0304-3800(98)00015-5

Mullins, D. T., & Duke, M. P. (2004). Effects of social anxiety on nonverbal accuracy and response time I: Facial expressions. *Journal of Nonverbal Behavior, 28*(1), 3–33. doi:10.1023/B:JONB.0000017865.24656.98

MySpace. (2008). Retrieved on December 4, 2008, from http://www.myspace.com/

Narciss, S., Proske, A., & Koerndle, H. (2007). Promoting self-regulated learning in Web-based environments. *Computers in Human Behavior, 23*(3), 1126–1144. doi:10.1016/j.chb.2006.10.006

Nass, C., & Moon, Y. (2000). Machines and mindlessness: Social responses to computers. *The Journal of Social Issues, 56*(1), 81–103. doi:10.1111/0022-4537.00153

Nastasi, B., & Clements, D. (1991). Research on cooperative learning: Implications for practice. *School Psychology Review, 20*, 110–131.

Nelson, G. (1998). Internet/Web-based instruction and multiple. *Educational Media International, 35*(2), 90–94. doi:10.1080/0952398980350206

Nesbit, J. C., & Winne, P. H. (2003). Self-regulated inquiry with networked resources. *Canadian Journal of Learning and Technology, 29*(3). Retrieved on November 4, 2007, from http://www.cjlt.ca/content/vol29.3/cjlt29-3_art5.html

New Media Consortium. (2008). *2008 horizon report.* [online]. Retrieved from http://connect.educause.edu/Library/ELI/2008HorizonReport/45926

Nielsen, J. (1994). Heuristic evaluation. In J. Nielsen & R. L. Mack (Eds.), *Usability inspection methods.* New York: John Wiley & Sons.

Nielsen, J., & Molich, R. (1990). Heuristic evaluation of user interfaces. *SIGCHI Conference on Human Factors in Computing Systems: Empowering People* (pp. 249-256) Seattle, WA.

Nonaka, I., & Takeuchi, H. (1995). *The knowledge-creating company: How Japanese companies create the dynamics of innovation.* New York: Oxford University Press.

Norman, D. A. (1988). *The design of everyday things.* New York: Basic Books.

O'Callaghan, P. M., Reitman, D., Northup, J., Hupp, S. D. A., & Murphy, M. A. (2003). Promoting social skills generalization with ADHD-diagnosed children in a sports setting. *Behavior Therapy, 34*(3), 313–330. doi:10.1016/S0005-7894(03)80003-5

O'Hanlon, C. (2007). The teacher becomes the student. *T.H.E. Journal, 34*(11), 20–21.

O'Reilly, T. (2005). Compact definition. O'Reilly radar. Retrieved on November 15, 2007, from [REMOVED HYPERLINK FIELD]http://radar.oreilly.com/archives/2005/10/web_20_compact_definition.html

O'Reilly, T. (2005). *What is Web 2.0: Design patterns and business models for the next generation of software.* Retrieved on December 15, 2006, from http://www.oreillynet.com/pub/a/oreilly/tim/news/2005/09/30/what-is-web-20.html

O'Reilly, T. (2005). What is Web 2.0: Design patterns and business models for the next generation of software. Retrieved on July 30, 2008, from http://www.oreillynet.com/pub/a/oreilly/tim/news/2005/09/30/what-is-web-20.html

Odling-Smee, F. J., Laland, K. N., & Feldman, M. W. (2003). Niche construction: The neglected process in evolution. *Monographs in Population Biology, 37.* Princeton University Press.

Olaniran, B. A. (2001). The effects of computer-mediated communication on transculturalism. In V. Milhouse, M. Asante & P. Nwosu (Eds.), *Transcultural realities* (pp. 83-105). Thousand Oaks, CA: Sage.

Olaniran, B. A. (2006). Applying synchronous computer-mediated communication into course design: Some consideration and practical guides. *Campus-Wide Information Systems, 23*(3), 210–220. doi:10.1108/10650740610674210

Olaniran, B. A. (2007a). Challenges to implementing e-learning and lesser developed countries. In A. Edmundson (Ed.), *Globalized e-learning cultural challenges.* Hershey, PA: Idea Group.

Olaniran, B. A. (2007b). Culture and communication challenges in virtual workspaces. In K. St-Amant (Ed.), *Linguistic and cultural online communication issues in the global age* (pp. 79-92). Hershey, PA: IGI Global.

Olaniran, B. A., Savage, G. T., & Sorenson, R. L. (1996). Experiential and experimental approaches to face-to-face and computer mediated communication in group discussion. *Communication Education, 45*, 244–259. doi:10.1080/03634529609379053

Oldenburg, R. (1997). *The great good place: Cafes, coffee shops, community centers, beauty parlors, general stores, bars, hangouts, and how they get you through the day.* New York: Marlowe & Company.

Onrubia, J. (2003). Las aulas como comunidades de aprendizaje: Una propuesta de enseñanza basada en la interacción, la cooperación, y el trabajo en equipo. *Cooperación Educativa Kikiriki, 68*, 37–46.

Onrubia, J. (2005). Aprender y enseñar en entornos virtuales: Actividad conjunta, ayuda pedagógica, y construcción del conocimiento [online]. *Revista de Educación a Distancia, n II*. Retrieved from http://www.um.es/ead/red/M2/conferencia_onrubia.pdf

Oravec, J. (2003). Blending by blogging: Weblogs in blended learning initiatives. *Journal of Educational Media, 28*(2-3), 225–233. doi:10.1080/1358165032000165671

Osborne, J. W. (2000). *Assessing metacognition in the classroom: The assessment of cognition monitoring effectiveness*. Unpublished doctoral dissertation, University of Oklahoma.

Osman, M. E., & Hannafin, M. J. (1992). Metacognition research and theory: Analysis and implications for instructional design. *Educational Technology Research and Development, 40*(2), 83–99. doi:10.1007/BF02297053

Owen, M., Grant, L., Sayers, S., & Facer, K. (2006). *Social software and learning*. Bristol, England: Futurelab. Retrieved on April 11, 2007, from http://www.futurelab.org.uk/resources/documents/opening_education/Social_Software_report.pdf

Owen, M., Grant, L., Sayers, S., & Facer, K. (2006). *Social software and learning* [online]. Opening Education, Futurelab. Retrieved from http://www.futurelab.org.uk/resources/publications_reports_articles/opening_education_reports/Opening_Education_Report199

Paavola, S., & Hakkarainen, K. (2005). The knowledge creation metaphor–an emergent epistemological approach to learning. *Science and Education, 14*(6), 535–557. doi:10.1007/s11191-004-5157-0

Palloff, R., & Pratt, K. (1999). *Building learning communities in cyberspace*. San Francisco, CA: Jossey Bass.

Palloff, R., & Pratt, K. (2003). *The virtual student. A profile and guide to working with online learners*. San Francisco, CA: Jossey Bass.

Palmer, E. J., & Hollin, C. R. (1999). Social competence and sociomoral reasoning in young offenders. *Applied Cognitive Psychology, 13*(1), 79–87. doi:10.1002/(SICI)1099-0720(199902)13:1<79::AID-ACP613>3.0.CO;2-Q

Palmer, S. (2000). On- and off-campus computer usage in engineering education. *Computers & Education, 34*, 141–154. doi:10.1016/S0360-1315(00)00014-2

Panini, S. (2005). Certificazione AIF del tutor e-learning: Metodo e stato dei lavori. *FOR. Rivista per la Formazione, 63*.

Papert, S. (1980). Mindstorms: *Children, computers, and powerful ideas*. New York: Basic Books.

Paris, S. G., & Winograd, P. (1990). How metacognition can promote academic learning and instruction. In B. F. Jones & L. Idol (Eds.), *Dimensions of thinking and cognitive instruction* (pp. 15-51). Hillsdale, NJ: Lawrence Erlbaum Associates.

Parise, S., & Guinan, P. J. (2008). Marketing using Web 2.0. *Proceedings of the 41st Hawaii International Conference on System Sciences*.

Park, S., Ji, S., et al. (2008). A new 3-dimensional comic chat environment for online game avatars. *Proceedings from the Second IEEE International Conference on Digital Game and Intelligent Toy Enhanced Learning* (pp. 18-22) Banff, Canada.

Parr, M., & Badger, G. (2004). *The photobook: A history* (Volumes I and II). London: Phaidon.

Pata, K. (2008). *Sociocultural and ecological explanations to self-reflection*. Retrieved on October 2, 2008, from http://tihane.wordpress.com/category/intersubjectivity/

Patterson, M. L. (2003). Commentary evolution and nonverbal behavior: Functions and mediating processes. *Journal of Nonverbal Behavior, 27*(3), 201–207. doi:10.1023/A:1025346132037

Pecher, D., & Zwaan, R. A. (2005). *Grounding cognition: The role of perception and action in memory, language, and thinking*. Cambridge University Press.

Penn, D. C., & Povinelli, D. J. (2007). Causal cognition

in human and nonhuman animals: A comparative, critical review. *Annual Review of Psychology, 58,* 97–118. doi:10.1146/annurev.psych.58.110405.085555

Pennebaker, J. W., Mehl, M. R., & Niederhoffer, K. G. (2003). Psychological aspects of natural language use: Our words, our selves. *Annual Review of Psychology, 54*(1), 547–577. doi:10.1146/annurev.psych.54.101601.145041

Percy, C. (2004). Critical absence versus critical engagement: Problematics of the crit in design learning and teaching. *Art, Design, & [ADCHE]. Communication in Higher Education Journal, 2*(3), 143–154.

Pereira, C. S., & Soares, A. L. (2007). Improving the quality of collaboration requirements for information management through social networks analysis. *International Journal of Information Management, 27,* 86–103. doi:10.1016/j.ijinfomgt.2006.10.003

Perkel, D. (2008). Copy and paste literacy: Literacy practices in the production of a MySpace profile. In K. Drotner, H. S. Jensen & K. C. Schroeder (Eds.), *Informal learning and digital media: Constructions, contexts, consequences* (pp. 203-224). Newcastle, UK: Cambridge Scholars Press. Retrieved on October 10, 2008, from http://sims.berkeley.edu/~dperkel/media/dperkel_literacymyspace.pdf

Pettenati, M. C., & Cigognini, M. E. (2007, July-September). Social networking theories and tools to support connectivist learning activities. [IJWLTT]. *International Journal of Web-Based Learning and Teaching Technologies, 2*(3), 39–57.

Philippin, F. (2008). *Reaktionen.* Retrieved on October 10, 2008, from http://www.lulu.com/content/3978261

Philips, M. (2008). It makes teachers touchy. *Newsweek, 152*(12), 10.

Piaget, J. (1975). *The equilibration of cognitive structures* (T. Brown, Trans.). Chicago, IL: The University of Chicago Press.

Picciano, A. G. (2001). *Distance learning: Making connections across virtual space and time.* Upper Saddle River, NJ: Merrill/Prentice Hall.

Pierce, M. E., Fox, G. C., Rosen, J., Maini, S., & Choi, J. Y. (2008). Social networking for scientists using tagging and shared bookmarks: A Web 2.0 application. *International Symposium on Collaborative Technologies and Systems.*

Pintrich, P. R. (Ed.). (1995). *Understanding self-regulated learning: Vol. 63. New directions for teaching and learning.* San Francisco: Josey-Bass.

Pintrich, P. R., & Schunk, D. H. (1996). *Motivation in education: Theory, research, and application.* Upper Saddle River, NJ: Merrill.

Pintrich, R. (2002). The role of metacognitive knowledge in learning, teaching, and assessing. *Theory into Practice, 41*(4), 219–225. doi:10.1207/s15430421tip4104_3

Poftak, A. (2006). Community 2.0. *Technology & Learning, 27*(144). Retrieved on October 31, 2007, from http://newfirstsearch.oclc.org/images/WSPL/wsppdf1/HTML/00427/2VVDD/1SW.HTM

Pór, G., & Molloy, J. (2000). Nurturing systemic wisdom through knowledge ecology. *The Systems Thinker, 11*(8). Retrieved from http://www.co-i-l.com/coil/knowledge-garden/kd/KE.pdf

Pór, G., & Spivak, J. (2000, May 23-24). *The ecology of knowledge: A field theory and practice, key to research, & technology development.* Paper presented at the Consultation Meeting on the Future of Organisations and Knowledge Management of the European Commission's Directorate-General Information Society Technologies, Brussels. Retrieved from http://www.co-i-l.com/coil/knowledge-garden/kd/eoknowledge.shtml

Putnam, R. (2000). *Bowling alone: The collapse and revival of American community.* New York: Simon & Schuster.

Qi, C. H., & Kaiser, A. P. (2004). Problem behaviors of low-income children with language delays: An observation study. *Journal of Speech, Language, and Hearing Research: JSLHR, 47*(3), 595–610. doi:10.1044/1092-4388(2004/046)

Quintana, J., & Higueras, E. (2007). *Les Webquests, una metodologia d'aprenentatge cooperatiu, basada en l'accés, el maneig i l'ús d'informació de la Xarxa*. ICE de la Universitat de Barcelona: Quaderns de Docència Universitària, 11.

Read, B. (2006). A week of change at Facebook, as it expands its membership. *The Chronicle of Higher Education, 53*(5), A35–A35.

Realo, A., Allik, J., Nolvak, A., Valk, R., Ruus, T., & Schmidt, M. (2003). Mindreading ability: Beliefs and performance. *Journal of Research in Personality, 37*(5), 420–445. doi:10.1016/S0092-6566(03)00021-7

Reisslein, J., Sullivan, H., & Reisslein, M. (2007, January). Learner achievement and attitudes under different paces of transitioning to independent problem solving. *Journal of Engineering Education*. Retrieved from http://findarticles.com/p/articles/mi_qa3886/is_200701/ai_n18706112

Rheingold, H. (1993). *The virtual community: Homesteading on the electronic frontier*. New York: Addison-Wesley Publishing Company.

Richardson, W. (2006). Blogs, wikis, podcasts, and other powerful tools for classrooms. Thousand Oaks, CA: Sage.

Richardson, W. (2007). Teaching in a Web 2.0 world. *Kappa Delta Pi Record, 43*(4), 150–151.

Ridley, D. S., Schutz, P. A., Glanz, R. S., & Weinstein, C. E. (1992). Self-regulated learning: The interactive influence of metacognitive awareness and goal-setting. *Journal of Experimental Education, 60*(4), 293–306.

Rizzolatti, G., & Arbib, M. A. (1998). Language within our grasp. *Trends in Neurosciences, 21*(5), 188–194. doi:10.1016/S0166-2236(98)01260-0

Rizzolatti, G., Fogassi, L., & Gallese, V. (2001). Neurophysiological mechanisms underlying the understanding and imitation of action. *Nature Reviews. Neuroscience, 2*, 661–670. doi:10.1038/35090060

Robbie, D., & Zeeng, L. (2008). Engaging student social networks to motivate learning: Capturing, analysing, and critiquing the visual image. *The International Journal of Learning, 15*(3).

Robbins-Sponaas, R. J., & Nolan, J. (2005). MOOs: Polysynchronous collaborative virtual environments. In K. St. Amant & P. Zemliansky (Eds.), *Internet-based workplace communications: Industry and academic applications* (pp. 130–155). Hershey, PA: Information Science Publishing.

Robins, B., Dickerson, P., Stribling, P., & Dautenhahn, K. (2004). Robot-mediated joint attention children with autism: A case study in robot-human interaction. *Interaction Studies: Social Behaviour and Communication in Biological and Artificial Systems, 5*(2), 161–198. doi:10.1075/is.5.2.02rob

Robinson, K. (2005). *Web 2.0? Why should we care?* Retrieved on January 11, 2006, from http://www.publish.com/article2/0,1759,1860653,00.asp

Roblyer, M. D., & Wiencke, W. R. (2003). Design and use of a rubric to assess and encourage interactive qualities in distances courses. *American Journal of Distance Education, 17*(2), 77–98. doi:10.1207/S15389286AJDE1702_2

Rockwell, P. (2000). Lower, slower, louder: Vocal cues of sarcasm. *Journal of Psycholinguistic Research, 29*(5), 483–495. doi:10.1023/A:1005120109296

Rodet, J. (2008). Tuteur à distance, entre function et métier. Retrieved on August 14, 2008, from http://jacques.rodet.free.fr/intjrci.pdf

Rogers, P. C., Liddle, S. W., Chan, P., Doxey, A., & Isom, B. (2007). Web 2.0 learning platform: Harnessing collective intelligence. *Turkish Online Journal of Distance Education, 8*(3), 16–33.

Rogoff, B., Paradise, R., Arauz, R. M., Correa-Chavez, M., & Angelillo, C. (2003). Firsthand learning through intent participation. *Annual Review of Psychology, 54*(1), 175–203. doi:10.1146/annurev.psych.54.101601.145118

Romero, M., & Wareham, J. (2009). Just-in-time mobile learning model based on context awareness information. *IEEE Learning Technology Newsletter, 11*(1-2), 4–6.

Rosen, J. (2006, June 27). The people formerly known as the audience. *PressThink* [weblog]. Retrieved on October 2, 2007, from http://journalism.nyu.edu/pubzone/weblogs/pressthink/2006/06/27/ppl_frmr.html

Rosenberg, M. J. (2001). *E-learning strategies for delivering knowledge in the digital age.* USA: McGraw-Hill.

Rotta, M. (2007). Il project based learning nella scuola: Implicazioni, prospettive e criticità. *Journal of e-Learning and Knowledge Society, 3*(1), 75-84.

Rotta, M. (2008). La conoscenza proibita ovvero la società del sovraccarico informativo. In P. Capitani & M. Rotta (Eds.), *Comunicare diversa-mente: Gli scenari della comunicazione e lo spazio dell'informazione.* Roma: Garamond.

Rotta, M. (in press). Learning³: Gli scenari dell'innovazione nelle strategie per la costruzione della cittadinanza digitale e della conoscenza in rete. In Istituto Pedagogico di Bolzano (Ed.), *Sviluppo delle competenze per una cittadinanza digitale attiva e responsabile.* Dobbiaco, 10-13 luglio 2008.

Rotta, M., & Ranieri, M. (2005). *E-tutor: Identità e competenze.* Trento: Erickson.

Rourke, L., & Anderson, T. (2002). Exploring social presence in computer conferencing. *Journal of Interactive Learning Research, 13*(3), 259–275.

Rowntree, D. (1995). Teaching and learning online. A correspondence education for the 21st century? *British Journal of Educational Technology, 26*(3), 205–215. doi:10.1111/j.1467-8535.1995.tb00342.x

Rudd, T., Sutch, D., & Facer, K. (2006). *Towards new learning networks.* Bristol, England: Futurelab. Retrieved on July 5, 2007, from http://www.futurelab.org.uk/resources/documents/opening_education/Learning_Networks_report.pdf

Rumelhart, D. E., & Ortony, A. (1976). *The representation of knowledge in memory.* La Jolla, CA: Center for Human Information Processing, Dept. of Psychology, University of California, San Diego.

Rumelhart, D., & McClelland, J. (1986). *Parallel distributed processing.* MIT Press

Russell, J. A., Bachorowski, J. A., & Fernandez-Dols, J. M. (2003). Facial and vocal expressions of emotion. *Annual Review of Psychology, 54*(1), 329–349. doi:10.1146/annurev.psych.54.101601.145102

Rutherford, M. D. (2004). The effect of social role on theory of mind reasoning. *The British Journal of Psychology, 95*, 91–103. doi:10.1348/000712604322779488

Ryberg, T. (2008). Challenges and potentials for institutional and technological infrastructures in adopting social media. In V. Hodgson, C. Jones, T. Kargidis, D. McConnell, S. Retalis, D. Stamatis & M. Zenios (Eds.), *Proceedings of the Sixth International Conference on Networked Learning 2008* (pp. 658–665). Lancaster, England: Lancaster University.

Saffer, D. (2005). *The role of metaphor in interaction design.* Master's thesis, Carnegie Mellon University, Pittsburgh, PA.

Saint-Onge, H., & Wallace, D. (2003). Leveraging communities of practice. Burlington, MA: Butterworth Heinemann.

Salaberry, M. R. (2001). The use of technology for second language learning and teaching: A retrospective. *Modern Language Journal, 85*(1), 39–56. doi:10.1111/0026-7902.00096

Salmon, G. (2000). *E-moderating, the key to teaching and learning online.* London: Kogan Page.

Salmon, G. (2002). *E-tivities, the key to active online learning.* London: Kogan Page.

Salomon, G., Perkins, D. N., & Globerson, T. (1992). Coparticipando en el conocimiento. La ampliación de la inteligencia humana con las tecnologías inteligentes. *Comunicación . Lenguaje y Educación, 13*, 6–22.

Salonen, P., Vauras, M., & Efklides, A. (2005). Social interaction–what can it tell us about metacognition and coregulation in learning? *European Psychologist, 10*(3), 199–208. doi:10.1027/1016-9040.10.3.199

Sancho-Vinuesa, T., & Gras-Martí, A. (in press). Case study: Teaching and learning (T&L) undergraduate mathematics in an online university. In W. Kinuthia & S. Marshall (Eds.), *Cases'n'places: Global cases in educational and performance technology.*

Sanger, D., Coufal, K. L., Scheffler, M., & Searcey, R. (2003). Implications of the personal perceptions of incarcerated adolescents concerning their own communicative competence. *Communication Disorders Quarterly, 24*(2), 64–77. doi:10.1177/15257401030240020301

Sanger, D., Hux, K., & Riztman, M. (1999). Female juvenile delinquents' pragmatic awareness of conversational interactions. *Journal of Communication Disorders, 32*, 281–295. doi:10.1016/S0021-9924(99)00003-9

Sanger, D., Scheffler, M., Drake, B., Hilgert, K., Creswell, J. W., & Hansen, D. J. (2000). Maltreated female delinquents speak about their communication behaviors. *Communication Disorders Quarterly, 21*(3), 176–187. doi:10.1177/152574010002100306

Sangrà, A. (2002). A new learning model for the information and knowledge society: The case of the UOC. *International Review of Research in Open and Distance Learning, 2*(2).

Sarris, A., Winefield, H. R., & Cooper, C. (2000). Behavior problems in adolescence: A comparison of juvenile offenders and adolescents referred to a mental health service. *Australian Journal of Psychology, 52*(1), 17–22. doi:10.1080/00049530008255362

Sarvas, R., Mäntylä, M., & Turpeinen, M. (2007). *Human-centric design of future print media.* Helsinki: PulPaper. Retrieved on October 10, 2008, from http://pong.hiit.fi/dcc/papers/FuturePrintMedia_PulPaper07.pdf

Scardamalia, M., & Bereiter, C. (2003). Knowledge building. In J. W. Guthrie (Ed.), *Encyclopedia of education* (2nd ed., pp. 1370–1373). New York: Macmillan.

Schick, S. (2006). Glendon puts end to server nightmare. *Computing Canada, 32*(15), 1–2.

Schmidt, K. L., & Cohn, J. F. (2001). Human facial expressions as adaptations: Evolutionary questions in facial expression research. *Yearbook of Physical Anthropology, 44*, 3–24. doi:10.1002/ajpa.20001

Scorolli, C., & Borghi, A. (2007). Sentence comprehension and action: Effect or specific modulation of the motor system. *Brain Research, 1130*, 119–124. doi:10.1016/j.brainres.2006.10.033

Segrin, C. (2000). Social skills deficits associated with depression. *Clinical Psychology Review, 20*(3), 379–403. doi:10.1016/S0272-7358(98)00104-4

Segrin, C. (2001). Social skills and negative life events: Testing the deficit stress generation hypothesis. *Current Psychology: Developmental, Learning, Personality, Social, 20*(1), 19–35. doi:10.1007/s12144-001-1001-8

Selinger, M. (2004). Cultural and pedagogical implications of a global e-learning programme. *Cambridge Journal of Education, 34*(2), 223–239. doi:10.1080/0305764040010001700589

Selwyn, N. (2000). Creating a "connected" community? Teachers' use of an electronic discussion group [electronic version]. *Teachers College Record, 102*(4), 750–778. doi:10.1111/0161-4681.00076

Sen, S., Lam, S. K., Rashid, A. M., Cosley, D., Frankowski, D., & Osterhouse, J. (2006). Tagging, communities, vocabulary, evolution. [*th Anniversary Conference on Computer Supported Cooperative Work*. Banff, Alberta, Canada: ACM.]. *Proceedings of the, 2006*, 20.

Sfard, A. (1998). On two metaphors for learning and the dangers of choosing just one. *Educational Researcher, 27*(2), 4–13.

Shayo, C., Olfman, L., Iriberri, A., & Magid, I. (2007). The virtual society: Its driving forces, arrangements, practices, implications. In J. Gackenbach (Ed.), *Psychology and the Internet: Inrapersonal, interpersonal, and transpersonal implications* (2nd ed., pp. 187-219). Boston: Academic Press.

Sheely, S. (2006). Persistent technologies: Why can't we stop lecturing online? In L. Markauskaite, P. Goodyear & P. Reimann (Eds.), *Who's learning? Whose technology? Proceedings of the 23rd ASCILITE Conference* (pp. 769–774). Sydney: CoCo, University of Sydney.

Sheridan, S. M. (1995). *The tough kid social skills book*. Longmont, CO: Sopris West.

Sherry, L. (2000). The nature and purpose of online discourse. *International Journal of Educational Telecommunications, 6*(1), 19–52.

Shih, W.-C., Tseng, S.-S., & Yang, C.-T. (2008). Wiki-based rapid prototyping for teaching-material design in e-learning grids. *Computers & Education, 51*, 1037–1057. doi:10.1016/j.compedu.2007.10.007

Shirky, C. (1998). And nothing to watch: Bad protocols, good users: In praise of evolvable systems. [-ff.]. *AMC Net Worker, 2*(3), 48.

Shirky, C. (2003, April 24). *A group is its own worst enemy: Social structure in social software*. Paper presented at the O'Reilly Emerging Technology conference, Santa Clara, CA. Retrieved on April 19, 2005, from http://www.shirky.com/writings/group_enemy.html

Short, J., Williams, E., & Christie, B. (1976). *The social psychology of telecommunication*. London: Wiley.

Siemens, G. (2004). *Learning management systems: The wrong place to start learning. E-learnspace*. Retrieved on October 1, 2008, from http://www.elearnspace.org/Articles/lms.htm

Siemens, G. (2005). *Connectivism: A learning theory for digital age*. Retrieved from http://www.elearnspace.org/Articles/connectivism.htm

Siemens, G. (2006). *Knowing knowledge*. Complexive Inc., Knowing Knowledge. Retrieved on August 14, 2008, from http://www.knowingknowledge.com/book.php

Siemens, G. (2006). *Knowing knowledge*. Retrieved from http://www.knowingknowledge.com/2006/10/knowing_knowledge_pdf_files.php

Slavin, R. (1990). *Cooperative learning. Theory, research, and practice*. New Jersey: Prentice Hall, Inc.

Smith, F., Hardman, F., & Higgins, S. (2006, June). The impact of interactive whiteboards on teacher-pupil interaction in the national literacy and numeracy strategies. *British Educational Research Journal, 32*(3), 443–457. doi:10.1080/01411920600635452

Smith, G. G., Torres-Ayala, A. T., & Heindel, A. J. (2008). Disciplinary differences in e-learning instructional design: The case of mathematics. *Journal of Distance Education, 22*(3), 63–88.

Smith, H., Higgins, S., & Miller, J. (2005). Interactive whiteboards: Boon or bandwagon? A critical review of the literature. *Journal of Computer Assisted Learning, 21*(2), 91–101. doi:10.1111/j.1365-2729.2005.00117.x

Smith, K. A. (2005). *Structure of the visual book*. Rochester, NY: Keith Smith.

Smith, M. K. (2002, 2008). Howard Gardner and multiple intelligences. *The encyclopedia of informal education*. Retrieved on August 9, 2008, from http://www.infed.org/thinkers/gardner.htm

Smokowski, P. R., & Hartung, K. (2003). Computer simulation and virtual reality: Enhancing the practice of school social work. *Journal of Technology in Human Services, 21*(1-2), 5–30. doi:10.1300/J017v21n01_02

Soderstrom, H. (2003). Psychopathy as a disorder of empathy. *European Child & Adolescent Psychiatry, 12*(5), 249–252. doi:10.1007/s00787-003-0338-y

Somekh, N., et al. (2006). *Making a difference with technology for learning*: *Evidence for college leaders*. Retrieved on August 20, 2008, from feandskills.becta.org.uk/download.cfm?resID=25958

Soukup, C. (2006). Computer-mediated communication as a virtual third place: Building Oldenburg's great good places on the World Wide Web. *New Media & Society, 8*(3), 421–440. doi:10.1177/1461444806061953

Soules, M. (2001). *Collaboration and publication in hybrid online courses*. Retrieved on October 7, 2008, from http://records.viu.ca/~soules/hybrid2.htm

Spitzberg, B. H., & Dillard, J. P. (2002). Social skills and communication. In R. W. Preiss, & M. Allen (Eds.), *Interpersonal communication research: Advances through meta-analysis* (pp. 89-107). Mahwah, NJ: Lawrence Erlbaum Associates, Publishers.

Squires, D. (1999). Educational software and learning: Subversive use and volatile design. Retrieved on December 10, 2007, from http://csdl2.computer.org/comp/proceedings/hicss/199/0001/01/00011079.pdf

Statistics Canada. (2008, April 3). *Canada at a glance. Statistics Canada catalogue no. 12-581- XPE*. Ottawa. Retrieved on July 29, 2008, from http://www.statcan.ca/english/freepub/12-581-XIE/12-581-XIE2007001.pdf

Stecconi, U. (2004). Interpretive semiotics and translation theory: The semiotic conditions to translation. *Semiotica, 150*(1/4), 471–489. doi:10.1515/semi.2004.056

Stern, S. (2008). Producing sites, exploring identities: Youth online authorship. In D. Buckingham (Ed.), *Youth, identity, and digital media* (pp. 95–118). Cambridge, MA: MIT Press. Retrieved on October 10, 2008, from http://www.mitpressjournals.org/doi/abs/10.1162/dmal.9780262524834.095

Stix, A. (1997). *Creating rubrics through negotiable contracting and assessment*. Retrieved on October 10, 2008, from http://interactiveclassroom.com/article_07.html

Stoyko, P. (2002). *Communities of practice: Lessons learned from the research literature and public service experience*. Strategic Research and Planning Branch, Canadian Centre for Management Development.

Stoyko, P., & Fang, Y. (2007). *Lost & found: A smart-practice guide to managing organization memory*. Canada School of Public Service Action-Research Roundtable on Organizational Memory. Retrieved on July 31, 2008, from http://www.csps-efpc.gc.ca/Research/publications/html/p137/1_e.html

Sullivan, S., & Ruffman, T. (2004). Social understanding: How does it fare with advancing years? *The British Journal of Psychology, 95*, 1–18. doi:10.1348/000712604322779424

Surowiecki, K. (2004). *The wisdom of crowds*. New York: Doubleday.

Takago, D., Matsuishi, M., Goto, H., & Sakamoto, M. (2007). Requirements for a Web 2.0 course management system of engineering education. *Ninth IEEE International Symposium onMultimedia, ISMW '07*.

Tammets, K., Väljataga, T., & Pata, K. (2008, June 30-July 4). Self-directing at social spaces: Conceptual framework for course design. In *Proceedings of ED-MEDIA 2008-World Conference on Educational Multimedia, Hypermedia, & Telecommunications* (pp. 6337–6342), Vienna, Austria. Vienna: Association for the Advancement of Computing in Education (AACE).

Taylor, J. S. (1969). *The communicative abilities of juvenile delinquents: A descriptive study*. Unpublished doctoral dissertation, The University of Missouri, Kansas City, MO.

Thalheimer, W. (2008, August 18). Evaluation e-learning 2.0: Getting our heads around the complexity. *Learning Solutions*.

Thomas, A. (2007). *Youth online: Identity and literacy in the digital age*. New York: Peter Lang.

Thorpe, M. (2002). Rethinking learner support: The challenge of online learning. *Open Learning, 17*(2), 105–120.

Tonnies, F. (2001). *Tonnies: Community and civil society*. New York: Cambridge University Press.

Treasury Board of Canada Secretariat. (2006). *Policy on learning, training, and development*. Retrieved on July 31, 2008, from http://www.tbs-sct.gc.ca/pol/doc-eng.aspx?id=12405&section=text

Trentin, G. (1999). *Telematica e formazione a distanza, il caso Polaris*. Milano: Franco Angeli.

Trentin, G. (2008). *La sostenibilità didattico-formativa dell□e-learning. Social networking e apprendimento attivo*. Milano: Franco Angeli.

Tufte, E. (1990). *Envisiong information*. Cheshire: Graphics Press.

Tulving, E., & Schacter, D. L. (1990). Priming and human memory systems. *Science, 247*(4940), 301–306. doi:10.1126/science.2296719

Turkle, S. (1996). Virtuality and its discontents: Searching for community in cyberspace. *The American Prospect, 7*(24).

Twitter. (2008). Retrieved on December 5, 2008, from http://twitter.com/

Ullrich, C., Borau, K., Luo, H., Tan, X., Shen, L., & Shen, R. (2008). Why Web 2.0 is good for learning and for research: Principles and prototypes. *Proceeding of the 17ʰ International Conference on World Wide Web*. Beijing, China: ACM.

Underwood, J., & Banyard, P. E. (2008). Understanding the learning space. *eLearning papers, 9*. Retrieved from http://www.elearningpapers.eu/index.php?page=doc&doc_id=11937&doclng=6

Väljataga, T., Pata, K., & Tammets, K. (forthcoming). Considering learners' perspectives to personal learning environments in course design. In M. J. W. Lee & C. McLoughlin (Eds.), *Web 2.0-based e-learning: Applying social informatics for tertiary teaching*. Hershey, PA: IGI Global.

Väljataga, T., Pata, K., Laanpere, M., & Kaipainen, M. (2007). Theoretical framework of the iCampFolio-new approach to evaluation and comparison of systems and tools for learning purposes. In E. Duval, R. Klamma, & M. Wolpers (Eds.), *Creating new learning experiences on a global scale* (pp. 349-363). Berlin/Heidelberg.

Vallance, D. D., & Wintre, M. G. (1997). Discourse processes underlying social competence in children with language learning disabilities. *Development and Psychopathology, 9*(1), 95–108. doi:10.1017/S0954579497001089

Vallance, D. D., Im, N., & Cohen, N. J. (1999). Discourse deficits associated with psychiatric disorders and with language impairments in children. *Journal of Child Psychology and Psychiatry, and Allied Disciplines, 40*(5), 693–704. doi:10.1111/1469-7610.00486

Van House, N. A. (2007, April 28-May 3). Flickr and public image-sharing: Distant closeness and photo exhibition. In M. B. Rosson & D. J. Gilmore (Eds.), *Extended Abstracts Proceedings of the 2007 Conference on Human Factors in Computing Systems, CHI 2007* (pp. 2717-2722) San Jose, CA.

Van Swol, L. M. (2003). The effects of nonverbal mirroring on perceived persuasiveness, agreement with an imitator, and reciprocity in a group discussion. *Communication Research, 30*(4), 461–480. doi:10.1177/0093650203253318

Vandermeer, J. (2008). The niche construction paradigm in ecological time. *Ecological Modelling, 214*, 385–390. doi:10.1016/j.ecolmodel.2008.03.009

VanMetre, S., Larson, L., Pearce, G., & Lewis, B. (2008). *Promethean activeclassroom: Integration for improving candidate academic performance*. Louisiana Board of Regents, Board of Regents Support Fund LEQSF (2008-10)-ENH-TR-38.

Varela De Freitas, C., & Valente, L. (2001). Uses of Internet in Portugal. *Educational Technology Research and Development, 49*(4), 117–120. doi:10.1007/BF02504953

Varela, F. J., Thompson, E., & Rosch, E. (1991). *The embodied mind*. Cambridge, MA: MIT Press.

Vasileva, J. (2004, August 30-September 3). *Harnessing P2P power in the classroom*. Paper presented at the ITS 2004, Maceio, Brazil.F

Veenema, S., & Gardner, H. (1996). Multimedia and multiple intelligences. *The American Prospect, 7*(29), 70–75.

Veenman, M. V. J., Wilhelm, P., & Beishuizen, J. J. (2004). The relation between intellectual and metacognitive skills from a developmental perspective. *Learning and Instruction, 14*(1), 89–109. doi:10.1016/j.learninstruc.2003.10.004

Von Wright, J. (1992). Reflection on reflections. *Learning and Instruction, 2*(1), 59–68. doi:10.1016/0959-4752(92)90005-7

Vrij, A., Akehurst, L., Soukara, S., & Bull, R. (2004). Detecting deceit via analysis of verbal and nonverbal behavior in children and adults. *Human Communication Research, 30*(1), 8–41. doi:10.1111/j.1468-2958.2004.tb00723.x

Vyas, D., & Dix, A. (2007, September 16). Artefact ecologies: Supporting embodied meeting practices with distance access. In *Proceedings of UbiComp (Ubiquitous*

Computing) 2007 Workshops, Innsbruck, Austria (pp. 117–122). University of Innsbruck.

Vygotsky, L. S. (1978). *Mind in society.* Cambridge: Harvard University Press.

Vygotsky, L. S. (1987). Thinking and speech (N. Minick, Trans.). In R. W. Rieber & A. S. Carton (Eds.), *Problems of general psychology, including the volume thinking and speech: Vol. 1. The collected works of L. S. Vygotsky* (pp. 39–285). New York: Plenum. (Original works published in 1934 & 1960).

Wall, K., Higgins, S., & Smith, H. (2005). The visual helps me understand the complicated things: Pupil views of teaching and learning with interactive whiteboards. *British Journal of Educational Technology, 36*(5), 851–867. doi:10.1111/j.1467-8535.2005.00508.x

Wang, M. (2007). Designing online courses that effectively engage learners from diverse cultural backgrounds. *British Journal of Educational Technology, 38*(2), 294–311. doi:10.1111/j.1467-8535.2006.00626.x

Ward, K. J. (1999). The cyber-ethnographic (re)construction of two feminist online communities. *Sociological Research Online, 12*.

Waterhouse, S. (2005). The power of e-learning: The essential guide for teaching in the digital age. Boston: Pearson.

Weber, R. P. (1990). *Basic content analysis, 2nd ed.* London: Sage Publications.

Wenger, E. (1998). *Communities of practice: Learning, meaning, and identity.* New York: Cambridge University Press.

Wenger, E., McDermott, R., & Snyder, W. M. (2002). *Cultivating communities of practice: A guide to managing knowledge.* Boston, MA: Harvard Business School Press.

White, J. (1998). *Do Howard Gardner's multiple intelligences add up?* London: Institute of Education, University of London.

White, R. W., Drucker, S. M., Marchionini, G., & Marti, H. M., & Schraefel, M. C. (2007). Exploratory search and hci: Designing and evaluating interfaces to support exploratory search interaction. *CHI '07 Extended Abstracts on Human Factors in Computing Systems.* San Jose, CA: ACM.

Wiley, D. A. (2002). *Connecting learning objects to instructional design theory: A definition, a metaphor, and a taxonomy. The instructional use of learning objects.* Bloomington, IN: Agency for Instructional Technology.

Wiley, D., & Edwards, E. (2002). Online self-organizing social systems: The decentralized future of online learning. OER Commons. Retrieved on August 14, 2008, from http://www.oercommons.org/matters/online-self-organizing-social-systems-the-decentralized-future-of-online-Learning

Williams, J. B., & Jacobs, J. (2004). Exploring the use of blogs as learning spaces in the higher education sector. *Australasian Journal of Educational Technology, 20*(2), 232–247.

Wilson, B. (1995). Metaphors for instruction: Why we talk about learning environments. *Educational Technology, 35*(5), 25–30.

Witherspoon, A., Azevedo, R., & Baker, S. (2007, July). *Learners' use of various types of representations during self-regulated learning and externally-regulated learning episodes.* Paper presented at a Workshop on Metacognition and Self-Regulated Learning at the 13th International Conference on Artificial Intelligence in Education, Los Angeles, CA.

Wong, W. K., Chan, T. W., Chou, C. Y., Heh, J. S., & Tung, S. H. (2003). Reciprocal tutoring using cognitive tools. *Journal of Computer Assisted Learning, 19*(4), 416–428. doi:10.1046/j.0266-4909.2003.00046.x

Wood, D. J., Bruner, J. S., & Ross, G. (1976). The role of tutoring in problem solving. *Journal of Child Psychiatry and Psychology, 17*(2), 89–100. doi:10.1111/j.1469-7610.1976.tb00381.x

Wood, D., Bruner, J., & Ross, G. (1976). The role of tutoring in problem solving. *Journal of Child Psychology and Psychiatry, and Allied Disciplines, 17*, 89–100. doi:10.1111/j.1469-7610.1976.tb00381.x

Wright, S. (1931). The roles of mutation, inbreeding, cross-breeding, and selection in evolution. In *Proceedings of the Sixth International Congress of Genetics, 1*, 356–366.

Wu, E. Hsiao-Kuang, Wu, Hubert, Chi-Yu, et al. (2008). A context aware interactive robot educational platform. *Proceedings from the Second IEEE International Conference on Digital Game and Intelligent Toy Enhanced Learning* (pp. 205-206) Banff, Canada.

Google, Inc. (2008). *Google docs.* Retrieved on December 4, 2008, from http://docs.google.com/

Wikipedia. (2007). Retrieved on August 10, 2007, from http://www.wikipedia.org/

YouTube. LLC. (2008). *YouTube–broadcast yourself.* Retrieved on December 4, 2008, from http://www.youtube.com/

Yahoo! Inc. (2008). *Welcome to Flickr–photo sharing.* Retrieved on December 4, 2008, from http://www.flickr.com/

Ylvisaker, M., & DeBonis, D. (2000). Executive function impairment in adolescence: TBI and ADHD. *Topics in Language Disorders, 20*(2), 29–57.

Young, J., & Upitis, R. (1999). The microworld of phoenix quest: Social and cognitive considerations. *Education and Information Technologies, 4*(4), 391–408. doi:10.1023/A:1009600528811

Zhang, J., & Norman, D. (1994). Representations in distributed cognitive tasks. *Cognitive Science, 18*, 87–122.

Zhang, J., & Patel, V. L. (2006). Distributed cognition, representation, and affordance. *Cognition & Pragmatics, 14*(2), 333–341. doi:10.1075/pc.14.2.12zha

Zimmerman, B. J., & Martinez-Pons, M. (1990). Student differences in self-regulated learning: Relating grade, sex, and giftedness to self-efficacy and strategy use. *Journal of Educational Psychology, 82*, 52–59. doi:10.1037/0022-0663.82.1.51

About the Contributors

Niki Lambropoulos is an experienced e-learning expert, researcher, consultant, HCI designer, and online communities manager. Her interests fall in the fields of E-Learning, and Idea Management for Distributed Leadership and User Innovation Networks. She was born in Ancient Olympia, Greece. She holds two BAs and a Diploma in Education from the University of Athens, Greece and an MA in ICT in Education from the Institute of Education, University of London. She finished her PhD at London South Bank University, UK. She started working as a Greek language teacher in Greece in 1989. She has worked as a Greek language, ICT teacher and ICT coordinator, and from 2002-2006 as a Project Manager mostly over the Net. She now works as a researcher in EU projects. Outside her office she likes Yoga, reading, arts, swimming, and cloud watching. She enjoys working collaboratively over the Net.

Margarida Romero is a specialist on e-learning and learning innovation, working as researcher, consultant and project manager. For the last 9 years she was a project manager in elearning and life long learning projects (ITIN University in Paris, IUFM French Guyana, Educational Ministry of Algeria…). In addition to her professional work she has developed her experience as learning facilitator being part-time lecturer at Universitat Ramon Llull (Blanquerna), Université de Limoges, Institut Universitaire Professionnalisé de Nîmes and Centre National des Arts et Métiers (CNAM). Active member of the most representative European educational associations, she leads Euro-CAT-CSCL, a research project within the FP7 Marie Curie IAPP actions. In 2007, she won the 3rd price on Technology Transfer from the EU Network of Excellence Kaleidoscope. In 2006, she won ex-aequo the Artificial Intelligence French Association Award for a communication claiming the need to introduce a metacognitive support into elearning systems.

* * *

Ruth Brown works at London South Bank University as an academic developer. She collaborated with Paula Roush in the development of the digital photography course which is the subject of this chapter. Her particular research interests in higher education are in the fields of eLearning, curriculum design and learning design, assessment (including eAssessment) and the student as a legitimate participant in the HE community. Her role as an academic developer requires that she keep abreast of developments in the sector which may enhance the student experience; one might say that she is a boundary scout!

Evelyne Corcos is an Associate Professor of Psychology at York University, Glendon Campus, Toronto, Canada. Her interests include issues surrounding the language, cognition, and social skills of children and adolescents with behavioral difficulties, as well as exploring and developing computer environments designed to address the concepts and skills associated with higher learning. She has written two books about creating a positive classroom environment by applying psychological principles to meet the academic and social needs of students. Her latest, *Teaching Children and Adolescents with Behavioral Difficulties: An Educational Approach,* is used in a third-year course entitled "The Psychology and Pedagogy of children and adolescents with behavior disorders".

Randall Dunn is an Assistant Professor of Education in the Department of Teacher Education at Liberty University (Lynchburg, VA). Dr. Dunn received his BA and MEd both from James Madison University, in History and Special Education respectively, and EdD from University of Bath, UK focusing on technology and education. He spent time as both a teacher in public middle education classrooms and in software development in the private sector. His research interests are in the areas of the use of technology in educational organizations, especially in reference to community formations and learning considerations in online environments. He is currently applying these interests specifically to researching virtual world contexts.

Anna Escofet Roig is PhD in Education. She teaches at University of Barcelona (Spain), in the area of education. Her research is focused on educational uses of ICT, distance learning and the impact of the digital divide in the society.

Núria Escudero-Viladoms holds a Mathematics degree (Universitat Politècnica de Catalunya), an Official Master degree in Research in Didactics of Mathematics and Science (Universitat Autònoma de Barcelona) and a Master degree in Pedagogical Qualification for Secondary School Mathematics Teacher (Universitat Politècnica de Catalunya). Nowadays, she is a PhD student in Didactics of Mathematics and Science at the Universitat Autònoma de Barcelona.

Wai-Tat Fu is an Assistant Professor research in the Human Factors Division at the University of Illinois at Urbana-Champaign. His research areas include learning in social media, Web 2.0 and education, cognitive modeling, learning and skill acquisition, adaptive behavior, human-technology interaction. His work has been published in *Psychological Review, Journal of Experimental Psychology, Cognitive Science, Psychological Research* and *Human-Computer Interaction.*

Mariève Gauthier, BA, has been working at the Canada School of Public Service since 2003. She began with the school as a French Second Language Teacher in 2003, after which she developed her expertise in the area of communities of practice. In 2006 she played a key role in establishing the Centre of Expertise in Communities of Practice located in the Quebec region where she is now the Supervisor of Client Services. Mariève has a Bachelors degree in French Language as well as a Bachelors of Education from the University of Ottawa. She is currently pursuing a Masters degree in Knowledge Management and E-learning at the University of Laval.

Yasemin Gulbahar is an assistant professor of Computer Education and Instructional Technology at Baskent University in Ankara, Turkey. She has taught many courses on educational technology, teaching methods, computer aided instruction, distance teaching and web design both at the undergraduate and graduate levels. Her research interests include e-learning, technology integration, web-based instructional design, adult education and technology planning.

Filiz Kalelioglu is a research assistant at the Department of Computer Education and Instructional Technology of Baskent University in Ankara, Turkey. She has completed M.S. degree in the same field at Middle East Technical University. And she is continuing her PH.D degree in Educational Technology department in Ankara University, Turkey. Her research interests are e-learning, technology integration, instructional design and software development.

Thomas Kannampallil is a research associate in the Human Factors Division at the University of Illinois at Urbana-Champaign. His research interests are in the area of user behavior in Web 2.0 systems, sequential processes in human behavior, strategies in problem solving behavior and software engineering. His work has been published in *Journal of American Society for Information Science and Technology* (*JASIST*), *ACM Conference of Computer-Human Interaction* (CHI), and *ACM Conference of Computer Supported Cooperative Work* (CSCW).

Linda Larson is an assistant professor in the Burton College of Education in the Educational Leadership and Instructional Technology Department at McNeese State University, in Lake Charles, Louisiana, where, in 2006, she received the Pinnacle Award for Teaching Excellence. Her most recent publications are *A Descriptive Study of Mentoring and Technology Integration among Teacher Education Faculty* (2009), *International Journal of Evidenced Based Coaching and Mentoring; Teachers Bridge to Constructivism* in K. McCauley & G. Pannozzo (Eds.) *Annual Editions: Educational Psychology 7/08 Twenty-Second Edition* and *Rubric to determine a quality on-line posting.* In Salmons, J. and Wilson, L. (Eds.) in *Handbook of research on electronic collaboration and organizational synergy.* Hershey, PA: The Idea Group. Her research focuses on professional development, mentoring, and technology integration in higher education and K-12 schools. She is currently conducting research the Promethean Activclassroom (interactive Whiteboard): Integration for Improving Teacher Candidate Academic Performance.

Mark J. W. Lee is an adjunct senior lecturer with the School of Education, Charles Sturt University, and an honorary research fellow with the School of Information Technology and Mathematical Sciences, University of Ballarat. Previously, he worked in a variety of teaching, instructional design and managerial roles within the private vocational education and higher education sectors. Mark has published widely in the areas of educational technology, e-learning and innovative pedagogy in higher education. He is presently chair of the New South Wales Chapter of the Institute of Electrical and Electronics Engineers (IEEE) Education Society, and serves on the editorial boards of a number of international journals in the area of educational technology and e-learning.

Andrea Mamers, BA, MA, began her career at the Canada School of Public Service as an intern in 2008. During her internship she designed and developed a large-scale evaluation strategy to evaluate communities of practice. She currently works as a Learning Advisor in the Research and Development sector of the Centre of Expertise in Communities of Practice. She has a Bachelors degree from Concordia University in Human Relations, as well as a Masters degree in Educational Technology from Concordia University. She specializes in needs assessments, evaluations and collaborative learning tools.

Catherine McLoughlin is an associate professor with the School of Education at the Australian Catholic University, Canberra. She also serves as the coordinator of the Australian Capital Territory branch of the Research Centre for Science, Information Technology and Mathematics Education for Rural and Regional Australia (SiMERR). With over 20 years experience in higher education in Europe, South East Asia, the Middle East and Australia, Catherine has experience and expertise in a variety of educational settings, with diverse students and across a wide range of cultural contexts. She is editor of the *Australasian Journal of Educational Technology* and an editorial board member of a several leading journals, including the *British Journal of Educational Technology.*

Marta Marimon Martí is PhD in Education. She teaches at University of Vic (Spain), in the area of Social Sciences and Education. Her research is focused on collaborative learning and educational uses of ICT in compulsory education.

Bev Mitelman, BA, MA, began her career in the Public Service as the Chief of Educational Technology for the Department of National Defence in 2005. In 2007, she was offered a new position at the Canada School of Public Service where she is currently the Manager of the Centre of Expertise in Communities of Practice. Prior to joining the Public Service, she worked in the private sector for Sun Life Financial and several high-tech companies. Bev specializes in people management, project management, communications and educational technology. Bev holds a Bachelors degree in Journalism and Mass Communication from Carleton University, and a Masters in Educational Technology from Concordia University. She also holds a number of additional diplomas and certificates in the areas of Multi-Media Development, Web Programming, Software Usability Design, Project Management, and Leadership.

Bolanle A. Olaniran is a Professor in the Department of Communication Studies at Texas Tech University. His research includes: Communication technologies and Computer-Mediated Communication, Organization communication, Cross-cultural communication, and Crisis Management and Communication. He has authored several articles in discipline focus and interdisciplinary focus Journals (i.e., Regional, National, and International) and edited book chapters in each of these areas. He has served as consultant to organizations at local, national and government level. His works have gained recognition such as the American Communication Association's "Outstanding Scholarship in Communication field," Who is who among College Teachers. He is also the recipient of TTU 2006 Office of the President's Diversity, 2007 President's Excellence in Teaching Awards and nominated for 2007 TTU Chancellor's Distinguished Teaching Award. His recent international invited lecture was a lecture series in Knowledge Learning, Information & Technology (KLIT) Workshop organized by Taiwan Normal University and the National Christian University in Taiwan and Technology science Innovation organized by the Russian Federation of Higher Learning, Ural State University, Ekaterineburg, Russia.

Peter Paolucci is a Special Assistant Professor of English at York University in Toronto, Ontario. He has interests in Shakespeare and the Renaissance, electronic texts (XML markup and editing), technology and teaching, computer applications in literary scholarship and editorial work, faculty support work through pedagogy and technology, usability testing, HCI (Human Computer Interaction), theory and practice of Interface Design, Project Management, and faculty support work (training and development).

Kai Pata received PhD in Education from University of Turku, Finland. She is currently working as a senior researcher in the Center of Educational Technology, Institute of Informatics, Tallinn University. Her main expertise is in learning management in distributed learning environments and social systems for self-directed learning, tutoring models and scaffolding elements in web-based collaborative learning environments, cognitive aspects of constructivist learning and model-based reasoning in inquiry learning environments, and science education. She has work experience as a teacher in science classrooms, science program manager in elearning portal Miksike, she has worked at research positions at the University of Tartu, Science Didactics Department, doing various science related ICT projects. She has contributed to the European 6th and 7th Framework Program projects (BioheadCitizen, iCamp, IntelLEO) as a pedagogical expert.

Mario Rotta is the Director of e-learning programs, E-Form Consortium Contract professor, at the University of Florence. He has worked as a partner in research activities of LTE, Educational Science Department, and has been a Professor in the post graduate course "Strategies for Online Learning", and now is currently a Professor in "Information Brokering" and "Online Tutoring", Master degree "E-Learning Project Management". He has also been a partner in ICT and e-Learning programs and research activity of ELEA, SDA Bocconi, CNR, Giunti, Garamond; a visiting professor in several courses on e-learning and multimedia education (Universities of Venezia, Macerata, Viterbo, Pavia, Chieti, Salerno); and a partner in research on certification of e-tutor professional profile for Cepas (ISO) and AIF (Associazione Italiana Formatori).

Paula Roush is an artist-educator-curator whose interests intersect practice-based arts research with critical cultural theory, and the role of the artist-theorist in contemporary media culture. She is senior lecturer in the BA (Hons) in Digital Photography at the London South Bank University (Arts, Media & English Department)-where she teaches courses on the archive and youth subcultures, artists publications and self-publishing practices, performativity and surveillance space. She also teaches the theory module for the MA in Art and Media practice at the University of Westminster (Media & Design Department). Current research : self-publishing practices and artists publications, digital writing and academic blogging, social media and the classroom of the read/write web, artists' uses of ethnographic methods and visual methodologies, globalisation and diasporic art strategies, synthetic worlds and virtual universities, site-specific work and locative media, cctv /webcam video technologies and use of live stream in installation.

Teresa Sancho-Vinuesa holds a PhD in Electronic Engineering (Universitat Ramon Llull) and a MS in Mathematics (Universitat de Barcelona). She is an Associate Professor of Mathematics in the Computer Sciences Department at the Universitat Oberta de Catalunya (Barcelona, Spain). She taught numerical analysis and the theory of probabilities and stochastic processes at La Salle School of Engineering, where she coordinated a research group on numerical methods to solve problems in fluid mechanics and electromagnetism. She directed the PhD program on Information and Knowledge Society at the Universitat Oberta de Catalunya. She has been involved in the Project Internet Catalonia (PIC), an interdisciplinary research project on the information society in Catalonia, co-directed by professors Manuel Castells and Imma Tubella. She has currently resumed her research activity on mathematics education in online engineering studies.

Hope Seidman, BA, MEd, PhD, began her career in the Public Service working for the Department of National Defence in 2006 as Chief of Educational Technology and Chief of English Curriculum. She then transferred to the Canada School of Public Service in 2008. She currently works as the Supervisor of Research and Development at the Centre of Expertise in Communities of Practice. She holds a Bachelors degree in Psychology from the University of Western Ontario, a Masters degree in Curriculum and Instruction from Pennsylvania State University and a PhD in Educational Technology from Concordia University. Over the past decade, Hope has worked for both the private and public sector within such domains as pharmaceutical, information technology and teambuilding and specializes in the application of learning theories, instructional design, professional development and technology-supported learning. She has presented at several conferences in North America and has led faculty development initiatives in India and Dubai. Her research interests include the design of instruction for critical thinking outcomes and the evaluation of informal learning in the workplace.

Sharon VanMetre is a professor in the Burton College of Education (BCOE) in the department of Educational Leadership and Instructional Technology. As department chair, Dr. VanMetre oversees the areas of Educational Technology, Educational Leadership, and Office Systems and Business Computing. Dr. VanMetre was the BCOE recipient of the Pinnacle Teaching Excellence Award at its inception in 2003. Dr. VanMetre's degrees include an Ed.D.in Educational Technology, M.Ed. in Secondary Mathematics Education, and B.S. in Computer Science. Her additional certifications include: Promethean Certification Levels 1&2; Universal Design for Learning LCET State of Louisiana; Compressed Video Certification Texas A&M University; QUEST / INTECH Louisiana Technology Certification; and Louisiana State Teacher Certification in Mathematics, Computer Science, and Technology Leadership. Dr. VanMetre is currently conducting research in the area of Interactive Whiteboard Integration for Improving Teacher Candidate Academic Performance.

Indi Marie Williams received her Masters in Communication Studies from Texas Technology University, Lubbock, Texas, USA. Ms. Williams received a BA in Sociology from the University of Texas at Austin and a second BA in English from the University of North Texas, Denton, Texas, USA. Her research interests include virtual learning communities, web 2.0 e-learning, instructional communication in distance education, human-computer integration, internet culture, and the anticipation of future interaction in online relationship development

Index